The Counter-Reformation Prince

The Counter-Reformation Prince

Anti-Machiavellianism or Catholic
Statecraft in Early Modern Europe

Robert Bireley

The University of North Carolina Press

Chapel Hill and London

© 1990 The University of North Carolina Press
All rights reserved
Manufactured in the United States of America

The paper in this book meets the guidelines for permanence
and durability of the Committee on Production Guidelines
for Book Longevity of the Council on Library Resources.

94 93 92 91 90   5 4 3 2 1

Library of Congress Cataloging-in-Publication Data

Bireley, Robert.
   The Counter-Reformation prince : anti-Machiavellianism or Catholic
statecraft in early modern Europe / by Robert Bireley.
      p.   cm.
   Includes bibliographical references.
   ISBN 0-8078-1925-5 (alk. paper)
      1. Political ethics—Europe—History. 2. Political science—
Europe—History. 3. Christianity and politics—Catholic Church.
4. Counter-Reformation. I. Title.
JA79.B54   1990
172'.094—dc20   90-31805
                                                          CIP

For Barbara, John and Joan, and the children

Contents

A section of illustrations will be found beginning on page 101.

Preface

"Machiavelli's theory was a sword which was plunged into the flank of the body politic of Western humanity, causing it to shriek and rear up. This was bound to happen; for not only had genuine moral feeling been seriously wounded, but death had also been threatened to the Christian views of all churches and sects." So wrote Friedrich Meinecke, the historian of Machiavellianism in 1924.[1] According to Machiavelli, at least as he was popularly understood, a ruler could not be successful, that is, create and maintain a powerful state, without departing from traditional Christian morality. Politics was necessarily "dirty" or compromising. So became broadcast a view that was not entirely new, to be sure, and still is prevalent in our day, as we see in the unfortunate connotation often attached to the word "politician." A conclusion to be drawn from it was that a sincere Christian could not participate in politics. But most Christians rejected this position, and an enormous literature was directed against "the Florentine secretary" in the late sixteenth and seventeenth centuries. So there was unleashed a widespread and intense debate about politics, morality, and religion that was often conducted around the term "reason of state." This debate itself became a significant feature of Baroque culture, and it remains very much alive, in different forms, in our society today. The relationship between politics, morality, and religion is a perennial issue, which was posed in unusually provocative form by Machiavelli and elicited a vigorous and widespread response.

Eventually there formed in the late sixteenth century a more narrowly defined international anti-Machiavellian tradition or school closely associated with the Counter-Reformation. It not only affirmed that a Christian could be a successful ruler or man of politics, indeed that he was much more likely to be so, but it endeavored to show in detail how this could be done, and so it proposed an alternative Christian program to Machiavelli's for the preservation and development of a state. This tradition is the subject of my book. It has rarely been studied. Yet two of its authors, the Italian Giovanni Botero and the Fleming Justus Lipsius, were perhaps the most widely read political writers of the first half of the seventeenth century, and it produced a political literature that is of immense importance for understanding the Counter-Reformation, the culture of the Baroque, and contemporary politics and diplomacy. Political culture in the seventeenth century can scarcely be understood without reference to it. Rulers and governmental figures like the Elector Maximilian of Bavaria, the leading prince of the Counter-Reformation in Germany, who governed from 1598 to 1651, and the two great rivals of the Thirty Years' War, Cardinal Richelieu and the count-duke of Olivares, chief minister of Philip IV of Spain from 1621 to 1643, made their practical decisions in an intellectual atmosphere of which anti-Machiavellianism was a major current. Political thought was also enriched by the anti-Machiavellians as they wrestled with issues of political ethics.

I have attempted to place the anti-Machiavellians in the context of their times. Chapter 1 describes the challenge issued by Machiavelli to contemporaries, looks at initial reactions, and outlines broadly the profound changes of the sixteenth century to which the anti-Machiavellians were also responding. Chapter 2 then describes in a general way the goals, methods, and appeal of the anti-Machiavellian writers and distinguishes them from the Scholastic authors from whom they borrowed and whose positions on major issues are briefly sketched. I chose then, instead of treating the authors collectively and anti-Machiavellianism topically, to devote each of chapters 3 to 8 to an individual anti-Machiavellian writer whom I consider essential to the tradition—Botero, Lipsius, the Spaniards Pedro de Ribadeneira and Diego Saavedra Fajardo, the German Adam Contzen, and the Fleming Carlo Scribani—while discussing others along the way. There is virtually nothing available in English on any of them as political thinkers, and the offerings in other languages are limited. In my opinion each merits to be studied individually as well as within the tradition. This method of proceeding also permits me to locate each author in his historical context, showing influences of his situation on his thought and indicating ways he in turn influenced thinking and policy. Needless to say, the treatment is far from exhaustive.

My intent is to lay out briefly the basic principles of each man and then analyze and evaluate his thought, usually organizing the discussion loosely around six characteristic topics: the relationship between virtue, reputation, and power; the uses of deceit; economic development; war and the military; the place of religion and toleration in the state; and the role of fortune or providence in history. Finally, in the last chapter, where it is a question of the more significant collective impact of the anti-Machiavellians, I suggest conclusions for our understanding of the Counter-Reformation and the culture of the Baroque.

Whether the interpretation given him by the anti-Machiavellians corresponded to the mind or intent of Machiavelli is a question with which this book is not directly concerned. Certainly, it was a historically significant interpretation, perhaps the most historically significant. This being said, in my opinion, their interpretation of Machiavelli, though unsophisticated, was, in essence, a faithful reading of his text, which still finds support from scholars today.

Several institutions and many persons have assisted me in the preparation of this book. Here I have the welcome opportunity to express my gratitude to them. The John Simon Guggenheim Memorial Foundation made it possible for me to devote the first seven months of 1983 to research and writing while residing in Cambridge, Massachusetts. A Senior Research Fellowship from the National Endowment for the Humanities and assistance from the Institute for Advanced Study in Princeton, New Jersey then enabled me to spend the academic year 1986–87 at the Institute, which provided an atmosphere most congenial to study, discussion, and writing. Indeed, I shall long treasure my years at the Institute for the people I came to know there and the new perspectives I acquired. In both 1982–83 and 1986–87 Loyola University also generously subsidized my work, and the university has provided significant financial assistance for the publication of this volume.

John Elliott read an early version of the book while I was in Princeton and made many helpful comments. I am also grateful to him and to his wife Oonah for their unfailing hospitality. I thank Felix Gilbert and Peter Paret for their comments on individual chapters and Irving Lavin and Robert R. Palmer, who were always willing to discuss a point. There are too many members of our "class of 1986–87" at the Institute to whom I am indebted for their conversation and hospitality to mention by name, but I will not forget our time together. John McManamon, S.J., John O'Malley, S.J., and Volker Press helped by reading individual chapters for me, and Simone Zurawski assisted with her expertise in matters of art history. Geoffrey Parker generously read the whole manuscript at a late stage and made many valuable criticisms and suggestions. To the anonymous readers of the University of North Carolina Press and to its executive editor, Lewis Bateman, who has always been encouraging, I also want to express my gratitude, as well as to the press's Ron Maner and Margaret Morse, for their editorial assistance.

My fellow Jesuits at Loyola University and at our Ignatius House community have given me much support in the nearly nine years I have worked on this book and have listened to me discoursing on Machiavelli and anti-Machiavellians. I want to thank them here.

To my sister Barbara, R.S.C.J., and to my brother John, his wife Joey, and their six children I dedicate this book.

Robert Bireley, S.J.
Chicago, September 1989

The Counter-Reformation Prince

Chapter 1

The Challenge of Machiavelli

For there is such a difference between how men live and how they ought
to live that he who abandons what is done for what ought to be done
learns his destruction rather than his preservation, because any man who
under all conditions insists on making it his business to be good will
surely be destroyed among so many who are not good. Hence a prince,
in order to hold his position, must acquire the power to be not good, and
understand when to use it and when not to use it, in accord with
necessity.

So proclaimed Niccolò Machiavelli in the trenchant fifteenth chapter of
The Prince, written in 1513.[1] Whereas writers for centuries according to
Machiavelli had been content to describe the ideal ruler or to outline a
utopian republic, he proposed to get to things as they really were, not as
they ought to be, and to deal with politics as men practiced it, not as they
ought to practice it. Central to this new gospel was the message that one
could not be a serious Christian and prosper in politics. In a world in
which men were generally "ungrateful, changeable, simulators and dissimulators, runaways in danger, eager for gain,"[2] a ruler or man of
politics could not survive without resorting to practices held to be immoral. Political success, Machiavelli elaborated in the *Discourses* several
years later, was not compatible with Christianity, at least as it was traditionally understood, because Christianity in its encouragement of humility and contemplation turned men away from that attention to this
world and pursuit of human achievement necessary for the creation of a
vigorous state.[3]

Examples illustrating Machiavelli's message startled his readers.
Held up for imitation in the *Prince* was the ruthless Cesare Borgia and in
the *Discourses* the legendary Romulus, fratricide and founder of Rome.

I

Borgia, supported by his father Pope Alexander VI in his efforts to carve a state out for himself in central Italy, appointed Remirro de Orco, known for his cruelty as well as his ability, to restore order in the turbulent Romagna. Once Remirro had completed the task, Borgia, "getting an opportunity for it, . . . had Messer Remirro laid in two pieces in the public square with a block of wood and a bloody sword near him." In this way the ruler deflected from himself the hatred and ill-feeling the harsh methods of Remirro had generated, and he "left those people at the same time gratified and awe-struck" and so more ready to support him.[4] Romulus had murdered his own brother, Remus, who otherwise would have shared authority with him in Rome. Machiavelli praised the deed as one carried out with necessity for the good of the young state. Neither a republic nor a monarchy, he argued, could be founded or effectively reformed except by one man. So it was necessary for the public good that Remus be eliminated.[5]

Many contemporaries strongly sympathized with Machiavelli's position. His friend Guicciardini agreed that it was impossible, at least in present circumstances, to govern states according to the Christian law.[6] There was a vigorous current within the Christian tradition that advocated great reserve toward politics and the active life in a sinful world. Spiritual writers popular in the sixteenth century approached Machiavelli's vision of the world and warned the sincere Christian about participation in its affairs. Such, for example, was suggested by the *Imitation of Christ* of Thomas à Kempis (1418), perhaps the most widely read book of the period after the Bible.[7] The principal interlocutor in Thomas More's *Utopia* (1516), the fictional Raphael Hythloday, argued that a good man's participation in government, instead of raising the tone of political life, would inevitably drag him down to its level.[8]

The prolific Spanish moralist and court bishop, Antonio Guevara, whose books were translated and widely read throughout Europe, published a volume with the revealing title *Contempt of the Court and Praise of Rural Life* (1539). While acknowledging in this and in his earlier *Guide for Princes* (1529) that one could save one's soul in any state of life, Guevara warned emphatically of the dangers of life at court, the center of government.[9] His books as translated into German and somewhat reworked by the Bavarian court secretary Ägidius Albertinus at the end of the century made him into a representative of contempt for the court and the world.[10] Nor can one overlook the example of Emperor Charles V who, as was popularly believed, preferred retirement to a monastery over endorsement of the Peace of Augsburg, which he felt would compromise his conscience, an example not without influence on the abdication of the pious Duke William of Bavaria in 1598.[11] Before that, Montaigne had expressed a distaste for public life because of the conflicts it involved between its demands and those of morality.[12]

But many Christians were unwilling to accept Machiavelli's vision of politics and his claim that a Christian could not participate in politics effectively. Among these were the anti-Machiavellian writers. They intended to show not only that Christianity and political achievement were compatible, but that being a Christian greatly enhanced one's chances of political success. Though some writers took up the pen against Machiavelli following the publication of the *Prince* and the *Discourses* in the early 1530s, the first two significant books in the anti-Machiavellian tradition with which we are concerned did not appear until 1589. These were the *Reason of State* of the Italian priest and one-time secretary to Charles Borromeo, Giovanni Botero, and the *Six Books on Politics* of the well-known Flemish humanist, Justus Lipsius, at the time professor at the University of Leiden but soon to return formally to Catholicism and to the University of Louvain. Botero, Lipsius, and the tradition they founded sought to elaborate a Christian statecraft or reason of state, that is, a Christian method for the preservation and development of a powerful state. Indeed, the title of Botero's volume helped popularize the term "reason of state"; he has been called the most frequently cited political writer in the first half of the seventeenth century.[13] Lipsius has recently been rediscovered as perhaps the most influential writer of the same period.[14] Together with the anti-Machiavellian authors who followed them, they represented a major current of thought within the Counter-Reformation, that is, the epoch in the history of the Catholic church stretching roughly from the mid-1540s, with the opening of the Council of Trent, to about 1700 and characterized by efforts at internal reform both personal and institutional, the defeat of Protestantism, and updating or accommodation to contemporary society and culture.[15] Not surprisingly, the anti-Machiavellians also displayed significant features of the Baroque culture that predominated in Catholic Europe from about 1590 to 1680[16] that was marked by the effort to establish intellectual and political order after the varied and profound changes of the sixteenth century.

According to his own testimony in the *Prince* and the *Discourses*, Machiavelli's outlook on politics developed out of two sources, his own experience and his reading of the ancient authors, especially the Romans. In both regards he was a son of the Renaissance, of the turbulent Italian politics of the era, and of humanism's fascination with Greece and Rome. Born in 1469, Machiavelli first entered public life in 1498, when he became second chancellor of the Florentine Republic. Four years before, all Italy had been thrown into confusion by the invasion of the French under Charles VIII, and the peninsula was to remain a battleground for the armies of France, Spain, and then the Holy Roman Emperor until 1559. During this period Milan changed hands eleven times, and in the forty years from 1490 to 1530 Machiavelli's native Florence underwent six major changes in its form of government. No wonder the search for stability characterized his political thought. His years in the chancery saw him carry on much of the official correspondence of the government as well as its correspondence with diplomats in the field, undertake major diplomatic missions himself to the French, imperial, and papal courts, and carry the responsibility for military administration, especially for the nagging war between Florence and Pisa.

With the collapse of the republic in 1512 and the return of the Medici to power, Machiavelli found himself without a governmental position, and despite his later efforts to acquire a post under the Medici, he was never successful. Thus the years until his death in 1527 were devoted principally to reading and writing, and in a fascinating letter he told a friend of the long evenings he spent in converse with the ancients, weighing their words carefully and adding his own reflections.[17] The *Prince* and the *Discourses on the First Ten Books of Livy* are his two books that concern us here. They are certainly the most important for his political thought, and they were the only ones really familiar to the anti-Machiavellian writers. The *Discourses* grew out of political discussions with friends and cronies in the Oricellari Gardens in Florence between 1515 and 1521, whereas the *Prince* was composed a little earlier as a gift for a Medici prince in the hope of an office as a reward. But a number of other works came from his pen in his later years, especially the *Art of War*, a discussion of military affairs complementing the *Discourses*; the *History of Florence*, a classic of the new humanist historiography; and the comedy *Mandragola*, still considered by many to be the most vital drama in the Italian language.

For Machiavelli the primary purpose of government, princely or republican, was the foundation and conservation of a powerful state.[18] The achievement of this goal reaped honor and glory for the ruler, or, in the case of a republic, for the citizens. Living amidst the volatile political situation of Italy, Machiavelli saw the public good largely in terms of order and security and the power necessary to guarantee them. His account of the origin of states emphasized that the primary reason people came together in a political community was the need for common defense.[19] He had relatively little to say about the goals of government beyond the continuing existence of an ordered state. Apart from the glory that citizens of a free and vigorous republic garnered for themselves, he did not elaborate on the benefits citizens or subjects might share, such as a fuller social life, economic development, educational and cultural activity, or moral growth—all elements of the common good in the Aristotelian tradition.

But to maintain a state was a greater challenge than to found one. The supreme human achievement was leadership of a state that endured in the face of the ravages of time, human nature, and fortune. To those who had a share in it belonged the highest glory of this world. Machiavelli emphasized the conservation of the state: its conquest of time in an environment where security was constantly threatened from within and from without.[20] His preference for a republican over a princely form of government was dictated by his conviction that a republic supported loyally by its citizens was more powerful and so more likely to endure over the long haul than a principality. The persistent threat to the state's existence, so evident to Machiavelli in contemporary Italy, came from the fickle and usually malicious nature of human beings and from the historical process itself.

The first presumption of the lawgiver had to be "that all men are evil and that they are always going to act according to the wickedness of their spirits whenever they have free scope."[21] They were characterized by an insatiable desire to possess more goods and untiring ambition to hold more power so as to render secure that which they already possessed. This incessant desire for more gives rise to "unending discontent in human minds and weariness with what is attained. Hence the present is blamed, the past is praised, and the future is desired, even though men are not moved to act in this way by any reasonable cause."[22] Thus men forever sought change, growing weary of even the prosperity they did possess; this pursuit of change and new satisfactions led to hostilities and wars, the ruin of one state and the rise of another. So human affairs remained in a continual state of flux, some states in ascent toward greater prosperity and power, others in decline.[23] The challenge to government was to maintain stability amidst this constant ebb and flow, and glory was the reward to be won.

The two major correlative factors in the historical process were, according to Machiavelli, fortune and *virtù*. The precise meaning of these terms is slippery and impossible to pin down. Fortune represented the power of heaven in human affairs; it was conceived after the fashion of the pagan goddess Fortuna rather than Christian providence.[24] Unpredictable, it always gave reason for hope and it always achieved its goals. This it did without fully determining man, though it did lessen his responsibility and freedom, so that "men who commonly live amid great troubles or successes deserve less praise or blame."[25] Man could not successfully resist fortune. What was within his power was to discern its designs, perhaps modify them to a degree, and then ride with their direction. He was enabled to do this by *virtù*, a term deriving from classical and Christian *virtus* but transformed by Machiavelli while retaining elements of its former character. Looked at from another perspective, fortune provided the opportunity (*occasióne*) for the exercise of *virtù*; without this chance to show itself, *virtù* would be wasted.[26]

In a well-known chapter of the *Prince*, Machiavelli used two images to explain what he meant by fortune and its interplay with *virtù*. Fortune was similar to a river raging in the springtime, overwhelming all that stood in its course. One could not make headway against the torrent, but one could foresee its coming and, to some extent, channel it to one's purposes through the skillful use of ditches and embankments. Fortune was also like a woman who yielded more readily to an aggressive suitor; it favored those who forced situations and seized the opportunities held out to them.[27] Thus foresight and boldness were inherent in Machiavelli's *virtù*, as well as the ability to adapt to circumstances and to attune one's actions to the ever-changing demands of the situation. *Virtù* could, then, within limits, manage to modify fortune. As Machiavelli put it, fortune displayed less power when confronted by *virtù*.[28] Reversing the verdict of Livy, he claimed that the success of Rome was due more to the *virtù* of its citizens than to the blessings of fortune. But there was a constant amount of *virtù*, Machiavelli reflected in the introduction to the second book of the *Discourses*, distributed differently throughout the world in different historical epochs. At one time it was concentrated among the Assyrians, then with the Medes, the Persians, and the Romans in that order. Once departed from Rome, it scattered among the barbarian kingdoms. The unforeseeable distribution of *virtù* contributed to the instability of politics, and the constant amount of its total reservoir meant that its appearance in one place indicated its departure from another. A new power always arose at the expense of an old one.[29]

Machiavelli's gloomy evaluation of human nature and fortune's uncertainties contrasted with the Renaissance optimism he displayed in the ability of men to meet the challenge of government. In the *Prince* and the *Discourses* he laid out his program for effective government. The *Prince* was concerned with one-man rule and the *Discourses* mainly with republican government, though the latter explicitly included considerable advice for princes too. His main sources were, as we have seen, his own experience and his reading among the ancients. Prominence among them was given to Livy, the historian of the Roman Republic, which Machiavelli considered to represent mankind's highest achievement. Better than any other state the Roman Republic had weathered the storms of time, and it was above all in its history that he sought the secrets to a state's endurance. Contemporary enthusiasm was unbounded, he wrote, for the art and literature of classical Greece and Rome, which served as models for artists and writers of the day. We even admired the political and military accomplishments of the ancients, but we failed to look to them for instruction and for models. This, however, was precisely the fruit to be gained from the study of history. Men remained essentially the same. "All cities and all peoples have the same desires and the same traits and . . . they have always had them. He who diligently examines past events easily foresees future ones in every country and can apply to them the remedies used by the ancients or, not finding any that have been used, can devise new ones because of the similarity of the events."[30]

Machiavelli's program can, for our purposes, be grouped under four headings: the qualities of an effective ruler—or in a republic, the qualities of the leaders or the citizen body itself—and the roles of law, religion, and the military in a powerful state. But first a word of caution is in order. Although we may systematize his work in order to discuss it, Machiavelli was not a systematic thinker, and it is unrealistic to expect consistency in him. His elusive use of fortune and *virtù* has been indicated. The *Prince* and the *Discourses* embody essentially the same vision of politics, but they obviously have different emphases. Machiavelli was a rhetorician, and he enjoyed in particular the use of hyperbole, which he apparently employed to shock his readers, as in the famous dictum in the *Prince* that men had to be "either caressed or else annihilated."[31] He deliberately overstated a position in order to make a point he modified elsewhere, and his critics often fastened upon such passages. One cannot fault them for this any more than one can fault Machiavelli for inconsistency.

Many characteristics of Machiavelli's ruler were comprised under *virtù*, fortune's counterpart. While preserving features of traditional moral virtue, in his hand the term took on new meaning. One modern writer has called it "whatever qualities are in practice needed to 'save the life and preserve the freedom of one's country.'"[32] *Virtù* meant political virtuosity. Three elements Machiavelli ascribed to it have already been pointed out: discernment of the course of fortune, boldness in seizing proffered opportunity, and flexibility in shifting circumstances. Certainly it included devotion to the public good. The man of genuine *virtù* had to place the public welfare above personal advantage and pursue it diligently as the highest good. When discussing a republic, it was above all in their allegiance to the common welfare that Machiavelli located the *virtù* of the citizen body.

Machiavelli's ruler had to know when to transcend traditional categories of right and wrong, to "acquire the power to be not good, and understand when to use it and when not to use it, in accord with necessity."[33] A new prince in particular could not "practice all those things for which men are considered good, being often forced, in order to keep his position, to act contrary to truth, contrary to charity, contrary to humanity and contrary to religion."[34] A republic as well as a prince had to learn, in the words of a figure employed by the Spartan statesman Lysander, to assume the role of a lion and a fox, that is, to apply force or fraud in an appropriate fashion in order to achieve desired ends. Fraud was often more effective than force, especially when a state had not yet developed sufficient resources to make proper use of force. "By no means can a prudent ruler keep his word—and he does not—when to keep it works against himself and when the reasons that made him promise are annulled. If all men were good, this maxim would not be good; but because they are bad, and do not keep their promises to you, you likewise do not have to keep yours to them. Never has a shrewd prince lacked justifying reasons to make his promise-breaking appear honorable." Model for the use of fraud was Pope Alexander VI. "Never was there a man more effective in swearing and who with stronger oaths confirmed a promise, but yet honored it less. Nonetheless, his deceptions always prospered as he hoped, because he understood well this aspect of the world."[35]

Machiavelli knew well that every government, princely as well as republican, needed a healthy democratic element, in the sense that it could not rule effectively without popular support. One could not long govern against the will of the people. Thus the ability to secure and retain popular support, to "make believers of the people," was essential to the art of rule. Government had to have leadership. One way to secure popular support was precisely through good government, for example, by keeping down expenditures in order to avoid burdensome taxes and above all by providing the order and security the people called for.[36] "Good government was good politics" one would say today.

But there was more to it than this. Machiavelli discussed the famous question of whether it was better for a prince or a republican government to be loved or to be feared, granting that it was desirable that both attitudes be found in the people. In both cases he came down on the side of fear. Because of their fickle nature, it was much more difficult to hold the allegiance of men through bonds of love than constraints of fear. Moreover, it was more in the power of the ruler to instill fear than love. One could compel people to fear but not to love. But at all costs a ruler had to avoid hatred and contempt. These were the twin sources of conspiracy. Machiavelli spent a long chapter in the *Prince* showing that it was by incurring the hatred or contempt of the people or of dominant social groups that many Roman emperors prepared their downfall.[37] Those whose support one could never hope to win should be simply destroyed, for example the remaining heirs of a dispossessed ruling house. In this context he made his well-known remark that "men are to be either caressed or annihilated," and he praised the thoroughness with which Cesare Borgia rooted out potential rivals.[38]

Popular support required the systematic cultivation of the ruler's reputation or image, according to Machiavelli. With some exaggeration he has been credited with first writing of reputation as a tool of government.[39] Reputation was crucial in politics. As we have seen, it was not possible for a successful ruler to avoid violations of the normal precepts of virtue and religion. On the other hand, his reputation, on which his popular support depended, demanded that he "appear merciful, trustworthy, humane, blameless, religious," and especially the last, which was judged of the utmost importance by the multitude. For this reason the ruler had to learn to "be a great simulator and dissimulator. So simpleminded are men and so controlled by immediate necessities that a prince who deceives always finds men who let themselves be deceived."[40] What was required was not that the prince be good but that he seem to be good. Appearance was what counted.

Reputation, in addition, demanded that the prince perform great and astounding deeds—military, certainly, but of other kinds too. The purpose was to make a firm and lasting impression on the people, to arouse in them admiration and amazement at his actions. Two examples of Ferdinand of Aragon made the point, his conquest of the Moors at Granada and his subsequent expulsion of Moors and Jews from Spain, the latter much more effective because it was performed under the guise of religion. An example of another sort was the return to her husband of a beautiful young Spanish woman by the Roman general Scipio Africanus when he might have kept her as a prize of war. "Above all, a prince strives to gain from all his acts notoriety as a strong man of superior ability." Moreover, whereas he ought to learn to mingle with the common people periodically and so manifest his humanity, he had always to be careful not to compromise "the dignity of his high position, because this he never at any time forgets."[41]

Machiavelli preferred republican to princely government, as is abundantly clear from the *Discourses*. A single individual was necessary for the foundation of a new state or the reform of an old one. But only a republic, with its larger measure of popular support, could endure over time and become truly great. The qualities required for government were much more likely to be found in a republic. To find more than two successive princes in a line who were endowed with a high degree of *virtù* was nearly impossible. A republic provided a greater pool of men of *virtù* from which to select officeholders, and the variety of their gifts made it easier for a republic to adapt to new situations than for a prince who was more liable to be set in his ways. Generally speaking, the people, when living under law, were wiser and more constant than a prince. Most important of all, only in republics did people really look to the common welfare. The reason was their participation in government and hence closer identification with the state. People supported more fully that in which they had an active part and interest. But republics, too, were inclined to corruption, that is, the subordination of the public good to private interest, and every republic would eventually decline and disintegrate. Rome had long parried the assaults of time only to succumb in the end.[42]

Proper laws were required for a vigorous state. In the *Prince* Machiavelli passed over a discussion of the role of law and turned directly to that of the military after remarking the reciprocal influence of the two. Laws were of little value without the power to enforce them, and the raising of an army required a well-organized state.[43] There was a thorough discussion in the *Discourses* of the fundamental law or constitution of the Roman Republic. This Machiavelli saw as a model, with its combination of monarchical and aristocratic elements although essentially popular in nature. Law served as the source of justice, and it balanced social interests. Rivalry and contention kept political awareness alive in a republic and were a sign of health provided they did not descend into factionalism; to prevent this was the function of law.

Indeed, law performed a function similar to religion for Machiavelli, though not as effectively. It was to inspire and even more to intimidate the citizens to display that *virtù* and especially that devotion to the common welfare without which a republic could not long remain vital. Law, after religion, was the antidote to corruption in a republic. Machiavelli acknowledged the difficulty in finding such laws, and for this reason he lauded the great figures who through their institution or revision of the laws had founded or reformed states, Numa, Lycurgus, and Moses.[44] Machiavelli encouraged the ruler or leading citizens to obey the law as an example to others. But although he seemed to be aware of the danger of too easily bypassing the law, he did not want it to stand in the way of remedying an evil. Piero Soderini, for example, should not have allowed respect for legal restraints to deter him from destroying his opponents and saving the Florentine republic from its enemies.[45]

Numa, the earliest Roman king and founder of the Roman religion, deserved a more prominent place in Roman history than did Romulus, the legendary founder of the state itself. So Machiavelli asserted the value of religion to the state. The *Prince* sought to impress upon the ruler the absolute necessity that he appear religious, because of the importance the people attached to religion. But it was in the *Discourses*, where he discussed the means to instill in the people that element of *virtù* which was devotion to the public good, that Machiavelli stressed the contribution of religion. He was unconcerned with truth; religion was for him solely a means of social control and a source of patriotism. "It is the duty, then, of the rulers of a republic or of a kingdom to preserve the foundations of the religion they hold. If they do this, it will be an easy thing for them to keep their state religious, and consequently good and united. Also whatever comes up in favor of religion, even though they think it false, they are to accept and magnify. And so much the more they are going to do it as they are more prudent and as they have better understanding of natural things."[46] Roman religion had been eminently successful in developing devotion to the public good, especially through its ability to inspire fear of the consequences should one act against that good. Christianity, on the other hand, was not suited to foster public spirit.

In his discussion of Christianity, Machiavelli raised criticisms to which Gibbon would later return. One reason for the recent decline in free states in Europe had been the influence of Christianity. It emphasized humility, placed a high premium on contemplation, and looked to man's fulfillment only in the next world. It disparaged the pursuit of earthly glory and riches and set up as models those who renounced them. Thus it diverted men from activity in this world and discouraged them from undertaking those great deeds on behalf of their country which would win them glory and fame. Christianity might have been interpreted in a different fashion, Machiavelli allowed, that would have rendered it more beneficial to the interests of liberty and patriotism. But the reform activity of Dominic and Francis in the thirteenth century had reinforced the traditional stress on humility and poverty.[47]

The papacy in particular came in for Machiavelli's strictures for its debilitating effect on Italian life. Decadence at the court of Rome had led to the decline of genuine religion in Italy. "Nor can a better estimate of its decline be made than by seeing that those peoples who are nearest to the Roman Church, the head of our religion, have least religion." More importantly, from Machiavelli's perspective, the papacy was responsible for the political plight of Italy, that is, its division into a number of smaller states that rendered it defenseless against invasions from without. The papacy, on the one hand, was not sufficiently strong to unite Italy under its aegis; on the other, partly because of its strategic position across the center of the peninsula, it was able to prevent any other state from doing so.[48]

Roman religion had succeeded where Christianity now failed. Roman citizens, individually or in a body, feared to break an oath more than they did to violate the laws; they were more in terror of gods than men. An incident following the Roman defeat at Cannae illustrated the point. A large group of citizens were preparing to flee to Sicily, thus abandoning the defense of their country. Hearing of this, Scipio rushed to the scene and with unsheathed sword compelled them to take an oath to remain and defend their country. "Thus those citizens whom love of their country and its laws did not keep in Italy were kept by an oath that they were forced to take." Religion induced them to act in the public interest.[49]

Well aware of the popular respect for religion, King Numa had always appealed to religious authority as the source of his enactments, and he pretended to regular conversations with a nymph. Machiavelli heartily approved this pious fraud and related other instances of successful religious deceit. No lawgiver among any people, he remarked, ever succeeded without the resort to religious authority and sanctions. For Machiavelli the foundation of Roman religion was the auspices, the attempt to divine the favor of the gods through the observation of the conduct of sacred birds or the position of their entrails. He showed how Roman leaders regularly manipulated these in order to secure popular support for actions or policies they considered to be in the public interest and especially to encourage and reassure soldiers on the eve of major battles. A distinctive advantage of Roman religion over Christianity to which Machiavelli pointed was the bloody nature of its sacrifices. At the sight of blood the people and especially the soldiers became ferocious and bold defenders of their country.[50]

The military was the foundation of the state for Machiavelli, and he devoted much attention to it in the *Prince* and in the *Discourses*. Had he not said that a ruler must be able to act as a lion as well as a fox? Contemporary Italy demonstrated a state's need for an effective military force. Machiavelli cited the oft-quoted words of Tacitus, "nothing is so weak or shaky as the reputation of a power that does not rely on its own strength."[51] Reputation alone would not suffice. A dictum Machiavelli refused to accept was that "riches are the sinews of war." Finances were vital, to be sure, but they were secondary to the formation of good soldiers. "For gold is not enough to find good soldiers, but good soldiers are quite enough to find gold."[52] One of the practical weaknesses of Machiavelli's thought was his nearly total neglect of economic growth and development as a basis for the power of the state. He did recognize the importance of an increasing population, but largely as a source of soldiers and of colonists for newly acquired territories. Rome might lose battles, but it always had the resources to put a new army into the field.[53]

Machiavelli had spent considerable time as a Florentine military administrator, and he had developed forceful views on the kind of army he felt necessary. He decried the use of mercenary troops, who had brought so much woe to Italy. Either they did not fight enthusiastically and were ineffective, or under a vigorous captain they won victories only to become a threat to the state that had hired them. Auxiliary troops, that is troops on loan from a friendly state, were little better; if they were successful in battle, they likewise became a peril for the state in whose cause they were engaged. Machiavelli insisted on an army made up of a state's own citizens or subjects. The failure to develop such forces was a main cause for the plight of Italy and was in sharp contrast with the practice of Rome. Only an army of native troops would fight vigorously in the service of their country, where they were battling for their own land, their own people, their own glory. This was especially true of a republic, where the citizens had a greater stake in the state. An army had to be kept in a state of constant readiness; the expense of such preparedness for a mercenary army was prohibitive. Only in an army of native soldiers did one have the common language and culture that fostered the development of a high esprit de corps.[54]

There was another reason for Machiavelli's passionate advocacy of a strong military. This was his conviction that a republic had to expand in order to survive and acquire glory. War was the normal means to this expansion and to the glory that it brought. As we have seen, Machiavelli considered the maintenance of a state a greater achievement than its foundation and long endurance possible only for a state with a republican constitution. But a republic also had to continue aggrandizing itself if it were to last. To be sure, Machiavelli distinguished two kinds of republics, those organized merely for preservation and those organized for conquest. Examples of the former were Sparta, Venice, and the contemporary German free cities; of the latter, Rome was the only feasible model. One could not stand still in a world that was in constant flux; one had to advance or move backwards. If a state was satisfied with its own extent and did not desire expansion at the expense of other states, they would take the offensive and force it into conflict and to the acquisition of new territory. Furthermore, if a state was not engaged in foreign war, domestic strife was bound to erupt and upset the social peace. Foreign war drew a state together and promoted unity. It brought to the helm of a republic leaders imbued with devotion to the state and the other qualities of *virtù*. Whereas in times of peace citizens out of envy often chose leaders of mediocre ability, in periods of imminent war they turned back to those figures really qualified for leadership. Thus war evoked the *virtù* of the citizens and spurred them on to the pursuit of glory in conquest.[55]

For Machiavelli as, according to Gibbon, for Livy, the Romans conquered the world in self-defense, that is, in the pursuit of security against domestic strife and potential foreign foes. The only reason the German free cities were able to avoid the alternative, expansion or decline, was that the emperor still possessed sufficient authority to mediate their disputes. Machiavelli did not really explain the long existence of Sparta and Venice; he made it clear that neither had chosen the path to dominion and glory. Sparta he criticized for failing to take measures that would have permitted it to carry out elements of the Roman program for aggrandizement he so admired. Venice Machiavelli faulted for its failure to arm its people and so to develop the needed military strength. If he did not succeed in demonstrating that expansion was essential to the long life of a republic, he did show that aggrandizement and war were a necessity for the republic he envisaged, covered with glory in the image of Rome. But even Rome had to come to an end, Machiavelli realized; no state could hope for eternal life.[56]

Neither the *Discourses* nor the *Prince* were published until the winter of 1531–32, four years after the author's death; then both appeared with the permission of the Medici pope, Clement VII. But long before then, in fact since the first appearance of the *Prince* in manuscript, controversy had swirled about his writings. The dedications of the early editions alluded to the polemics they had already generated in Florence. Yet there were in circulation approximately fifteen editions of the *Prince* and nineteen of the *Discourses* and French translations of each before they were placed on the Index of Paul IV in 1559, a measure which nearly stopped publication in Catholic areas except for France.[57]

Three principal writers took the field against Machiavelli between the publication of his works and their condemnation in 1559 and again by the Tridentine Index in 1564. These were the English cardinal Reginald Pole and the Portuguese bishop Jeronymo Osorio, both of whom lived for many years in Italy, and the Italian humanist and later bishop, Ambrogio Caterino Politi. Pole and Caterino were important figures at the first two sessions of the Council of Trent, 1545 to 1547, and 1551 to 1552. All three grasped clearly Machiavelli's challenge to Christianity, even though their acquaintance with his work was incomplete. They focused on elements of his thought to which the later anti-Machiavellians would subsequently return.

Pole in his *Apology for Emperor Charles V*, written in the late 1530s but not published for over two centuries, issued a warning against Machiavelli that had European significance. He told how he had been introduced to the *Prince* by Thomas Cromwell, Henry VIII's chief minister and enemy of More. Cromwell had explained to him that the view of politics in the schools was all right in its place, but that it had no relationship to the actual government of a state, where experience had to be the guide. He then spoke of the *Prince* and offered to obtain a copy for Pole. But the cardinal did not get his hands on one until a later visit to Florence, where he raised the issue of Machiavelli with friends. Immediately he realized that the *Prince* embodied a philosophy of life at odds with Christianity that amounted to practical atheism. He singled out Machiavelli's reduction of religion to a means of control of a ruler's subjects, his elevation of utility to the sole measure of political action, and his effective denial of the Christian vision of divine providence. Only Satan could be the author of such a doctrine, Pole claimed, and he called Machiavelli more pernicious than the heretics or schismatics. In fact, he argued, Henry VIII had followed the teaching of the *Prince* in the introduction of the Reformation into England and in the shameless way he had broken faith with the rebels at the time of the Pilgrimage of Grace.[58]

Having spent time in Italy in the 1530s, Bishop Osorio returned to Rome for some years before his death in 1580, during the pontificate of Gregory XIII, and earlier works of his were reissued late in the century. His *On Christian Nobility* (Lisbon, 1542), comprised "the first published attack" on Machiavelli.[59] But it was in a later edition, published in Florence itself in 1552, that he took issue with Machiavelli in a manner showing familiarity with the *Discourses* as well as the *Prince*. While making the same arguments as Pole, he introduced new ones. Having understood Machiavelli to have blamed Christianity for the downfall of Rome, he rejected this argument. All things human must come to an end, he contended as had Augustine in the *City of God*. Moreover, the causes of Rome's demise had been at work in Roman society long before the advent of Christianity. Military virtue had not suffered at the hands of Christians. The fact was that Machiavelli equated bravery with a certain animal ferocity inspired by the bloody pagan sacrifices and superstitious fear of the gods. This was far from Christian courage.

Osorio went on to serious distortions of Christianity he found in Machiavelli. He made a crucial if traditional distinction between private and public affairs, which was scarcely new in the sixteenth century, Thomas Aquinas having made it back in the thirteenth.[60] Machiavelli wrote as if Christ had taught that one must always return a kindness for an insult, failing to distinguish between persons and circumstances.

Christians were encouraged to show patience and moderation in private matters, "but in times of public danger they are energetic, vigorous champions of the public good and of liberty, especially when the dignity of religion is involved. In the latter case they look upon meekness as a shameful disgrace and patience as a serious crime."[61] Moses and David had shown this spirit, as had a number of unnamed Christian emperors. Christ himself was terribly severe with those who made a mockery of temple worship. Osorio rejected the position that participation in war was prohibited by the New Testament. Christianity certainly approved the use of force in a just war involving the public good or religion and in situations calling for the preservation of domestic order. Contrary to Machiavelli's assertion, through its encouragement of the martial virtues Christianity fostered the public good.[62]

Ambrogio Caterino—or Lancelotto Politi, as he was known before his entrance into the Dominicans in 1517—had developed from a humanist into a significant theologian and was active at the first session of the Council of Trent, during which he was made Bishop of Minore in Italy. His denunciation of Machiavelli appeared at the end of a short work, *Books to be Hated by a Christian and to be Completely Eliminated from Christendom*, published in 1552, a year before his death and intended for the use of the Fathers at Trent.[63] For him a refutation of Machiavelli was not really necessary; it was enough for a Christian to become familiar with the doctrine of the *Prince* and the *Discourses* to realize it was unacceptable. Caterino pointed especially to Machiavelli's effective denial of the Christian conception of divine providence and to his reduction of religion to a means of government control. Particular offense was taken at Machiavelli's encouragement that the ruler learn to act as a lion and a fox. Caterino cited the pertinent passage from Cicero's *Moral Obligation*, where Machiavelli had presumably gleaned the image, and showed that Cicero had condemned both types of conduct as inhuman. The teaching of Machiavelli was at odds not only with Christianity but with humanity and reason.

Thus by the early 1550s the anti-Christian character of the *Prince* and the *Discourses* had been recognized, and Machiavelli was considered a dangerous author in the Catholic world. Yet there was a general awareness that he was being read, especially by rulers and those with political influence, and the publication of his works confirmed this. Caterino had called attention to the fact. Thus it was not surprising that his works appeared on the Index in 1559 and five years later on the Tridentine Index. This took place despite the efforts of partisans of Machiavelli to prevent such a step. Even their attempt to secure approval for an expurgated edition of the *Discourses* and of the *Art of War* fell short. Still, there was as yet no general campaign against Machiavelli. Many of the Fathers at Trent had thought it best simply to ignore him.[64]

Events of the religious wars in France, and especially the Massacre of St. Bartholomew's Day, August 24, 1572, then had a profound effect on Machiavelli's standing. French translations of the *Discourses* and the *Prince* (in two versions) along with the *Art of War* had appeared by 1553. The original French reaction was mixed. The humanist and constitutionalist Estienne Pasquier writing in 1560 considered the *Prince* to be "worthy of the fire," and Estienne de La Boétie, poet and friend of Montaigne, shared his view.[65] But Jean Bodin's first comments, found in his *Method for the Easy Comprehension of History*, published in 1566, were positive. Machiavelli was the first person to have written intelligently about government in nearly twelve hundred years. Then came the St. Bartholomew's Day Massacre, with its over five thousand Huguenot victims in Paris and the provinces. Many Frenchmen allotted the responsibility for it to the Italian Catholic Queen Mother, Catherine de Medici. They tended to see it as the product of a typically Italian statecraft that was best embodied in the works of Machiavelli. Thus the attacks on Machiavelli that began to appear were often also manifestations of an intense feeling against Italians. Of these the most important was the *Discourse against Machiavelli* by the Huguenot Innocent Gentillet, published in Geneva in 1576.[66] It was the first attempt at a systematic refutation of Machiavelli and was to have a far-reaching influence on Catholic as well as Protestant authors. Catholic writers like Pole associated Machiavelli with the Protestants, whereas Protestant authors saw him as Italian and Catholic.

Gentillet divided his book into three parts, each containing maxims drawn from the *Prince* or the *Discourses*—Gentillet saw the latter as a commentary on the former—which were then discussed at varying length. Altogether there were fifty maxims, each discussed in a separate essay. Gentillet explicitly forewent the Scriptures as a means to refute Machiavelli; this was too easy. His sources were the classical writers and the historians of France. Often enough he distorted Machiavelli's thought in the selection and formulation of his maxims, but he recognized as clearly as had the Catholic theologians its essentially anti-Christian character. Machiavelli was an "atheist." Evidence for the dissemination of Machiavelli's books was given when Gentillet referred to them as the bible—or as he put it—the "Koran of the courtiers."[67]

Right at the start, in his dedicatory epistle to Francis, Duke of Alençon, the king's brother, from whom the Huguenots hoped to receive support, Gentillet made it clear that the primary task of the ruler was to support and maintain the Christian religion. He was never to approve or encourage false religion as Machiavelli advised. Both the Catholics and the Reformed deserved to be called Christians, according to Gentillet, and except for a few remarks, the Catholics did not come in for the diatribes one might have expected. Machiavelli was clearly a greater danger to church and society than were the Catholics. Gentillet did attack the papacy vigorously—one of the points on which he agreed with Machiavelli was his criticism of its religion—and he went out of his way to pillory aspects of the mendicant life. But under the obvious influence of current events he deplored religious wars, whether they were meant to impose religion within the ruler's own country or to propagate it elsewhere. Gentillet seemed to have some hope for religious reconciliation in France.[68]

Two further themes characterized the *Discourse against Machiavelli*. Gentillet insisted on the limits to governmental authority imposed by the law of God, the natural law, and the fundamental laws of the kingdom, especially the right of private property, and he contrasted Machiavelli's thought with the French juridical tradition.[69] The other theme was to be substantially developed by the Catholic anti-Machiavellians: immoral or irreligious conduct was ultimately counterproductive. It either brought down God's punishment on the state or ruler or it produced by its very nature the opposite of the desired effect. Gentillet listed, for example, a number of rulers who had been entangled in their own deceits, and he argued that fidelity to one's word was the basis of any society. Machiavelli's recommendations were not only immoral, they were ineffective.[70]

Jean Bodin's magnum opus, the *Six Books of the Republic*, appeared in 1576, the same year as Gentillet's *Discourse*. Bodin wrote in the preface that one goal of the volume was to combat the nefarious effects of Machiavelli's doctrine, and he had certainly altered his position toward Machiavelli since the publication of the *Method for the Easy Comprehension of History* ten years before. Bodin shared Machiavelli's respect for experience and sense for the importance of history in the study of government. But for Bodin experience and history both pointed to the existence and validity of law. A purpose in his major writings was to uncover what was common to all cultures and so served as the basis for a universal and natural law. Bodin's knowledge of history was much broader than Machiavelli's. Whatever his ultimate religious beliefs, he was a deeply religious and moral man. For him the final goal of the state was the development of virtue in the people, first the moral virtues, then the intellectual ones that flowered into contemplation of God's creation and then God himself. Bodin's ruler, fitted out with sovereignty as he was, was definitely subordinate to divine and natural law and to the basic laws of the kingdom.[71] Catholic anti-Machiavellian writers contested Bodin on many issues, but they were in agreement with him on the moral purpose of the state. They drew on him, often without acknowledgment.

By the time Botero and Lipsius published their anti-Machiavellian works in 1589, change had transformed the general scene in Europe from what it had been when Machiavelli composed the *Prince* and the *Discourses*. The new situation could not help but influence their response to him; indeed the anti-Machiavellians were responding to the changing times as well as to Machiavelli.[72]

The first half of the sixteenth century constituted an important chapter in the emergence of the modern state. The France of Francis I, the Spain of Ferdinand and Isabella and then Charles I, and the England of Henry VII and Henry VIII all saw a significant increase of royal authority vis-à-vis its principal competitors, the feudal nobility, the towns, and the church. In the long run the Reformation resulted in greater governmental control of religion in Catholic as well as Protestant states, but in the short run in France and elsewhere it stirred civil conflict among competing religious, social, and political groups. France under Francis I had been for Machiavelli, and in reality, the most powerful state in Europe, but after the sudden death of Henry II in 1559 there erupted the religious wars that tore France apart and that approached their climax in the 1580s. By that time Spain under Philip II was the leading power in Europe, partly because of the internal conflict weakening France. As a result of the Italian Wars that had stretched out from 1494 to 1559, and under the shadow of which Machiavelli had lived and worked, Spain, in control of Milan and Naples, dominated Italy.

But to the north the Dutch rebellion had broken out in 1566, and the Netherlands soon became the running sore of the Spanish Empire, draining Spain of money and resources. At the same time the conflict disrupted the southern Netherlands, one of the most prosperous areas of Europe, and provoked widespread emigration, especially to the northern states of the Dutch Republic and to Germany. Lipsius himself was among the emigrants. But in the late 1580s, under the leadership of the Duke of Parma, the Spanish position improved, and this despite the defeat of the Spanish Armada in 1588. In 1580 Philip II had brought Portugal under his dominion and so added to the crown's colonies in America and the Far East those of the Portuguese. Thus the Spanish monarchy could boast of the most extensive empire the world had yet known. The sun never did set on it. England, meanwhile, now directed by the firm hand of Elizabeth and committed to the Protestant cause, had risen to become the chief European rival of Spain. Having for a time cautiously supplied aid to the Huguenots in France and the rebels in the Netherlands, England then rescued the cause of Protestantism in northwestern Europe with the stunning defeat of the Spanish Armada in 1588, an event that struck a severe blow at Spanish morale and confidence.

Germany and Italy, each still made up of many medium- to small-sized states, had passed through difficult times during the first half of the century. Germany had had its civil war between Emperor Charles V and the mostly Protestant states; this strife finally ended with the Peace of Augsburg in 1555. Italy suffered through the long ordeal of the Italian Wars, fought largely by Habsburg and Valois. Both then enjoyed a period of relative peace and prosperity during the second half of the century, which saw the increasing consolidation of political power in the larger territories and princely states like Bavaria and Saxony, Savoy and Tuscany. The Augsburg settlement provided Germany with a fragile political stability that lasted until the outbreak of the Thirty Years' War in 1618. By giving the princes the authority to determine the religion in their territories, Lutheran or Catholic, the Peace greatly increased the power of the princes vis-à-vis the emperor and the territorial estates, thus further fixing the direction of German political development.

But Germany, and to a lesser extent Italy, were threatened by the advance of the Ottoman power, which had been pushing forward since the late fourteenth century. The Turks controlled most of southeastern Europe, and in 1529 they had pushed to the very gates of Vienna. They remained a constant peril even after the death of the great sultan, Suleiman the Magnificent, in 1566. They and their Muslim allies in North Africa challenged the Christian forces in the Mediterranean, raiding the European coast, and their presence in the Mediterranean remained strong even after the legendary victory of the Christians over the Turks at Lepanto in 1571. One reason most Italians remained relatively content with Spanish domination of the peninsula after 1559 was that the power of Spain alone could provide effective protection from the Turks.

Perhaps the most visible change that had come over Europe since the composition of the *Prince* and the *Discourses* was the Reformation. It brought in its wake intensified interest in perennial questions regarding the relationship between church and government as well as decidedly new twists to these questions; it brought to the fore issues of toleration and the treatment of dissidents. Lutheran expansion peaked in Germany in the 1570s, by which time Lutheranism had become the established religion in the Scandinavian countries and advanced into Bohemia and Hungary. But by Calvin's death in 1564 Geneva had become known as "the Protestant Rome," and Calvinism the more dynamic form of Protestantism. The Calvinists had gathered strength in France, where they helped provoke the vicious religious wars; in the Netherlands, where they played a decisive role in the rebellion against Spain; and in Scotland, where they ousted Mary, Queen of Scots, and established the Presbyterian church. Calvinism also spread into Germany, especially the Palatinate, and into Bohemia and Hungary. England under Elizabeth had created its own Anglican "via media," which left both Catholics and incipient Puritans unhappy. Then there were the sects, mostly Anabaptist, who because of the distance they wished to maintain from the state were seen as particularly dangerous by Catholic and Protestant governments alike. The fiasco at Münster in 1534–35 confirmed the suspicions of many and earned them an undeserved reputation as subversives. There the unbalanced John of Leiden had proclaimed himself king and introduced a community of property and wives, to be defeated only by a combined Catholic and Protestant army. By the 1580s many Anabaptists had emigrated to eastern Europe, where they found freedom in Poland and then in Moravia and Russia.

As for the Catholic church, the Council of Trent, which convened for three sessions between 1545 and 1563, consolidated and strengthened many of the forces for reform. The pontificates following the council, those of Pius V from 1566 to 1572, Gregory XIII from 1572 to 1585, and Sixtus V from 1585 to 1590, saw a reinvigorated papacy take its place at the head of Catholic Reform and acquire renewed influence in international politics. The successful challenge to the Turks at Lepanto was undertaken at the initiative of Pius V, and the popes continued to warn Christendom of the Turkish threat. They encouraged Catholic rulers to take measures against heretics and to pursue the initiative against Protestant countries. The new Society of Jesus, founded in 1540, numbered several thousand members by the 1580s, and its schools were spreading across Catholic Europe. Finally, the Church of Rome had dispatched large numbers of missionaries to America and to the Orient, to India, the Malay Archipelago, Japan, and in 1582 the first permanent mission was established by the Jesuits in China. Botero's *Universal Relations*, a multivolume series undertaken in the 1580s at the request of the papacy, was initially an attempt to evaluate the situation of the church and the prospects for evangelization throughout the world. Continued work on the mammoth St. Peter's, that masterpiece of the Renaissance and the Baroque, and the renovation of the city itself undertaken under Sixtus V, displayed the renewed self-confidence of Rome.

European influence spread phenomenally across the globe during the sixteenth century. This had gone out from the Iberian Peninsula and in the 1580s was largely under the control of Spain, the Spaniards having brought the Portuguese Empire under their nominal direction by their conquest of Portugal. Neither the Dutch nor the English nor the French had as yet begun serious colonizing activity, but they were challenging Iberian claims to monopoly on trade with America and Asia. Information about life and customs there, often communicated through reports of the missionaries, stirred the interest of European readers and broadened their horizons. As early as 1512 the debate had begun in Spain over the monarchy's moral and legal obligations toward the peoples of America, and political writers of the sixteenth century like Bartolomé de las Casas and Francisco de Vitoria expended much effort in the attempt to relate the peoples across the sea to European Christendom and to lay the basis for an international juridical order that would comprise newly discovered non-Christian peoples.

The sixteenth century was, generally speaking, one of economic and demographic expansion in Europe, and it saw the inauguration of a world economy taking in America and much of Asia. Already by 1500 the commercial and financial center of Europe had shifted from Italy to Antwerp, where Baltic, Iberian, and Mediterranean trade converged. The Atlantic ports Seville and Lisbon bustled with activity along with the growth of Iberian overseas trade. But by 1585 Amsterdam was on the verge of the phenomenal growth that enabled it to succeed to Antwerp's role by 1600, and the Dutch were on the threshold of their rapid expansion into a dominant economic power. Overall, the economy in Germany continued to prosper, particularly in the city-states, if not to the degree it had at the start of the century when Augsburg was the wealthiest city in Europe and Nuremberg not far behind. Most Italian states as well, having recovered from the wars and from the blow to Levantine trade delivered by the Portuguese ventures to the Orient, flourished during the last third of the century. The intensification of traditional European commerce plus the growth of trade with the East and America, the influx of treasure from America into Spain and its dispersal throughout Europe, and an obvious, yet to many, mysterious inflation—prices tripled at least—marked the century.

Accompanying economic expansion was a substantial if regionally uneven growth of population, especially in the cities, to which people migrated from the countryside, particularly in southern Europe. The Baroque was an increasingly urban culture. Rome's population jumped from about fifty-five thousand at mid-century to nearly one hundred thousand by its end.[73] From the early sixteenth to the early seventeenth century Madrid's population soared tenfold to 150,000 as it became the capital city of the Spanish monarchy, attracting folks from rural areas and so contributing to the depopulation that set in elsewhere in Spain around 1590.[74] Population growth strained the capacity of agriculture and opened opportunities for landowners, including many east of the Elbe who could supply demand, but peasants rarely benefited from this and overall their lot declined in the course of the century, especially as they became subject to increasing demands from landowners and governments alike. Opportunities for wealth promoted a greater degree of social mobility. The number of merchants and entrepreneurs grew, many of them eventually pursuing admittance into the ranks of the nobility, which for its part retained social dominance. The new wealth was not spread out over the population, and the gap between rich and poor widened. Increasing numbers of poor became noticeable in the cities, and vagrancy and crime emerged as more serious problems. As early as 1526 the Spanish humanist Juan Luis Vives, living in Bruges and acquainted with circumstances in the Netherlands and England, published the first book on relief of the poor.[75]

Inflation, the gradual swelling of court and bureaucracy, and above all war—in the Netherlands, in France, and with the Turks in the Mediterranean and Hungary—and the threat of war and pursuit of security elsewhere led to escalating costs of government. Princes and rulers were increasingly hungry for revenue and new sources of revenue. All these developments drew the attention of political writers to economic issues, and the anti-Machiavellians were to be among the first to emphasize the importance of economic development and demographic growth for the creation of a powerful state. They were to be among the first mercantilists.

Chapter 2

Anti-Machiavellians and Scholastics

Few authors have stirred as much comment, discussion, agreement, and opposition as Machiavelli. Nearly every serious writer on politics since has had to deal with issues he raised, especially the dichotomy he found between ethics, or at least Christian ethics, and politics. Largely because his books were on the Index, much acquaintance with his writings in Catholic lands during the sixteenth and seventeenth centuries was garnered second-hand from his enemies. With minor exceptions, no edition of either the *Prince* or the *Discourses* was published after 1559 in Italy, nor did any edition of either come out in Spain or in the Catholic areas of the Empire.[1] French translations, on the other hand, appeared with a certain regularity, the *Prince* and the *Discourses* each coming out about fifteen times between 1559 and the mid-1660s. All Latin translations were published at Leiden or in the Protestant areas of the Empire, the first Latin version of the *Prince* seeing the light of day at Basel in 1560, with about eleven editions following before 1660 and fewer of the *Discourses*. Only one edition of each work appeared in English before 1660 and none in German.[2]

Still, even in Catholic areas, the *Prince* and the *Discourses* were read.[3] Nor was all the reaction negative. Some like Bodin initially and the maverick Gaspare Scioppio, who circulated an *Apology* for Machiavelli in 1618–19, saw in him as in Aristotle a political scientist who described political reality as it actually was; others like the Englishman James Harrington, writing in the 1650s, embraced aspects of his republicanism.[4] Yet, the response was overwhelmingly anti-Machiavellian. Already in the time of Marlowe and Shakespeare the word *Machiavellian* had assumed for the Elizabethan stage the sinister connotations it retains today.[5]

My intention is to use the term *anti-Machiavellian* in a restricted sense, so that it applies to only a portion of the many books and pamphlets published against "the Florentine secretary," as he was dubbed by those who shunned even the mention of his name. *Anti-Machiavellian* can be applied to any book and author clearly responding negatively to Machiavelli with the stated or strongly implied purpose of refuting him or at least substantially modifying his position.

Secondly, and distinctively, an anti-Machiavellian volume must contain a program in some detail showing how to maintain and develop a powerful state without departing from Christian morality. It must not only be written against Machiavelli, it must put forth a counterprogram for political success. This use of the term excludes from consideration many authors who took to the barricades against Machiavelli like Pole, Osorio, and Caterino. All three perceived keenly the anti-Christian character of his thought, but none even began to draw up an alternative program for state building. The idiosyncratic Dominican friar Tommaso Campanella, who sat in a Neapolitan prison from 1600 to 1629 because of his suspect political and theological views, directed his *Atheism Conquered* against Machiavelli and in particular his misuse of religion; the original Italian title of the treatise, written in 1605 but published only in 1631, read "The Philosophical Recognition of the True, Universal Religion against Machiavellian Anti-Christianism."[6] But this work, as well as his *Political Aphorisms* written about 1600, was far from a treatise on state building, and Campanella's thought as reflected in his *City of the Sun* and *Monarchy of Spain*, both originally published in Germany in the early 1620s although written much earlier, was much too utopian and universalist to qualify him as an anti-Machiavellian writer in the sense intended here.[7]

Two other authors who rank among the prominent opponents of Machiavelli fall outside the narrower definition of anti-Machiavellian: the Oratorian and disciple of Philip Neri, Tommaso Bozio, and the peregrinating Jesuit, Antonio Possevino, both close to papal circles in Rome. During the 1590s Bozio published four books against Machiavelli, three at Rome, each dealing at exhaustive length with a particular issue. His *On Military Strength and the Illustrious, Enduring Catholic Kingdoms* (1593) took up Machiavelli's case against a Christian military, his *On the Fall of Peoples and Kingdoms* (1594) argued against Machiavelli's conception of fortune, and his *On the Situation of Italy in Ancient and Modern Times* (Cologne, 1595) dealt with his attack on the papacy. Closest to an anti-Machiavellian work in our sense was his *On the Rule of Virtue or That Kingdoms Ought to be Ruled by Genuine and not by Counterfeit Virtues* (1593).[8]

Possevino, who undertook various diplomatic missions for the papacy, including journeys to Stockholm and Moscow, first published his *Judgment of Various Writings of the French Soldier Noue, Jean Bodin, Philippe de Mornay, and Niccolò Machiavelli* at Venice in 1592 at the request of the short-lived Pope Innocent IX himself.[9] It was frequently republished, in Protestant Germany sometimes bound with a Latin edition of the *Prince*—to which it presumably served as an antidote—in which case Machiavelli's name was placed before the others in the title.[10] Machiavelli received considerably less attention than Bodin in Possevino's short treatise; in one edition seven pages were devoted to Machiavelli along with an excerpt of eighteen pages from Osorio, whereas thirty-seven pages were given to Bodin, whose unorthodox religious views and qualified acceptance of toleration were severely criticized.[11]

Possevino's treatment of Machiavelli was of a singular poverty.[12] In some editions he admitted that Machiavelli displayed "talent and cleverness" (*l'ingenio e l'acutezza*), while lacking piety and experience. He wrote to show the "execrable bestiality" of Machiavelli, so that Catholics would lose their taste to read him themselves.[13] Much of the exposition of Machiavelli's position was taken without acknowledgment directly from Gentillet's *Discourse*, and the maxims allegedly drawn from Machiavelli were allowed to stand as self-condemnatory. Machiavelli's doctrine led inevitably to the destruction of the state, Possevino argued. Experience showed that it was piety and the true Catholic religion combined with wise counsel, truth, and humility that raised up and preserved empires. Examples were brought forward to prove this, from biblical times Moses and Joshua, from more recent history Charles V, who had defeated the Lutherans at Mühlberg, and the Duke of Parma, who was then making gains against the rebels in the Netherlands. Possevino did discuss at length Machiavelli's understanding of fortune. The world was governed, he argued, not by fortune but by God's providence, which gave ultimate victory to God's champions. But then, as if to concede that this ultimate victory did not necessarily encompass great worldly success, he added, citing Aquinas's *On the Government of Princes*, that the true, present happiness of a ruler did not consist in a long reign and many victories but in just government itself, the control of his own passions, and a firm hope in eternal life.[14] Possevino also attacked Machiavelli's bellicose proclivities; war was allowed only to defend church or country.

Six authors among the host of anti-Machiavellian writers serve as the focus of this study. Besides Giovanni Botero and Justus Lipsius, we look closely at Pedro de Ribadeneira, a Spanish Jesuit whose *Christian Prince* appeared in 1595; Adam Contzen, a German Jesuit and subsequent confessor to Maximilian of Bavaria, whose *Ten Books on Politics* was first published in 1620; Carlo Scribani, a Flemish Jesuit whose *Christian Politician* came off the press in 1624; and the Spanish diplomat and literary figure, Diego Saavedra Fajardo, whose *Idea of a Christian Prince* dates in its final form from 1643.

I have chosen these six authors because their works generally enjoyed a wide circulation beyond national borders, some more than others to be sure, and so they came to constitute the main vehicles of an international anti-Machiavellian tradition or school. By this I mean a group of authors who shared a common goal, who featured similar themes, who discussed similar issues, and who, for the most part, were familiar with the previous works in the tradition as it developed. They belong to the tradition by virtue of the content of their writings; as we shall see, there was substantial difference in form. In addition, these six have been selected because they had contact with figures of court and government in various states and most participated in government themselves at least as occasional consultants. They both wrote for those in government and reflected their views; thus they reveal much of the political culture of the times, that is, the principles and attitudes in the light of which policies were formulated and decisions taken. Other anti-Machiavellians will come up for discussion in passing, for example, the Florentine intellectual Scipione Ammirato, the canon of Liège Jean de Chokier, and the Spanish Jesuit Juan de Mariana, whose *The King and the Education of the King*, was published at Toledo in 1599. This celebrated volume of Spanish political thought seems not to have found a widespread audience in its day. Although it went through four Latin editions by 1640, three were issued in Germany, and there were no translations until the nineteenth century. Its circulation was restricted by the Jesuit Order, which suffered from the controversial position on tyrannicide advanced by Mariana.[15]

Characteristic of the anti-Machiavellian tradition was the desire to meet Machiavelli on his own terms, that is, on the level of practice. His agenda, anti-Machiavellians were determined to demonstrate, could only ruin and not preserve or advance the state. They assumed and usually treated in a cursory fashion the theological and metaphysical arguments to the effect that Machiavelli was unchristian and immoral. For these they looked to the Scholastic writers. Their intent was to develop a detailed, practical program that showed how a ruler or statesman operating with solid Christian principles could maintain and develop a powerful state and so be successful politically. The charge to which they were most sensitive was that they were utopians or idealists far removed from the realities of power in a hard world.

Thus the anti-Machiavellians represented a salient element of Counter-Reformation spirituality: the full Christian life could be lived amidst secular activity. This assertion was a major element in the response of the Catholic church to a widespread desire for a deeper religious life in the world, which was a source of both Reformation and Counter-Reformation. It distinguished the spirituality of Ignatius Loyola, as seen in his *Spiritual Exercises*, and of Francis de Sales, as found in his classic bestseller, *The Introduction to a Devout Life*, published in 1608, probably the two most influential devotional works of the Counter-Reformation.[16] The full Christian life was not only for monks and nuns and perhaps some clerics who withdrew from the world. It could be led in the world by lay people, clerics, and members of religious orders. A flood of books followed de Sales's *Introduction* off the presses, pointing the way to Christian living in various callings, like the four-volume Spanish *Perfection of the Christian in All States [of Life]* by Luis de la Puente (1612–16) or the French *The Holy Court* by Nicolas Caussin (1624), both of which circulated widely.[17] A dominant aim of the Europe-wide Jesuit theater was to exalt the active life in the world and to exhibit the harmony between it and the Christian virtues.[18] Thus, the anti-Machiavellians reaffirmed a major strain of the Renaissance: that the active life and especially participation in politics was a noble Christian calling. Counter-Reformation writers recommended the political life to citizen and prince alike as a way of Christian living.[19]

Contemporaries read the anti-Machiavellians because they addressed a problem keenly experienced during the Baroque: tension between the demands of the good (*bonum honestum*) and the useful (*bonum utile*) made by life in the world and especially by life in the world of politics. The perception of this tension, or at least its articulation, was owed in no small part to Machiavelli, for whom the claims of the good and the useful in politics were ultimately irreconcilable. By the late sixteenth century, in many quarters a pejorative connotation had attached to the word for politician or man of politics in different languages: *politicus, politico, politique*. This probably derived from the French *politiques* who were thought to place political considerations above religious ones.[20] As we shall see, Ribadeneira in 1595 seems to have been the first major writer to apply the term *político* to Machiavelli. In 1600 Duke William of Bavaria warned his nephew, Archduke Ferdinand of Inner Austria, the future emperor, against the "politicians, . . . false Christians with their illusory fears,"[21] and in 1606 the English Catholic writer Thomas Fitzherbert compared the etymology of the word *politicke* to that of *tyrant*, which had originally meant only monarch. At one time, he wrote, politician designated "such a one as practices that part of human prudence which concerns state"; now however, "by the abuse of such as profess the same it begins in all languages to be taken in evil part, and is commonly applied only to those, who framing a policy after their own fancy, no less repugnant to reason than to conscience and religion, change all the course of true wisdom and prudence."[22]

Drama in France from roughly 1600 to 1660, especially the Jesuit drama and Corneille, could not be understood without awareness of the anti-Machiavellian writers with whom playwrights expected the audience to be familiar. This was the case even though no significant anti-Machiavellian author was French; they were widely read in France as part of the international tradition.[23] Gabriel Naudé in his *Advice for the Development of a Library*, prepared for Cardinal Richelieu in 1627, remarked that politics and morality occupied the majority of the best and most vigorous spirits.[24] Germany and Italy were little different.[25] Books dealing with political ethics predominated in the libraries of the European elite.[26]

In 1604 the new duke of Feria, who held major administrative positions under Philip IV, addressed a telling letter to the Augustinian theologian Juan Marquez. After indicating that his concerns were shared by many others and praising the work of university theologians, by whom he probably meant the Scholastics, Feria lamented their failure to speak to lay people. Some writers on public affairs seemed to think that "all runs smoothly and easily, without seeing the contradictions of the useful [*lo util*] with the good [*lo honesto*], the burden of those things that are not so good or the human means that go beyond the limit and, on the other hand, [without seeing] that a little something is necessary of which the minister neither hears nor approves." Moreover, those who wrote on prayer or provided "spiritual exercises" required so much time that it was impractical for a man of affairs to attempt to follow their teaching. If learned men were to write for people in different states of life, it would seem appropriate, Feria went on, to deal with governors and political figures, "thus to purify at its source the spring from which the people had to drink." Feria asked Marquez to be the "master of those of us who have the obligation to know how to govern." But he made two special requests about the approach to be employed. The doctrine was to be drawn from Scripture and to be illustrated with examples. This explains why Marquez constructed his anti-Machiavellian treatise, *The Christian Governor* (Salamanca, 1612) around the lives of Moses and Joshua.[27]

A similar tension between the good and the useful is found in *The Ambassador*, a dialogue first published in 1620 by Juan de Vera y Figueroa, a member of Olivares's circle and later ambassador himself to Venice, Savoy, and Rome; it was destined to become the classic guidebook for diplomats.[28] The question was raised at one point, what should an ambassador do when the prince he represented was in the wrong and the ruler to whom he was accredited had justice on his side. To this the interlocutor replied that "in giving a satisfactory answer to this question, the greatest difficulty of this material will have been solved," involving as it did, "what is an ordinary thing in government, the clash of the useful with the good."[29] A long discussion followed in which different views were expressed and a novel distinction introduced between a good man in an absolute sense and a good man in a relative sense. The former could not function as a statesman. He would be like Cato, who had lived in the city of Romulus as if it were the city of Plato and caused infinite trouble. Better for him who sought absolute goodness to retire to the country and a life of contemplation. No clear resolution was given to the problem in the dialogue.[30]

Although their view of human nature retained a solid dose of Machiavelli's pessimism, the anti-Machiavellians' vision of the world was fundamentally an optimistic one. They were convinced that the good and the useful belonged together, that a good Christian could be a successful ruler or man of politics, and that in fact many historical instances demonstrated this. This was the basic point. But not rarely anti-Machiavellians went beyond this to display a further optimism. They often gave the impression that attachment to Christian principles virtually guaranteed success to a ruler or statesman, provided of course he possessed intelligence and skill. Machiavelli had contended that in order to succeed the ruler had, at least eventually, to do evil. Anti-Machiavellians now appeared to claim the obverse, that if a ruler governed in a Christian fashion, he would with near inevitability enjoy success. Thus they approached a position analogous to what is normally called the Puritan ethic, that godliness combined with virtue and talent brought success in one's calling.[31] Such a position seemed to contradict experience, to look away from the message of the cross in the Gospel, and to betray an artificiality often associated with the Baroque.

Yet this point should not be pressed. The anti-Machiavellians were not facile optimists and were far from Pollyannas. They were well aware that commitment to the cause of justice or religion did not always advance the political fortunes of a ruler or his people. This was particularly so for Spanish writers after the defeat of the Armada in 1588. A grappling with the mystery of providence and a poignant consciousness of the clash of the good with the useful constituted an anti-Machiavellian, and Baroque, strain that ran counter to the extreme optimism of a Catholic version of the Puritan ethic.

Two types of argument characterized anti-Machiavellian efforts to reconcile the good and the useful. They can be called providentialist and intrinsic or immanent pragmatism, the former requiring faith, the latter resting on reason alone. Both were interpretations of history. The writers took for granted, of course, that only moral, Christian conduct was useful, in the ultimate sense that it alone bestowed genuine peace of heart in this world and flowered into eternal life beyond the grave. But this was not their principal concern. Providentialist pragmatism argued from God's providence and required the anti-Machiavellians to wrestle with the concept of fortune, dear to the Baroque as well as to Machiavelli. God bestowed victory and success in this world, at least in most cases, on rulers and peoples that served him faithfully and uprightly. This he did either through a direct, miraculous intervention in the course of events or, much more likely, through his skillful guidance of secondary causes. Such an argument presupposed the capacity to discern God's hand in history and led in the direction of a theology of history.

Intrinsic pragmatism argued from the nature of the act itself, apart from any divine intervention. Moral action by its very nature was useful; immoral action was counterproductive. A standard example was the lie, which was always unprofitable, because in the long run it undermined trust and confidence in its perpetrator. This position led to the assertion that moral action was reasonable, whereas immoral action contravened reason. Machiavelli was unreasonable as well as irreligious and immoral. Another way of putting it was that violation of the natural law, which was based on reason, inevitably brought its own retribution on states as well as individuals.

The anti-Machiavellian concern with practice fostered the moral analysis of individual actions and the careful application of general principles to them, in other words, casuistry, which during the Baroque became increasingly a feature of Catholic, and Protestant, moral theology.[32] The anti-Machiavellians asserted that one could succeed in politics without acting immorally. But what, precisely, was immoral action, for example, in the case of deceit? To be sure, an outright lie was wrong, but was it deceit to mask one's intentions, to mistrust another, to feign an attack from one direction in order to lead the enemy into an ambush from another? Casuistry has unfortunately acquired a negative connotation, and it can be overdone. In his *Provincial Letters* of 1656–57, Blaise Pascal pointed out brilliantly the pitfalls to which casuistry was liable while at the same time grossly exaggerating the degree to which contemporaries were ensnared by them.[33] Casuistry is a necessity in any complex society, especially at times when changing situations demand the rethinking and reapplication of moral norms, as was the case during the Baroque.

Both types of pragmatism, providentialist and intrinsic, called for the use of history. Just as Machiavelli made his case through examples drawn from ancient and contemporary history, so did the anti-Machia-vellians. But they greatly surpassed him in the variety of historical peri-ods and the number of historians on which they drew, calling especially on histories of the late Roman Empire and the early Middle Ages and the historical books of the Bible. In this they exhibited a vast learning as well as a lack of critical sense similar to Machiavelli's. Their multiplication of examples, a typical form of Baroque argument, was intended to over-whelm the reader and so compel his assent in much the same way that the façade of a Baroque church or palace was meant to impress and evoke the allegiance of the beholder. Nor can we lose sight of the rhetori-cal force of the illustrative example. The Duke of Feria had requested just such examples from Marquez.

By emphasizing the need for a powerful state, Machiavelli focused the attention of political thinkers on power and the means to obtain it.[34] The anti-Machiavellians in their turn contributed to the growing concen-tration of political thinkers on power. Living as they did during the religious wars, they recognized the need for a state that could provide the order, internal and external, so much desired in the Baroque era. Power was not evil. It was, as Machiavelli declared, an absolute necessity for a prince or a state in a hostile and chaotic world. A ruler had a genuine obligation to develop a powerful state. The question was, how was this to be done? The anti-Machiavellians sought to elaborate a realistic ethics of power. Indeed, in their effort to show that a ruler need not resort to immoral methods, they pointed to a legitimate means to power over-looked by Machiavelli, namely, economic development, and, in general, they advocated increasing government activity. In doing this they exhib-ited a confidence similar to Machiavelli's in the potential of government to build and maintain a state.

In their pursuit of a morality of power and in the allied development of casuistry, the anti-Machiavellians were part of a much larger move-ment within the Counter-Reformation, the attempt to update the Catho-lic church to meet the challenges of early modern Europe, which was in turn a major feature of church reform.[35] In every age the church must determine its attitude toward contemporary society and culture. In the early centuries the need was to come to terms with the prevailing Greco-Roman culture, in the Middle Ages to confront and adapt to the barbar-ian tribes. The Counter-Reformation church was called upon to propose and foster a form of Christianity that was suitable to a changing Europe. The Council of Trent sought to reformulate Catholic teaching in re-sponse to the Protestant challenge, and it endeavored to reform and update the pastoral practice of the church. Missionaries were dispatched to gather in a harvest from the far corners of Asia and the Americas. The spirituality of Ignatius Loyola and Francis de Sales was an effort to outline a style of Christianity for the increasing number of Christians active in the world.

Yet, in every age the church's relationship to the prevailing culture has been a source of tension and even conflict within the church. Some, in their enthusiasm for contemporary achievement and their desire to participate in it, open themselves to the charge of being "too worldly." Others tend to see any change or reapportionment of emphasis as a betrayal of the Gospel. It is in this context that we must see in early modern times the conflict over usury and, more generally, business ethics, the discussion of religious toleration, and the debate over the new science that culminated in the Galileo Affair. Another contemporary example was the prolonged controversies over the Chinese and Malabar Rites, where the fundamental issue was the degree to which Catholic Christianity could incorporate native customs and traditions into its own tradition.[36] The main issue between Jesuits and Jansenists was precisely over the relationship of the Christian to the world and by extension to human values generally. In their search for a modern Christian statecraft, the anti-Machiavellians definitely belonged on the side of those inclined to accommodation.

The anti-Machiavellians, then, concentrated on practice or statecraft, an emphasis that grew out of their concern to meet Machiavelli on his own terrain. Their approach did not mean that they were not interested in broader issues of political philosophy—some were. But the moral and Christian unacceptability of Machiavelli was evident to them, and on the theoretical level the Scholastic writers had demonstrated this to their satisfaction.[37] They did take up such questions as the origin of the state and its purpose, often merely in passing, but in this area they were not original and for the most part depended on the Scholastics. The one exception was their general espousal of princely absolutism and their severe restriction of the right of resistance. This was in response to the civil conflicts of the time just as it was with Bodin. But to understand the anti-Machiavellians we must take a look at the general theory of the state with which they operated implicitly or explicitly. This is to be found in the writers of what has been called the Silver Age of Scholasticism in the sixteenth century.

The early sixteenth century saw a turn away from the Nominalism that had dominated in the universities in the later Middle Ages and a revival of the Thomistic tradition. The movement, which began at the University of Paris at the turn of the century, flowered in Spain, where Francisco de Vitoria brought it in 1522 after long study in Paris. As professor of theology at Salamanca from 1526 until his death in 1546, the Dominican Vitoria exercised a great influence upon numerous students, even though no work of his was published until his lectures appeared in 1557 at Lyons. First the Dominicans and then the Jesuits served as the leading carriers of the movement; both orders formally took Thomas Aquinas as their master. Among the important Dominicans was Domingo de Soto (1494–1560), who also studied in Paris and then for many years taught alongside Vitoria in Salamanca. The leading Spanish Jesuits were Luis de Molina (1535–1600) and Francisco Suarez (1548–1617), the latter having studied at Salamanca and then taught at Rome from 1580 to 1585. Other important Jesuits were the Belgian Leonard Lessius (1554–1623), who taught for many years at Louvain, and the Italian Robert Bellarmine (1542–1621), who taught in Rome from 1576 to 1588, when he became a consultant to the papal curia, and in 1592, a cardinal.[38] Suarez and Bellarmine, both of whom were active in Rome in the 1580s, were the most influential contemporaries of the first anti-Machiavellians.

In the tradition of Aquinas, the sixteenth-century Scholastics put forth a total vision of man and the universe based on Christian revelation and natural law. They were both theologians and philosophers, distinguishing still more carefully than their medieval predecessors the realms of faith and reason. Their greatest achievements came in the area of the philosophy of law and politics—Mesnard considers Suarez's writings the apogee of sixteenth-century political thought[39]—but these must always be seen against the background of their complete vision of the world. For the Scholastics the realm of politics fit into a hierarchy of human activities, within which it found its meaning; this characteristic immediately separated them from Machiavelli. They represented another aspect of the church's effort at accommodation during the Counter-Reformation, concerned as they were as political philosophers to develop an ethic that would recognize the changes of the sixteenth century: the emergence of the sovereign state, the European discovery of new peoples in America and other parts of the world, the progress of the Reformation. How were these sovereign states to relate to one another? What were the rights of the Amerindians vis-à-vis the Christian nations attempting to colonize and evangelize them? What were the church's rights toward heretics in lands that were still Catholic and in others where the ruler had become Protestant?

Vitoria and Suarez have been credited with major contributions to the development of international law.[40] Suarez's philosophy of law and politics was set forth most completely in his *On the Laws and God as Legislator*, published in 1612, by which time he was teaching at Coimbra in Portugal, but many of his leading ideas seem to have been worked out well before then.[41] The chief source for Bellarmine's thought is his famous *Controversies*, first published between 1586 and 1593.[42] But in each case we must look to other writings too. Both Suarez and Bellarmine composed major works dealing with the conflict in the early seventeenth century between the papacy and James I of England, which grew out of James's advancement of his theory of the divine right of kings and the imposition of a new Oath of Allegiance on the English Catholics, and both took up the defense of the papal position during the dispute with Venice over the Interdict from 1605 to 1607.[43] Then, at the end of his life, Bellarmine produced an undistinguished anti-Machiavellian work, *On the Duty of a Christian Prince*, for the young Polish prince Vladislav, who would rule from 1632 to 1648. It appeared in 1619 at Rome, and translations into French, Italian, and Spanish soon followed.[44]

Thomas Aquinas built his political philosophy on Aristotle, transforming his doctrine in accord with the Christian revelation. The sixteenth-century Scholastics further refined the thought of Aquinas, with Suarez playing the prominent role. Initially, Aquinas distinguished the happiness of the present life from the happiness of the future life or Beatific Vision, with the former happiness ordained to the latter, which was man's final and ultimate goal. To the happiness of the future life the church had the responsibility to direct its members, and it was superior to the state because the goal to which it led was man's transcendent and ultimate one. Suarez then further distinguished happiness of the present life into spiritual happiness or the natural happiness of individuals as private persons and temporal happiness of the community and of individuals as members of this community. Spiritual happiness lay outside the competence of the state. Its goal was temporal happiness, which was identical with the common good, and to which Suarez gave the term "political happiness" (*felicitas politica*). It comprised the same three elements as Aquinas's common good: peace, justice, and security in an ordered community; a sufficiency of material goods; and "that moral uprightness which was necessary for this external peace and happiness of the state and for its continued conservation." Thus the state was to make good citizens rather than good men or, in other words, to make people virtuous to the extent that the virtues were essential for a viable society. Suarez then discussed individual virtues from this perspective.[45]

For the Scholastics, consent was at the basis of government. Men joined together in a political community in order to participate in the benefits of the common good. Political authority had its origin in God, but it came to those who held it through the consent of the community. No individual possessed by nature authority over another; the community as a whole was the original bearer of authority. It was up to the community to determine what the form of government was to be and what persons were to exercise its authority. While asserting the moral indifference of the three traditional forms of government, the Scholastics generally expressed a decided preference for mixed monarchy, that is, one incorporating democratic and aristocratic elements as a check on the king.[46]

Of great interest during the sixteenth century, especially in France after the outbreak of the religious wars, was the right of resistance to a ruler. Under what conditions might subjects withdraw consent, oppose a ruler and, if necessary, even take his life? The Spanish Jesuit Mariana caused a sensation when in 1599 he declared that as a last resort, if it was not possible for the representatives of the community or people properly to convene in order to take action, an individual acting in the name of the people might kill a legally constituted prince who had become a tyrant. This presupposed, however, that the decision that the ruler was in fact a tyrant represented a popular consensus, not merely the assassin's view. Mariana's position brought down upon him, and to a degree on the Society of Jesus, the wrath of many of Europe's crowned heads, particularly perhaps because of the sympathetic tone with which he discussed the murder of Henry III of France by Jacques Clément in 1589. But Mariana was only carrying a bit further a doctrine with a long tradition. Interestingly, his book brought no protests from Spain, where it was published and dedicated to Philip III.[47]

Traditionally, two types of tyrant had been distinguished. One was the usurper who seized power and had no legitimate title to it. The sixteenth-century Scholastics generally asserted that as a last resort a private person acting in the name of the community could take the life of a usurper. This was the community's legitimate self-defense. The only consideration in this case was the prudential one, would assassination lead to a chaotic situation worse than the tyranny? The second type of tyrant was the ruler who had become tyrannical by systematically placing his own good before that of the community.

Bellarmine's treatment of this issue became more rigid with time, perhaps in an attempt to distance himself from the French monarchomachs and to avoid opening himself to the charges of James I and his apologists that he was a fomenter of rebellion. In an early unpublished work he allowed for the killing of a usurper by an individual acting in the name of the community, but he then later rejected this opinion. He consistently followed Aquinas's position in *The Government of Princes* that a private person could never take the life of a tyrant with a legitimate title,[48] and he later backed off from an earlier view that the people might depose a tyrant on the grounds that he had violated his agreement to work for the common good, provided the action did not provoke a worse state of affairs. The only way to get rid of a tyrant, in Bellarmine's mature view, was through the intervention of papal, ecclesiastical authority, in other words, from above, not below. Bellarmine was moving toward absolutism.[49]

The Spaniard Suarez was not as restrictive as Bellarmine in his treatment of resistance to tyranny. The people or any part of them might revolt against a usurper, and a private individual might take his life on the supposition that the injustice of his title was clear. Such tyrannicide had to be a last resort and unlikely to generate a worse state of affairs. A legitimate monarch turned tyrant might never be killed by a private person on his own authority. But the whole community might take up arms against him precisely because he had not governed for the common good that it was his duty to foster. But his tyranny had to be manifest. In addition, there had to be solid grounds that the rebellion would succeed and proportion observed between the suffering caused by the rebellion and the situation it sought to overthrow.[50]

The principal instrument by which government directed the community toward the common good was law. To be valid, this human law had to be in accord with justice as found in the natural law. It was in his discussion of human law that Suarez mentioned Machiavelli by name, the only time he did so in all his works. He summarized Machiavelli's position, which he equated with that of contemporary *politici*: "The lay power and the civil law look per se to the state and its conservation and growth; as a result the content of the laws is what contributes to the state, its conservation and its growth. In pursuit of this goal laws are made that seem useful to the temporal state regardless of whether they are rooted in a genuine uprightness or merely a counterfeit and apparent one and with the disguise of those laws that are unjust." In other words, the civil power was not constrained by moral considerations in its pursuit of the interests of the state.

Machiavelli's presupposition, Suarez went on, was that a state could not be preserved without departing from the path of virtue. Suarez's response was twofold. The first was expressly a priori. The natural law prohibited any law or action that was immoral. The *politici* who taught the opposite were heretics or, still worse, atheists. Anyone with some realization of who God was would readily concede that God's law must take precedence over any commandments of men. Suarez's second argument was that of the anti-Machiavellians, based on providentialist and intrinsic pragmatism. Virtuous action, by its very nature, was necessary for the peace and temporal happiness of a kingdom. Moreover, experience showed that there was nothing more useful for maintaining states than the practice of the Catholic faith. For the latter statement Suarez referred his readers to Ribadeneira's *Christian Prince*.[51]

The sovereign state arrived in the sixteenth century. The Scholastics accepted it much as did Bodin, while at the same time seeking to retain elements of an international authority. Already in Vitoria there was a rejection of any imperial authority extending beyond Germany and any direct papal power in temporal affairs (apart from the Papal States). Vitoria merely came to terms with the status quo. Yet there were still proponents of imperial authority and especially of the temporal power of the papacy; Bellarmine himself fell into disfavor with Pope Sixtus V for restricting the latter.[52] The essential element in sovereignty for Vitoria was the right to make war; for Suarez, it was supreme legislative and judicial power within a given territory. Bellarmine combined both. According to him a sovereign state was one that could defend itself, that is, make war, issue laws, and hand down judgments from which there was no appeal to a higher instance within its own order.[53]

The last phrase is important. A state was supreme in the temporal order, but just as the goal of the state, political happiness, was subordinate to man's ultimate goal, the happiness of the Beatific Vision, and just as reason was subordinate to revelation, so the state was ultimately subordinate to the church. This led to the famous indirect power of the papacy in temporal affairs, a teaching developed by the sixteenth-century Scholastics from Aquinas's position on the relationship between church and state. The temporal ruler was to govern in his sphere in such a way that he fostered or at least did not obstruct the attainment of man's ultimate goal. Should he fail to do so, the pope might intervene in the government of the state and in extreme cases, such as heresy, excommunicate and depose civil rulers, release subjects from their allegiance, and call upon other princes to carry out these measures. This was the indirect power in temporal matters. The theory was a throwback to the High Middle Ages, when the European states were in their infancy, and it no longer had a place in the political world of the late sixteenth century. Understandably, it appeared ominous to Protestant princes, especially after the excommunication and deposition issued against Elizabeth of England by Pius V in 1570, offering as it did a justification for religious war. Obviously, the Scholastics expected great prudence would be exercised in the use of this power. But the pope had to possess it, they argued, if the church in its turn was to be a perfect community, that is, outfitted with all the means required to bring its members to eternal life. Otherwise temporal rulers could frustrate the pursuit of its goal.[54]

What were to be the relationships among sovereign states? How was some form of order to be maintained among them? Machiavelli had set out to show what an individual state had to do in order to protect itself and to flourish in the intense competition among states. For the Scholastics the further concern was to establish a principle of unity on which to base an international order of justice that would regulate the relations among the states and preserve peace. Two such principles or bases for international relations were located, the one specifically Christian, the other growing out of the human solidarity that followed from the universal natural law. Both had their roots in Aquinas's position on the relationship of the church to the temporal power and his conception of natural law and the law of nations or *ius gentium*. Vitoria, who was very much alert to the problems raised by Spain's conquests among the non-Christian peoples of the New World, gave a decided impetus to natural human solidarity as the foundation of international relations. He recognized clearly the sovereignty of the non-Christian peoples overseas.[55]

Both principles of unity were found in Bellarmine and Suarez, with the Christian principle more developed in Bellarmine and the natural law principle in Suarez. For Bellarmine, whose acceptance of the sovereign state seems to have been reluctant, Christendom or the *respublica christiana* remained a guiding concept. It provided the principal foundation for the unity among states, as well as a further justification for the intervention of the pope in individual states. Bellarmine's basis for harmony and order among states was thus more historical and theological, and it applied first of all to Europe, whereas Suarez's was more philosophical and universal. Ideally, Bellarmine would have preferred a form of single, federal state as the temporal counterpart of the papacy, but he was conscious this was not to be realized. Suarez considered a universal state simply impossible. Christendom was then for Bellarmine that area in which the papacy represented the spiritual power, could guide the temporal power as the soul did the body, and as a result intervene in the affairs of states when this was necessary for the spiritual good. The unity of states was Catholic and its center in Rome.

For both, papal jurisdiction extended de facto and de jure to heretics and to Jews and Muslims living in Christian lands. It extended de jure but not de facto to former Christian areas now held by the Turks, such as Greece; thus it allowed readily for war against the Turks. Papal jurisdiction did not reach to peoples who had never been Christian or held Christian territory, but even in pagan lands under certain circumstances the pope might intervene in order to protect Christians or to compel the admittance of Christian missionaries.[56]

In their concern to develop a framework for international relations, the Scholastics inevitably took up the issue of war and peace. Following a Christian tradition dating back at least to Augustine, they accepted the reality of war, which Suarez defined as "an external contest at arms which is incompatible with external peace when carried on between two sovereign princes or between two states." It could not be avoided, given the present human condition. As for Machiavelli, a state would inevitably have to make war in order to assure its independence. Suarez made a common distinction between two kinds of just war. A defensive war was the immediate response to an actual enemy attack, an aggressive war a means to redress a grievance, assert a right, or even punish another nation. Both were allowed, and sometimes even commanded, by the natural law. They could not be opposed to the Gospel, because it in no way derogated from the natural law. But Suarez was far from glorifying war. "While a war is not in itself evil," he wrote, "nevertheless, on account of the many misfortunes which it brings in its train, it is one of those undertakings that are often carried on in an evil fashion, and therefore it requires many [justifying] circumstances to make it righteous."[57] The Scholastics rejected pacifism as a realistic alternative. Their goal was to humanize war and bring it under the control of law to the degree possible.

The Scholastics, then, set out to determine, as had so many Christian thinkers, what constituted a just war.[58] The question applied, for Suarez, only to an aggressive war, since the right to defend oneself against an unjust attack actually in progress was conceded to everyone. The first qualification was that war be waged by a legitimate authority, that is, by a sovereign prince or a state with no superior in temporal matters. Suarez pointed to the mediatory role of the pope that followed from his indirect temporal power. He had the authority to require that a dispute be submitted to him for arbitration and that rulers abide by his judgment "unless his decision be manifestly unjust." But the pope did not always choose to exercise this option "lest perchance greater evils result," Suarez went on, showing an understanding for the political reality of the sixteenth century, nor were princes bound to seek his authorization to wage war.[59]

The second requirement for a just war, according to Suarez, was that its cause or reason be just. To this Bellarmine added, following Aquinas more closely, that the intention of the ruler be good, that is, that his goal be peace and the restoration of public order.[60] "A just and sufficient reason for war," Suarez wrote, "was the infliction of a grave injustice which cannot be avenged or repaired in any other way." He then listed three main types of injuries or injustices: the seizure of property and the refusal to restore it; the denial without good cause of the rights commonly accorded nations, such as the right of transit over highways; and grave damage to a prince's or nation's reputation or honor. Suarez denied that justice could be on both sides in a war; one was in the right, the other in the wrong. In addition, the cause of the war had to be proportionate to the effort and suffering the war would entail. This involved, as Suarez elaborated, that the prince be at least reasonably certain of victory.

Suarez allowed that a war might also be undertaken to punish a state for a serious violation of justice or even to protect innocent persons within another state, though he was aware of the abuses to which this could lead. His justification in these cases revealed his concern for an international order. There existed no effective higher power to inflict such punishment, but without some power of this sort to deter princes, the various states of the world could not live in harmony. Thus "war of the kind in question [punitive] has been instituted in place of a tribunal administering just punishment." He dealt with the objection from Paul's Epistle to the Romans (12:17–19), "do not render evil for evil," by saying that this applied to private persons and to doing evil for its own sake. Suarez then discussed at great length, as was his custom, the type of certitude about the just character of a war that a ruler, the leading men and generals, and the common soldiers had to have before they could legitimately participate in it.[61]

The third requirement for a just war related to the manner of carrying on the conflict. Prior to undertaking an aggressive war, a prince or state first had to notify the opposing prince or state of his claim and to seek compensation. If the potential enemy offered adequate compensation, he was obliged to desist from launching an attack. What Suarez would allow in the course of the war was rather extensive. "Hardly anything done against the enemy," he wrote, "involves injustice, except the [direct] slaying of the innocent. For all other damages are usually held to be necessary for attaining the end to which the war is directed," and if the goal of the war, victory, is allowed, so are the means. Included under "innocent," a term on which he elaborated, were by the natural law women, children, and all those unable to bear arms, by the law of nations ambassadors, and by canon law clerics; in some circumstances those capable of bearing arms might be considered innocent, "if in other respects they have not shared in the crime or in the unjust war." Once victory had been won, a prince might inflict upon the defeated state losses adequate to "a just punishment and satisfaction" and require full compensation for all his losses. In extreme cases this punishment might even extend to the execution of a large number of people. But the victor must always observe a just proportion and also take into account the need to win over the defeated for the future peace and not merely stir up lust for vengeance.[62]

The difficult issue of a prince's fidelity to an agreement was treated by Suarez in the context of the just war. His discussion was rooted in a tradition that was realistic and remarkably flexible and that might have surprised even Machiavelli. To break faith with another state was not permitted, provided an agreement had been undertaken in a valid fashion. But if one side refused to abide by an agreement, so might the other consider it abrogated. Changing circumstances might also release a ruler from an agreement if it meant that "the promises in question cannot be kept without grave loss." According to Suarez, "the equity of law demands that this condition be understood to exist" as part of an agreement, namely, that it was not binding if adherence to it involved "grave loss" to one party. In this case the prince had to warn the other party that it was impossible for him to keep his commitment. Once he had issued such a declaration, he was freed from his obligations. But such declarations were rarely to be permitted. As to the use of military stratagems, Suarez agreed with Aquinas that they were permissible "in so far as relates to the prudent concealment of one's plans, but not with respect to the telling of lies."[63]

With the Reformation religious toleration became a major issue in the sixteenth century. Should heretics be tolerated in a Catholic state, and if so, under what conditions and how—by tacit approval or formal recognition? In their response to this question, the Scholastics did not show the same spirit of adaptation that they generally displayed in their attitude toward the sovereign state and their efforts to create a framework for international relations that would include the non-Christian peoples of Asia and the Americas. Perhaps because they resided in Spain and Italy, where heresy made little headway, neither Suarez nor Bellarmine conceded a Catholic state any right to tolerate heretics. They shared the view of many Catholics that the Reformation remained a temporary phenomenon and were confirmed in it by a look at history, which recorded the demise of most heretical groups in the Western church. Time was on the Catholic side. Concessions would only prolong the existence of heresy.[64]

The impetus toward toleration came from the hard-pressed north of Europe, as might have been expected. The lukewarm Catholic acceptance, under political duress, of the Peace of Augsburg in 1555 was a step in this direction. Shortly thereafter Sigismund II August of Poland granted limited toleration to the Polish nobility in 1556, to be expanded by the Warsaw Confederation of 1573, and Emperor Maximilian II made concessions to the Protestant nobility of Lower and Upper Austria in 1568 and 1571 respectively.[65] In the 1560s French Catholic *politiques* like Catherine de Medici's chancellor Michel de L'Hospital and François de Montmorency anticipated Bodin in advocating toleration out of political necessity, that is, lest the French monarchy be torn asunder by religious conflict.[66] Bodin distinguished between the public practice of religion and private belief. In his *Six Books of a Republic* in 1576, he certainly preferred unity of public practice in a state, and he urged its legal enforcement and the suppression of dissenting views. Toleration was called for only when it became clear that the effort at enforcement merely stirred conflict and undermined the state. But normally government ought not to interfere with private belief; attempts to compel people to believe or to force their consciences only resulted in atheism.[67]

Early Catholic theologians to argue in toleration's favor were the professors at Louvain, Joannes Lensaeus (Jean de Lens) and Joannes Molanus (Jean Vermeulen), who did so in 1578 and 1584 respectively, following the short-lived Pacification of Ghent in 1576, by which the States General in the Netherlands extended limited freedom of religion to the Calvinists of Holland and Zeeland. Both applied to contemporary Protestants a principle invoked by Aquinas in his discussion in the *Compendium of Theology* "whether the rites of unbelievers may be tolerated" in Christian lands. The issue was worship or public practice not belief, and the principle was that an evil might be permitted, not committed, for the sake of a greater good or the avoidance of a still greater evil like conflict (*dissidium*) or the creation of obstacles that would make eventual conversion more difficult. "For this reason," Aquinas concluded referring to medieval practice, "the church has sometimes tolerated the rites of heretics and pagans when there was a great multitude of unbelievers."[68] Lensaeus and Molanus, developing this line of thought, concluded that in contemporary circumstances Protestant heretics might be tolerated, and Molanus insisted that any agreements made with them to this effect had to be honored.[69] Thus for practical purposes they adopted the position of the *politiques* who advocated toleration as the only alternative to the destruction of the French monarchy.

In his *On the Three Theological Virtues*, published in 1621, Suarez gave a classic defense of the traditional position that the church could take measures against heretics up to and including the death penalty. The church had the primary responsibility for this because the matter belonged to the spiritual realm, but states were expected to assist "as protectors of the church and according to the determination of the same church."[70] Suarez carefully worked out the definition of heretic. He was one who while professing to be a Christian clung willingly and pertinaciously to doctrine contrary to the teaching of the Catholic church. A heretic was thus clearly distinct from such nonbelievers as the Amerindians, who had never known the faith and could not be compelled to accept it precisely because faith had to result from a free act. A heretic was a baptized person who had defected from the faith. Suarez extended the term to include second- or third-generation Protestants, once they had rejected the opportunity to learn about the Catholic faith. The Catholic church claimed jurisdiction over all heretics by virtue of their baptism, whereas it disclaimed jurisdiction over nonbelievers. One reason for the severity toward heretics was precisely the feeling that they had betrayed a faith they had once possessed.[71]

Suarez argued that the use of force was a "licit and suitable means falling within the power of the church" to get heretics to abjure their heresy and that stubborn heretics who refused to return to the faith after sufficient instruction might be put to death. "For without these [punishments], spiritual [punishments] alone usually move carnal men but little." Suarez explained his position. It becomes more intelligible if we realize his assumption that profession of the Catholic faith was necessary for eternal salvation and recall his view that the church had a responsibility for heretics that it did not have for nonbelievers whose fate could be left more readily to the mercy of God. Heresy was, Suarez wrote, a most serious public crime, harmful to the *respublica christiana*—he used the term in this context—which called for punishment and satisfaction as did any crime. Such punishments were an example and a deterrent to others and, apart from the death penalty, a means to the correction and conversion of the heretics. To support his argument he called upon an array of authors and church practice. That corporal punishments diminished in any essential way the freedom necessary for faith he denied in a tortuous argument that contrasted with his evident concern to protect the freedom of nonbelievers being evangelized by Christian missionaries.[72] In any event, it was a "lesser evil" that heretics were brought to belief under such pressures than that they simply did not believe at all. He acknowledged that sometimes false conversions took place, but this happened *per accidens* and could be permitted because of the greater evils that were thus avoided.[73]

The toleration of religious dissidents was to be a serious problem for rulers of the sixteenth and seventeenth centuries, Protestant as well as Catholic. Machiavelli had strongly advocated the religious unity of the state for utilitarian purposes, though in a much different context. Anti-Machiavellian writers would have to deal with the issue in their turn.

Chapter 3

Giovanni Botero: Founder of the Tradition (1589)

"Botero is marvelous. He has so accommodated morality, justice, and obligation with the advantage of the prince as to merit in this respect immortal praise." So wrote Apollinare de' Calderini of Ravenna in the essays or *Discorsi* on Botero's *Reason of State* that he published at Milan in 1597.[1] He touched the secret to the success of Botero's volume, which had first appeared eight years before in Venice and had become "the book of the day" on its way to a position as a bestseller of political literature.[2] In showing the harmony of the useful with the moral, Botero advanced a predominant thesis of the Counter-Reformation: one could live as a good Christian and succeed in the world, specifically in politics; indeed, adherence to Christian principle greatly enhanced the likelihood of success. Botero had refuted Machiavelli, or so it seemed. This explains the immense popularity of the *Reason of State*, which inaugurated a new genre of political writing, the anti-Machiavellian treatise.[3]

By the early 1590s the *Reason of State* was already well known at the three major Counter-Reformation courts of Madrid, Munich, and Graz, not to mention Rome. Calderini reported that Philip II of Spain had had the volume translated for his heir—in fact the first Spanish translation dates from 1591—and that Duke William of Bavaria had set his son Maximilian to studying its text. Maximilian, as the leading German prince of the Counter-Reformation, would reign until 1651 and emerge from the Thirty Years' War as an elector of the Empire.[4] It was the papal secretary responsible for Bavarian affairs and former emissary to Germany, Minuccio Minucci, who recommended Botero's volume to Munich, probably also in 1591.[5] Shortly afterward the book was known in Graz at the court of the still teen-age Archduke and future Emperor Ferdinand II, which is not surprising given the contacts between Munich, Graz, and Rome. Later there were clear echoes of it in the anonymous *Essential Prince* (*Princeps in Compendio*), published first in 1632 and again in 1664 and often attributed to Ferdinand, a small volume that had a major part in the education of Habsburg princes well into the eighteenth century.[6] But its influence was by no means restricted to Catholic lands. The well-known German Protestant professor Hermann Conring lauded Botero's Christianization of Machiavelli in the introduction to his Latin translation of the *Reason of State*, published at Helmstedt in 1666, and the book was to have an influence on the Cameralists or German mercantilist school.[7]

But there were critics. Already the charge could be heard that in his zeal to refute Machiavelli, Botero had approved questionable practices and so, it was implied, become tainted with Machiavellianism himself.[8] Admittedly, he was at times unclear, inconsistent, and excessively flexible; yet the charge is wide of the mark. He never departed from his fundamental anti-Machiavellian position.

Botero was a child of the Italian Counter-Reformation. Enthusiasm for Catholic reform and restoration ran high in Italy as he undertook studies in the years following the Council of Trent, and his most creative period, from 1586 to 1595, was spent in Rome, during the pontificates of Sixtus V (1585–1590) and Clement VIII (1592–1605). By then the rejuvenated papacy had recovered much of the universal vision and moral prestige lost during the Renaissance, and the city of Rome began to take on its triumphalist Baroque face. Born at Bene Vagienna in Piedmont in 1544, at the age of fifteen Botero was sent to Sicily to study at the Jesuit college in Palermo, where his uncle was on the staff. The following year he transferred to the college in Rome, where he then entered the Jesuit novitiate. His first years in the Society were spent studying in Rome, where Robert Bellarmine was a classmate, and teaching rhetoric and philosophy in small Jesuit schools in Italy and then at Billom in France. His assignment to Paris for much of 1568 and 1569 gave him the chance to observe at first hand what he later designated the greatest city in Christendom.[9] But Botero, who suffered from moodiness and ill-health, had trouble settling down in the Jesuits even after his ordination to the priesthood in 1572, and he quietly and honorably left the Society in 1580.[10]

At this low point in his life, Botero was picked up by Charles Borromeo, the saintly, activist Archbishop of Milan, who gave him a curacy, a pastorate, and then brought him to Milan in 1582 as his secretary. The two years he served in this capacity until Borromeo's death in November 1584, left a strong impression on him, and he published a widely circulated account of the saint's death and burial. In 1583 he had dedicated to Duke Charles Emmanuel of his native Savoy the *On Kingly*

Wisdom, which anticipated in an amateurish fashion themes of the *Reason of State*. Machiavelli he referred to as "a truly gifted man but little Christian," and he opposed to Machiavellian *virtù* Christian piety rather than the understanding of *virtù* which he himself later developed.[11] After Borromeo's death there began an association with the Savoyard dynasty that was to be important for the rest of his life. Much of 1585 he was in France accompanying Charles Emmanuel's ambassador on a mission, probably to make contact with the Catholic League. This second stay in France included a long sojourn in Paris shortly after the Duke of Anjou died, leaving Henry of Navarre in line for the throne. So Botero experienced the French Religious Wars at their peak. It was also during this period that he read Bodin's *Republic*, which was to exercise a major influence on him.[12] Upon his return, he accepted a position as tutor and councillor to the twenty-two-year-old Federico Borromeo, cousin of Charles, and accompanied him to Rome in late 1586.

When Botero arrived in Rome, Suarez had just returned to Spain after five years teaching at the Jesuits' Roman College, recently reendowed by Pope Gregory XIII, and Bellarmine continued as a popular professor there. Sixtus V was just embarking on "a programme of urban development without parallel in any other European city."[13] Botero's contacts there included the humanist Piero Maffei, the philosopher Francesco Patrizi, the Florentine Scipione Ammirato, and his association with Borromeo, who was created a cardinal in 1587, gave him entrée to high ecclesiastical circles. As a councillor to Borromeo, he participated in four papal conclaves, three in the year of the three popes, 1590–1591, and the fourth that elected Clement VIII in 1592.[14]

The first of Botero's three main works, *The Causes of the Greatness of Cities*, was published at Rome in 1588. This small book numbers only 66 pages in the modern Firpo edition compared to the 289 pages of the *Reason of State*, with which it was often published. As the title indicates, its concern was cities rather than principalities, but these were frequently the Italian city-states, so that the line between cities and states was often blurred and many themes of the two books overlapped. Botero's reputation as the founder of demographic studies is based largely on this volume; he was well aware of the swelling population in sixteenth-century Europe. The strength of a city or state, he contended, was measured above all by the size of its population, a position he discussed more fully in the *Reason of State*. But he also theorized how disease, famine, and war restricted population growth and how inherent limits on productive capacity set bounds to the population of a region and provoked the movement of peoples to new areas of settlement. There appeared in the *Greatness of Cities* his interest in America and Asia and especially in

China, to which he attributed a population of sixty million. He shared with many contemporaries a utopian view of the Chinese Empire, which had brought order and prosperity to a population that greatly surpassed the most populous European state, France, with roughly fifteen million people.[15]

The *Reason of State* first appeared in Venice in 1589. Two years later Botero published in Rome the first part of his third major work, the *Universal Relations*, with subsequent parts appearing there in 1592, 1595, and 1596. This work seems to have begun as a response to Borromeo's request for information about the state of Christianity worldwide. It was a compendium of contemporary knowledge rather than a creative effort like the *Reason of State*, a vast mine of information about the known world—physical, geographical, anthropological, economic, political, and religious. Its attempt to gather positive data was of particular importance, and its concern with numbers contributed to the development of an early science of statistics. Botero went further than Bodin in his stress on climate and geography as factors in history. He had at his disposal many travel accounts as well as the reports of missionaries from the field. The first edition of all parts together appeared at Bergamo in 1596, and for nearly a century the *Relations* were "the true and proper geopolitical manual of the whole European governing class," various parts going through eighty editions and translations into Latin (1596), German (1596), English (1601), Spanish (1603), and Polish (1609) before the end of the seventeenth century.[16] Later Botero published other *Relations* independently, for example, the *Relation on the Sea* (*Relazione del Mare*, Rome, 1598), which has been called "the first Italian oceanographical treatise."[17]

The *Relations* were filled with digressions on topics discussed in the *Reason of State*, and there were modifications of Botero's thought, generally in the direction of greater unity for Christendom. He came to embrace explicitly positions close to Bellarmine's on the *respublica christiana* and the indirect power of the papacy in temporal affairs, and he himself acknowledged a new, qualified preference for a great empire like the Spanish over the medium-sized state he had favored in the *Reason of State*. There was also praise for the Spanish expulsions of the Jews and Moors in 1492, for which Botero saw God rewarding the Spaniards with the conquest of the New World, whereas little enthusiasm was shown for these measures in the *Reason of State*, where they were considered from an economic perspective.[18]

The reason for these shifts lay partly in a providentialism less prominent in the *Reason of State* because of Botero's intent there in his response to Machiavelli to focus on intrinsic pragmatism. There is also some evidence that Botero was put under pressure by unknown persons in Rome to move in this direction.[19] Most important was probably the growing emphasis in Rome on Catholic universalism. Possevino included in his massive *Select Library* (*Biblioteca Selecta*), published at Rome in 1593 with a preface by Clement VIII, an ambitious plan for world evangelization, and Campanella advocated universal monarchy in several writings—his *Monarchy of Spain* (*Monarchia di Spagna*) may well have been composed at this time.[20] After the Christian victory at Lepanto in 1571, ardor for war against the Turks had cooled in Venice and then in Spain but not in Rome.[21] Especially after the outbreak of war between the emperor and the Turks in 1593, to last until 1606, Botero shared the perception that a mobilization of Christendom against the Turks was needed. This would be more effective if Christendom's unity were greater. His last political work, the *Discourse on the League against the Turks* (*Discorso della lega contro il Turco*, Turin, 1614), summoned at least Catholic Europe to a common effort to confront the Turkish danger.

When Federico Borromeo returned to Milan as archbishop in late 1595, Botero accompanied him. Three years later he left Borromeo's service, and after a brief stint in Rome he answered a summons to Turin from Charles Emmanuel to oversee the education of his sons. There he resided at court as a tutor and councillor, except for a year in Spain in 1605–6, accompanying three of the Duke's sons, until his retirement in 1614, allegedly for reasons of health but perhaps because of a new anti-Spanish twist to the duke's policy.[22] He died at Turin three years later at the age of seventy-three and was laid to rest in the church of the Jesuits, with whom he had always remained on good terms.

There was a notable jump in the number of books on politics published in Italy after about 1580.[23] This was occasioned neither by a political crisis nor by immediate problems facing individual states. Rather it grew out of increasing consciousness of that sixteenth-century phenomenon, the developing state, and fascination with "reason of state," the term popularized by Botero but well in use before him.[24] Small groups assembled, for example, in the 1590s in Rome and Genoa to discuss "*cose di stato.*"[25] Issues raised by Machiavelli, especially the relationship between politics and ethics, and reason of state approached from different perspectives served as topics for authors who both reflected and wrote for the contemporary situation in Italy. Here it was a period of relative stability after the chaos of the first decades of the century, with widespread acceptance of the Spanish presence in the Peninsula. Demographic growth and economic expansion characterized the

Italian states during the second half of the century, and both contributed to a revived urbanism. Botero was obviously impressed by the rising population in the Italian cities and especially in Rome, where it nearly doubled to one hundred thousand between 1550 and 1600 and brought with it increasing numbers of beggars and vagrants in the streets.[26] Tempered absolutism was the rule in principalities and, in general, in both principalities and republics there were efforts to elicit more active support for government at least from the elite.[27]

Of these Italian political writers who included Ammirato, the Venetian Paolo Paruta, Girolamo Frachetta, Ciro Spontone, and a score of others, Botero was easily the most prominent and influential.[28] Many took their cue from him. His *Reason of State* was an immediate and undoubted success from its publication in 1589. Fifteen Italian editions appeared before 1700, ten before the death of the author in 1617. Translations followed, into Spanish (Madrid, 1591; six editions by 1606), French (Paris, 1599–1606), Latin (Altdorf, 1602; three more editions by 1666), and, much later, German (Frankfurt, 1657–1664). From 1589 on, as we have seen, the *Causes of the Greatness of Cities* was often printed with it, and after 1598 the *Additions to the Reason of State*, five essays elaborating on themes of the *Reason of State*, was added.[29]

Botero did not write with a view to any one prince or principality. His purpose was a more general one characteristic of most Italian writers. As he explained in his dedication to Wolf Dietrich von Raitenau, a distant relative of the Borromeos who had been elected Archbishop of Salzburg in 1587, in the course of his travels he had frequently heard the term "reason of state," especially in connection with two authors, Machiavelli and the Roman historian, Cornelius Tacitus. He was in fact the first writer to link Tacitus with Machiavelli as an apostle of a nefarious reason of state, for which he was later criticized by his former acquaintance in Rome and fellow foe of Machiavelli, Ammirato, in his *Discourse on Tacitus* (Florence, 1594).[30] Botero was astonished at the discovery that anyone could so oppose government to the law of God or so completely separate what was allowed by reason of state from what was permitted by conscience as did these two authors. There was nothing "more irrational or more impious," he asserted, placing irrationality before impiety and so hinting at the nature of his argument. This attitude had produced chaos in Christendom, by which he seemed to mean the Reformation and all that followed it. He hoped to help remedy the situation by elaborating a reason of state that was Christian.[31] This was the purpose of his book. It was intended to serve as a handbook for Christian government.

Botero's vision was broader than the vision of his Italian contemporaries. It reached beyond Italy to France and Spain and even to Asia and the New World, and it had a clear eye for the significance of the economy. His periods of residence in France equipped him with knowledge of that country, and his perceptive comments about Spain, especially its shaky economic condition, earned his volume great popularity there, especially with advocates of reform like the *arbitristas*, who issued proposals especially at the start of the reigns of Philip III and Philip IV, and with Olivares himself, who used it as a source for his famous memorial on the "Union of Arms."[32]

Still, Botero too wrote essentially from the perspective of the contemporary Italian states, and he considered medium-sized states like them the most viable political entities. Much of what he wrote about government's need for popular support, the importance of economic development and the role of population, the treatment of heresy, and other topics also reflected current practice and thinking in the states of Italy.[33] He drew more from those which had grown out of an original urban base like Tuscany, Venice, or the Papal States than from those like his native Savoy, which had been princely territorial states from the start, without an urban tradition to hinder the creation of a centralized bureaucracy.[34] Botero had little to say about bureaucratic organization or structure. He scarcely mentioned Sixtus V or the contemporary government of the Papal States, but sometimes his remarks can be interpreted as a commentary on the policies of Sixtus.

Two key terms were clarified right at the start of the *Reason of State*. Botero defined state as "a firm rule over people [*dominio fermo sopra popoli*]," much in the manner of Machiavelli in the first chapter of the *Prince*.[35] "Reason of state" he designated as "knowledge of the means suitable to create, preserve, and expand a rule so established." His use of the term was to prove influential. It was, consciously, much more positive and much more general than the usage of many contemporaries for whom the term meant, as he himself noted with a certain vagueness, "those things which cannot be reduced to an ordinary or common reason."[36] This was the case with Ammirato or Spontone, for example, where reason of state signified the need to override, for the sake of the common good, ordinary practice or positive law but not natural or divine law.[37] For others like the satirical republican Traiano Boccalini in his *Reports from Parnassus* (1612) it retained the infamous sense of "a law useful to states but in everything contrary to the law of God and of men."[38]

The term *reason* had a further implication for him. The anti-Machiavellians argued from what we have called providentialist and intrinsic pragmatism. Botero concentrated on the latter and really did not elaborate systematically a position on providence. The gist of his argument was that the ruler who sought a powerful state did best to seek the well-being of his subjects in a moral and intelligent fashion. Botero did not spend time exhorting the prince or reminding him that he was the servant of his people, as did so many authors on princely government. He merely showed that for a prince whose ambition was a powerful state, the reasonable way to govern was the way he recommended. Machiavelli's immoral means were in the end counterproductive and therefore unreasonable. They simply did not work.

Statecraft, or the method of government, was Botero's concern, and his perspective that of a prince intent upon a powerful state. He cannot be faulted for failing to elaborate a political philosophy; this he presupposed from the contemporary Scholastics.[39] He accepted the modern state in much the same way as Bellarmine, his former classmate. In the *Reason of State* he presupposed some form of subordination to the papacy, but the treatment was too cursory to attribute to him the theory of indirect or direct papal power in temporal matters. From the start it was evident Botero had in mind a state ruled by an absolute prince or king. Nowhere did he discuss the merits of the different forms of government, and he showed little of Machiavelli's interest in the constitutional structure of the state. Like Bodin, he was a part of the trend toward vigorous princely government as the only viable response to the disorder and wars of the late sixteenth century, which he had personally experienced in France. The only restraints he placed upon the ruler were moral not constitutional, though, as we shall see, he warned the prince of his need for popular support. Nor did he distinguish clearly between the ruler and the state. The prince was, as it were, the artisan, the state the material.[40]

Yet Botero esteemed republics and paid his respects to their love of liberty, Venice being frequently mentioned with favor in the *Reason of State*. The ideal was the medium-sized state, precisely because it was more durable. Two examples were Sparta and Venice, which Machiavelli had reproached for not pursuing expansion and glory effectively. They remained within their limits, and so were less exposed to the envy and violence of others and less subject to the vices and passions that came with great wealth and power. Small states such as the republics of Ragusa or Lucca could not maintain genuine independence, and large states such as Spain or the Turkish Empire would fall from their own inner corruption. Rome's decline began with the conquest of Carthage.[41]

Botero's interest was the maintenance, then the expansion of the state; he had scarcely anything to say about its foundation. All three stages, however, he attributed to the same causes.[42] Machiavelli's chief concern, certainly in the *Discourses*, had been the preservation of the state in a hostile environment and against the ravages of time. Botero had few illusions about the environment. When discussing prudence, he introduced the concept of princely interest (*interesse*) or advantage, perhaps borrowing it from Guicciardini's *Maxims and Reflections (Ricordi)*, which was circulating by then in printed and manuscript versions.[43] He contrasted it with friendship, blood relationship, obligations to allies, or "any other bond," and he warned the ruler "to take it for a settled matter that in the deliberations of princes interest is that which overcomes every other consideration."[44] To preserve a state was a greater work than to create one, precisely because of the variability of things human. Power was often gained by accident or by force, he wrote, sounding like Machiavelli, "but to maintain what one had acquired was the fruit of an outstanding *virtù*" and called for great wisdom. The Spartan custom of punishing those who in combat lost not their swords but their shields showed their esteem for preservation.[45]

Botero's predilection for medium-sized states showed that for him it was not a question of conquest and glory or mediocrity and probably extinction, as Machiavelli seemed to argue. He distinguished, formally, between maintenance and expansion, and he devoted the last four books of the *Reason of State* to the latter. But the purpose behind the distinction was to show that within a Christian, moral framework it was possible for a prince to enlarge his state and so to acquire the resultant glory. Botero creatively forged a new concept of expansion that had much less to do with military conquest than Machiavelli's.

Botero argued from historical example much as did Machiavelli and Bodin, and he frequently called to the bar the ancient writers, especially the Romans. Despite his assignment to a place alongside Machiavelli, Tacitus was cited seventy-three times, much more frequently than Livy, the author next in line with fifty-six citations. No Scholastics were cited, nor were any medieval or Renaissance historians or political writers except Machiavelli and Polydore Vergil, who each appeared once.[46] But these figures are deceptive. Botero used many examples, historical and contemporary, without citing any source, and these were balanced about equally between the ancient world and more recent history, that is, the Renaissance and the sixteenth century. He alluded as well to medieval events.

Distinctive of Botero and of the anti-Machiavellian school was their understanding of *virtù* or virtue, reputation, and power, and the relationship among them. The anti-Machiavellians provide a key to understanding these concepts, which were central to the political culture of the Counter-Reformation and the Baroque. The Spanish council of state reminded Philip III in 1616, when war in Italy threatened, that "religion and reputation . . . are the two great matters which sustain states," and on them there could be no compromise.[47] Reputation played an important role in the policy-making of Olivares and Richelieu, and *reputation* and *puissance* were found throughout the cardinal's *Political Testament*, where *vertu* has generally been replaced by the more specific *prudence* or *raison*, as was often the case once we move into the seventeenth century.[48]

Both Machiavelli and Botero highlighted the role of the ruler's *virtù*, which was for both a congeries of qualities that enabled him to win and retain the support of his people. But Botero reunited Christian moral virtue with the political skill and panache of Machiavelli's *virtù*. This was fundamental to his position. The ruler of *virtù* was both virtuous and virtuoso. At the heart of his thought then was the connection between *virtù*, reputation, and power; never stated explicitly, it served as an implicit substructure revealing the congruence of the good and the useful. *Virtù* produced reputation, understood as the support of the people, and reputation constituted the cardinal element in the ruler's power, which in turn augmented his reputation. Immoral conduct as well as political ineptitude—the two nearly overlapped in Botero—subverted the prince's power by undermining his reputation. The word *potenza* for power was not nearly as much a part of Botero's vocabulary as were *virtù* or *riputazione*, but the reality was as central to his thinking as virtue or reputation.[49]

Virtù was a constant theme throughout the *Reason of State*'s ten books. Botero devoted most of book 1 to princely *virtù*, book 2 to its vital components, prudence and valor, and then books 3 to 6 to a further elaboration of the way *virtù* enabled the prince to secure the support of his people. Book 7 then began his treatment of the state's expansion, the discussion of the last four books revolving around the "instruments of prudence and valor" or *virtù*, the tools of expansion. These were the prince's resources (*forze*), which he reduced to "men and money," and they too were basic elements of his power and likewise a source of reputation. Machiavelli had made nearly the same reduction, subordinating the need for a full treasury to the necessity for loyal troops, however, and understanding people largely in terms of these troops.[50]

Without the support of his people, a prince could not rule for any length of time; it consisted in their love (*affezione*) for him and his reputation (*riputazione* or *stima*) among them. These were "the foundations of every government of a state."[51] So Botero introduced a non-juridical form of popular consent into government, thus incorporating the democratic element in princely rule affirmed by Machiavelli and the role of consent insisted on by the Scholastics. Love could be elicited by benefits and moderate *virtù*, reputation only by outstanding *virtù* displayed in matters that were vital to the people. These Botero summed up in a triad which comprised much of the traditional notion of the common good, "abundance, peace, and justice." A people could not but be content "who without fear of foreign or civil war and without fear of being violently assassinated in their homes had the necessary food available at a good price."[52] The prince who carried out his obligation to provide for the common good would enjoy his people's support. Good government was good politics because it helped secure reputation.

Botero developed his concept of reputation more fully in the *Additions*. He did not directly discuss its role in a ruler's foreign relations, yet the connection between domestic and foreign policy seems to have been evident to him, reputation abroad being dependent upon reputation or support at home. A crucial measure of a prince's weight in international affairs was the support or lack of it from his own subjects. Reputation now became a composite of love and fear that existed in them. It was to a prince what reverence was to a holy person. It designated a sense of awe and wonder in the subject generated by the ruler's *virtù*, which "had something of the outstanding and wonderful about it and which elevated the prince above the earth and removed him from the number of the citizens." So the prince shrouded himself in an element of mystery that his people could not fathom.

Botero then asked which was more important in reputation, love or fear. Like Machiavelli, and with a certain sadness, he came down on the side of fear. Given the world as it was, no government was more uncertain than one based on love. It was nearly impossible for a prince to satisfy all his subjects and unite thousands in the love of himself. Subjects tended to murmur and long for change. The subjection that followed from fear was necessary. Moreover, it lay within the power of the prince to create fear in his subjects, whereas to elicit love was often beyond him. But fear was a far cry from hatred, Botero warned, as had Machiavelli and Aristotle long before him. Hatred as well as contempt had to be avoided at all costs, since they soon undermined government.[53]

For Botero reputation had to be based on genuine *virtù*. Here his discussion with Machiavelli led him into the favorite Baroque topic of the relationship between appearance and reality. Feigned *virtù* would not long convince. One simply could not successfully counterfeit piety over a long period of time, as Machiavelli suggested. Botero distinguished natural reputation, which corresponded to the *virtù* of the ruler; artificial reputation, which resulted from conscious exaggeration of his *virtù*; and adventitious reputation, which exaggerated the prince's reputation but was not the result of a conscious effort to do this. Neither of the last two would endure, and they could lead to trouble. The condottiere Carmagnola had been executed by the Venetians because he failed to prevail in a battle that his reputation had led them to think he should have won.[54]

But, Botero added, this did not mean a prince could not or should not polish his image. Certainly it was a fault if his reputation was less than he deserved, he went on, perhaps seeking to dispel in pious rulers false notions of humility. He suggested that a prince improve his image, for example, by hiding his weaknesses, assigning unpopular tasks to others, or "without ostentation making his power manifest." A prince's image was like a painting. Just as a painter might exceed the limits of truth as long as he remained within those of verisimilitude, so might the prince in developing his image, wrote Botero drawing on contemporary art theory. But in the last resort enduring reputation had to be based on reality, appearance was never enough.[55]

Botero broke princely *virtù* down into three pairs of virtues, justice and liberality, valor and prudence, and temperance and religion. The last pair he treated as qualities of the people as well as the ruler; they were essential for both if the state were to endure. But valor and especially prudence were the predominant virtues for the prince because they secured reputation. Valor was of the hand, corresponding roughly to Machiavelli's lion; prudence was of the eye, corresponding to Machiavelli's fox.[56] The overwhelming amount of space devoted to prudence in the *Reason of State* indicated that the eye was more important than the hand, and prudence soon became for the anti-Machiavellians the cardinal virtue of the ruler or politician, combining moral goodness with political skill, as it had long done in the Aristotelian and Thomistic traditions.[57] The prince garnered the love of his subjects especially by justice and liberality, the virtues "which were directed completely to their benefit." Botero discussed two forms of justice distinguished by Aristotle and usually treated by the Scholastics: distributive, which dealt with the fair allocation of honors and burdens in the state, and commutative, which protected the subjects from violence and fraud at the hands of one another. They had to obtain in those areas where the hand of government touched most regularly the lives of subjects, in the collection of taxes and in the administration of justice, where people wanted above all fairness and speed. Botero's criticism of the sale of offices, summarized in the phrase, "whoever sells offices wants thieves as officeholders," certainly applied not only to France but to Rome, where the practice was more advanced at the time.[58] The prince should pay judges well and refuse them permission to accept any gifts at all. Botero praised the way the Chinese prepared their officials, and he lauded the system of spies used by Cosimo de' Medici, Grand Duke of Tuscany, to keep tabs on his judges.[59]

Liberality had two foci, relief for the poor and patronage of the arts. No work was more praised in Scripture than care for the unfortunate, nor was there any activity "more suited and more effective to win over the people's hearts and create in them an obligation to their lord." The good and the useful were in harmony. The prince should manifest his concern especially at times of such natural disasters as earthquakes. Botero added the Machiavellian advice that at the time of such calamities the ruler should not allow any private person to become too prominent in the relief effort, since this could easily create a popularity for him threatening to the government.[60] So the Gracchi brothers had risen to influence in ancient Rome. Secondly, liberality was exercised by fostering the *virtù* of subjects, where *virtù* meant their literary and artistic abilities. The ruler should be a patron of the arts and sciences, as indeed many contemporary princes were, thus binding prominent personalities to the state. Nor did Botero fail to add the admonition that the prince should not be so liberal with his gifts that he notably increased the tax burden and thus stirred discontent.[61]

Prudence and valor made up the leading components of *virtù*. They were the source of reputation, the two columns "on which every government ought to be founded." Prudence was acquired above all through experience. For Botero as for Machiavelli, a major part of a prince's or statesman's education was the study of history. It enabled him to draw on the experience of others as well as his own; it was "the broadest stage one could possibly imagine." Botero then took up an idea from Bodin that he developed much more fully in the *Universal Relations*. Peoples were different. Their character was greatly affected by their geography and their climate. Those who inhabited mountainous areas, for example, tended to be fierce and wild, those who dwelt in valleys to be soft and even effeminate. It was up to the prince to acquire an understanding of the peculiar nature of his own and other peoples.[62] So Botero implied an individualized reason of state, or means to construct and maintain a state, tailored to the population and situation of particular states, and he thus helped prepare for the further evolution of thinking about reason of state and the interests of particular states.[63]

Botero mentioned under prudence a number of precepts or maxims that are impossible to summarize but that were of the utmost importance for his political position. Many have a Machiavellian ring and reflect a pessimistic vision of the world, but they do not at any point recommend clearly immoral conduct. Reference has already been made to the first of his "headings of prudence [*capi di prudenza*]," "Let [the prince] take it for a settled matter that in the deliberations of princes, interest is that which overcomes every other consideration." Polybius and Plutarch were cited in support of this principle of conduct. The prince was never to trust anyone who had actually been offended or felt himself to have been offended by him. The desire for revenge remained latent and came to the surface when the opportunity presented itself. Botero advised princes against wars with powerful republics unless they were certain of victory. The love of liberty was rooted so deeply in the hearts of the citizens that it was difficult to defeat them and almost impossible to keep them in subjection. "The enterprises and counsels of princes die with them, the designs and deliberations of free cities are as it were immortal," he wrote, sounding much like the republican Machiavelli. Nor should a ruler enter into conflict with the church. Rarely did he have justice on his side, and he would always appear to be acting against religion, thus gaining nothing. Milan, Florence, Venice, and Naples had emerged with no benefits from their wars with the popes.[64]

For Botero, as for Machiavelli, a sense of timing was fundamental in politics. Nothing was more unworthy of a prudent ruler than to commit himself to the whim of chance or fortune. Here Philip II of Spain provided the outstanding example. But a prince had to know when to act, "because nothing was of greater moment than a certain period of time, which was called opportunity [*opportunità*] and was nothing other than the coming together of circumstances that rendered a project easy [to carry out], which either before or after that point in time remained difficult." As for Machiavelli, a ruler had to know when to exploit the occasion (*occasióne*), a term used later by Botero in a similar context and divorced from any connection with fortune.[65] Botero warned especially against sudden changes, which always had something of the violent about them, "and rarely did violence succeed and never did it produce a lasting effect." Especially at the start of his reign a prince ought to be careful about making changes. When they were necessary, they should be made in imitation of nature, which did not move rapidly between summer and winter but passed through fall and spring. Charles Martel had demonstrated this by the way he gradually prepared the way for his son Pepin to assume the Carolingian throne.[66]

Faithfulness to agreements was a part of prudence and an essential element in a ruler's reputation. Yet Botero's treatment of it was unsatisfactory, given his assertion that in the world of politics, interest, as a matter of fact, always prevailed. His outstanding example of fidelity was Alexander Farnese, Duke of Parma, Governor of the Netherlands and commander of Philip II's army there from 1578 to 1592, who had been successful in taming the Dutch rebels and who served it seems, consciously or unconsciously, as Botero's counterpart to Cesare Borgia. Nor should one promise what one could not deliver; this too undermined confidence. Later Botero pointed out the necessity for a ruler to remain faithful to the terms on which another people had submitted to him. Any other policy could stir up fears and with them trouble.[67] To build on any other foundation but truth and fidelity to one's word was counterproductive. Yet Botero failed to offer any guidance regarding the circumstances when a changed situation involving newly perceived interests might allow a ruler to withdraw from an agreement. The Scholastics had exhibited flexibility in this regard. Botero merely left side by side his insistence on fidelity and his assertion of the factual predominance of interest.

Botero gave much less space to valor, the second source of reputation, and he often blurred the line between prudence and valor. More narrowly, valor meant boldness (*ardire*). Together with prudence it brought forth "astonishing deeds." Their common achievement for Botero as for Machiavelli was that they captured the subjects' attention and energies, whether by exciting their wonder and awe at the prince's undertakings or by keeping them occupied and so from causing trouble. A prince ought never to undertake an enterprise that was not certain to result in success with honor, nor take up projects of little moment that were ill-suited to magnify his reputation. There ought to be something "outstanding and heroic" in all his deeds.[68] Two types of deeds were the military and the civil, with the former meriting emphasis. Among the civil were building projects distinguished by their "grand scale or marvelous utility," such as the aqueducts, bridges, and roads of the Romans or the Propylaeum of Pericles in Athens. So Botero appeared to endorse the building program of Sixtus V, one of whose major achievements was the completion of the aqueduct called *Acque Felice* that carried water to Rome from twenty kilometers east of the city, and another, the construction of a new system of streets within the city.

But gradually Botero's perspective shifted from the grandeur of the undertakings themselves to their ability to keep the people occupied, and by people he now meant primarily the increasing urban population and especially the urban poor, who were by nature unstable and desirous of novelties. He envisioned the capital cities first of Rome and then of Paris, Madrid, and elsewhere, where there was need to control a restive population and Baroque culture was later at home.[69] Pope Sixtus's building program was a great source of employment in Rome.[70] In a passage where he uncharacteristically demonstrated enthusiasm for war, he approached Machiavelli's traditional view that foreign wars were useful to keep the peace at home, and he explained the domestic peace enjoyed by Spaniards and Turks partly in terms of their faraway wars. Christians had at hand a constant, traditional enemy against whom they always could make war legitimately, as he was later to point out. The popular entertainments employed by many rulers like the Medici in Florence were useful to distract the people. Ideally, they should educate as well as entertain and so combine pleasure (*piacere*) with uprightness (*onestà*)—Botero was highly critical of the contemporary theater, but he lauded the ecclesiastical pageants of Carlo Borromeo in Milan. "In short, it is necessary to do this in such a way that the people have some occupation, pleasurable or useful, at home or abroad, that engages them and so keeps them from impertinent actions and evil thoughts."[71] This was another tool of Botero's statecraft.

He subsequently divided subjects into three groups, the nobles or the wealthy (*grandi, opulenti*), the middling sort (*mezani*), and the poor (*poveri, miseri*). The middling sort he passed over quickly as a peaceful lot who posed no threat and turned to the others who did. Recommendations for dealing with the urban poor we have already seen. Here he anticipated his program for economic development by showing the need for the poor to be given opportunities in agriculture or a craft, which would in turn give them a stake in the state. Among nobles, three types could be dangerous: princes of the blood, great feudal lords, and those outstanding by virtue of their valor. Generally speaking, Botero was concerned about the threat to the prince's rule from the overmighty, a threat that the wars in France had brought home to him. Offices that carried too much authority ought not to be created, and existing ones—like the Great Constable of France—suppressed. Rulers should avoid alienating offices by granting them in perpetuity, like the governorships in France, so that incumbents could be removed. There should be a clear distinction between members of the royal council, who enjoyed no jurisdiction, and officials with jurisdiction, such as governors, generals, and captains of major fortresses. Ferdinand the Catholic, Botero noted, never assigned the governorship of a province to the general who conquered it.[72]

Religion and temperance were the last pair of virtues under *virtù*, sustaining the others and so preserving the state. They were qualities needed in the people as well as in the prince. Religion was the mother of virtues, temperance the wet-nurse. Botero feared excessive wealth much as did the republican Machiavelli, who saw it as undermining civic loyalty.[73] He advocated luxury taxes and sumptuary laws limiting expenditures on food and clothing, not to promote Christian simplicity of life nor to preserve social distinctions, as was the case with many contemporaries, but to forestall dangers to the state. Without temperance the people fell into indulgence, luxury, and ostentation, which blinded the mind, weakened resolve, and brought public and private ruin. This was true of Rome, where luxury and softness made possible the tyranny of a Tiberius and a Caligula. Portugal, overrun with the delicacies of the East, was heading in the same direction. Botero placed much of the blame on women, "the ladies being much more apt to corrupt the men than the men to restrain the ladies; few men were masters of their own wives." All great empires had fallen because of luxury, and "avarice is born of luxury and luxury of women." Moreover, as a mercantilist Botero was sensitive to the loss of money to the state caused by the purchase of imported jewels, perfumes, finery, and other luxury goods.[74]

Botero saw religion from the perspective of providentialist and intrinsic pragmatism; it was valuable because of the divine aid it won for the state and for the virtues it engendered in the subjects, especially obedience. Like Machiavelli, he pointed to the importance attached to religion by the Romans, who undertook no enterprise without first consulting the augurs and seeking the favor of the gods. Like the Carolingians and Capetians before them, the Habsburg rulers owed their prominence to their piety. Botero related a tale, already a part of Habsburg lore. Back in the thirteenth century, Count Rudolph of Habsburg had assisted a priest bringing Viaticum to a peasant in the midst of a terrifying storm. The priest's grateful blessing brought the House its subsequent good fortune. God rewarded a prince's piety.[75]

"Religion is the foundation of all princely rule," Botero continued as he turned to the subjects. The ruler must encourage piety among them. Religion was useful in many ways. It encouraged bravery in battle, civic responsibility, and a spirit of obedience. "Nor was there any law more favorable to princes than the Christian [law], because it subjects to them not only the bodies and property of their subjects, where this is suitable, but also their minds and consciences, and it binds not only their hands but also their affections and thoughts; it requires that they obey not only disciplined princes but dissolute ones, too, and suffer everything rather than disturb the peace."[76] According to Christian teaching, God was the source of all authority. Christians were bound in conscience to obey even unworthy rulers, except when a command stood in opposition to the law of God, and even then, Botero added coming as close as he ever did to a discussion of the right of resistance, a "clear break" with the ruler should be the last resort. Christians had demonstrated long-suffering and patience under the Roman persecutions. At present Catholics endured with patience their trials in France, the Netherlands, England, and Scotland, in contrast to the Protestants so often inclined to rebellion, he contended, overlooking activities like those of the Catholic League in

France.[77] Christianity and specifically Catholicism was a bulwark of the state, Machiavelli notwithstanding.

Despite his apparent opposition to the increasing intervention of rulers in ecclesiastical matters, Botero accorded the prince a major role in church affairs when he assigned him responsibilities for religion, thus opening the door for an expansion of the state's activity that was typical of the Counter-Reformation. Indeed the increased role of government in ecclesiastical affairs that characterized the Counter-Reformation, and the Reformation, was as important to the development of the state as a standing army or a nascent bureaucracy.[78] Botero laid out a program of reform and Counter-Reformation. The prince should serve as an example to his people by genuinely and intelligently practicing his faith, avoiding pretense and superstition. He should see to it that the people had good pastors and preachers, care for the material needs of the clergy, and provide suitable churches, and he should promote church programs with his authority and his funds.[79]

The problem of religious dissidents had become acute following the Reformation. For Botero as for many of his contemporaries, religious differences were the main source of division within states, and religious unity essential to a state's power. Botero discussed policy toward dissidents not under religion but under the means to reconcile newly acquired subjects to the government of a prince; it was more a political than a religious matter. The ideal was their conversion, and Botero recommended many ways to approach this. Good missionaries, men of solid doctrine and exemplary life, were the first requirement. Education was a way to win over the parents as well as the children, and Botero praised the Jesuit schools in Germany, India, and the New World. When necessary, as Suarez had argued for unbelievers as well as for heretics, one could legitimately bring pressure to bear by the concession or denial of such privileges as tax exemption. Nor should one underestimate the effectiveness of charity or almsgiving.[80]

But what about the irreconcilables who proved immune to all efforts at conversion? For Botero, these were the Muslims among the unbelievers and the Calvinists among the heretics. The Calvinists in particular, whom he knew from his travels in France, generated constant unrest and were to blame, according to a passage he later deleted, for the war in France, the rebellion in the Netherlands, and the overthrow of Mary Stuart in Scotland.[81] The prince had to take stern measures when it was evident they were not going to convert and intended to resist the new arrangements. But, it should be noted, these measures of government were aimed not directly at conversion but at the prevention of rebellion. Botero first suggested a number of ways to take the spirit out of dissidents, for example, by denying them the use of the horse, as the Turks did the Christians, or by requiring them to wear distinctive dress. Secondly, the prince was to weaken their resources, that is, their supplies of men and money. He should deny them arms and fortified places, and impose special taxes. The Turks took Christian youths to serve in the Janissaries; Christian rulers might have to result to similar measures. Lastly, one ought to sow dissension among dissidents, cut off their contacts with foreigners, and keep out preachers and subversive publications, and in extreme cases one might have to relocate populations, as the Assyrians had done with the Jews.[82] Significantly, Botero did not hold up as an example in this context the expulsions of the Jews and Moors from Spain.

But, inevitably, troubles would break out. As he took up the topic of actual rebellion, Botero approached the position of Bodin and the *politiques* and showed his aversion to religious civil war. If rebellion could be suppressed quickly by force, this should be done, the more quietly the better. The part of prudence was to know when to take a hard line and when to yield. Botero made a number of suggestions about handling a mob. One was simply to dissimulate, that is, overlook a provocation; another was to let the mob exhaust its energy for lack of leadership. But if it appeared that these and other expedients would not work, it was normally better to yield in part or in full before actual hostilities began. In this way the prince retained the affection of his subjects, if not his reputation—he distinguished the two here—and even his reputation, if he could make it appear that he was granting concessions freely. Once civil war broke out, it was very difficult to bring it to a close without compromises, he wrote, perhaps with the French experience in mind. Better to make concessions at the start, Botero seemed to imply. He was not prepared to fight a war for the suppression of heresy. The sum of wisdom in the matter was to resist beginnings. Trouble could usually be foreseen well ahead of time; it rarely started with a full-scale rebellion.[83]

Preservation of the state was owed to the prince's *virtù* and its expansion to the "instruments" of his *virtù*—his resources (*forze*), which were central features of his power. But the methods for enlarging the state were basically the same as for preserving it. The distinction between the two was a nominal one made, it would seem, to highlight that a Christian prince could win the glory of expanding his state without engaging in military conquest. Such conquest figured but little in Botero's scheme of things, since his ideal was the medium-sized state. He distinguished further between the extensive, or quantitative, and the intensive, or qualitative, enlargement of a state. The former was essentially its economic development, the latter its military preparedness. The prince's resources comprised items such as munitions, arms, and horses, but they were reduced ultimately to men and money.[84] Men were more important than money, as they were for Machiavelli. Whereas for Machiavelli "men" were essentially soldiers, Botero included soldiers, but took "men" to comprise the general population, which was the most fundamental resource of a state because it produced the state's wealth, which in turn was the source of the prince's treasure. Botero the emergent mercantilist did not lose sight of the importance of military strength, but he possessed a broader vision of state power than did Machiavelli.

The literature of reason of state recognized with particular clarity the connection between the increasing functions of government and the need for revenue. Botero more than any other was responsible for this insight.[85] A prince needed to accumulate treasure, by which Botero meant ready funds in the form of precious metals. He distinguished it carefully from the wealth or economic resources of a state, which were more important as the source of treasure. Reputation required treasure, Botero insisted and then added, indicating his awareness of the change in thinking since the days of Machiavelli, "because the power [*potenza*] of states is adjudged today no less by the supply of treasure than by the size of the territory."[86] Perhaps he learned this lesson from Sixtus V. To the wonder of contemporaries, this pope during his brief pontificate stored up a treasure of four million scudi in Castel Sant'Angelo for use in emergencies. In the long run, however, his achievement had disastrous results for papal finances, partly because it was not adequately coordinated with a broader economic policy as it was in Botero's writings. Sixtus overburdened his people with taxes, against which Botero explicitly warned.[87]

Treasure was necessary in time of peace but especially in time of war. Botero cited the familiar dictum rejected by Machiavelli, "money is the sinews of empire,"[88] perhaps having in mind the disasters to which financial shortfalls had brought the Spaniards. One had to have funds on hand. To try to raise money when hostilities were imminent was too late, usually meant borrowing at high interest rates, and so resulted in higher, burdensome taxes.[89]

Maximilian of Bavaria was one of Botero's most prominent students in this respect. As he wrote in 1598 to his father, who had just abdicated, "ecclesiastical as well as secular princes look only to '*ragion di stato*,' and he is respected who has much land or much money. Since we do not have the former, we will never have any authority with the Italians or others, until we do better in financial matters, . . . to which we ought to give the highest priority."[90] Maximilian's ability to build up and then maintain an *aerario* with ready funds even during the Thirty Years' War explains much of his political success. But his economic policy had its shortcomings too, as we will see later.

How much treasure ought a prince to gather? This Botero realized was a thorny question, but his answer made eminent economic sense and pointed to the weakness of papal policy. Obviously, the amount of treasure necessary was greater in time of war, especially if the prince planned an aggressive war, than in time of peace. A solid reason for avoiding war was precisely to prevent straining the economic resources of a state and so making prosperity impossible.

The desirable amount of treasure was proportionate to the total economic resources of a state, which were the source of the ruler's treasure. Thus it varied widely from state to state. The King of Poland's *aerario* should contain considerably less than that of the government of the Netherlands. As a firm rule for peacetime, a prince should never accumulate funds in his coffers to the point that the money he withdrew from circulation hindered the availability of funds for the normal course and development of agriculture, industry, and commerce. This was to restrict economic activity and so harm the state in the long run by lessening its wealth. More precisely, a ruler ought never to take into his treasury more than the amount by which the inflow of treasure into the country surpassed the outflow. This presupposed, Botero noted, careful record keeping. He wanted a favorable balance of payments, and the prince should never draw into the treasury more than the amount by which the balance was favorable. Should the outflow presently exceed the treasure coming into the state, the prince should forego the accumulation of treasure for the time being and concentrate on developing the state's productivity, a point which Botero extensively elaborated.[91]

But the limitations of Botero's economics were shown by his failure to take note of the current currency fluctuations and inflation, which Bodin had addressed in 1568,[92] and by his prohibition of interest or usury, which he saw as taking money out of circulation, just as the ruler's treasure did, in addition to violating church directives. Yet thanks to the availability by this time of other sources of credit and the narrow interpretation of the prohibition of usury, the ban on it hindered economic development very little if at all.[93]

How was the prince to raise funds? Certainly there were patrimonial lands as well as unexploited land within the principality, which ought to be developed vigorously. Then there were import and export levies. One reason the prince should foster trade was that it meant greater revenues from duties; he should try to put the burden on foreigners as much as this was feasible. Loans were a further source of funds, for which he had to take care to maintain his credit. He could also call on the church for help. This was justified before God by papal approval and before the people by necessity. Extraordinary sources of revenue were, in the case of one's own subjects, confiscations, indemnifications, gifts, in the case of foreigners, tribute, pensions, and other awards. At first blush, Botero's assertion that a prince's power ought to be measured more by his ability to gather funds from extraordinary than from ordinary sources is surprising; but most princes had sold or otherwise committed their ordinary revenues and lived from the extraordinary ones, he claimed.[94] In 1592 two-thirds of the revenue of the papal government went to pay interest on the *monti* or government bonds promoted by Sixtus.[95] His remark realistically reflected the situation of many contemporary rulers, whose ability to impose and, perhaps more important, to collect taxes was limited.[96]

But Botero advocated as the chief source of revenue regular taxes on the wealth of subjects. In this he pointed the way to the future. The most important step in the development of state finance was the gradual movement of such taxes from the margin to the center of government revenues, not contingent upon necessity or upon a particular set of circumstances but as an ordinary source of funds.[97] To be sure, regular impositions existed before Botero, like the French *taille* or the Florentine *decima*, but they were still considered extraordinary sources of revenue by many.[98] Botero was one of the first political writers to affirm that regular impositions should be an ordinary source of revenue. Perhaps he came to this position by observing the rise in taxation in the Italian states during the sixteenth century; in the Papal States it nearly tripled.[99] Such taxes were licit and just, "because all reason dictates that private goods serve the public good, without which they [private goods] cannot be secured." They should be levied on property, not persons; otherwise there would be clear exploitation of the poor. With conscious reference to the Netherlands, where Philip II's attempt to tax movable property had fomented rebellion, Botero urged that taxes be levied only on land. Should there arise a need to tax movable goods, this should be done in a manner similar to that employed in the German cities, where the citizens themselves assessed the value of their own property and paid accordingly.[100] Botero made no suggestions about an apparatus for the collection of taxes.

A powerful prince had to have treasure at his disposal. Even more important was a large population. Valuable as a source of soldiers, it was still more necessary for the wealth it produced. A large population was both the cause and result of the state's wealth and the prince's treasure.

The ruler should actively foster agriculture and industry. Agriculture was the basis for all demographic growth; first one had to feed the population. The prince should encourage it with the development of the "infrastructure," for example with irrigation and drainage projects as the Romans had done, with the importation of new seeds and plants, and with rewards to those who farmed their lands well. The Chinese with their efficient use of land functioned as good examples.[101]

But industry was still more vital than agriculture. It supported more people—according to Botero two-thirds of the Italian cities lived by the silk and wool industries—and produced more wealth. In a highly enthusiastic passage, which had appeared originally in the *Greatness of Cities*, Botero exalted the ability and ingenuity of human beings in the production of goods. Look what they had done with the excrement of worms! People were more important than natural resources. Those who worked materials always gained greater rewards than those who gathered them. Neither Italy, nor the Netherlands, nor France possessed extensive natural resources, yet they were the wealthiest areas of Europe. Certainly they did not have anything like the mines of the New World.

Botero stood out as an early critic of Spain's economic situation and especially its failure to develop industry. He was perhaps the first to call attention to the signs of demographic decline in Spain and its threat to productivity.[102] Here Ferdinand the Catholic's expulsion of the Jews and Moors, which Machiavelli had lauded as a great deed, came in for Botero's implicit criticism because of its removal of groups valuable to the country's economy. He praised instead rulers like the Grand Dukes of Tuscany, who recruited foreign workers and artisans to help the growth of industry and peasants to locate on sparsely settled land.[103] Spanish social attitudes disdainful of farming and industry were harmful, and the widespread Spanish permission for the export of raw materials imprudent in the extreme.[104] In Rome Pope Sixtus did make an effort, ultimately unsuccessful, to develop the textile industry, having a large wool-weaving mill constructed near the Trevi Fountain and encouraging the peasants of the Campagna to raise sheep and to turn to the cultivation of the silkworm.[105]

Foreign trade also promoted the wealth of a state. In the *Reason of State* Botero had little to say about it, but in the *Greatness of Cities*, against the background of the discoveries and European expansion, he inserted a lyrical passage in praise of God who had created the various peoples dependent on one another for goods in order to lead them to mutual love and union. Thus he revived an idea that dated back to Libanius, a teacher at Antioch in the fourth century, where it was picked up by the Church Fathers Chrysostom and Basil and then to appear sporadically in subsequent writers until the sixteenth century, when Botero propagated it anew.[106] "In truth it appears that God has created the water not only as an element necessary for the perfection of nature but more so as a most suitable way to carry goods from one country to another, because, having willed that men embrace one another as members of the same body, he divided the goods [of the world] in such a way that he did not give everything to any country, so that this people needing the goods of that people and that people the goods of this people, there would be born of these needs communication, and of communication love, and of love union." So, in God's plan, commerce served to unite the world. States grew not so much at the expense as with the help of others.[107]

Throughout Botero's treatment of princely finances and his advocacy of economic development, the argument from intrinsic pragmatism served as the implicit framework of his thought. The prince who fostered the economic prosperity of his subjects, their "abundance," increased his own power. Their wealth served as his tax base. Botero never harangued the prince about his obligation to promote the welfare of his subjects. This was not his method. He showed that the economic well-being of his subjects corresponded to his own advantage. The good and the useful went together. So he opened up a legitimate Christian road to state power that was more likely to lead to success than Machiavelli's path.

Botero did not overlook military power. When he turned to war and the military, he touched on just war theory and discussed many of the military issues raised by Machiavelli. Writing of discipline, he stressed the need for rewards and punishments and again pointed to the Roman example. From this perspective the writing of history was important, since one of its functions was to preserve the memory and honor of soldiers, which was one of their rewards. Botero praised the contemporary Portuguese in this regard, undoubtedly with the *Lusiads* in mind, and faulted the Spaniards for their failure to record the deeds of their heroic century. Soldiers had to have confidence that they would be cared for if they were wounded or when they retired and to know that the prince would look after their wives and children should they fall in his service. In this regard the Spaniards had already begun to lead the way, although Botero did not note it. They opened the first permanent military hospital at Mechelen in the Netherlands in 1585, under the Duke of Parma, and eleven years later they established a public trust to execute the testaments of deceased soldiers.[108]

But Botero's vision of human nature came through when he claimed that punishments were still more important than rewards. Virtue was to a degree its own reward, with its own satisfactions. In war, if the prince did not reward, he would not be loved; if he did not punish, he would not be obeyed, and there was nothing worse than that. Botero cited with favor the horrible military punishment of the Romans, the decimation, and recounted the Spartan adage that a soldier should fear his commanding officer more than the enemy. Like Machiavelli, he contended that soldiers fought best under pressure, or what Machiavelli called necessity (*necessità*), with their backs against the wall. This heightened their valor and *virtù*. Commanders should endeavor to maneuver them into such situations.[109]

Botero agreed with Machiavelli that a prince had to draw his army essentially from his own subjects, and he endorsed the current practice in Venice and Savoy of maintaining native militias, a practice to which the Habsburgs and other German princes also turned increasingly in the last decades of the sixteenth century.[110] To be sure, there were dangers in arming one's own subjects, "but in human affairs and especially in the management and government of peoples, it is not possible to avoid all troublesome situations. It is the task of the wise king to escape the most difficult and dangerous ones." The chief reason for an army composed of subjects was that it promoted the independence of the prince; reliance on foreign troops was not compatible with such independence. In addition, the interests of foreign mercenaries were essentially different from those of the prince. They were often vehicles for undesirable foreign influences; they had brought heresy to France. But Botero had nothing against the use of foreign soldiers as accessories in a secondary capacity. Subsequently and somewhat inconsistently, he observed—perhaps with the Duke of Parma's forces in the Netherlands in mind—that the most effective armies of the day were multinational ones that combined, for example, "the prudence of the Italian, the diligence of the Spaniard, the steadfastness of the German, and the vitality of the French." Thus he parted from Machiavelli's view that similarity of language and culture was basic to the unity and esprit of a fighting force and made a concession to what an earlier observer had called the Noah's Ark armies of the day.[111]

To know that they were fighting in the cause of justice greatly increased the valor or fighting effectiveness of troops. "He fights with greater spirit and vehemence who redresses a wrong than he who inflicts one." Right made might. He who acted unjustly knew that he had God in opposition, and this was enough to demoralize troops. A general had to make certain that his soldiers were aware of the justice of their cause. Prayer was also highly recommended. This guaranteed the army divine protection and communicated to them a sense of confidence and the assurance of eternal life should they fall in combat. Botero did not allude explicitly to Machiavelli's criticism of Christian soldiers, but his statement that hope in eternal life greatly stimulated their boldness was certainly made with it in mind. Botero even went so far as to claim that those who were more closely united to God displayed greater valor.[112]

A formidable asset of a general was his reputation for good fortune (*felicità*), which Botero defined as "assistance of the divine *virtù*, with which His Majesty accompanies those whom he chooses as ministers of his justice or executors of his will." This was a magnificent inspiration to soldiers. Joshua, Cyrus, and Alexander the Great all enjoyed it. "If God is pleased with the Prince or the Captain, and the sins of the people do not stand in the way of this good fortune, then one cannot doubt of victories and triumphs, and even though good fortune does not always accompany this *virtù*, because God also favors Gentiles, Turks, and Moors against bad Christians, nevertheless this is the way things ordinarily turn out." To support his case, Botero pointed to the victories of Charles V and the more recent ones in the Netherlands and France of the Duke of Parma, whom he hailed as the ideal commander.[113]

In the final chapter of the *Reason of State*, entitled "Against whom ought [rulers] turn their forces," just war theory shone through. Botero might have had Suarez before him as he wrote, except that he had little to say about the moral limits on the manner of fighting wars and nothing on the protection of the innocent. But his real interest lay elsewhere. "If a defensive war is just and an offensive [that is, aggressive] war is just only insofar as it is defensive in nature, then there is no case in which it is licit to take the offensive except to defend [the state]. How therefore will I—someone might say—be able to expand my state?" Having already shown how a prince might enlarge his state by promotion of the economy, Botero now wanted to point out that there was always an opportunity at hand to engage in war for the public good if a ruler was intent on doing so for the sake of military glory. The public good here, however, was the public good of Christendom, not of his own state. First there were the heretics, more pernicious enemies than the Turks. "But because war is the ultimate recourse that ought to be used against the heretics, it is not as universally licit to make war on them as on the infidels." Botero was not an advocate of religious war against domestic heretics, as we have seen. Much less did he champion intervention against heretics in a foreign state. Perhaps this explains the absence of any mention in the *Reason of State*, or for that matter in the *Universal Relations*, of the Spanish Armada, which sailed to its defeat the year before the *Reason of State*'s publication. "But he who wants to go to war cannot excuse himself for the lack of a public enemy against whom to demonstrate his valor."

Earlier Botero had assured the prince there would always be enemies against whom one could employ a restive population. These were the Turks, the enemies of Christendom, against whom the Christians always possessed a legitimate claim to wage war, because of Turkish occupation of Christian lands in southeastern Europe. Here Botero's sense of Christendom, an international community beyond the sovereign state, came to the fore in the *Reason of State*. War with the heretics was still a civil war within Christendom. Botero shared the concern about the Turkish danger and the enthusiasm for a crusade against the Turks that had not died out at Lepanto. The Empire's forces would take up the challenge in 1593 and remain in the field until 1606. Botero concluded the *Reason of State* with an impassioned summons to a campaign against the Turks, which paralleled Machiavelli's call in the last chapter of the *Prince* to a war to drive the foreigners out of Italy. Machiavelli was an Italian patriot, Botero here a European one. Surely one would find divine support and assistance for such a magnificent venture.[114]

Once again the good and the useful were joined. The utility to the prince in terms of the glory to be won, the distraction of his population, and perhaps the expansion of his state harmonized with the enterprise of a full-scale campaign against the Turks, the enemies of Christendom.

Chapter 4

Justus Lipsius: Founder
of the Tradition (1589)

The year 1589, when Botero's *Reason of State* appeared at Venice, also saw the publication at Leiden of an equally influential anti-Machiavellian tract, the *Six Books of Politics or Teaching on the State*, by the Flemish humanist Justus Lipsius. Lipsius has usually been considered primarily a scholar and philologist, known for his editions of Tacitus and Seneca and for his dissemination of Neostoicism in the late Renaissance. But recent scholarship has shown the enormous impact he had on European political thought during the Baroque Age through the *Politics* and its two companion volumes, the *Two Books on Constancy* (Leiden, 1584) and the *Political Advice and Examples* (Antwerp, 1605).[1] Indeed, there were similarities between Lipsius and his fellow humanist and Netherlander, Erasmus. Both were internationally recognized scholars; both carried on a vast and often public correspondence with leading European figures—the inventory of Lipsius's letters includes more than 4,300 entries and 700 correspondents, among them Montaigne, Philip Sidney, and Philip Rubens, brother of Peter Paul who immortalized Lipsius in his painting *The Four Philosophers* (see Ill. 1);[2] both sought to reconcile the classical tradition with Christianity in a synthesis that would speak to contemporaries; and both were staunch advocates of peace.

But times had changed since the death of Erasmus in 1536. The cleavage between Protestant and Catholic had deepened, new Protestant churches had emerged, and religious conflict had spilled over into war, especially in France and the Netherlands. These changes greatly affected Lipsius personally, and he belonged among those writers who looked to a powerful and unified state as the way out of the civil and religious chaos he saw engulfing himself and his world. He wrote explicitly with Machiavelli in mind and showed respect for his thought; in the introduction to the *Politics* he acknowledged Machiavelli's "genius . . . , sharp, subtle, fiery."[3] His concern was to elaborate a vision of practical politics, in response to Machiavelli, that would be moral, Christian, and effective in the circumstances of the late sixteenth century. He deserves to be considered along with Botero the founder of the anti-Machiavellian tradition of the Counter-Reformation.

Justus Lipsius, or Joest Lips, came into the world on October 18, 1547, at Overyssche (Isque), a small town between Brussels and Louvain.[4] His parents sent him to the new Jesuit college in Cologne in 1560, but fearful that he might enter the Society of Jesus, they arranged his transfer to the University of Louvain in 1563. Probably while studying in Cologne and Louvain Lipsius acquired the knowledge of Aquinas that showed through in his later political writings.[5] His mother and father both died two years after his matriculation at Louvain, leaving their son very little to live on. He had displayed great promise as a classicist, and in 1569 he published at Antwerp a small volume discussing variant readings of ancient authors. In the meantime, Cardinal Granvelle, who had been a dominant figure in the Council of State in the Netherlands at the beginning of Philip II's reign, took the young scholar with him on a mission to Rome. There Lipsius spent nearly two years, from 1568 to 1570, shortly after the seminarian Botero left the city. He came to know the intellectual world of Machiavelli and Guicciardini, and the great classical scholar Marc Antoine Muret introduced him to Tacitus and Seneca, the two ancient authors he was to make available in marvelous editions.

By the end of 1570 Lipsius was back in Louvain. But civil war between the Dutch and their Spanish rulers now threatened, and Lipsius soon joined the trail of émigrés looking for a place at one of the courts in peaceful Germany. Having failed in Vienna at the court of Maximilian II, he was soon made professor of history and eloquence at the University of Jena in the Lutheran state of Saxony-Weimar. This post he held from 1572 to 1574, and during this period he went over to Lutheranism, a move that he later claimed to regret.[6] His motive is unclear. It seems to have been a mixture of aversion to Spanish policy in the Netherlands— these were the years of Alba's harsh regime there—and the desire to accommodate himself to the local situation. At the end of 1574 he returned to Flanders, where he published at Antwerp his edition of Tacitus that has remained standard up to our own day.[7] This made his international reputation. He remained in the southern Netherlands for several years, after marrying a solidly Catholic widow from Louvain in 1575.

But Lipsius was wary of the Inquisition, and in 1579 he accepted a professorship in history, which was initially meant to be temporary, at the new University of Leiden, which had been founded only four years before by the fledgling Dutch Republic as its answer to Louvain. He was to endow it with its lasting reputation for philological studies.[8]

Here in 1584 he published the *Two Books on Constancy*, which was an attempt to combine Stoicism and Christianity in a philosophy that would help the individual to live through the difficult period of the religious wars that caused Lipsius himself such agony. The volume brought him fame and reached a wide international readership as it went through more than eighty editions between the sixteenth and eighteenth centuries, over forty in the original Latin and the rest in translation into all the modern European languages, including fifteen French editions.[9]

Lipsius later claimed that during his years in Leiden he never actually departed from the Catholic faith and never participated in heretical services or in any form of political activity. This may well have been the case. We must recall that in 1589 only 10 percent of the population of the Dutch Republic were members of the official Reformed church and that there were Catholics at the university.[10] On the other hand, had he admitted otherwise, he would have been liable to prosecution as a relapsed heretic, for which the penalty was severe, though such prosecution was extremely unlikely.[11] In any event, as early as 1586 he was engaged in efforts to leave Leiden. Three years later he published the *Politics* there. Its success surpassed that of the *Constancy*; it became "a manual on government and statecraft which was the most widely read in the seventeenth century," appearing eventually, if we include the translations from Latin into all the modern European languages, in ninety-six editions, the overwhelming majority before 1650. Until the outbreak of the Thirty Years' War in 1618, a new edition was issued nearly every year, and during the reign of Henry IV alone ten editions of the French translation left the presses.[12]

A bitter controversy over positions he took in the *Politics* with the Dutch Protestant writer and advocate of general religious toleration Dirck Coornhert made him more determined than ever to leave Leiden.[13] Finally, under the guise of taking the cure at Spa, he departed the city and eventually made his way to Mainz. There, helped by Jesuits with whom he had remained in contact, he was fully reconciled with the Catholic church. There can be no doubts about the sincerity of his return to Catholicism.[14] Shortly afterwards he made his peace with Spain, and in 1594 Philip II named him a royal historian. But he remained active in the cause of peace for the Netherlands until his death.[15]

His third major work on politics, the *Political Advice and Examples*, appeared in 1605, and if not the success of the earlier two, reached a circulation of ten to eleven thousand within two years of publication and counted altogether twenty-six editions along with translations into French, Dutch, and Polish.[16] In his last years he also brought out two volumes on which he had long been working, his *Introduction to the Stoic Philosophy* (1604) and his edition of the works of Seneca (1605). Death overtook him at Louvain on March 23, 1606, where, among others, he was attended by his fellow Fleming, the Jesuit theologian Lessius, who had served as his confessor for over a dozen years.[17]

Lipsius's *Constancy*, *Politics*, and *Advice* must be seen in relationship to one another; this is the way he himself saw them. At the start of the *Politics* he wrote that "as in the *Constancy* we educated citizens to bear up and to obey, so here [we educate] those who rule to govern."[18] The *Advice* then, he declared at the beginning, was meant to respond to the many requests he had received for exempla to illustrate and confirm the doctrine of the *Politics*, which was usually expressed in pithy maxims and directives.[19]

There was a development in Lipsius's thought over the course of the three books; it is especially evident when one considers the new editions of the *Politics* along with the explanatory notes he added in response to his critics and the short treatise *On One Religion*, which he first issued at Leiden in 1591 to elaborate his views on toleration against Coornhert.[20] But it would be a serious mistake to stress the points of development so as to miss the basic consistency of his thought. There was no substantial reversal of field by Lipsius. He was a Christian humanist who, because of inclination and because of fear of ecclesiastical authority, avoided dogmatic issues and, for the most part, the use of Scripture. His writings betrayed no serious theological differences with Catholics or Protestants. But his thought did tend to become more explicitly Catholic, which is not surprising given the course of his life.

Lipsius's audience was the politically active elite in Europe, rulers together with those who in other ways shared in government. Tacitus, his favorite ancient writer, had seen himself carrying on the educative role of Cicero's orator in the new circumstances of the Early Empire; so Lipsius considered himself called to provide moral instruction for princes, councillors, magistrates, officials, military officers in the increasingly absolutist states.[21] The *Constancy* was dedicated to the consuls, senate, and people of Antwerp. His regular use in the *Constancy* and the *Politics* of the term citizens (*cives*) rather than subjects connoted the Early Empire if not the Republic or Renaissance Florence. Lipsian Neostoicism extolled participation in public affairs. Not surprisingly the Jesuits often made use of his volumes in their schools, from which many magistrates and government officials emerged. As we have seen, the *Spiritual Exercises* of

Loyola underlined the validity of a Christian life in the world, and a hallmark of the Jesuit drama was its emphasis on active participation in civic life.[22]

Lipsius's view of Tacitus obviously differed from Botero's. Whereas for Botero Tacitus stood for a reason of state similar to Machiavelli's, even though Botero cited him frequently, for Lipsius he revealed in his histories "as it were a theater of the present day" and was, as Lipsius wrote a Spanish theologian in 1600, "a gift bestowed by eternal Providence . . . for exemplifying and directing thoughts and plans" at the present.[23]

Lipsius sought for himself and for others, he wrote in the preface to the *Constancy*, the way to peace and tranquillity of soul amidst the calamities of the time. These were primarily the religious wars, especially the conflict between the Dutch and the Spanish that was ravaging the Netherlands. He had long labored on the *Constancy*, and he called it at the time "the best and greatest of my literary work." His intent was to provide his readers with something simpler than contemporary philosophy, of which he was bitingly critical for its excessive subtlety.[24] In response to charges that his book was not sufficiently religious and did not make adequate use of Scripture, Lipsius insisted in a preface added to the second edition of 1585 that he was a philosopher not a theologian. Theology went beyond philosophy, he recognized, but Christians had also to imitate the Greek and Latin Fathers in putting philosophy at the service of the faith. "I know the advice of Augustine," he wrote, "to collect what the Philosophers had written and to claim for our use what had been seized by those unjust possessors." Indeed, shortly after the publication of the *Constancy* he had reassured the humanist Laevinus Torrentius, soon to become Bishop of Antwerp, "I wanted to accommodate the old philosophy to our [Christian] truth."[25] His response to the accusation that he relied excessively on reason elicited the admission that he did emphasize reason as became a philosopher, but a reason "directed by God and enlightened by faith."[26] No Thomist could have put it better.

The *Constancy* was written in the typically Renaissance form of the dialogue. There were two characters. The first was Lipsius himself, who has decided to flee the troubles in the Netherlands, the second an old friend, Charles Delanghe or Langius, a canon of Liège, with whom he stayed the first night of his flight.[27] Delanghe gradually convinced Lipsius that flight from external ills would not solve his problems. Only internal change made it possible to live contentedly amidst the turmoil of the world. Delanghe made the case for a Christianized Neostoicism without ever adverting to the New Testament, though he did several times call upon the Old. Constancy was the virtue to be cultivated, "an upright and steadfast strength of soul that was neither elated nor cast down by external or fortuitous events."[28] It did not, however, lead to withdrawal from public affairs and retreat into private life. Lipsius, who was cosmopolitan in both the Stoic and Christian traditions, criticized severely contemporary forms of patriotism as thinly disguised selfishness. But having made this point, he argued that "we ought to be good citizens in order to be good men." Citizens were obliged to do what they could to help the state; at the same time they had to realize the limitations to what they could achieve and yield to the plan of God.[29] Gradually the dialogue moved toward its main topic, one of much contemporary interest, the providence of God and man's conduct in the face of it.

Lipsius's doctrine on providence is most important if he is to be understood as an anti-Machiavellian. Machiavelli had elaborated his own conception of the role of fortune in history, and the relationship between free will and divine providence or fate remained a topic of great interest to sixteenth-century thinkers, the Italian philosophers Pompanozzi, Geronimo Cardano, and Patrizi, as well as the Reformers Luther and Calvin.[30] Botero showed scant interest in the issue. But Lipsius developed a philosophy of history that was to have a great impact on the Baroque outlook on life. He expounded it chiefly in the *Constancy*, and he presumed it in the *Politics* and his subsequent works. His assumption that he had not come into conflict with the Catholic church on this issue was essentially correct. With only slight changes the *Constancy* later received ecclesiastical approval.[31]

Inscriptions at the start of the *Politics* set the tone for the book: "Man attains nothing more excellent than Political Virtue." No task was as demanding or as difficult as the ruler's, nor was any as vital to the welfare of the community. To meet his responsibilities the ruler had to apply reason to government but first to his own life. "If you desire to subject all things to yourself, subject yourself to reason. You will rule many if reason rules you. From it learn what you ought to undertake and how to undertake it."[32] But Lipsius never employed the term *reason of state* in his writings.

His topic was strictly the rule of principalities, he explained in notes added in 1590, but the first part of the *Politics* applied to states in general, and throughout there were "precepts for all civic life."[33] Many others had written on the topic, he was well aware, but Plato, Aristotle, and most other ancient writers had dealt more generally with the state, not with principalities. Lipsius added that medieval and more recent writers had little to offer the present time. The one exception was Machiavelli. "Would that he had led his Prince along the right way to the temple of virtue and honor. But he too often strayed, and while he intently pursued the paths of utility, he wandered from this royal way." Lipsius's book was practical, not speculative, and in this respect fit the anti-Machiavellian pattern. He intended to elaborate general principles but to avoid any concrete applications of them. There was no attempt in the *Politics* to deal with specific contemporary issues. But the implications were clear enough. As Lipsius wrote, he who understood the principles would know how to apply them.[34]

Lipsius addressed two unusual features of the style of the *Politics* in the preface. At least half the book's content was made up of quotations from ancient writers. In this respect it was a tour de force and displayed the author's mastery of classical literature. The fourth, the most extensive of the six books, included 750 quotations. Of these, not surprisingly, Tacitus was the most frequently called upon, with 174 citations. The authors summoned forth most frequently after Tacitus were Cicero, 103 times, and Seneca, 92 times. Major authorities also included Sallust, Aristotle, and Livy, as well as the Patristic writers Augustine, Basil, Gregory the Great, and Tertullian.[35] But as Lipsius emphasized, the *Politics* was not a mere compilation. He had organized them. They carried the authority of the ancients, but they represented his thought. "So we [have created] from some thousand particles this uniform and coherent body."[36] His correspondent Montaigne seems to have concurred when he referred to the *Politics* as "this learned and carefully woven fabric."[37]

Secondly, Lipsius acknowledged the concise and sometimes obscure style of the *Politics*, and he asked the reader to take the time to allow the text to sink in. "The form of our work is such that I scarcely promise that when first looked at it will please, more so [do I promise that it will please] when it is examined." The obscurity, he alleged, resulted from the writers he cited and, as he wrote at the start of book 4, from the complexity of the material, that is, statecraft.[38] In fact, Lipsius was the major figure in the transition from a clearer, more diffuse Latin style often associated with Cicero to the pithy, subtle, and often obscure style of Tacitus and the Silver Age, which was increasingly preferred by Baroque writers. One function of this style was to challenge the reader and to draw him into reflection on the writer's thought.[39] In this sense difficulty and an element of obscurity were stylistic virtues. We will meet them again in Carlo Scribani and Saavedra Fajardo.

Lipsius's extensive use of the ancient writers should not lead us to believe that they were the only or necessarily the principal sources of his thought. He knew the writings of Aquinas, and he drew on them at particularly crucial points, such as the treatment of the just war, and he was familiar with the Spanish Scholastics. Bodin and Machiavelli were

others with an obvious influence on him.[40] His method was not induc-
tive and did not purport to be so. There were few historical examples; in
fact, the *Advice* was written to supply these. Lipsius himself supplied the
definition and analysis of terms in a manner that suggested Ramist
method.[41] Virtues, for example, were defined and then progressively
broken down into further categories, as with prudence, the leading
princely virtue. Generally speaking, Lipsius was more exhortatory than
Botero.

The *Politics* was divided into six books. The first two treated the
virtues of the prince as well as the purpose of government and its various
forms in a generally traditional fashion. The third turned to the distinctive virtue of the prince, "political prudence [*prudentia civilis*]," and
took up his choice of councillors and officials and his relationship to
them under the heading "prudence [acquired] from others [*prudentia ab
aliis*]." Under the heading "prudence proper to the prince [*prudentia a
se*]," the fourth and by far longest book was devoted to the most difficult
problems of government—the arcana as it were—for example, how to
handle religious dissidents. This was the heart of the *Politics*.

Under "military prudence" books 5 and 6 took up matters of defense, the military, and civil war. Together with Lipsius's other writings
on military matters, especially his *Five Books on the Roman Military, A
Commentary on Polybius* (1595–96), they greatly influenced military
thinking in the seventeenth century, particularly toward the development
of military discipline and a military ethic. He was fortunate to have
known at Leiden Count Maurice of Nassau, son of William of Orange,
and his cousin Count William Louis, who employed his ideas in the
reform of the Dutch army, whence they spread to Sweden, the German
territories, and beyond. Even after his return to Louvain he kept up
correspondence with Dutch military reformers. In the rival camp of
Spain Lipsius contributed already in the 1590s to a civilianizing of the
military virtues and a revival of a sense of service to the state on the part
of the nobility.[42]

Even before the *Politics* was off the press, Lipsius was preparing
himself for the onslaught of criticism he expected. Both Catholics and
Protestants attacked the book for its position on toleration, and it appeared on the Roman Index of 1590, partly because of its leniency toward heretics who were not activists. But the most severe attack came
from Coornhert, who accused Lipsius—unfairly—of supporting the procedures of the Inquisition and, furthermore, of being a Machiavellian.
The second edition of the *Politics* in 1590 included the *Brief Notes* on
the first three books. The following year there appeared the *On One*

Religion written against Coornhert; it was a commentary and elaboration on the three chapters of the fourth book where Lipsius discussed the relationship of the state to the church in general and toleration in particular. Following his return to the Catholic church, he issued another edition of the *Politics* in 1596 with changes to meet the objections of Roman officials and with further explanatory notes.[43] These elaborations and changes must be taken into account in any discussion of the *Politics*, but none of them amounted to a change in his role as an anti-Machiavellian.

In 1605, the year prior to his death, Lipsius published the *Advice*, which as we have seen was intended primarily to provide exempla for the principles laid out in the first two books of the *Politics*. Two similar volumes were projected for the remainder of the *Politics*. He explained in the preface that he was now publishing the first volume because he felt death would prevent him from ever completing the whole project, and it did.[44]

Stylistically the *Advice* did not match the *Constancy* or the *Politics*. There were new emphases but no departure from the main lines of Lipsius's thought. He appears more outspokenly Catholic and more sharply opposed to Machiavelli, for example, in his vigorous rejection of Machiavelli's admonition that the ruler simulate virtue.[45] His new relationship to Spain was shown by his designation of Archduke Albert, who with his wife Archduchess Isabella had become coruler of the Netherlands in 1598, and indeed the whole Habsburg family as exemplifying the qualities of the ideal ruler.[46] There was a much more decided tendency to find God's providence at work in history. Lipsius illustrated divine reward for the deserving prince with the familiar tale, found also in Botero, of Rudolf of Habsburg's assistance to a priest bearing Communion to the sick and his resultant rise to power.[47]

Except for his firm espousal of nascent absolutism, Lipsius's ideas about fundamental issues of political philosophy were generally traditional and taken over from the Scholastics. He presumed the existence of the sovereign state. With a number of arguments in the *Politics* he defended princely rule as the best form of government, the chief being that it provided greater unity to the state. Further, the people were not competent to enjoy liberty and few were eager for it, he wrote, provided their rulers governed with justice.[48] His observation of the situation in the Dutch Republic clearly pushed him in this direction. His correspondence at the time showed him deploring the lack of a single, strong leader after the assassination of William of Orange in 1584 and hoping for the emergence of a prince or king in place of the many-headed regime then in power.[49] He saw the ruler as the representative of God and even as a god himself; the Christian and ancient conceptions of the ruler merged to exalt his status.[50]

But the prince was expected to obey the law and to submit to the administration of justice. There was no provision, however, to compel him to do so, the estates having been set aside by Lipsius.[51] He avoided a direct discussion of a right to resist a tyrannical ruler, while acknowledging that those who had overthrown despots deserved praise and glory. But the better course was to bear up under rather than overthrow tyrants (*ferre* rather than *auferre*). Several reasons pointed to this conclusion, but the clinching argument was one Lipsius had learned from history and from his own experience. The efforts of a private person or of a public institution to eliminate a tyrant almost always led to a situation worse than tyranny itself. In the words of Plutarch, "Worse and more miserable than tyranny or unjust rule is civil war."[52]

Lipsius's thought revealed the same anti-Machiavellian pattern as Botero's. As he wrote late in life in the *Advice*, "A good description and precept, be just and virtuous, and from the depths of the heart will issue forth upright [*honesta*] and useful [*utilia*] counsels. Let us not separate these two, that is, the upright from the useful. The doctor from Italy errs who teaches otherwise, who creates petty tyrants, not legitimate kings or princes."[53] But normally the good and the useful did not harmonize as easily for him as they did for Botero, and he often felt keenly the tension between them. His pragmatism meant that Lipsius had to assess or reassess the morality of many current political practices, and this exercise of casuistry brought him perilously close to Machiavellianism himself. Lipsius paid virtually no attention to the economy. This does not mean he ignored it. Rather it was for him an area of human activity that stood outside politics, the topic he was discussing.[54]

The prince governed through the exercise of prudence and virtue. Together they constituted that political virtue lauded at the opening of the *Politics*. They were the two directors (*rectores*) of civic life, with prudence mentioned before virtue. Prudence "without virtue would be cunning and roguery and anything other than prudence; although it is the rudder that properly steers civic life, [it cannot do this] without the use and assistance of that magnet [virtue]."[55] So for Lipsius as for Botero, moral virtue was joined with political dexterity. At the start of the fourth book, he adverted much as had Botero to the difficulty of writing at all systematically about political prudence. "Prudence in the strict sense, that is the prudence we want in the prince, is difficult to tie down in directives. It is broadly diffuse, flexible, hidden. Thus we lay down some instructions regarding it, but we do not exhaust the topic."

Prudence was not a science; it dealt with continually changing matter, and many of the factors involved came from "on high," an apparent allusion to providence.[56]

In Lipsius we find the fundamental relationship among virtue, reputation, and power characteristic of the anti-Machiavellians, with the more specific prudence often replacing virtue. A ruler had to have the support of his people. This was as evident to Lipsius as to Machiavelli or Botero. Prudence then for Lipsius, as for Botero, taught the ruler how to understand his own and other peoples and showed him how to win their support. Lipsius shared the negative view of the people found in Machiavelli and Botero, but he made no significant distinctions among their groups or classes as had the two Italians. They were pretty much the mob, unstable, prone to extremes, credulous, easily swayed by demagogues, interested only in their private interests. Nor did rulers themselves come off much better. Different peoples and different rulers had distinctive characteristics, Lipsius went on, and it was a part of prudence to master these. Like Botero he implicitly accepted an individualized reason of state. But, in accord with his practice, he provided no examples for individual countries.[57]

Lipsius discussed many of the most important aspects of government precisely from the perspective of popular support. In the fourth book he called this support itself virtue (*virtus*), in what he admitted was a use of the term "a little other than the popular one." It was defined as "a praiseworthy and useful disposition about the king or toward him brought about by his rule." Lipsius then broke virtue down into benevolence (*benevolentia*) and authority (*auctoritas*), both of which though taking their origin in the ruler, "nevertheless had their seat and home in the souls of the people." Benevolence in turn was "a ready inclination and love of the subjects toward the king and his state," authority "a sense of awe [*opinio reverens*] impressed upon subjects and foreigners alike toward the king and his state." Authority was then further defined as a combination of wonder (*admiratio*) and fear (*metus*).[58] Virtue when used in this sense by Lipsius amounted to the same as Botero's reputation, composed as it was of love and fear. It also carried with it connotations of the *virtù* that Machiavelli in the *Discourses* wanted to glow in the hearts of republican citizens.

Lipsius did not explicitly take up the question of whether benevolence or authority was more vital to virtue, but he appeared to incline to authority, especially when he remarked that it was impossible for a ruler to avoid all hatred. One could not win the love of all. Authority was absolutely essential. "In truth, who would rule otherwise? 'The power [*vires*] of the government,'" he cited from Livy, "'rests in the consent of the obedient [subjects],' which in turn results from esteem [*aestimatione*]," in the context a synonym for authority. "Take this [esteem] away, you take away the kingdom."[59] With regard to foreigners, authority as combination of wonder and fear predominated even more clearly over benevolence, but Lipsius did not elaborate its role in foreign policy.

Lipsius developed at considerable length specific qualities or measures to win the "virtue" or support of the citizens. A certain mildness or gentleness of bearing was desirable to win their benevolence, along with a prudent liberality, that is, one where the prince did not later have to resort to undesirable means to recoup what he had given away. Then there was indulgence, the provision of food and entertainment, bread and circuses, to the extent this could be done without the corruption of popular morals.[60] So Lipsius endorsed the public amusements and diversions so popular during the Baroque Age. But for him they were not so much as for Botero a means to occupy and divert the energies of the people as they were a way to win popular affection.

Yet a prince required a certain severity to balance his gentleness and to guarantee his authority. The proper mix of rigor and mildness was crucial to princely rule. An excessively familiar prince or easy-going government could prove disastrous, given the unpredictable and volatile nature of the mob. It was also important that the prince act in such a way that the people were well aware that he was actually in charge and not manipulated by councillors, favorites, or others.[61]

For Lipsius as for Botero, any government that collected taxes and administered justice to the satisfaction of subjects was well on the way to securing its reputation with them. Taxes were the main source of subjects' ill will. The experience of the Netherlands, where Philip II's tax policy had been a major cause of the rebellion, was certainly on his mind. Lipsius did not advocate one type of tax over another, much less recommend a tax program as had Botero. Apart from the counsel to moderation lest the sources of revenue dry up, his advice was limited to principles aimed at provoking the least possible negative reaction to taxes. The necessity of taxes must always be evident to the people, as well as the good uses to which they were put. Careful provision was to be made to prevent fraud or extortion in tax collection. Fairness was to be observed, not in the sense that all social classes were to be taxed equally but that individuals were not to be given special privileges or required to bear special burdens. Lipsius recommended regular appraisals of property for tax purposes, and he reflected and perhaps influenced widespread contemporary practice when he advised that the people be allowed to choose the assessors in order to guarantee fairness. In many states, for example, in Bavaria and the Austrian lands, long after the prince had established his political dominance, the representative body of estates continued to administer the collection of taxes.[62] Nor should a prince always be sniffing about for new sources of tax revenue. This was unworthy of him.[63]

Power (*potentia*) was treated in this context as a means to authority or reputation rather than the other way around. It was "the direct and royal way to solid authority." Without it the prince had no authority and without authority he could not rule. The prince should have no scruple about seeking power, which Lipsius defined as "the capability and resources to preserve what is one's own and obtain what belongs to others."

Power was divided into five components. The first was wealth, which was not as for Botero the wealth of the whole people but the financial resources necessary to put an army in the field. A well-equipped army was the second element, and Lipsius discussed it at length in the last two books of the *Politics*. Two further elements were good counsel and the assistance of allies. Finally, there was good fortune, which pointed to Lipsius's sense of providence. Who would deny, he asked in the words of the Roman historian Curtius, that the greatest glory and power was more often the benefit of fortune rather than virtue. It lay beyond human control, as was evident from an example Lipsius gave, childlessness, which often caused contempt. Later Lipsius used the same word to designate a military officer's good luck that Botero had employed in its Italian form in the same context, *felicitas*. There was nothing like the smile of the gods and the belief that the ruler enjoyed the smile of the gods to augment his power and authority. Yet he should keep in mind that fortune was fickle and uncertain and that "nothing could long endure that was not based on reason."[64]

The prince's morals were also critical to his authority, in particular his piety. The people were well-disposed to a prince they felt enjoyed the favor of the gods and certainly much more reluctant to plot against him. Negatively, Lipsius warned the prince against immorality, licentiousness, drunkenness, all of which undermined his authority, as did incompetence, slowness of mind, and inability to speak well.[65] To forestall the interpretation that the appearance of virtue might suffice to secure a ruler's authority, Lipsius had insisted in the first two books of the *Politics* on the necessity of true virtue. He urged the ruler to "prefer to be than to seem to be upright," a point he elaborated on in the *Brief Notes* and in the *Advice*.[66] But nowhere did he really stress the argument that the ruler could not fool the people with feigned virtue.

Under the heading "mixed prudence" Lipsius attacked the most delicate issues of statecraft in the final two chapters of the fourth book of the *Politics*. Here more than anywhere else we sense the clash between the demands of the good and the useful. At first blush he might seem to approve what could be understood as Machiavellian procedures. But careful analysis combined with a look at his later statements seems to preclude this conclusion except perhaps in one or two instances. As he wrote, he did not want to depart "completely from the good [*honestum*]."[67] His treatment was at times unclear and inconsistent. What he labored at was the application of traditional principles to thorny problems in the effort to arrive at a realistic ethic. If he failed at some points, this was a far cry from surrendering to Machiavelli's assertion that a ruler could not be successful without departing from traditional morality.

Lipsius opened his discussion with a description of the political world reminiscent of Machiavelli. "Among whom do we live? truly cunning and evil men, who seem to consist totally of deceit, falsehoods, lies." The prince had to survive in the world as it was. "Nor should we condemn so quickly the spotted Italian [*Maculonum Italum*], the poor man whom everybody scourges nowadays." There was, after all, as St. Basil declared, a certain "honest and praiseworthy cunning." Lipsius employed a familiar figure. "Where the lion's skin does not achieve [the goal], it is necessary to put on that of the fox." This was not a separation of the good from the useful but a mixing of the two. Another figure made his point. "Wine does not cease to be wine if it is lightly tempered with water. Nor does prudence cease to be prudence if a little drop of deceit is in it. I always understand [that it is done] moderately and for a good purpose."[68] A note in the margin claimed that he was "walking around the way of virtue, not departing from it."[69] Perhaps his later statement from the *Advice* that we ought never dissociate the useful from the good as did Machiavelli was a further attempt to make himself clear.[70]

Lipsius became more specific in the next chapter as he clarified what he understood by deceit; he seemed to agonize as he tried to arrive at norms that would be realistic and at the same time moral. Deceit (*fraus*) he defined as "an artful design departing from the way of virtue and the laws for the good of the king or the kingdom." This was nearly the same as what Botero recognized to be the meaning of reason of state for many contemporaries. He then divided deceit into three categories: "slight, lightly sprinkled by the dew of malice, which departs not at all far from virtue," comprising mistrust and dissimulation; moderate, "which curves further from virtue so that it approaches the borders of vice," including bribery and deception (*deceptio*); great, "which departs not only from virtue but from the laws and is of a vigorous and perfect malice," taking in perfidy and injustice. The first he recommended, the second he tolerated, the last he condemned.[71] But what Lipsius categorized under deceit was obviously not always immoral nor did he consider it such, even though he saw it as a departure from the fullness of virtue.

Lipsius the casuist now went to work. With regard to slight deceit, he showed convincingly why in the world of court and politics the prince had to be slow to trust or believe others. Dissimulation was the natural companion of mistrust; by it one "looked to be frank but concealed one's thoughts." Here there was no question of positively seeking to deceive another but merely to hold back information one was not bound to divulge. Lipsius cited the contemporary dictum also found in Botero and usually attributed to Louis XI of France, "he who does not know how to dissimulate does not know how to rule."[72] Such conduct was unacceptable in private relationships but necessary in public affairs.[73] At this point we are dealing not with a departure from morality but with an intelligent application of moral principles. There was no obligation to trust everyone nor to reveal all one's thoughts.

Lipsius spent few words on bribery, or corruption as he called it, the first form of moderate deceit that he seemed to take for granted. By it he meant efforts to secure support in the camp of a rival prince, not attempts to obtain favors from officials, much less to influence judges at home. One could always find men, and women, at hostile courts willing to betray their prince.[74] Lipsius judged it more in accord with human nature to conquer "with reason and intellect" than "with force and strength,"[75] that is, he preferred the fox to the lion.

But if he spent little time on bribery, the opposite was the case with deception, which caused him the most difficulty. Deception he defined as "when you persuade another to your advantage by the use of misinformation or a lie," without drawing a clear line between dissimulating and lying. Later when discussing the suppression of rebellions, he stated explicitly that a ruler could lie or make false promises to their leaders in order to induce rebels to lay down their arms. This procedure was preferable to a slaughter and presumed that the prince would deal with them mercifully.[76] Lipsius noted that many authors, including Plato, approved lying for the sake of the subjects, just as a doctor sometimes lied for the sake of his patients. Rulers practiced deception all the time. "There is scarcely any other way for a good prince to protect himself and his people against so many conspiring [against him]."[77] Thus Lipsius allowed a lie for the good of the state.

But he was still uneasy. Lying was not in accord with divine law. A number of quotations from Scripture were adduced to show this, one of the few times he turned to Scripture, as were the words of Augustine, "It is not allowed to lie even for the praise of God." Lipsius saw the dilemma. "Indeed, I [can] scarcely extract you, or myself, from this except through what the same Bishop [Augustine] suggested, 'there are certain types of lies in which there is not great fault but which yet are not without fault.' In this category we consider little cases of corruption [*Corruptiunculas*] and deception [*Deceptiunculas*]; and this at least then when employed by a good and legitimate king against evil men, for the sake of the common good; otherwise they [lies] are a sin and a great sin, however the old hands at court may ridicule me."[78]

Finally, there was serious deceit, perfidy and injustice, both of which Lipsius condemned. Few approved these practices openly, he wrote, but many employed them often. Fidelity or faithfulness (*fides*) he had earlier discussed under justice, which he defined as "the effect in us of what we have said or promised." He roundly condemned those "who poison the ears of princes arguing 'that they may overlook all that is right and honest provided they gain power.'" He defended fidelity largely on the basis of utility, and this of two kinds. Fidelity to one's word was essential to the reputation of a prince. It was also the basis of any human society. He even went so far as to cite St. Ambrose, "even with the unfaithful faith must be kept."[79] Yet, as we have seen, he did allow a ruler to make promises he did not intend to keep in order to disarm rebels. One can explain this by his hatred of rebellion, which grew out of his personal experience.

Injustice for Lipsius was "when they [rulers] increase their power and property dishonestly rather than cunningly, in violation of rights and laws." Examples were the exile or even elimination of individuals or the timely occupation of a foreign province. As we have noted, for Lipsius the prince was subject to the law, though he did not initially make a distinction between natural and human law. In this context, despite his condemnation of injustice, he made a modest concession. "A prince may in extremely distressing and contrary situations pursue not what sounds plausible but what is actually necessary; then, I say, he may depart slightly from the laws, but only for the sake of preserving his own [state], never enlarging it. For necessity, the great defense of human weakness, breaks all law," he added citing a dictum of Seneca well known to contemporaries. Later, in the 1596 edition of the *Politics*, he inserted the word "human" before laws, thus explicitly excluding any departure from natural law.[80] Such a position was in reality quite conservative and was in line with the Thomistic position.

But Lipsius remained uneasy here also. "This [I write] fearfully," he added, and again with Scripture quotations he showed God's displeasure with injustice. He even went so far as to declare that the current troubles of Europe were God's punishment for the practice of injustice.[81] No wonder he was furious when Coornhert accused him of "Machiavellizing," advocating fraud, murder, and perjury in the *Politics*. "I call God and men to witness [that] since the birth of calumny no one has been attacked by a more vile and open calumny. Did I approve or clear the way for these things? Rather in explicit, clear words I condemned, detested, repudiated them; I never wrote about them except to condemn them."[82]

His discussion of mixed prudence showed Lipsius more rigorous than traditional Scholastic teaching, except in his allowance of a lie, and in the instance of a lie to rebels, he did not advert to the respectable position that promises made under duress did not necessarily bind. Significantly, his concern for princely reputation, or in other words the useful, pushed him toward strictness. In discussing perfidy he overlooked a Scholastic position that one need not keep a promise under vastly changed circumstances. Both Aquinas and Suarez allowed for a new situation that would permit a ruler to withdraw from a treaty. According to Suarez, any agreement included the tacit understanding that if circumstances changed to the point that grave loss would result from fidelity to a treaty, a party might withdraw after giving suitable notice. But unilateral withdrawal was to be resorted to rarely.[83] With regard to departure from the law, Aquinas himself had taught that necessity was not subject to law, that is, human law, and it was a commonplace of the schools that human law ceased to bind when it no longer served the common good.[84]

For Lipsius as for most of his contemporaries, religion constituted an essential bond among the subjects and was basic to the unity of the state. Only religion and the fear of God held states together. "Let the prince seriously reflect on this: the neglect or decline of religion has always dragged the state down with it and will do so [in the future]."[85] Only religion provided adequate deterrence from crime, Lipsius elaborated in the *On One Religion* and the *Advice*, and it fostered a spirit of obedience among the subjects.[86] Personal piety was of special advantage to a ruler, because people were generally wary of offending those whom they thought to be close to the gods. But his was an active not a contemplative vocation, and he should not spend too much time in prayer.[87]

Specifically, the religion Lipsius had in mind was Christianity. This is evident from his reference to the Scriptures or "sacred letters" in the first book of the *Politics*, where he called piety the first part of virtue. "Before all else it is necessary to know that highest divinity (inasmuch as it is given to man [to know him]) and having known him, to venerate him piously and purely. The true light for this is found in the sacred letters, though I see certain flashes of it scattered throughout profane literature, which I will gather [here]."[88] Lipsius adhered to his policy of avoiding issues of Scriptural interpretation or Christian theology and of putting the ancient classics at the service of Christianity.

To be sure, only in the 1596 edition of the *On One Religion* did he commit himself explicitly to Catholicism, a commitment that became much clearer in the *Advice*.[89] But nowhere did he attempt to prove that Christianity as a religion was more advantageous to the state than other religions. Missing also was the frequent anti-Machiavellian assertion that Christian soldiers were braver than others. Christian princes certainly could not make use of superstitions to control their subjects, Lipsius made clear, but he did not deny that false religion could be useful to government. He was keenly aware of the social role religion had played in the history of the Jews, whom he greatly admired. On the other hand, pagan practices like the worship of animals or human sacrifice were socially debilitating.[90]

What responsibility did the prince have for religion, beyond giving good example to his subjects? This was the general issue on which Lipsius locked horns with Coornhert. The prince was not to intervene in the internal affairs of the church, much less to meddle with doctrinal issues. He did not have a "free right" in sacred matters, but he could look in on or investigate them, a point Lipsius made in the *Politics* and developed further in the *On One Religion*, with references to Augustine and Pope Leo the Great. This seems to have meant the encouragement and protection of religion along with oversight of the church's external order to prevent fraud and corruption. But above all the prince was to care for the unity of the church. The prince and the state had a great interest in unity; religious differences inevitably led to civil discord. After citing examples from beyond Christendom to support this, Lipsius claimed that there never had been such vicious wars over religion as in the present, when each side claimed to be fighting on the side of God. The prince should forestall any religious innovation or departure from religious tradition, Lipsius argued, much as had Bodin.[91]

Thus he arrived at the treatment of toleration, a critical issue of the day and a challenge to his prudence. He offered his solution as a way of ending the religious strife in Europe. It did not differ much from that of the *politiques* or Molanus, except that he also adopted Bodin's distinction between the public and private exercise of religion, which as refined and developed by Protestant jurists would find its way into the Peace of Westphalia in 1648.[92] Lipsius distinguished between two types of heretics or those "who sinned in religion." The first group were those who sinned publicly by attempting to win converts, and so, often caused trouble. The second were those who sinned only privately, that is, they kept their dissenting beliefs to themselves. For them he recommended toleration. One could not force belief, he argued, and to attempt to do so would create only external observance and often hypocrisy. Better to rely on good example and active evangelization. Moreover, Lipsius opposed inquiries into people's consciences; such activity was often the cause of rebellion, he wrote, perhaps with the procedures of the Inquisition in the Netherlands in mind.[93]

But the treatment of active dissidents was another matter. They were responsible for the strife tearing Europe apart. There was "no place for mercy here." Severity was the only way to put a stop to nascent discord. In this context Lipsius used the phrase exploited by Coornhert, "Burn, cut, as the whole body [of the state] is of more value than some members." Penalties, Lipsius suggested, should be dealt out according to circumstances, and in *On One Religion* he proposed a hierarchy of punishments, ranging from fines through exile and in extremely rare cases, death.[94] But this was all understood of a situation where it was realistically possible to suppress dissent. Once the dissidents reached a certain strength, this could no longer be done without civil war inflicting still greater harm on the state. This was the case in many countries, he suggested, and he went on to urge that in this situation it was certainly better to practice toleration and wait to see what solutions time would bring, as the *politiques* advised. Thus Lipsius advocated toleration for dissidents who practiced their faith quietly and for those whose numbers were such that they could no longer be put down without warfare. But vigorous measures were to be taken against active dissidents who threatened to disrupt an existing unity in the state.[95]

Lipsius encountered opposition to his position from two sides, from the Protestant Coornhert and from the Roman Inquisition. Nor had his distinction exhausted all possibilities. How should the prince deal with those, for example, who did not actively proselytize but who did want to worship publicly, that is, have their own churches? In his response to both sides Lipsius did not substantially alter his position. He pointed out for Coornhert that the phrase "burn, cut," which he did regret using, was a well-known medical phrase of the ancient world found in Cicero that did not imply the barbarity it seemed to suggest. His dispute with Coornhert upset him not only because of the misinterpretation he had suffered but because of his opponent's failure to recognize his sorrow at the bitter wars in Europe.[96] Lipsius made some accommodations to the Roman authorities in order to avoid the placement of the 1596 edition of the *Politics* on the Index. He agreed that in the case of peaceful dissidents pressure brought upon them initially might open them up to subsequent instruction and the acceptance of the faith. Thus pressure might sometimes be justified. But the change was not as significant as some of his critics have argued. Essentially he remained opposed to prying into people's consciences.[97]

Military power was a necessity for a prince, according to Lipsius, to keep order at home and to provide protection against the constant threat from foreign states; it was fundamental to the reputation without which the prince could not govern. But military power was of little use unless controlled by "military prudence." Lipsius's interest in the army did not mean he was a militarist. On the contrary, his description of the horrors of war, drawn to an extent from his own experience, and his encomium of peace showed exactly the opposite. He devoted much more space than Botero to guidelines for entrance into war and for its conduct, which were obviously taken from the Scholastics. Throughout his discussion there appeared clearly the attempt to combine the moral with the useful. His recommendations for military organization and discipline were not only an effort to create an effective army as a necessary buttress to the state, they were also an attempt to impose an order on the military that would diminish war's suffering and make it a little less horrible. Like his fellow Netherlander and younger contemporary Hugo Grotius, who drew upon him, Lipsius accepted the inevitability of war and sought, during a period when the size of armies was increasing dramatically— tenfold between 1530 and 1710—to establish rules of conduct that would mitigate its horrors.[98] Perhaps nowhere did his opposition to Machiavelli come through more clearly than in his effort to fix some form of morality on war.

Lipsius earnestly warned the prince that he must avoid injustice in undertaking and waging war. Fighting for a just cause, he added, gave the best hope of triumph, but he was careful to avoid a necessary linkage between the justice of the cause and victory.[99] Following Aquinas as elaborated by the sixteenth-century Scholastics, Lipsius laid out three requirements for a just war. First, only a sovereign prince or sovereign authority could carry on a war. Secondly, the cause had to be just. Here Lipsius like Suarez distinguished two types of just war. The first was a defensive one in which the prince had actually been attacked by an enemy. One might also come to the aid of innocent parties who were the victims of such aggression. But the prince had to avoid pretexts, and Lipsius criticized the Romans for using the defense of allies as a pretense for conquest. The second type of just war was an "invasion." This occurred when the prince opened hostilities himself in order to avenge an injustice or to reclaim what was rightfully his according to the law of nations. The third condition for a permissible war was a good intention or goal, which could only be peace and protection (of the state or the order of justice). A prince might have a legitimate cause for waging war, but to do so would still be sinful if his goal, as such, was revenge, glory, or mere conquest.[100]

But even if all three requirements were met, this did not permit the prince to go to war. In his own way Lipsius made the Scholastic argument that the injustice to be remedied had to be proportionate to the suffering to be expected in the war. The prince should keep before his mind's eye all the evils war entailed: death and suffering, crimes, financial exhaustion. Even a just war was to be hated. Those at court who pushed for war, Lipsius warned, often pursued their own advantage.[101]

Several statements made by Lipsius previously when discussing power as a leading element in a ruler's authority or reputation seemed to contradict the position he took here. "It may seem improper to state it, but sometimes it is useful to say clearly," he wrote citing the German king Tiridiates from Tacitus: " 'to secure one's own characterizes a private house, to fight for others' property brings praise to kings.' " So Lipsius made a concession to the princely need for military glory, and he then asserted baldly that in the international arena where the weak and powerful contended, a preventive war was sometimes the best course of action, even it seemed at the expense of justice. "I acknowledge that it is more desirable to protect the extent [of one's state] with justice. 'More desirable' [I say]. For who is always able [to do this]?" Further, "I add . . . that no great state can long remain at rest; if it does not have a foreign enemy, it will find one at home."[102] So he wrote, apparently embracing elements of Machiavellianism in his determination to be a realist.

But we can argue that he presumed, in most cases here at least, that there was just reason for a war, that it was a case where the prince might choose to take up a just cause or not. Botero urged a Turkish campaign for the ruler who sought military renown and the distraction of his subjects. The Jesuit Mariana claimed that there was always a just cause available for the ruler who wanted one.[103] This was probably the thought of Lipsius, too. Yet he also argued that sometimes it was necessary, given the struggle for survival among states, to launch a preemptive attack, even if some injustice were involved. Here while allowing the contradiction to stand as a sign of the tension Lipsius felt between the good and the useful, we must recall his grudging admission when dealing with mixed prudence that necessity sometimes compelled injustice for the good of the state, where at least after the clarification of the 1596 edition injustice meant a departure from human but not natural law. Presumably it meant the same in this context. Furthermore, what he said in the explicit context of the just war must take precedence over what he said elsewhere on the topic, especially when he prohibited unjust war so vehemently.

A war also had to be fought in a just fashion. Lipsius turned to a topic that virtually all writers on the morality of war touched upon, the use of stratagems, which involved some type of deceit. He cited the same passage of Augustine that Aquinas had. "When a just war has been undertaken, whether one fights openly or from an ambush has no reference to justice."[104] Conquest by reason and intellect was more suitable for human beings than conquest by brute force, Lipsius argued, as he had when advocating bribery of an enemy. He outlawed the use of hired assassins or poison as beneath the dignity of a ruler, and, interestingly, in early 1632 both emperor Ferdinand II and Philip IV of Spain rejected a proposed plot to assassinate Gustavus Adolphus for much the same reason.[105] Lipsius made no effort to define the category of innocents in war or to fix clearly rules of conduct toward them, but the discipline he hoped to introduce into the army certainly was to their benefit.

Lipsius had advice for the victor and vanquished in the peace-making process. It was wiser for a triumphant ruler to make a moderate peace than to press forward with war in the hope of a still more complete victory. War's fortunes were uncertain and liable to unexpected changes. Such a procedure showed that the prince had genuinely undertaken the struggle with a desire for peace and redounded to his reputation. Finally, it was always good policy to grant favorable terms to an enemy and so to avoid driving him to desperation and revenge. As for a defeated prince, his goal should be a decent peace, that is, one with tolerable conditions. "For any peace, even an unjust one, is more useful than war." Lipsius understood that a manly ruler would at all costs shun a settlement that meant slavery for himself and his people. "It would seem better to fall with dignity than to serve with ignominy." But, generally speaking, it was wiser to sue for peace on the best terms possible. Lipsius concluded the discussion with a moving prayer for peace that drew on Jeremiah the prophet and Paul the apostle.[106]

The influence of Machiavelli was evident in the treatment of military organization and training in the *Politics*. But Lipsius went beyond Machiavelli when he insisted upon the maintenance of a standing army made up of regular, professional soldiers, the *miles perpetuus*, to use the term he coined.[107] The practice had begun to appear in France and in several Italian states in the fifteenth century,[108] and it played a vital role in the coming of the modern state. The size of forces would differ, Lipsius wrote, according to state and circumstances, but he gave a general figure of 6,000 of whom 400 would be cavalry. They were then to be complemented by a body of reservists, similar to the militia advocated by Botero and increasingly found in German and Italian states, which could quickly be called up for service.[109]

Lipsius, too, argued for native troops because their loyalty would undoubtedly be superior to that of foreigners. The ruler might employ some foreigners to supplement them, but only a tyrant would fear arming his own subjects and so rely chiefly on foreigners.[110] The troops' quality was to be assured by careful selection, for which Lipsius supplied criteria, including a preference for country over city boys, and by a system of training and discipline, defined as "rigorous formation of the soldier in hardiness and virtue." He insisted that the officers possess an authority with their troops similar to that of the prince with his subjects. One element contributing to this for Lipsius as for Botero was good fortune (*felicitas*), which in turn was associated with God's providence. "It was indeed often accompanied by counsel and reason, yet it was bestowed a little more generously by God on some. For he was its author; no one could attain it by himself." There was nothing like a record of triumphs attributable to divine favor to secure for a general the respect of his troops.[111]

Lipsius's system of discipline was his most significant contribution to military thought, and it spread across much of Europe as a literature of military science developed. For this he drew on his detailed knowledge of the Roman army, in what was an outstanding example of the influence of the ancient world on practical affairs in early modern Europe.[112] The first element in military discipline was drill or exercises. Just as other arts needed practice, so did the military art. This involved regular exercises with weapons, marches carrying equipment, practice digging in and fortifying positions, and mock battles. Only with disciplined, well-drilled troops could an army employ the new volley method of fire introduced by the Dutch in the mid-1590s. It called for the first rank of troops to fire their muskets in unison and then to retire to the rear of the unit to reload while the next ranks stepped forward to fire in their turn and so to maintain a continual volley of fire.[113] Secondly, an army had to be organized into units of descending size, each with its own officer, and have a clear hierarchical structure and a definite chain of command. Only then, Lipsius contended, could an army be effectively deployed in a battle or campaign.

Thirdly, there was a moral code to be instilled in the troops. Under continence Lipsius meant moderation in food, drink, and sex, and he noted that the army of Hannibal after overcoming the rigors of winter while crossing the Alps had themselves been conquered by the delights of Italy. Modesty comprised a number of qualities but principally obedience, an obvious necessity in an army. As the Roman Curtius wrote, soldiers ought to be "attentive not only to the order but to the nod of their commander." Lastly there came abstinence, a quality that certainly served to protect the innocent. By it Lipsius meant that the soldiers refrain from harming or plundering the civilian population and make every effort to live in peace with them. A system of rewards and punishments for the enforcement of proper military conduct constituted the last element of Lipsius's discipline. Both were of great importance, rewards perhaps more effective when the troops were actually engaged in battle, punishments more necessary when they were encamped with time on their hands.[114] Oddly, Lipsius did not make the statement that was virtually ritualistic with other writers: the troops had to be paid on time. Perhaps this was another manifestation of his determination to avoid specific applications to his own day.

Up to this point we have been looking at Lipsius from the perspective of intrinsic pragmatism. Now we turn to providentialist pragmatism, that is, to Lipsius's conception of divine providence as it operated in history, rewarding or punishing the prince and his people according to their deeds. Thus we come to a philosophy, or theology, of history, although Lipsius was still careful to avoid topics he considered the proper domain of the theologian. His Neostoic conception of providence and fate left its stamp on the Baroque vision of life, and his universalism was another aspect of his Neostoicism not to be overlooked. Machiavelli's distinction between the foundation and conservation of the state was missing in Lipsius, as was Botero's between its conservation and expansion. His interest was in the survival of the state over time. Still for Lipsius the individual human being and the human race were written larger than the state. Thus its demise was not the tragedy it was for Machiavelli. The individual survived and the human race benefited, as we shall see.

Lipsius approached the topic in the *Constancy* with reverence and humility, conscious that God's providence, though always benevolent, was often mysterious and beyond human understanding. He argued that disasters such as plagues, famines, and wars, in particular the war in the Netherlands, were ultimately necessary and meant to be useful to man. Calamities came from a good and loving God and so, either directly in natural catastrophes or indirectly through human agency as in wars, were always ordered to man's ultimate benefit. Lipsius cited Augustine's

Enchiridion, "He [God] judged it better to draw good from evil rather than to permit no evils." They were intended to test, to warn, to punish, to heal. Had not the ferocity of Attila served to call forth the virtue of Christians immersed in pleasures and luxury?[115]

Lipsius took over the Stoic notion of fate but clearly subordinated it to the Christian conception of providence, which was "the ever watchful and perpetual care (but a care nevertheless secure) by which God looked at all things, was present to them, and knew them; and by which he directed and governed them in a succession that was unchanged and unknown to us."[116] Fate was "the unchangeable decree of providence, inherent in changeable things, which assigns individual things their order, time, and place."[117] It was in things and ascribed to them, whereas providence was in God and attributed to him alone. Later in the *Politics* and the *Advice* he dropped the distinction and virtually identified fate with providence.[118] But this was a move of only secondary theological importance, since fate for him had always been subordinate to providence.

Two main statements summarized Lipsius's providentialist pragmatism. The first was that, by necessity, all things human were moving toward decline and death. The implication was that decline and death need not be interpreted as punishment; they were part of the fundamental order of things that ultimately issued in good. "In this [necessity]," he wrote, "you would not seek an empty consolation in your sorrow."[119] Necessity he understood to be "the firm ordinance and power of an immutable providence." It existed as a natural tendency in all created things by which "they were carried toward change and death as by an innate force." It was virtually the same as fate. All created things were destined for "death and destruction," of which public calamities were often the "ministers and instruments."[120]

Lipsius described how necessity operated in the natural world and then turned to its working in political bodies, towns, states, kingdoms. "As individual human beings pass through adolescence, adulthood, old age, and death, so do these [political bodies]. They have beginnings, grow, stand firmly, flourish, and all this so they may fall." The ancient monarchies of the East had flourished, as had the great empire of Rome, but all succumbed eventually to the necessity that lay within their very natures.[121] In the *Politics* Lipsius recognized in fate a remote cause of the fall of kingdoms, for which there was no remedy, "because it is certain from the history of every age, God brings to an end almost ritually great empires in this fashion."[122] All things passed through the stages of birth, growth, decay; there was no escape.

But in the face of fate Lipsius did not advocate passivity and the abandonment of public affairs as had the ancient Stoics. Fate operated through secondary causes, and citizens were to make use of them. Just as in the case of an individual's illness one did not know whether it was fatal or not and did all in one's power to heal it, so the prince or citizens worked to bring the state through its crisis and to preserve it. Lipsius applied to the state the proverb, "so long as the soul is in the sick person, hope." But once the signs were clear, one had to yield to time and to God.[123] In fact, Lipsius pointed out, while admitting that he saw less clearly here, this necessity within things contributed to the preservation and development of the human race. At this juncture his Stoic, and Christian, universalism came through in a manner totally foreign to Machiavelli. "The ruin of this country or kingdom will be the rise of another; the downfall of this town the raising up of a new one; nor does anything perish in the strict sense, it changes." Where would the French and Germans be today had they not been brought under the yoke of Rome? The Spanish campaigns in the New World had opened up a new culture for the Indians. In a variation on this line of thought, Lipsius approached a primitive Malthusianism. The finite earth could not support an unlimited number of people. Public calamities were, he suggested with great tentativeness, the way in which the number of people in the world was scaled back for the good of the whole universe.[124]

Lipsius's second statement about providence asserted that God saw to the reward and especially to the punishment of princes and nations, though in a manner that often transcended human understanding. Overcoming to a degree his reluctance to take up theological issues, Lipsius first asserted in this context that all men were sinners. They had been touched by original sin and they continued to ratify it with their further personal sins. Only God could judge the state of an individual soul; it was impossible for a human being to do so even in his own case, Lipsius affirmed, following the teaching of the Council of Trent whether he realized it or not.[125] Thus it was not within man's competence to claim that a punishment had not been deserved. "Nor has there ever been even in the best men such purity that there did not remain some stains to be washed away by the salty water of disasters."[126]

Lipsius distinguished three types of punishment. First, there were the internal ones, "the punishment of a crime associated with, indeed natural to every crime." They afflicted the soul while it was still united with the body; among them were fear, anxiety, and remorse. Then there were the posthumous ones. They overtook the soul after it had left the body and culminated in the eternal punishment of hell, a topic Lipsius excused himself from elaborating, because it was properly the territory of the theologians. Third, there were the external ones that tormented the body, such as poverty, exile, pain, sickness, and death. These followed from public disasters and were most closely related to providentialist pragmatism. All three often went together, especially the first two. But "if the third is lacking when the first two have been imposed, who will justly accuse the heavenly justice? But they are not lacking. Nor does it ever happen (certainly rarely) that manifest criminals who oppress others do not pay for this with visible punishments for all to see. Some sooner, some later; some in themselves, others in their [successors]." Proud Caesar was stabbed to death beneath the statue of Pompey. Augustus suffered at the hands of his own children.[127]

Thus for Lipsius external punishments did not inevitably overtake evil princes or sinful peoples. But they usually did, especially if one took the long-range perspective and kept in mind the social nature of man. Lipsius's most far-reaching example in this regard was Adam himself, whose sin led to the punishment of all his posterity. Curiously, perhaps because of his desire to avoid theology or of his focus on punishment instead of reward, Lipsius failed to mention the counterpart of Adam, Christ, whose good deed on the cross led to the salvation of all. Families, towns, and kingdoms should not be seen as diverse or unconnected entities but as a body or natural unity. The family of the Scipios, the city of Athens, the Roman Empire all constituted unities across space and time. The members of these respective societies shared in their rewards and punishments. Just as an individual might be punished in old age for a crime of his youth, so might a state encounter retribution only after decades of its history. A whole nation might be punished for the sins of its leaders, as were the Jews for David's. On the other hand, sometimes a few bore the punishment for the many, a procedure that could be interpreted as a merciful justice for the many. Thus Lipsius suggested a role for vicarious suffering in history. Here he might have been expected to introduce the instance of Jesus once again. But he cut off with a warning about attempting to penetrate the secrets of God. "Many judgments of God are hidden, none are unjust."[128]

Providentialist and intrinsic pragmatism now merged. The disaster that overtook a people or its ruler could be considered the intrinsic result of sinful actions or the punishment imposed by God. The revolution with which a subject people turned against the cruelty of long-time oppressors might be viewed as the natural consequence of cruelty or as the retribution of divine providence. So Lipsius rested his case for virtue and prudence in politics.

Lipsius and Botero launched the anti-Machiavellian tradition of the Counter-Reformation. They found a wide audience because they dealt with issues that agitated their contemporaries; they both reflected and molded attitudes of the day. Neither Bodin's *Six Books of the Republic* (1576) nor Johannes Althusius's *Politics Methodically Set Forth* (1603) enjoyed anywhere near the circulation of Lipsius's volumes, and they also remained behind Botero's.[129] Lipsius's works crossed confessional lines more readily than Botero's; his *Politics* circulated essentially in two versions, the original Leiden one in Protestant lands and the 1596 Louvain one in Catholic territories.[130] His greatest popularity seems to have been reached in France and Germany, Botero's in the Latin lands. His *Politics* was published ten times in French translation during the reign of Henry IV, as we have seen, and it served as a major source of the political thought of the influential *On Wisdom* (1601) by Pierre Charron.[131] Maximilian of Bavaria was as familiar with Lipsius as with Botero; texts of his were scattered throughout the prince's political testaments.[132] Lipsius may have outshone Botero even in Spain. According to Marcel Bataillon, he was as popular in Spain in the first half of the seventeenth century as Erasmus had been in the first half of the sixteenth.[133] The well-known Spanish diplomat under Philip II, Bernardino de Mendoza, translated the *Politics* into Spanish in his retirement—the translation appeared in 1604—and the author of *The Ambassador*, Don Juan de Vera y Figueroa, drew so heavily on Lipsius that he was accused of plagiarism.[134] Lipsius and Botero each had an impact on Richelieu and Olivares, the two great rivals in the Thirty Years' War, Richelieu making use of Lipsius in his *Political Testament*, and Olivares taking on Lipsius's Neostoicism, especially after the death of his daughter in 1626.[135]

Botero and Lipsius did much to set the tone for the political culture of the early seventeenth century. Both favored absolute government and believed in its ability to get things done, and both insisted on the ruler's need for popular support, that is, reputation. It was the key requirement for a ruler, and virtue was essential to its acquisition. Both writers sought to limit war and impose restraints on it while at the same time showing how a prince intent on war could find an outlet for his energies. For both religious unity constituted the ideal, but they were ready to allow for toleration under certain circumstances, Lipsius more so than Botero. Each advocated the expansion of government. Peculiar to Botero was the emphasis on economic development as a way to power and to Lipsius the advocacy of a disciplined standing army as a means to the same end. Perhaps one reason for this difference was Botero's outlook, which took in the Italian cities and included European expansion into Asia and the New World, and Lipsius's narrower focus on the states of northwestern Europe afflicted by the religious wars. Lipsius felt much more keenly the tension between the good and the useful in politics—Botero seemed scarcely to notice it—and he endured the problem of providence in history as a poignantly personal issue with which he wrestled himself as he encouraged his contemporaries to constancy.

Ill. 1. Rubens's "The Four Philosophers" or "Justus Lipsius and His Pupils," dating from about 1615 and now in the Pitti Gallery in Florence, shows Lipsius the teacher with two of his favorite students, Philip Rubens, the painter's brother, at the left and Jan Woverius at the right. Rubens himself stands at the far left. Above to the right is a bust thought to be of Seneca. Courtesy of Alinari/Art Resource, New York, and Palazzo Pitti, Florence

Ill. 2. This title page conceived by Rubens for the first volume of Lipsius's *Opera omnia* (Antwerp, 1637) emphasizes his Roman Stoicism. Courtesy of the Newberry Library, Chicago

PIETRO
RIBADENEYRA
Della
Compagnia di Giesú;
della Religione
del
Prencipe Christiano

CONTRA
li
Macchiauellisti

RELIGIONE   RAGIONE DI STATO   VERITA

IN BOLOGNA PER PIETRO PAVLO TOZZI. 16

. 1621

Ill. 3. Religion and Truth characterize a Christian reason of state according to the title page of an Italian translation of Ribadeneira's *Christian Prince* (Bologna, 1621). Courtesy of the Newberry Library, Chicago

Ill. 4. The comprehensive nature of Adam Contzen's *Ten Books on Politics* (Mainz, 1621) is clear from this marvelous title page. Courtesy of the Newberry Library, Chicago

Ill. 5. This portrait of the Jesuit Carlo Scribani by Anthony van Dyck reveals him to be a man of substance. Courtesy of the Kunsthistorisches Museum, Vienna

CAROLI SCRIBANI

E SOCIETATE IESV

POLITICO-CHRISTIANVS

PHILIPPO IV.

HISPANIARVM REGI

DD.

APVD MARTINVM NVTIVM
ANNO M.DC.XXIV.

R. pinxit.

Cor. Galle sculpsit.

Ill. 6. Christian Politics and Abundance or Prosperity were partners, according to this title page created by Rubens for Scribani's *Christian Politician* (Antwerp, 1624). Courtesy of the Houghton Library, Harvard University, Cambridge, Mass.

Ill. 7. The motto of emblem no. 31 from Saavedra's *Politico-Christian Prince* reads "Resting upon reputation," and the figure shows a royal crown atop a Corinthian column representing reputation, as the author elaborates in his accompanying essay. Government depends upon reputation or popular support. This and the following figures are taken from Saavedra's own translation of his book into Latin (Brussels, 1649). Courtesy of the Newberry Library, Chicago

Ill. 8. Emblem no. 43's motto, "That he might know how to rule," alludes to the advice allegedly given by Louis XI of France to his heir: "He who does not know how to dissemble does not know how to rule." The ruler must know how to combine force, represented by the lion's skin, with cunning or prudence, represented by the serpents coiled about his head. Saavedra's prince disdains the malicious deceit recommended by Machiavelli, which the fox would symbolize. Courtesy of the Newberry Library, Chicago

Ill. 9. "Near to Jupiter and his thunderbolt" reads the motto of emblem no.
50. So the *valido* or favorite rises above others and is close to Jupiter or the king,
but he is also exposed to his wrath. Courtesy of the Newberry Library, Chicago

Ill. 10. "Trust and distrust" translates the motto of emblem no. 51. The art of government consists, Saavedra writes in his essay, in knowing when to place trust in another and when to deny it. Courtesy of the Newberry Library, Chicago

Chapter 5

Pedro de Ribadeneira: Origins of the Tradition in Spain (1595)

Lipsius had composed his *Constancy* and *Politics* as the calamities of war visited his beloved Netherlands. Against the background of this conflict he worked through the problem of providence in history and expounded a program for effective, moral government to suit the times. The defeat of Spain's Invincible Armada in 1588 and the shadow it cast over the Golden Age of Spain provided the backdrop for the first Spanish anti-Machiavellian. The tragic outcome of the Armada generated a crisis among Spaniards, expressed in the words allegedly spoken by Philip II, "I sent my ships to fight against men and not against the elements." God's providence seemed to have abandoned those who trusted in him, especially when one considered the part played by ill weather in the defeat of the Spanish force. *Desengaño* or disillusionment began to spread in Spain.[1]

The Jesuit Pedro de Ribadeneira published his *The Christian Prince* at Madrid in 1595. His response to Machiavelli was an attempt to articulate a Christian statecraft or reason of state that would prohibit a repetition of such a disaster. He was the first of the *arbitristas*, those writers who put forth programs of reform for Spain beginning in the late sixteenth century,[2] and he demonstrates a connection between their activities and the defeat of the Armada. The *Christian Prince* served as a vehicle for restating ideas of Botero, whose *Reason of State* was already well known in Spain among reformist writers, but it was more concerned with the issue of God's providence than Botero's or even Lipsius's books had been and more focused on providentialist pragmatism. *The Christian Prince* betrayed the influence of Lipsius's *Politics* in several places, but Ribadeneira's thought was little indebted to him. Themes from Seneca echoed in his *Treatise on Tribulation* of 1589, but they do not seem to have been taken from Lipsius. The Roman Stoic's writings had long been popular in Spain.[3]

But the *Christian Prince* was not written merely for Spain; it was to have a European impact, if not nearly to the extent of Botero's *Reason of State* or Lipsius's *Politics*, and for this reason it belongs to the broader anti-Machiavellian tradition. Ribadeneira's volume was the first and, apart from Saavedra's later work, the most distinguished of the anti-Machiavellian treatises originally written in Spanish.

Until well into middle age, Ribadeneira gave little indication that he would become a leading Spanish writer with a volume all to himself in the *Biblioteca de Autores Españoles*. Born at Toledo in 1526, he came to Rome at the age of thirteen as a page in the service of Cardinal Alexander Farnese.[4] In 1540 the homesick lad found a new home at the recently opened Jesuit house in Rome and a second father in his fellow Spaniard, Ignatius Loyola, who took an immediate liking to him. Soon he entered the Society of Jesus, and he was ordained a priest in 1553. Most of the four years between 1556 and 1560 he spent in the Netherlands, where he had been dispatched to establish the young Society of Jesus and to secure its formal approbation by Philip II, who still resided there. He became acquainted with the Court of Brussels, and he sojourned in England as a companion of the Spanish ambassador, the duke of Feria, during the crucial winter of 1558–59, which saw the death of Philip's wife, Mary Tudor, the ascent of Elizabeth to the throne, and negotiations for the Peace of Cateau-Cambrésis, when there was talk briefly of Philip's marrying Elizabeth.[5] This stay in England, together with his later friendship with the English Jesuit Robert Persons, helps explain his acute interest in the affairs of the church there.[6] During the next fourteen years Ribadeneira held major Jesuit administrative positions in Italy: provincial superior of Tuscany (1560–62), when Robert Bellarmine was a seminarian,[7] and then of Sicily (1562–65); rector of the Roman College (1565–71); and assistant to the superior general for the provinces of Spain and Portugal (1571–74). Thus he had spent considerably more time in Rome than either Botero or Lipsius, both of whom had resided in the Eternal City during their formative years.

Pope Gregory XIII's desire to reduce the influence of Spanish Jesuits in Italy and Ribadeneira's own ill-health combined to force him to return to Spain in 1574. There he devoted himself almost exclusively to writing, residing in Toledo until 1586 and then in Madrid until his death in 1611. His literary activity and semiretirement did not prevent him, however, from maintaining contacts with leading Spanish figures. Cardinal Quiroga, Inquisitor General of Spain and Archbishop of Toledo, consulted him on personal as well as public matters, and in a memorial prepared for him in 1580 Ribadeneira advised against war with Portugal over the succession.[8] He was on good terms with Juan de Idiáquez, royal secretary, member of the Council of State, and adviser on English affairs,[9] and with various members of the powerful house of Mendoza. Within the Society of Jesus he acquired a position of authority as one of the few, and then as the only, surviving Jesuit to have known Ignatius intimately. Jesuit superiors general consulted him on matters of internal government, and his opinion was respected in Rome.[10]

Ribadeneira's return to his homeland was a gain for Spanish literature. Marcelino Menendez y Pelayo, the great nineteenth-century Spanish historian of literature, ranked him with the classic Spanish prose writers, and others have concurred with his judgment. He combined a pure classical style of the Renaissance with a mentality colored by the *desengaño* following 1588 that was a feature of the Spanish Baroque.[11] His contemporaries looked upon him primarily as a historian. In the year of his death, Lope de Vega addressed to him the following encomium:

You have ascended to that level of honor
to which a sacred pen may aspire,
Illustrious Ribadeneira, saintly Livy,
Honor the verses of my humble song.[12]

His *Life of Ignatius Loyola*, a classic of humanist biography, first appeared in Latin at Naples in 1572, then in Spanish at Madrid in 1583, and it soon became the standard biography of the founder of the Jesuits.[13] His *Bouquet of Saints (Flos Sanctorum)*, popular lives of the saints, began to appear in 1599 and became a common possession in Spanish families for generations. In addition to a number of devotional works and publications dealing with the early Jesuits, Ribadeneira published the first bibliography of Jesuit writers.[14]

Three of Ribadeneira's most important publications were related directly to the Armada, *The Ecclesiastical History of the English Schism*, the *Treatise on Tribulation*, and *The Christian Prince*. The first part of his *English Schism* was an attempt to prepare the Spanish people for the coming Armada.[15] It was published in 1588 at Madrid, Valencia, Zaragoza, Barcelona, and Antwerp. Essentially a translation and thorough revision of the manuscript of an English priest, Nicholas Sanders, edited by Persons, it told the story of the English Reformation from a Spanish Catholic perspective up through 1587. It proved extremely popular in Spain and for two centuries remained the principal source for the Spanish view of the Reformation in England.[16]

Far from being the triumph the Spaniards—and Ribadeneira—expected, the Armada ended in disaster. In his *Exhortation for the Soldiers and Captains Who Are Going on the Expedition against England, in the*

Name of Their Captain, which he originally intended to be the concluding chapter of the first part of the *English Schism*, Ribadeneira revealed a
conception of the Armada that he shared with many leading Spaniards,
including Philip II himself.[17] The *Exhortation* struck the note of a national effort to defend the faith in Europe, vindicate the reputation of the
king and the nation, and protect the Spanish homeland itself. Spain had
the honor of bearing the faith to the New World and restoring it in the
Old. "There is not under heaven anyone who can aid them [the English
Catholics] except the unconquered Spanish army, sent as help from
heaven for the Catholic King, Philip." Divine providence would make
victory easy, since rarely had the issue been so clearly joined between
God and evil. "Let us proceed to an enterprise that is not difficult, since
God Our Lord, whose cause and most holy religion we defend, goes
before us."[18] Thus the enterprise of England took on features not only of
a just war in defense of religion but of a holy war undertaken at God's
behest with special promise of divine assistance. That Ribadeneira himself had reservations about this militancy or at least its public expression
is shown by his suppression of the chapter and his directive not to reveal
its authorship when he sent a copy to Ana de Guzmán, wife of the duke
of Medina-Sidonia, captain-general of the Armada, after she had learned
of its existence.[19]

The catastrophe of the Armada provoked questions about God's
providence. How could the Lord allow the defeat of a venture so clearly
undertaken to defend the faith? In first taking up the issue, Ribadeneira
sounded the note of Christian, Neostoic resignation that was to characterize a seventeenth-century Spain becoming increasingly aware of its
own inevitable decline. The *Treatise on Tribulation*, his greatest ascetical
work and his principal artistic triumph, was published in Madrid the
year after what a monk of the Escorial called "the greatest disaster to
strike Spain in over six hundred years."[20] "The hardships and calamities
of these times," Ribadeneira wrote, indicating his purpose, "are such
that they oblige me to write this *Treatise on Tribulation* to provide some
consolation and remedy for them." The treatise's first part dealt with
personal sufferings, the second "with those general calamities of these
our days."[21] The latter opened with the statement that God punished not
only individuals but also cities, provinces, and kingdoms for their sins.
Even the virtuous suffer in this situation, for their own good. "Yet a
greater cause for wonder is that an Armada, great and powerful, which
appeared invincible, prepared to defend the cause of God and his holy,
Catholic faith and accompanied by so many prayers, supplications, and
penances of his faithful servants, was destroyed and lost in such a strange

way, that no one can deny that it was a severe punishment and chastisement from the hand of the Most High."[22]

Ribadeneira made a valiant effort to show why God allowed heresy. His power was glorified in the victory over it; his wisdom was manifested in that he raised up teachers to refute the heretics; his goodness was revealed in that he inspired men to die for the faith; the presence of heresy was a test of faith. But only God could answer fully the question of why the heretics flourished while the Catholics suffered. It was a mystery of his providence to be endured and accepted as a punishment for sins. Courage, reform, and trust in the face of God's inscrutable designs was the attitude the Christian should take toward the apparent victory of heresy.[23]

The second part of the *English Schism*, completely the work of Ribadeneira, first appeared at Alcalá in 1593. It took up the events between 1588 and 1593, and was loosely unified around the attempt to refute the charge, reiterated in Elizabeth's edict of 1591, that the Jesuits and seminary priests were political enemies of England. Featured were accounts of the sufferings of English Catholics at the hands of the English government. Toward the end Ribadeneira entered an impassioned plea for the toleration of Catholics in England, but with little hope that his words would be heeded. In the final chapter he returned to the basic question of the *Treatise on Tribulation*, why did God permit this. He referred the reader expressly to the earlier work and applied the more general answers given there to the English situation.[24] The problem of evil posed by the defeat of the Armada remained in the forefront of his thought. It would recede but not disappear in *The Christian Prince*, where the Armada was not explicitly mentioned.

The *Treatise on the Religion and Virtues Which a Christian Prince Ought to Have to Govern and Conserve His States against That Which Niccolo Machiavelli and the Politicians of this Time Teach* was first published at Madrid in 1595 and appeared two years later at Antwerp. Second editions came out at Madrid and Antwerp again in 1601, and translations followed into Latin (1604), Italian (1608), French (1610), and English (n.d.).[25] But *The Christian Prince* did not enjoy the widespread popularity of some of his other works. It was well received at the Spanish court and became a favorite of the future Philip III, to whom Ribadeneira dedicated it.[26] Maximilian of Bavaria counted a copy of the Latin translation in his own private collection, apart from the ducal library,[27] and the volume was highly regarded in some English Catholic circles.

In his "Memorial on the Conversion of England" of 1596, Persons recommended *The Christian Prince* with much enthusiasm to the Catholic ruler who, he hoped, would lead England back to the faith after the death of Elizabeth;[28] and the émigré, courtier, and sometime English secretary to Philip II, then priest and later Jesuit, Thomas Fitzherbert, in his *Whether There is Advantage in Crime or the Misfortune of the Machiavellian Prince against Machiavelli and the Politicians His Followers* (Rome, 1610), dedicated to the Count of Castro, then Spanish ambassador in Rome, added that he knew no one "who had written more elegantly or more richly about the Christian prince" than his friend Ribadeneira.[29] Two mammoth, tedious English volumes by Fitzherbert, the first and second parts of a *Treatise Concerning Policy and Religion* (Douai, 1606–10), showed traces of Ribadeneira's influence, but he was not named in them.[30]

The *Christian Prince* comprised a program of reform, instructing the future Philip III and Christians generally about how to govern so as to obtain God's favor and to avoid catastrophes like the Armada, which Ribadeneira had interpreted as a punishment for sin. In a letter of late 1588 to an unidentified minister, probably Juan de Idiaquez, but evidently intended for Philip II, Ribadeneira had listed specific sins for which the defeat was a punishment: despoliation of the poor by government ministers under pretext of gathering materials for the Armada, insufficient zeal for the spiritual good of the English, and excessive desire to profit commercially by the venture.[31]

Principally to blame for the increasing ills of Europe, Ribadeneira claimed in the dedication to Prince Philip, were the *políticos* or politicians, a term he professed to apply with regret to such figures because it dishonored the noble art of politics. He was the first, it seems, to associate Machiavelli with the *políticos*, a term hitherto reserved in its pejorative sense for the French *politiques*. The chief characteristic of the *político* for him was their contention that the successful government of a state was not possible without departing from God's law.

Ribadeneira found two features of Machiavelli especially difficult to stomach, his use of religion as a means of social control and his denial of Christian providence, and the Spaniard devoted considerably more space to the place of religion in the state than had Botero or Lipsius. In the preface to *The Christian Prince*, Ribadeneira lumped Tacitus, Bodin, and the French Calvinists François de la Noue and Philippe du Plessis-Mornay with Machiavelli as representative *políticos*, but the four were of secondary importance to him. Tacitus he probably took over from Botero, who in his *Reason of State* had designated him an apostle of malicious politics. Indeed Ribadeneira was the first Spaniard to attack

Tacitus, and he has been credited with giving him a bad name in Spain.[32] That not all Spanish anti-Machiavellians shared this view can be seen from the recommendation given him by Ribadeneira's friend and colleague, Mariana, as "a suitable author, whom neither princes nor courtiers should ever lay aside, but day and night should study."[33]

Bodin and the two Calvinists had been listed alongside Machiavelli by Possevino in his 1592 *Judgment of Various Writings of the French Soldier Noue, Jean Bodin, Philippe de Mornay and Niccolò Machiavelli,* and Ribadeneira probably followed this lead, which is not to say he had not read the writers in question, since he cited Bodin often and du Plessis-Mornay, too. Possevino had seen the heretics as a greater danger than the *políticos* and in a sense as their offspring; Ribadeneira, with greater insight, was more concerned about the *políticos* than the heretics, who at least preserved some elements of religion.[34]

There were two reasons of state, Ribadeneira affirmed in his preface, as had Botero in the dedication to the *Reason of State*; one looked to man's higher purposes and recognized God's law and providence, the other looked only to the preservation and growth of the state and allowed the use of any means, just or unjust, including the manipulation of religion, in pursuit of this goal. The second was profoundly unreasonable, ultimately in opposition to reason as well as faith. His purpose, Ribadeneira declared, was to refute the arguments of those who taught that the claims of religion and politics were irreconcilable and to outline the general features of a Christian reason of state. He defended his competence as a priest and religious inexperienced in government to undertake such a task. St. Thomas, Giles of Rome, and other learned religious had done the same. But he acknowledged that he was not suited to lay out many particulars of a program for state building, and he left them to the experts.[35] Thus he usually did not descend to the detail of Botero or Lipsius.

History was vital to Ribadeneira, who was determined to show that the principles he advocated worked and were not speculations for an ideal world. All that was necessary to refute Machiavelli were the examples of rulers who had governed successfully according to Christian principles and so demonstrated that this was possible and not really rare. His examples were also intended to inspire the reader to imitate the virtue of the princes who were proposed as models. Modern Christian rulers could equal and even surpass the glory won by Christian kings and statesmen of the past. Ribadeneira seemed to overwhelm his readers with examples, sometimes devoting whole chapters to illustrating principles he elucidated in several sentences.

Ribadeneira drew on a wider variety of historical sources than had

Botero or Lipsius, let alone Machiavelli. Usually examples were taken first from ancient Greek and Roman historians, including Tacitus. Since they did not have the light of faith, they exemplified in particular the reasonable character of Ribadeneira's policy. There followed then the biblical writers, especially of the Old Testament, and such historians of the early church as Eusebius and Sozomenes, who were favorites of Ribadeneira. Finally there came a wide range of medieval and modern writers, including another favorite, the church historian Baronius; Philippe de Commynes, author of the early sixteenth century *Memoirs of the Reigns of Louis XI and Charles VIII*; and Guicciardini. Only twice did he refer to Mariana's multivolume *History of Spain*, which was to become a popular source for Spanish anti-Machiavellians. Perhaps its only recent appearance in 1592 had made it difficult for him to use.

The *Christian Prince* also belonged to a genre popular at the time, especially in Spain, which dealt with the education of the prince and which had been nourished by Erasmus's *Education of a Christian Prince*. This genre had roots in the medieval tradition of the mirror of princes, of which the two thirteenth-century works of Aquinas and Giles of Rome with the same title, *On the Government of Princes*, were landmarks.[36] They both are mentioned in *The Christian Prince* at crucial points, as is Aquinas's *Compendium of Theology*. Other writers to whom Ribadeneira turned fairly often were Aristotle and, despite his status as a *político*, Bodin. In addition to Aquinas, Ribadeneira depended for his basic principles of political philosophy on the contemporary Scholastics, whom, however, he barely mentioned. Lipsius's *Politics* he cited three times, and there is evidence for further influence of the Fleming,[37] but his impact on Ribadeneira was much less than Botero's, who is only mentioned once and then as source for a historical example. Machiavelli's *Prince* and *Discourses* he had certainly read.

Ribadeneira passed over many fundamental issues of political theory, although he often gave hints of his position as he discussed other topics. He presumed a sovereign monarchy without taking up alternative forms of government. Nowhere was there any mention of the power of the pope, either direct or indirect, in temporal affairs, a trait *The Christian Prince* shared with Mariana's *The King and the Education of the King* and Juan Marquez's *The Christian Governor*. But before we conclude that this was typical of Spanish writers, we should note the extreme papalist views of the politically influential Juan de Santa María's *Treatise on the Commonwealth and Christian Policy* (Madrid, 1615).[38]

Ribadeneira's discussion of the relationship between the spiritual and temporal power asserted the role of popular consent in the origin of the latter, as was common with the Scholastics, and his treatment of taxation implied a body from which the ruler sought consent for it. But he explicitly avoided a more precise treatment of the need for popular approval, leaving it up to the "experts."[39] Thus he differed sharply from Mariana, who stated clearly his preference for the vigorous estates of Aragon over the flaccid *cortes* of Castile.[40] Ribadeneira warned the ruler against tyranny, but he completely avoided a discussion of the right of resistance, which brought Mariana into so much trouble four years later.

The whole first of the two equally long books of *The Christian Prince* was devoted to the religion of the ruler and the state. The difference between the *políticos* and the Christians was that the former saw in religion only a means to strengthen the state. For Christians, Ribadeneira wrote, God had given the princes power "so that their subjects might be blessed here below with temporal happiness (which is that toward which the political government is directed), and above with eternal [happiness], to which our temporal [happiness] looks and is directed as to its goal and ultimate end, and [the princes] ought to keep their eyes fixed on God and his holy religion before all other things."[41] The direction of man to his final goal was properly the function of the church, but the state had the duty to assist it. Certainly, in the pursuit of its immediate goal, the temporal happiness of its subjects, the state could never undertake any action that would violate God's law and so hinder man's realization of his, and the state's, final end, eternal happiness.

This, of course, was not a pragmatic argument. But Ribadeneira turned to providentialism when he affirmed that God gave "a good outcome to those endeavors undertaken for his service,"[42] and he went on to provide many examples, first of rulers who had been favored by God in return for their care for religion and then of others who had suffered as a result of neglecting it. To the former group belonged the Christian emperors Constantine and Theodosius, as well as Charlemagne and Hugh Capet, and Rudolf of Habsburg. Closer to home there were Ferdinand and Isabella, whose expulsion of the Jews and Moors was lauded (in contrast to Botero's lack of enthusiasm for it in the *Reason of State*) and, most recently, Charles V, whose long and eloquent response to Luther at the Diet of Worms Ribadeneira had cited at great length in the dedication to Prince Philip. Among those punished for neglecting religion were the Hebrew King Jereboam; Duke John Frederick of Saxony, who had favored Luther; and the French kings Francis I, Henry II, and Henry III, all of whom had at some time aided the heretics. Even Mary Stuart had lost her crown for her toleration of heretics, although her subsequent courage had brought her the reward of martyrdom.[43] But Ribadeneira was well aware that matters did not always work out this way, as the outcome of the Armada had brought home to him. We shall return to his further discussion of the mystery of God's providence.

The ruler's obligation to foster religion Ribadeneira understood in a broad sense. It included active encouragement of Catholic practice and of the observance of moral principles, as well as suppression of heresy. So there came to the fore a crucial issue of the day, religious toleration, to which Ribadeneira devoted a good third of the first book. His adversaries were the *políticos*, whom he criticized as "ministers of Satan . . . [who] teach that kings and temporal princes ought to pay no attention to the faith and belief of their subjects but maintain them in justice and peace, and govern the commonwealth in such a way that each one follows the religion he wants, provided he is obedient to the civil laws and does not disturb the peace of the commonwealth."[44] Did Ribadeneira wish to include here among the *políticos* Lipsius, who advocated more clearly than Bodin that those who sinned privately in religion be left alone? Quite possibly. Whether the *políticos* answered fully to his indictment was doubtful. Certainly Bodin and Lipsius preferred unity of religion in a state and urged its enforcement up to the point that this became impracticable, proving more disruptive than religious diversity. But Ribadeneira sensed, correctly, that the state's indifference to religious truth induced a dynamic toward "liberty of conscience," in which every individual could believe as he wanted so long as he obeyed the laws.

He now brought forward a multiplicity of arguments against toleration, some presented in several sentences and others developed with examples at great length. As an anti-Machiavellian he was concerned to point out the benefits that unity in the Catholic faith brought to the state. But in this case, his pragmatic approach was to result in an unexpected conclusion. Ribadeneira saw the very presence of heretics in a kingdom as sufficient to call down God's wrath on prince and people, and he related a number of historical incidents to support this argument. But his emphasis was on the argument against toleration as disruptive of civil peace, and his survey of recent history enabled him to marshal a strong if exaggerated case for religious unity. Confessional differences had brought to most European states a strife from which Spain had remained relatively free. Calamities had overtaken Germany, Bohemia, Poland, Transylvania, Scotland, and other states on this account. The sects had fought with one another in Germany, and nearly one hundred thousand perished when they rose against the princes. But to see that religious discord usually ended in civil war it was not necessary to look far afield. It was enough to consider neighboring France, he argued, which had remained obedient to its king until it opened the door to heretics for reasons of state.[45]

Ribadeneira clearly foresaw the use of force to preserve religious unity against the inroads of heresy. But he did not lay out any suggestions or norms for its application, as had Botero and even Lipsius. He further clarified his position by making the traditional distinction between heretic and nonbeliever. Faith was a free act; it could not be forced. The nonbeliever was not to be compelled to make it. The heretic had made a commitment in baptism on which he had then gone back. The Scriptures referred to heretics as wolves and thieves, who sent men to perdition with their doctrine, and they were to be treated as such. Ribadeneira invoked a number of authorities in his favor, including Augustine, who had sanctioned the use of force against the Donatists after first refusing to do so.[46]

This did not mean that other measures, especially good example and preaching, were not preferable. They certainly were. Moreover, one had to distinguish those who had been deceived in their simplicity from those who were malicious deceivers. But if lenient measures failed, then the prince had to turn to greater rigor, but, he continued in a surprising tone,

in order to do this quietly and without harm to the Catholics, he ought attentively to consider the state of his kingdom, and whether there were many or few heretics in it, because when the whole kingdom or the greater part of it is composed of heretics, and the tares cannot be uprooted without also uprooting the wheat or without serious danger of revolutions or wars, Christian prudence teaches to look the other way [*dissimulare*] in order not to do more harm than good, according to the teaching of St. Augustine, who says: *non propter malos boni deserendi, sed propter bonos mali tolerandi*; one ought not abandon the good for the sake of the bad but tolerate the bad for the sake of the good.[47]

Here Ribadeneira took a decisive new turn, to which he was led by his pragmatic approach. He spoke of wars and revolutions, that is, the obverse of civil peace. Civil peace with religious toleration was to be preferred to the unrest stirred up by further efforts to enforce religious unity.

So Ribadeneira interpreted the Gospel parable (Matt. 13:28–29) in which the harvest master allowed the tares or weeds to continue to grow lest in tearing them out damage be done to the wheat crop. Whether he meant by this mere tacit toleration or a formal, legal toleration is not clear, but both his subsequent remarks and the logic of his argument pointed to the latter. Without apparently realizing it, he had accepted essential elements of Bodin's and Lipsius's position. His ideal, too, was national unity of faith, and he encouraged the quashing of dissent by force if this could be done with more or less ease, but toleration was to be preferred to "the dangers of wars and revolutions."

In support of his concession, Ribadeneira cited Aquinas's *Compendium of Theology*, where Aquinas allowed the toleration of pagan, and even heretical, rites in order to avoid still greater evils such as civil strife.[48] Thus Ribadeneira advanced well beyond Suarez. There is no evidence that he was influenced in this by either of the two Flemish theologians, Lensaeus or Molanus, who had espoused a similar position. For that matter, Ribadeneira was unexpectedly reticent about the Dutch War throughout his writings, perhaps out of a hesitation to criticize Spanish policy; despite frequent discussion of the issue at court, the Spanish government, like the Dutch, consistently refused to bend on toleration. Negotiations for a truce had collapsed again in 1594, partly over this matter.[49] He showed much more interest in the affairs of England and France and, indeed, the situation of Catholics in these two lands was undoubtedly behind his thinking. Had he not just pleaded for toleration of Catholics in England? He sided with those English Catholics who recognized that the Catholic ruler who as they hoped would soon return to the throne of England would have to exercise toleration.[50] His stance can also be seen as justifying Spain's withdrawal from its support of the Catholic League in France, which indeed took place in 1598, the year of Philip II's death.

Never at a loss for historical examples, Ribadeneira called up two instances from the eighth-century historian Paul the Deacon to vindicate his argument. The sixth-century Pope John I had implored the Emperor Justinian not to confiscate the property of the Arians in Constantinople so as not to give the Arian King Theodoric a pretext to destroy the Catholic churches in Italy. Nor did the same pope hesitate to consecrate Arian churches in Constantinople, lest Theodoric pillage all Italy. In such situations, Ribadeneira went on, the prince must act with prudence, seeking to enlighten the ignorant, lead back the strayed, and win their good will.[51]

But Ribadeneira was quick to add that all this did not alter the situation in those Catholic countries where a few heretics caused disturbances, and he embarked upon a tirade against toleration. If he had been a Frenchman, he probably would have given much more prominence to the far-reaching concession he did make to religious toleration. In France the heretics had acquired a solid foothold, and in such a case toleration was in order. Logically, Ribadeneira would have had to approve, at least in principle, the Edict of Nantes issued by Henry IV in 1598. Nowhere did he explicitly refer to it. But in the 1605 edition of the *English Schism* he inserted several paragraphs in which he spoke highly of the progress Catholicism was making in France and of the peace the country now enjoyed.[52] But Ribadeneira was determined to impress upon the Spaniards, and especially upon the future king to whom *The Christian Prince* was dedicated, the need for religious uniformity at home, if Spain were to continue to enjoy internal peace and to maintain itself as a world power.

For Ribadeneira, then, the ideal of religious unity in a state was not above compromise. Unity in the Catholic faith was a source of Spanish political strength, from the perspective of both providentialist and intrinsic pragmatism. But this was not the case everywhere. In countries like France and England, limited toleration with the peace it brought was more useful to both church and state than was continual effort to impose uniformity. Thus the anti-Machiavellian concern for the pragmatic, useful good, for church as well as state, led to support for toleration. It was precisely in the development of this line of thought that a Catholic position favorable to the toleration of heretics was developing. In Spain itself there now seemed to be two theological opinions about the treatment of heretics in areas of unrest like the Netherlands. Marquez in *The Christian Governor* of 1612 followed the position of Ribadeneira, citing the same texts of Augustine and Aquinas.[53] Mariana, however, in 1599 had given little indication that he allowed for toleration,[54] and Juan de Santa María in his *Treatise on the Commonwealth and Christian Policy* of 1615 rejected it explicitly.[55]

The virtue, or virtues, of the ruler formed the topic of the second book of *The Christian Prince*. The development followed loosely the four moral virtues—justice, temperance, prudence, and courage, in this order—with economic development falling under justice and military affairs under courage. Temperance received slight treatment. If we take all the virtues together as a composite, with prudence serving as guide, then this composite constituted the virtue of the prince and was a blend of moral uprightness and political skill, as for Botero and Lipsius. Throughout there remained the underlying pattern of thought that virtue was useful from its intrinsic nature and from the assistance of God that it brought the ruler. Although a connection was occasionally drawn between virtue, reputation, and power, it was not a featured theme, as it had been in Botero and Lipsius.

Ribadeneira's insistence that virtue be genuine was obviously directed against Machiavelli, and a long citation from the famous chapter 18 of the *Prince* was inserted in this context. Fictitious virtue could never garner true glory; Cicero had correctly asserted this long ago. Nor was it possible, in the long run, successfully to deceive the people about the ruler's virtues. When the deception was uncovered, "the prince is that much the more hated to the extent they understand he sought to deceive them," and he is grievously damaged in his reputation. Moreover, the ruler could not win divine favor through simulated virtue. In fact God had a particular aversion to hypocrites, as Christ's strictures against the Pharisees showed.[56]

Prudence stood out for Ribadeneira as a key virtue for the ruler, but it did not predominate as it had for Botero or Lipsius. It was to be a Christian and not a political (*política*) prudence, where political obviously designated the *políticos*. Nor was it to be confused with a "deceptive cleverness."[57] It enabled the prince to distinguish true from false utility. An advantage that was obtained only at the expense of the good (*lo honesto*) was useful only in appearance (*aparente utilidad*). But Ribadeneira did not offer a concise definition of prudence; rather, like Botero he described it through a number of functions it performed and precepts it provided. The development was not at all systematic. Nor was the role of prudence in securing popular support central to Ribadeneira.[58]

One instruction of Ribadeneira on prudence seems clearly to have been directed to the future Philip III and meant to encourage a departure from the practice of his father, the Prudent King, who was known for concentrating decision-making power in his own hands and tarrying over decisions. A ruler had to be deeply involved with government; he could not delegate his responsibility beyond a certain point. Yet a primary characteristic of the prudent person was the recognition of his need for counsel and advice, owing to the weakness of his own understanding and to his passions. This applied especially to a ruler who was "an absolute lord and great king and monarch of the world," for whom "it was not possible to understand all his affairs himself" any more than it was possible to manage all the state's affairs himself. Such was certainly the king of Spain. Lipsius had advised the prince to make sure the people knew he was in charge. Ribadeneira rather saw the ruler as attempting to undertake too much himself. The prince had to be able to distinguish important from less important matters and to know what to do himself and what to entrust to others. Nor should prudence be confused with indecisiveness or the inability to reach decisions.[59] In the event, an indolent Philip III adapted an excessively "hands off" policy, leaving responsibility with his ministers, especially the duke of Lerma, who became the royal favorite or *valido*, and Olivares later expended much effort on making Philip IV into a working king.[60]

One specific reason for seeking counsel was to obtain backing from the people, who were always more willing to stand behind a policy about which they knew the ruler had sought advice. Especially in making changes or introducing reforms the ruler had to proceed slowly, testing the reaction of the people with what today would be dubbed "trial balloons." To move too quickly was to leave the people behind and lose their support. But there was another side to this. The prince should try to rule so that no one could reasonably criticize him. But, Ribadeneira pointed out, as had Botero, it was not possible to avoid all criticism. The lot of the prince was "to do good and be criticized." He had to learn to put up with this, "because the populace is a many-headed beast and is not able to understand the reasons and motives why the prince does what he does," Ribadeneira continued, displaying his view of the people. The approval of the knowledgeable ought to be the prince's goal.[61] Prudence taught him to learn about the peoples whom he governed and to study other peoples, to have a clear idea of his own resources and of other rulers', to be familiar with their ways of thinking and of their councillors', in order to be better able to formulate policy toward individual states. Timing was also an essential of prudent statecraft. "It is unbelievable how quickly opportunity (*ocasión*) comes and goes."[62]

Ribadeneira took on the role of casuist when he discussed the discernment of true from false utility in the employment of forms of deceit described by Lipsius, whom he did not mention by name in this context.[63] The role did not fully suit him, and he failed in clarity. He was well aware of the real world of politics. Machiavellian rulers and statesmen abounded who regularly took on the appearances of lions and foxes. Christian princes had to find a way "so that on the one hand they were not deceived and their sincerity, openness, and truthfulness were not mocked, on the other, that in order to avoid this, they did nothing against the law of God."[64] This was a classic statement of the problem.

Ribadeneira permitted and advocated what Lipsius had recommended as slight deceit—mistrust and dissimulation. But he stated clearly at the start Augustine's teaching that a lie, either in word, which was a lie strictly speaking, or gesture, which was normally called simulation, was never permitted. Thus he rejected the lie that Lipsius, with misgivings, had tolerated in extreme circumstances. But what was a lie and what was dissimulation? That was the issue. A ruler had to be careful whom he trusted. Nor was he obliged to indicate through his facial expression that he did not trust another, since this would undermine confidence in him and harm the state. On the contrary, a certain impassiveness of expression was a desirable trait and amounted to laudable dissimulation. The same was true when a ruler or minister looked the other way or acted as if he did not see something, even though this created the impression that he was ignorant of it. At times prudence required this. Nor was it a lie, in the interest of preserving secrets vital to government, not to reveal all one knew, even though others might draw false conclusions from this. Ribadeneira distinguished from a lie, and permitted, equivocation or what was later called a mental reservation in the broad sense,[65] "when necessity or great utility called for it." This practice, which Lipsius had not mentioned, involved making a statement that was in itself ambiguous, that is, open to two understandings, when one knew it was likely that the listener would take it in other than the true sense.

Thus far Ribadeneira was clear, except that he had given no definition of a lie or distinguished it properly from dissimulation. His concluding passage, drawn from the sixteenth-century *Manual of Confessors* of Martin de Azpilcueta, "the Doctor of Navarre," only confused matters. "There are two types of simulation and dissimulation: one is practiced by those who without reason or advantage lie and pretend that that exists which in fact does not or that that does not exist which in fact does; the other by those who without evil deception or lie prudently give to understand one thing for another when necessity or utility require it."[66] This mystifying passage did not adequately distinguish between the nature of the act and its purpose. It designated simulation, to "pretend that that exists which in fact does not" and dissimulation, to "pretend that that does not exist which in fact does." But simulation was usually considered by writers who followed Aquinas to be lying through actions rather than words. This was so with Botero and Marquez,[67] and Ribadeneira himself had just used it in this sense. He had reiterated Augustine's stand that lying by word or gesture, that is, simulation, was never allowed. Now both simulation and dissimulation seemed to be a lie when practiced "without reason or advantage." This was the first type of simulation or dissimulation in the passage. But who ever acted without reason or advantage? Neither was then a lie, it appeared, when practiced "when necessity or utility required it." This was the second, acceptable type of simulation or dissimulation. The passage hid other puzzles, too.

Ribadeneira concluded his discussion with a figure like Lipsius's drop of water, or deceit, which did not spoil the wine of truthfulness. Dissimulation was similar to a drug that was taken against a viper's poison and was composed of the same content. It should be used "only when necessity required it, and let it be of a small quantity in dose and measure," and according to the law of God. Otherwise it would poison the one who took it. A lie was never permitted.[68]

One form of Lipsius's serious deceit, unfaithfulness to promises, Ribadeneira treated under justice. He insisted on the obligation of the ruler to be faithful to his word, seeing himself in sharp contrast with Machiavelli and the *políticos* on this point. The Christian prince had to be careful about making commitments, but once made, he had to stick to them. Ribadeneira stressed the advantage to be gained from a reputation for fidelity. It increased the ruler's wealth, for example, since it enabled him to secure military supplies or to borrow money when necessary, because his credit was good. "So he became more powerful, more obeyed and feared."[69] But Ribadeneira advised the ruler not to be afraid to withdraw from an enterprise when circumstances called for it and added that "necessity was a weapon so strong and powerful that it could not be resisted, and it excused that which otherwise would not be able to be excused." Guicciardini was called upon to support the point.[70] But this seems to have been little more than the Scholastic principle that allowed for the withdrawal from a commitment under greatly changed circumstances, which Lipsius had also invoked.

Ribadeneira passed over two types of Lipsius's deceit. One was bribery, for Lipsius a form of tolerable, moderate deceit used to garner support in the ranks of other rulers. Perhaps he either disdained this practice or, in the other extreme, simply took it for granted. Injustice or the violation of positive law under pressure of necessity, Lipsius's second form of serious deceit, Ribadeneira did not have to discuss directly, since for him the prince was not bound to positive law in any event and was advised to adhere to it only as a means of giving good example to his subjects.[71]

Justice was the virtue most essential to the ruler after religion and piety.[72] Ribadeneira's implicit thesis was that just, honest government paid off in the support of subjects and God's blessing on the prince and the state. As for Botero and Lipsius, the virtue was exercised chiefly in two areas, the administration of justice and the distribution of benefits and burdens, especially taxes; thus the traditional commutative and distributive justice, which touched the subjects directly through the courts and the tax collectors.

The delicate question of privileges for the nobility, especially their access to office, came up when Ribadeneira turned to the apportionment of dignities and wealth in a kingdom. He walked a fine line, insisting on appointment on the basis of merit and talent, yet recognizing out of necessity the claims of nobility. To bestow rewards and offices according to merit was in the interest of the prince and the state. Otherwise one diminished the motivation to serve the state, and particularly in times of crisis when competent persons were needed, they were hard to find. A secret of Roman success had been their system of rewards for service to the republic. The prince had to keep alive the hope of the ambitious and the fear of the ensconced. But Ribadeneira quickly added, his remarks did not mean that certain groups should not receive preferred treatment. To give the nobles special consideration was both reasonable and just, and besides, to do otherwise could cause discontent and stir up serious political trouble. But certainly non-nobles who merited rewards of the state should not be set behind nobles who did not. True nobility consisted, after all, in virtue.[73]

Taxes were the principal burden of the state. The subjects had the duty to support the kingdom, but there were limits to what the prince could require. Ribadeneira was much more reserved about the rights of a ruler to collect taxes than Botero or Lipsius. He inclined to the older tradition, very much at home in the Spanish kingdoms, which required consent. The ruler was not the absolute lord of his subjects' wealth. The fact that tax grants were called *servicios* or *donativos* indicated they were voluntary, not obligatory. Presently the ruler had his patrimonial revenues as well as the *servicios*. When these did not suffice, he might in justice call upon his subjects for further revenues. But, as we have seen, Ribadeneira omitted any further discussion of royal rights to demand taxes or of subjects' to limit them. He also passed over any discussion of the suitability of particular taxes or of a concrete program for taxation such as Botero had outlined.[74]

But Ribadeneira was only warming up to the topic. He argued that it was to the prince's advantage not to load his subjects with taxes but to foster their wealth as the necessary prerequisite for their continuing ability to pay taxes. "This is more than an obligation of justice; it is a matter of great utility for the prince himself and the whole commonwealth." The ruler had to manage his finances well and not engage in immoderate spending, "since just as it is fitting that a prince be rich, so it is necessary that he be circumspect in the way he accumulates his riches and much more so in spending them." Perhaps Ribadeneira had the Spanish experience of government bankruptcies in mind when he followed Botero in warning against borrowing at high interest rates. His passing advice that the prince uphold the value of the currency touched an issue that Botero had overlooked and that was to be a vital one throughout the first half of the seventeenth century. In 1609, at the age of eighty-five, Mariana spent nearly a year in jail for his criticism of the currency manipulation practiced by the Spanish government.[75]

Ribadeneira's chapter advocating the prince's promotion of the economy strengthened his claim to be the first *arbitrista*. Certainly his recommendations were an implied criticism of Spanish policy. Like Botero, he was an early mercantilist, yet there were differences between them. Ribadeneira stressed agriculture and trade, and he neglected industry. Nor did he advert at all to the importance of population growth for the economy or to the incipient population decline in Spain. About the Spanish income from the New World, which peaked in the 1590s, he remarked that "it requires planning only that the fleets come and go on time" and were well protected. He prescinded from discussing this source of revenue further, almost as if to agree with what Botero had implied, that it was artificial and not to be relied upon. All in all, Ribadeneira was much less detailed than Botero, and perhaps his goal was merely to impress upon the prince the need to look to the development of his country's economic resources as a morally acceptable method of advancing the state's power without indicating in more than a cursory fashion the way this might be done.

Ribadeneira was particularly enamored of the manner in which the advancement of commerce had fostered communication among nations and contributed to the opening up of new areas and the growth of a world economy. His treatment was reminiscent of the enthusiastic passage in which Botero greeted the growth of world trade as promoting contact and interdependence among all the nations of the world. Merchants brought to Europe new knowledge of faraway peoples. "A man standing in his own kingdom is as an inhabitant and citizen of the universe." Trade increased the wealth of the nation, but the prince must be careful that it did not undermine native customs—Ribadeneira showed a sense for the cultural impact of development—and result in harmful luxury. Also, one should prevent the departure of too much money from the country; a positive balance of payments was essential to economic health. He noted the recommendation of some that customs duties be used to control imports, but he took no position himself on the issue.[76]

Ribadeneira's first concern in dealing with courage was a typical anti-Machiavellian one, to refute Machiavelli's contention that pagans were better soldiers than Christians. On the contrary, Christians made outstanding soldiers. What Machiavelli thought to be courage was really "a barbarian and inhuman ferocity."[77] If participation in bloody pagan sacrifices made the pagans more courageous fighters, then cannibals ought to make the best troops of all. Courage was rather a moral virtue that accompanied the other three.

Machiavelli had a grossly distorted view of Christianity and saw in it only qualities like humility and meekness. According to Aristotle and Cicero, the brave man was characterized by his contempt of external matters, his endurance for the sake of virtue, and his performance of arduous and dangerous deeds. Christianity brought out these qualities.

More than anything else, the hope of eternal reward stirred men to bravery. Ribadeneira pointed to the martyrs, both men and women, as Christian exemplars, but should Machiavelli not accept them as representatives of courage, then let him look at the many soldiers and generals that Christianity had produced. This was Ribadeneira's trump card, and he played it well. He let a parade of Christian heroes march by, most from the sixteenth century, featuring Columbus and Charles V, and he pointed in particular to the European achievements in the New World. Great Christian soldiers and men of action there had undoubtedly been. Ribadeneira went so far as to assert that "as they were more devoted and bound to God and dependent upon him, so much the more brave, triumphant, and glorious they were, so that it was understood that the Lord was the source of their courage and success." Machiavelli's assertion was, for Ribadeneira, simply ridiculous.[78]

The ruler had to uphold the honor and prestige of the military profession. War was inevitable, a necessary evil in the current order of things. Ribadeneira left to others the discussion of military organization and strategy, but he did provide several precepts for the prince regarding the military. Education, he agreed with Machiavelli, was a principal factor in developing courage in the citizens. In recent years it had become "soft and dissolute," he agreed further, and it was likely to lead to decadence as it had in the later days of the Roman Empire. This was not the fault of Christianity as Machiavelli declared, but Ribadeneira did not pursue the line of thought further.[79] He insisted on the need to maintain strict discipline among the soldiers, lest the wrath of God be provoked. The key to this was to treat them well and, especially, to pay them promptly. Evidently, Ribadeneira was aware of the riots of the Spanish soldiers in the Netherlands caused by the failure to pay them on time and the disastrous effects of these riots in the area. Ministers and officials who obstructed payment of the troops ought to be severely punished.[80]

Ribadeneira was sensitive to the horrors of war. The first reason he had given to dissuade Philip II from going to war over the Portuguese succession had been "the dangers and calamities that wars bring with them while they last as well as those that follow them."[81] Nor did Ribadeneira, like Botero and Lipsius, claim that there were reasons a prince could find to wage war legitimately so that he might distract or unite his people or gain the glory of a warrior king. Yet there would always be internal and foreign enemies with whom a prince had to contend. A ruler's goal was, to be sure, peace, but often "one cannot secure or maintain a good peace without a good war." So it was in the world. A ruler need have no scruples about engaging in war, Ribadeneira reassured the prince. One way God showed his providence was through the victories he gave those who fought in his cause. Many heroes had received triumphs from the Lord, from Gideon in the Old Testament through Constantine and Clovis to Joan of Arc and Don Juan of Austria at Lepanto. But the prince had to assure himself of the justice of his cause. Precisely how to determine this Ribadeneira remitted explicitly to those more expert than himself.[82]

But if he did not elaborate on the just war, he did allow for a type of war generally ignored by the Scholastics, the holy war. By this was meant a war fought usually but not necessarily for a religious goal, that is, the defense or expansion of a religion or religious interests, but more importantly, at the direction of God or at least with the promise of special divine assistance. The Scholastics allowed for the possibility that the pope exercising his indirect power in temporal affairs might authorize a ruler to suppress heresy in another kingdom or principality. This was a religious not a holy war, that is, one fought for a religious goal but not at divine behest or with the guarantee of divine aid.

Ribadeneira had conceived of the Armada as undertaken against the English heretics, if not because of a divine call, then at least with the assurance of God's help. There was no mention of the pope in his *Exhortation* for the Armada or in *The Christian Prince*. "By the wars which God has ordered his holy captains to wage," he wrote in the latter, "by the victories he has given them, and by the laws he published for his people, teaching them the way to wage war, one sees that war can be made in a holy fashion [*santamente*]."[83] This passage was intended in the first instance to show that war was a legitimate activity for a ruler. But the expression and the subsequent examples drawn from the Old Testament and the Late Christian Empire connoted more; they pointed to a holy war. Before Jericho an angel appeared to Joshua and responded to his query with the words, "I am nothing other than the leader of the Lord's army who come to help you."[84] God had bestowed victory on Constantine through the standard of the cross. This appropriation of Old Testament concepts of the holy war was not at all uncommon among both Catholics and Protestants, especially the Puritans, during the Wars of Religion.[85] Ribadeneira appears to have exemplified it, though not as clearly as Adam Contzen, the German Jesuit we will see in the next chapter. Neither Mariana, nor Marquez, nor Juan de Santa Maria came as close as Ribadeneira to advocating holy war, nor had Botero or Lipsius, although there were overtones of it in Botero's call for a campaign against the Turks.

Ribadeneira argued well the case that the art of politics could be practiced morally and successfully, and his call for reform in Spain was

eloquent. In this respect he was clearly optimistic. But Machiavelli's denial of God's providence in history had most incensed him, and it was in
response to this that the note of resignation in the face of God's plan,
which set the tone for the *Treatise on Tribulation* and the second part of
the *English Schism*, sounded briefly in *The Christian Prince*. Throughout
it he repeatedly argued that God in a special way looked after princes
who were faithful to him and punished those who were unfaithful to
their commitments or harbored heretics. But it was as obvious to Ribadeneira as it was to Augustine and Aquinas that God did not always
reward the pious and upright prince with political success and military
victory. The world was not that simple, and the fate of the Armada had
brought this home forcefully to him and to Spaniards generally. Twice he
turned to this issue explicitly, once in book 1, when dealing with the
place of religion in the state, and again in book 2, when he responded to
Machiavelli's charge that Christians by their humility and meekness had
abandoned the world to malicious and evil rulers.

Lipsius had sought to reconcile Christian and naturalist, Stoic conceptions of providence in his vision of the historical process. All things
including kingdoms and states shared a natural tendency toward decline
and death. Spanish writers of the early seventeenth century, including
arbitristas, took up this theme in their effort to understand the perceived
decline of Spain. They often resorted to the analogy between the state
and the human body already found in Lipsius, as did Jerónimo de
Ceballos, for example, writing in 1623.[86] Later Saavedra proceeded in
the same manner. But naturalist elements were not to be found in Ribadeneira's treatment of providence in *The Christian Prince*, and for this
reason it was more hopeful. There was no natural process of the rise and
fall of states into which divine providence intervened; in this sense,
providence was more free, as it were.[87]

Ribadeneira's first discussion of the alleged failure of God to look
after his own followed lines similar to Possevino's *Judgment of Various
Writings* of 1592, and drew on medieval authors. He relied heavily on
Aquinas's *On the Government of Princes*, but he also turned to Giles of
Rome's treatise of the same name and to Augustine's *City of God*, which
Aquinas himself had employed. Belief in providence was "the foundation
on which ought to be built the government and confidence of the pious
prince," he wrote. The good Christian ruler knew himself to be envel-
oped by God's providence, and he trusted in it. "When God accedes to
his desires, he gives thanks; when he does not, he holds for the best any
happening directed to him by that source of wisdom and goodness,
whom he esteems so much that it appears the most contemptible and
mean thing to offend him or to abandon him for all the states and

empires of the world." God did, always, look after the Christian prince, but he did not always bestow on him political success.[88]

What was then the true happiness of kings and the reward God gave them for their efforts? This could not ultimately be success in this world. "If the reward was exhausted in these [worldly] goods, they [the rewards] would not be the great goods that they are but short-lived, low, and of little value. And many times there would be no difference between the Catholic and the heretic, the good king and the bad, the Christian and the pagan, if one measured their happiness by these alone; but the Lord grants these to the one and to the other in order to show the little esteem we ought to have of them." God gave worldly honor and political success to both good and bad rulers precisely to show their relatively meager value. Just rule was its own reward, in that it brought the prince the peace and joy of a good conscience and the firm hope of eternal life.

At this point Ribadeneira went beyond providentialist pragmatism. He had endeavored to render principles of government as flexible as possible within the framework of God's law. A prudent prince would not allow events to develop to the point where he was confronted with a choice between the apparent preservation of the state and adherence to God's law. But should this happen, the prince was obliged to "risk all the states, kingdoms, lordships, and possessions he had in this world," and trust in God's providence come what might, rather than offend God.[89] Here Ribadeneira's most profound difference with Machiavelli was revealed. Machiavelli was an atheist in the sense that he denied any effective providence of God in the world and beyond. Ribadeneira's position made sense only to one with a deep trust in God's loving care for the ruler and the world. The preservation of the state was not the ultimate good.

His treatment of courage was the setting for Ribadeneira's second lengthy discussion of providence. He had already demonstrated that Christianity had produced many outstanding princes and conquerors who did successfully resist evil with force and advance the cause of good. His concern here was to explain the instances when those fighting in God's cause had encountered defeat. The matter of the Armada was evidently on his mind. This time he drew on the tradition of the Old Testament and related defeat and failure to sin.

God was master of history, and he distributed kingdoms as he willed, according to the prophet Daniel. He transferred rule from one nation to another because of injustices, wrongs, and deceits. Was it not written in Proverbs that God "makes use of evil princes and tyrants, who are ministers of the demon, to execute his healing anger, to purify the dross from the gold and to destroy the evil, and then afterwards punishes those tyrants of whom he has made use." So God used Sennacherib, Nebuchadnezzar, and Cyrus at different times to discipline his people and summon them to reform. Defeat and subjection to tyranny were to be seen as punishments for sin and calls to reform. So Ribadeneira had interpreted the catastrophe of the Armada. But God later settled the score with the tyrant who had served as the instrument of his chastisement. God's providence was often mysterious, Ribadeneira confessed. Often we did not know why he allowed tyrants to remain in power or heretics to triumph. Here he returned to the earlier argument of Aquinas. God gave the happiness of heaven only to those who served him, whereas he bestowed the kingdoms of this earth on the pious and the impious to show that man's final end was not reached here below. But God was in charge. The world was not given up to the power of evil princes as Machiavelli claimed. Good princes did succeed in preserving and maintaining states. When this was not the case, it had to be considered either a punishment for sin or attributed to a providence that was ultimately benevolent yet beyond human understanding.[90]

So the anti-Machiavellian Ribadeneira ended his general sketch of a Christian reason of state and the reform of which not only Spain was in need. A Christian ruler operating within the constraints of God's law could be successful in maintaining a powerful state. Indeed a Christian statecraft pointed the most direct way to lasting success. Significantly Ribadeneira said nothing about the expansion of the state; conservation was the concern in Spain. He generally did not descend to the detail of Botero or Lipsius, partly because he realized the limitations of his competence. But he devoted more attention than they did to the points in Machiavelli that had stirred the initial writers—Pole, Osorio, Caterino, and later Possevino—against him. These were Machiavelli's denial of providence and his manipulation of religion, and to a lesser extent for Ribadeneira, his claim that Christians did not make good soldiers or men of action or were otherwise unsuited to life in the world. The debacle of the Armada intensified his interest in the problem of providence. Two points in particular deserve special mention. Most important was his acceptance of religious toleration; here he was a reluctant pioneer led to his advance by his concern for utility. Secondly, there was his role as an early *arbitrista*, with a call to reform and to economic development. Perhaps in this last regard he was principally a channel for ideas of Botero.

Ribadeneira well realized that the Christian ruler did not always succeed, either because of his sins or the sins of his people, because of God's desire to educate both to the transitoriness of worldly achievement, or because of other reasons known to God alone, a God who nevertheless always cared for his own. Spain was now entering a period where it would have to cope with failure and decline. The call was to reform, that is, to the practice of a Christian reason of state, to trust, and to resignation to God's will come what might. Ribadeneira was leading the way into the Spanish Baroque.

Chapter 6

Adam Contzen: German Anti-Machiavellian (1621)

In 1638 the popular writer and court preacher of Maximilian of Bavaria, the Jesuit Jeremias Drexel, drew up a canon of recommended books on politics. All were published in Latin. In addition to Aquinas's *On the Government of Princes*, Lipsius's *Politics* and *Advice*, and Bellarmine's *On the Duty of a Christian Prince*, they included Jean Chokier's *Thesaurus of Political Aphorisms* (Rome, 1611), Adam Contzen's *Ten Books on Politics* (Mainz, 1621), and Carlo Scribani's *The Christian Politician* (Antwerp, 1624).[1] All except for Aquinas's were anti-Machiavellian works. Scribani we will see in the next chapter.

Chokier was a cleric of Liège who died in 1656, having for thirty-four years administered the diocese as vicar-general for two Bavarian prince-bishops. He had been a favorite student of Lipsius at Louvain, studied law at Orléans, and then with the blessing of his mentor journeyed to Rome to pursue his interest in antiquities. There his tome, large and unwieldy, first appeared, along with a letter written by Lipsius shortly before his death, dated March 5, 1605, endorsing Chokier's undertaking. Five subsequent Latin editions were issued, all but one in Germany and the last posthumously in 1687, and there were two pirated German translations published at Nuremberg.[2]

The volume was much more explicitly Catholic than Lipsius's *Politics*, but the master's influence was clear in the structure as well as the content. The good will (*benevolentia*) of the subjects or citizens and reputation (*fama*) and authority (*auctoritas*) with them were essential to government, indeed more so than resources (*vires*), and they were the fruit of piety and virtue, especially "political" virtue; prudence was not featured to the degree it was in Lipsius, nor was there any "mixed" prudence.[3] Chokier expanded the one book that Lipsius devoted to councillors and the prince's relationship to them into three of his own, and they in turn served as the basis for Lorenzo Ramirez de Prado's

Council and Councillor of Princes (Madrid, 1617), dedicated to the duke of Lerma.[4] The last of Chokier's six books included a theory of the rise and fall of states, using terms from Lipsius like necessity, fortune, and fate, which were to be understood, as the author stated in the preface, in a Christian sense. There was nothing on the contemporary issue of religious toleration, nor the economy, nor the military, though usually published with the *Thesaurus* was *The Commander* of Onasander, a brief military treatise by a first-century Roman general popular in the Renaissance, along with Chokier's *Notes or Comments*. The *Thesaurus* was nowhere nearly as thorough nor as open to new developments as Contzen's *Ten Books*, nor does it seem to have had a similar impact, even though it enjoyed more editions.

The publication of the German Jesuit Contzen's *Ten Books on Politics* at Mainz in 1621 marked a milestone in the development of the anti-Machiavellian tradition. It came on the heels of the unexpected and decisive Catholic victory over the Bohemian rebels at the White Mountain outside Prague, two years after the outbreak of the Thirty Years' War. Much European history had coursed by since the publication of Ribadeneira's *Christian Prince* in 1595 in the wake of the Armada's defeat. The Edict of Nantes ended the French Wars of Religion in 1598, and the Twelve Years' Truce of 1609 put a temporary halt to the struggle between the Spanish and the Dutch in the Netherlands. The principal scene of politico-religious conflict shifted to the Empire, where Catholicism had recovered its élan. The successful campaign in 1583 of the Bavarians, the pope, and the Spaniards to prevent the fall of the crucial Archbishopric of Cologne into Protestant hands marked a turning point politically, and by 1600 Tridentine reforms were beginning to show results in Germany. The Wittelsbach duke Maximilian of Bavaria and the Habsburg archduke Ferdinand of Styria both came to power in 1598, with Ferdinand destined to assume rule of all the German Habsburg lands except the Tyrol and Anterior Austria in 1617–18 and the imperial title in 1619, and Maximilian to be named an elector by Ferdinand in 1623. Both were ardent supporters of the Counter-Reformation and especially of the Jesuits, whose colleges now dotted Catholic Germany.

The *Ten Books* echoed the new, confident spirit in the German Counter-Reformation. Its dedication was to Emperor Ferdinand II, the victor of the White Mountain, and a second, slightly expanded edition appeared at Mainz in 1629, when Contzen was at the height of his influence as confessor to Maximilian, a post he assumed in 1624, and Maximilian's prestige as a Counter-Reformation prince was at its peak. The volume was the most thorough and most effective confrontation with Machiavelli from the pen of any German or Jesuit up to that time.[5]

More than other anti-Machiavellian works, which focused on the virtue of the prince, the elite, and perhaps the soldiery, the *Ten Books* shared with Machiavelli's *Discourses* the determination to inculcate virtue in all the citizens (*cives*), a term he frequently used, as had Lipsius and Chokier. In their active virtue lay the strength of the state. Contzen repudiated the views of those who wanted to restrict prudence to the ruler and his government and who "preferred that the citizens be ignorant, dull-minded, and as they say, simple."[6]

Contzen believed in the ability of church and government working together to mold a pious, industrious, and competent people. This described a goal of many German rulers at the time, Catholic and Protestant, who pursued increasing discipline of the population, especially through religion, legislation, and education, and so advanced the development of the territorial state.[7] Thus we have the growth of Catholic and Protestant schools as well as legislation like the detailed Bavarian Law for Religion and Morality issued in 1598, the first year of his reign, by Maximilian, and then in 1616 the new Code of Maximilian, which with few changes was adopted several years later by Ferdinand of Cologne, Maximilian's brother, for the Archbishopric.[8] The *Ten Books* soon became an influential blueprint for a Catholic state, especially in Central Europe, a position it would hold into the early eighteenth century.[9]

Contzen belonged to the second generation of anti-Machiavellians. He had been born in 1571 at Monschau, a village in western Germany not far from Aachen, and from an early age he was familiar with the persistent religious conflict between Calvinist and Catholic in Aachen and across the border in the Netherlands. After study at the Jesuit college in Cologne, he entered the Society of Jesus in 1591 and was ordained a priest prior to 1603. Then came assignments in Cologne and Würzburg before his appointment in 1609 as professor of biblical studies and then in 1612 as professor of controversial theology at the Jesuit academy in Mainz.

The decade between his appointment to Mainz and the publication of the *Ten Books* saw nearly a book a year come from his pen. They were generally theological and polemical in character, several occasioned by the exchanges surrounding the centennial of the Reformation in 1617. After his move to Munich, his pen continued to be active. Apart from biblical commentaries, he produced two volumes dealing with politics. The *Instruction on Civic Doctrine or a History of the King of Abyssinia* (Cologne, 1628) was a political novel in which the semilegendary figure of the Ethiopian king was used to demonstrate principles of government.[10] The *Mirror of the Court, or On the State, Life, and Virtue of*

Courtiers and Magnates (Mainz, 1630) was a guide to Christian living for government councillors and courtiers.[11]

Contzen's magnum opus, the *Ten Books*, was a massive, encyclopedic volume of 837 folio pages, 943 in the second edition, dwarfing in size earlier anti-Machiavellian works. It was meant to be comprehensive, and it was. The full title conveyed the scope of the volume while at the same time revealing an order of treatment similar to Lipsius's *Six Books on Politics*: *Ten Books on Politics, in which are discussed in a fashion suitable for common use and life the form of the perfect commonwealth* [book 1], *its virtues and vices* [books 2–3], *the education of the citizens* [book 4], *the laws* [book 5], *ecclesiastical officials* [book 6], *civil officials* [book 7], *the power of the commonwealth* [book 8], *sedition* [book 9], *and war* [book 10] (see Ill. 4). The tome was extremely diffuse, loaded with examples and digressions, and sometimes simply undisciplined.[12]

Neither the *Ten Books'* thickness, however, nor its diffuseness should blind us to its essentially simple purpose: to refute Machiavelli's claim that a ruler could not be a good Christian by setting forth a complete, workable program for the development of a Catholic state. Perhaps no sentiment echoed more loudly through Contzen's political writings than the conviction that moral conduct could and should permeate political life. In the dedication to the *Mirror of the Court*, he contended vigorously that sanctity could be achieved at the center of government and branded as "a pernicious error of the stupid" the view that a life of virtue was only for religious or those in orders. He considered it his task in the *Ten Books* to show "how all things human, private as well as public, were to be directed to the highest good and ultimate end," or in other words, to integrate political activity into the context of a total Christian life.[13] Machiavelli and his other adversaries were dubbed "Pseudopoliticians [*Pseudopolitici*]," a term which set in relief his esteem for the vocation to government, "the lord of all the arts."[14] The Machiavellians did not deserve to be called men of politics or politicians (*politici*), a word here charged with highly positive content.

Contzen very much saw himself dealing with the real world, and he dreaded being written off as a utopian. Like Aristotle, he wrote of the possible.[15] Before his eyes was the situation in Germany. Unlike Botero, Lipsius, and Ribadeneira, he had never been to Rome; to our knowledge, he never left Germany. Despite his wide reading and interests, his world was that of the German territorial states and cities, and the Holy Roman Empire. Much of his program for state building came out of the German states and was meant for them, whereas his vision of the Counter-Reformation encompassed the whole Empire, and his discussion of constitutional matters often reflected its peculiar issues, such as the right of the princes to make war. A nascent German patriotism can be heard in his references to "German fidelity" and his hostility to the encroachment of foreign fashions.

The *Ten Books* was directed to rulers and men of politics but also to the youth, especially students in Jesuit colleges, who would later assume responsibility for government. Its purpose was to engender esteem for participation in government as well as solid principles of rule.[16] Whether the *Ten Books* was read by many students or not, it undoubtedly influenced their teachers. Contzen's subsequent *Instruction on Civic Government* grew out of a special desire to reach students. Familiar with them from his early Jesuit days as a dormitory prefect in the colleges of Münster and Cologne, he hoped by using the novel form, as did other Jesuits through the drama, to render attractive topics that students often found boring.[17]

Like other anti-Machiavellians, Contzen stressed the weight of reason, man's "most certain light,"[18] in his argumentation, a reason he assumed to be in accord with faith and superior to experience. He sounded almost Cartesian. Authorities he certainly called to the bar, but he criticized modern authors including Lipsius, who he felt attached too much importance to the ancients at the expense of recent history and fresh insight. He took up the relationship of reason to experience when discussing his own competence to write of political and military affairs. Neither Plato nor Aristotle, nor Lipsius, possessed any meaningful experience in politics, and most military writers were politicians, not generals or officers. More valuable than personal experience was the experience garnered from the thoughtful reading of history. But historical experience in its turn took a backseat to reason. Certainly neither statecraft nor military science could be constructed inductively; there were too many instances of which to take account. His many historical examples, he stated, were intended to teach, illustrate, and confirm the doctrine arrived at by reason.[19]

An enormous number of sources—ancient, biblical, medieval, and modern—were utilized in the *Ten Books*. In the list of authors cited at the start, Contzen included 376 names plus 59 ecclesiastical councils. Of the modern authors, by far the most prominent was Lipsius, whom we have just seen mentioned alongside Plato and Aristotle. His influence was regularly acknowledged, as when Contzen stated that seven chapters in book 10 were a summary of Lipsius's *On the Roman Military*.[20] But Contzen was not afraid to disagree with him, and the *Ten Books* breathed a different spirit than the *Politics*. Contzen did not mention Botero by name, but his influence is unmistakable in book 8's treatment of economic development. Four Latin translations of the *Reason of State* had appeared in Germany by 1615, two at Cologne, and they cannot all have eluded Contzen.[21] He does not seem to have known Ribadeneira's *Christian Prince*, but he did make use of Mariana's *The King and the Education of the King*, of which a second edition appeared at Mainz in 1605. Surprisingly, Chokier did not appear in his roster of authors, and evidence of his influence is unconvincing, even though editions of the *Thesaurus* were published at Mainz in 1613 and at Frankfurt in 1619. Contzen listed Bodin among the authors he cited, but the Frenchman does not appear to have exercised a significant influence on him. Contzen clearly knew Machiavelli's *Prince* and *Discourses*, and even *The Art of War*, to which he frequently referred in his later chapters on military affairs. He was not afraid to learn from Machiavelli.

Contzen was not a speculative thinker. His expertise lay in the science of state building and in the analysis of concrete issues and their ethical evaluation. He was a political scientist and moralist rather than a philosopher or theologian. But his aim at comprehensiveness meant that he had to discuss all the basic issues of traditional political philosophy: the origin of the state, the nature and variety of law, and the relationship between the spiritual and temporal power, for example. Such questions he treated in an eclectic and occasionally inconsistent fashion, usually without departing from traditional Scholastic positions. But there were exceptions to this, all in the direction of strengthening the sovereign state. As we shall see below, Contzen seemed to expand the responsibility of government for the formation of citizens in virtue beyond the general Scholastic position, in order to accommodate the contemporary desire for discipline and order.

But the chief exception was Contzen's espousal of absolutism. He was the first major Jesuit author to take this step, and he did so not by a violent break with the tradition, which had been tending in this direction, but by new emphases and careful omissions.[22] His reasons were practical. They grew out of his perception that strong government was the only antidote to the political and religious chaos of the times, a view he shared with Bodin, Lipsius, and others. Never had legitimate authority been under such vicious attack, he declared in the dedication. For this he blamed the Calvinist "pseudotheologians," another set of adversaries, who had incited the revolt in Bohemia and were now girding themselves for a fight to unseat James I in England. Never had it been so necessary to insist on the Pauline teaching of obedience to legitimate authority.

Government was based on consent, he agreed. The people might reserve certain powers to themselves, but, Contzen noted significantly, in his day monarchical power had become more absolute because of controversies and unrest.[23] He spoke of checks on the ruler and the ruler's obligation in conscience to obey the law, a law, however, that the ruler himself was able to alter.[24] His evaluation of the estates was almost totally negative. They ought to be consulted, and their consent sought especially in matters of taxation, if only to forestall discontent or worse, but taxes were not in the last resort dependent on their approval.[25] The crucial point was that there was no way in which either the people, an individual, or a foreign prince could coerce a king. Though Contzen seemed at times to hold in theory a curialist position on papal authority, wherein he further disagreed with contemporary Jesuit Scholastics, he never mentioned papal measures that might be taken against a ruler. Resistance to kings could not be justified.[26] Contzen's argument was dictated by the chaos to which resistance had led in recent times more than by any theory of monarchy. "Let the commonwealth choose a man [as ruler] who has limited desires, since much is permitted him." Abuses had to be tolerated; only God could punish kings.[27]

In the *Ten Books* Contzen never spoke directly in the abstract of the harmony of the good with the useful as did other anti-Machiavellians, but this argument underlay the discussion of many issues. It could be found just under the surface in a wide variety of forms.[28] In fact, he was the most optimistic of the anti-Machiavellians, with the possible exception of Botero, coming closest to the obverse of Machiavelli by affirming that Christian, moral action assured political success. In contrast to Lipsius and Ribadeneira, he devoted scarcely any space in the *Ten Books* to instances where God's providence seemed to have abandoned the good prince. But in 1632, after the decisive Catholic defeat at Breitenfeld at the hands of Gustavus Adolphus, he was forced to confront a situation similar to the catastrophe of the Armada for Ribadeneira. To his providentialism we shall return.

Contzen's intrinsic pragmatism and especially the important connection he found between virtue, reputation, and power came out most clearly at the start of book 8. The topic of the book was power (*potentia*), a concept central to his political thought as a result of his confrontation with Machiavelli. "Without it [power] we cannot protect the country; the number of the avaricious and the malicious is very great, and the commonwealth cannot overcome injustice without power." Nor could one act effectively in the international arena without a firm power base at home. To preserve the state was more difficult than to expand it; one could conquer with military strength, but one could govern citizens and maintain the state—for Contzen as for Lipsius—only with "prudence and virtue."[29]

Piety and virtue were the most important elements in power. This stood out in a key passage where Contzen employed terms taken from Lipsius and Botero. "The resources [*vires*] of a state consist in piety and the virtues, then in those things which follow from the virtues in a principality, the first of which is authority [*auctoritas*], or reputation [*fama*] or majesty [*majestas*], then love [*amor*] of the citizens. Thirdly, [there comes] wealth [*opes*], arms [*arma*], men [*viri*], fortresses [*arces*], cities [*urbes*]."[30] The first element in a state's power (*potentia* was the term used in the chapter's title) or resources (*vires*, Botero's *forze*) was piety and the virtues, where Contzen used the plural to designate a composite of moral qualities and political skills.[31] Of the virtues, prudence predominated. Thus Contzen reversed the roles Lipsius had assigned to piety and prudence. For the Fleming, prudence and virtue were the two directors of civic life, and piety the first part of virtue.[32] For Contzen, piety and virtue held this position, and prudence was the first of the virtues.

The next two elements in power followed upon piety and virtue: authority, further explained by reputation and majesty and later in the chapter by esteem (*aestimatione*) and good reputation (*bona reputatione*), and love of the citizens. These corresponded to Lipsius's authority and goodwill (*benevolentia*) and Botero's reputation (*riputazione*) and love (*amore*). They were attitudes in the citizens. Piety and virtue led by prudence elicited them. They also brought forth "wealth, arms, men, fortresses, cities and alliances," that is, concrete economic and military power expressed in the terms of Lipsius and Botero. In speaking of power, Lipsius spoke of "wealth, arms, advisers [*consilia*], alliances, and fortune."[33] Contzen dropped, significantly, fortune and also advisers, which he treated elsewhere. He added, certainly under Botero's influence, men and cities, where men stood for people or population as well as soldiers. In books 2 and 3 Contzen focused directly on the virtues, showing in the process how they contributed to the prince's reputation and material power. Book 8, and books 9 and 10, too, started with reputation and material power and related these to the virtues in a reverse process. So he followed the same procedure as Lipsius.

Piety or religion was thus the first characteristic of a powerful state. Machiavelli had claimed that only fear would produce virtuous action in the citizens and that religion served as a formidable instrument to instill it. Contzen argued that only fear of God's judgment and punishments together with hope of eternal reward would sustain virtuous action in the body of the citizens. Without religion the moral order in the state would collapse.[34] So religion was for Contzen also, though certainly not only this, a means to induce fear and inspire virtuous living in the citizens. He contested vigorously Machiavelli's argument that Christianity lessened people's bravery and legitimate desire for freedom.[35] The prince's task was to protect and foster religion at the behest of the clergy, whose role it was to direct religious affairs. The temporal power was subordinate to the spiritual, he asserted, but he drew no practical consequences from it in the *Ten Books*.[36] On the contrary, while Contzen, like other anti-Machiavellians, condemned the manipulation of religion, he so stressed the state's interest in it that in the long run he fostered state control of it. This coincided with the mind of Maximilian, who with the connivance of Rome exercised considerable control over the church in Bavaria, often to the consternation of local ecclesiastical authority.[37]

To the necessity of religious unity Contzen devoted many chapters of the *Ten Books*. The weight of his case rested on contemporary evidence, from the Netherlands, France, England, Scotland, and, to a lesser extent, Germany itself. Religious differences inevitably led to social and political upheaval. Contzen generally went easy on the Lutherans; he consciously sought to separate them from the Calvinists, whom he felt to be the real incendiaries and with whom he felt there could be no peace. Every country where they established a foothold soon approached chaos. Their demand for religious liberty was only the first step toward the acquisition of sufficient power to impose their own settlement. By introducing new views, these pseudotheologians created uncertainty about religion among the people. The proliferation of theological positions and sects brought religion into contempt and ended in the atheism of the pseudo-politicians, argued Contzen, as had Ribadeneira. These were then worse than the heretics, who at least for the most part were in good faith. Without religion, rulers lost the trust of their people and so made their own government more difficult. All in all, a prince's duty and his interest lay in the preservation of a renewed Catholicism and his own exemplary practice of it.[38]

There was, then, in Contzen's scheme of things no place for religious toleration, at least over the long run, although he did recommend patience in the restoration of Catholicism. He did not allow for a situation where the ruler was faced with the choice of practical toleration or continued civil war, at which point Lipsius, Ribadeneira, and apparently Botero permitted concessions to heretics. Martin Becan, Contzen's teacher and predecessor in Mainz, a leading German Jesuit theologian, and from 1619 to 1624 confessor of Emperor Ferdinand II in Vienna, had consistently defended limited concessions to Protestants for the sake of a greater good—civil peace or greater likelihood of their conversion. This he first did with a reference to Molanus in his *On Keeping Faith with Heretics* in 1608,[39] and in 1620 he supported the concessions Ferdinand made to the Protestant nobility of Lower Austria.[40] But Contzen took no such step, probably because he felt confident in the gathering force of the Counter-Reformation in Germany. Protestantism had lost its impetus. It was dividing into ever more groups and sects, and this gave hope for the general return to Catholicism Contzen envisioned.[41] Indeed, a significant number of conversions to Catholicism among prominent figures marked the decades following the turn of the century.[42] The Catholics were riding the wave of the future; the victory at the White Mountain confirmed this.

Measures for the preservation of Catholicism in a state and for its introduction into newly acquired territories belonged to Contzen's program for state building. His remarks allow us glimpses of the psychology employed by Counter-Reformers, and they also cede to the prince in practice considerable freedom to intervene in religious matters. The ruler ought to promote the prestige and wealth of ecclesiastical dignitaries, who needed to be free from material needs in order to devote themselves to pastoral work. Contzen advised the prince who was intent upon keeping the faith vigorous in his lands to foster the moral life of his subjects—heresies arose from moral failures—and to see to the orthodoxy of preachers and teachers. There were times when forms of force and pressure were in order. "I know it seems hard," he wrote, "to impose laws on free minds and to constrain consciences." God himself did not compel people to accept salvation. Contzen recognized the danger of creating hypocrites. He saw the difficulties with the use of force, but he then justified it by quoting the well-known passage of Augustine arguing against the Donatists. People sometimes had to be led to what was good for them; after an initial reluctance, they would accept it interiorly.[43]

Many of the same recommendations turned up in the program for the restoration of Catholicism in Protestant territories acquired by a Catholic prince. Great stress was placed upon the example of the ruler and the clergy as the most effective means of re-Catholicization. The prince was to proceed slowly but firmly and with consideration of popular psychology. Weak points in heretical positions and differences among heretics were to be exploited. Heretical preachers and teachers were to be expelled quickly. This was the most severe measure recommended in the *Ten Books*, and it was one granted the ruler by the Peace of Augsburg, which permitted the expulsion of all dissidents as well as giving them the right to emigrate. Pressures to convert were to be applied, although apart from preachers and teachers the heretics should be dealt with leniently except where there was imminent danger to the state. The bestowal or removal of honors and privileges were useful tools. Many people were attracted by the use of music in the services.

Contzen returned to the argument from Augustine, responding more fully to the charge that force created hypocrites. Force at least prevented the mocking of Catholic practice and the cultivation of the devil. External observance was better than no observance at all, and in the long run the regular performance of external actions eventually led to the corresponding internal attitudes. A person who attended Mass each Sunday under pressure would eventually grow to appreciate it. This was especially true of young people, as could be seen in Bavaria and Inner Austria, where the Jesuit colleges were producing results.[44] Contzen looked to the long term, and indeed the Counter-Reformation has been called a youth or generational movement.[45] But he and other Counter-Reformers simply could not grasp the fact that people could reject the brief for Catholicism in good conscience when it was presented to them clearly and attractively. Undoubtedly there were many genuine conversions, but overlooked by Contzen was the profound resentment that pressures to convert created. The great Upper Austrian Peasants Rebellion of 1626, during the Bavarian occupation, was primarily the result of Counter-Reformation measures, especially the forced removal of Protestant pastors.[46]

After piety or religion, Contzen turned to the four cardinal virtues as a source of state power: prudence, justice, temperance, and fortitude, which constituted a blend of moral qualities and human skills guided by prudence.[47] Under diligence, a subdivision of prudence, Contzen insisted as had Lipsius on the personal government of the ruler. The prince's life was one of work and called for a careful allotment of time. Contzen even drew up a daily schedule for a prince, thirteen hours for work, seven for sleep, two for eating, and two for recreation. Thomistic fortitude Contzen nearly identified with Lipsius's constancy, and he lauded Lipsius's treatment of the virtue. His discussion of these virtues then passed over at the end into an exhortation to charity, to that love of God and neighbor that supported all the virtues. A prince was called to care for his people with genuine love; they would usually recognize this and requite him in the same coin. Charity served as a bond among all the subjects, uniting them with one another; this was the most firm basis for a solid community.[48]

Contzen was particularly careful to distinguish prudence from astuteness (*astutia*), which he defined as "a habit of soul that deceived in order to harm others." In this context he turned explicitly to the types of deceit taken up by Lipsius under mixed prudence. As for a healthy mistrust of others, which for Lipsius belonged to slight deceit, Contzen saw it as a virtue rather than a vice, especially for one who was involved at court or in government. But he was vague and unclear about the differences between dissimulation and a lie. When dissimulation merely involved the concealment of one's thoughts, for example, as when a prince responded with a friendly silence to what was manifestly a foolish proposal, it was clearly permitted. But to go beyond this to the use of ambivalent or ambiguous words was to stray beyond the permitted. Thus Contzen appeared to outlaw the mental reservation admitted by Ribadeneira under certain circumstances. While asserting with Augustine that a lie was absolutely forbidden, Contzen never did define one. He also left the door open a bit, as had Lipsius and even Augustine himself, by noting that lies were in some cases not serious sins. Bribery, tolerated by Lipsius as moderate deceit, Contzen considered a suitable means to win support from those in the service of another government or prince. Better to win wars with money than with blood, he commented, echoing a frequent anti-Machiavellian sentiment. The pursuit of diplomatic negotiations as a means of gaining time, even when one had no intention of arriving at an agreement, was also a legitimate practice.[49] But Contzen denounced the definition of a diplomat as "a good man, experienced in lying and prepared to lie for the commonwealth," which seems to have been a paraphrase of the definition of the Englishman Sir Henry Wotton, "a man sent to lie abroad for the good of his country."[50]

Lipsius had condemned two forms of grave deceit, the breaking of one's word and injustice or illegal action, while appearing to permit them at times of overwhelming necessity. Contzen differed, but not to a great extent. He insisted on fidelity to agreements, even those made under pressure with rebels. To act otherwise was to subvert trust and go counter to that faithfulness which was the peculiar characteristic of the Germans. But, Contzen added, echoing Botero, agreements were rarely kept should the ruler encounter serious financial difficulties or, for that matter, were treaties or alliances long adhered to when they ceased to serve the interests of both parties.[51] Oddly, Contzen, like the other anti-Machiavellians, did not mention the position of both Aquinas and Suarez that in greatly changed circumstances promises and agreements might no longer bind. For Contzen a prince could never violate the divine or the natural law, and he was bound in conscience to the positive law, which, however, he himself could change.[52]

After religion and virtue, reputation was the second element in princely power. It was the product of virtue and included many ingredients: love, a good name, praise, fear, reverence. It was an attitude toward the prince that was at the root of his popular support and also of his international influence. Fear and love seemed to find a balance. Earlier, when treating clemency, Contzen had preferred love to fear, expressly rejecting Machiavelli's position.[53] Now, when dealing with reputation, Contzen acknowledged, as had Botero, that one could never hope to please everyone. There would always be detractors, and the implication was that certainly in their case fear would have to predominate. Moreover, many people only performed their duty out of fear; this point Contzen had made in his treatment of religion. Yet loyalty, especially when sacrifice was called for, could only be sustained by love.[54]

Appearances were of great importance in politics. "More was accomplished by [the force of] opinion than reality. For what if your reputation was so great that you won the battles at hand because your enemy did not dare to harm you?" The prince not only had to be a man of virtue; he also had to have the reputation of being a man of virtue. Citing Augustine, Contzen urged the ruler to set aside any scruple he might have about pursuing praise and reputation. Reputation was "a means to the public welfare." Certainly if one could seek wealth and even kill for the public good, one could take measures to secure reputation.[55]

The first and essential way to reputation was "that your life be such as you desire your reputation to be." One simply could not feign virtue, as Machiavelli had recommended, for a long period of time. A prince was too much in the public eye to permit this. He might fool some people for a time, but he could not deceive all the people all the time. "Hence the good reputation of a wicked man would not last long," and when such deception was uncovered, the prince was left with the stigma of hypocrisy and forfeited the trust of the people. The prince should legislate and judge in such a way that few if any retractions were necessary, since they usually hurt reputation. In other words, he should govern well. Like Botero and Lipsius, Contzen showed how the prince might enhance his image. One way was the creation of a certain aura of mystery about himself, a measure Contzen did not emphasize as much as Botero. If a ruler did not have a venerable appearance, at least he ought to be serious and never to laugh. Those who attacked the prince's reputation or made public what might be his secret sins ought to receive severe punishment.[56]

But neither a prince nor a state could survive on religion, virtue, and reputation alone. Material power was absolutely essential. This was for Contzen, as it had been for Machiavelli and most anti-Machiavellians, reducible in principle to military and economic power, or "men and money," where men could mean either soldiers or a productive population. Like Botero and to a lesser degree Ribadeneira, Contzen emphasized economic development as the way to state power. Here he showed Botero's influence most clearly. But there were differences between them, and Contzen merited recognition himself as a pioneer mercantilist and German Cameralist.[57]

Contzen insisted that the prince make it a priority to fill the state treasury or *aerarium*. His future penitent, Maximilian, had already taken this lesson to heart from his reading of Botero. But Contzen was not alert to the danger of excessive withdrawal of funds from circulation and so did not attempt to put a cap on the treasury as had Botero. As with reputation, Contzen went out of his way to dispel any scruples a prince might have arising from a misunderstood asceticism. Personal avarice was not involved here. Kings in the Old Testament had certainly sought wealth, and Joseph had built up Pharaoh's treasury. To keep it filled "was a pious and holy duty of the prince and the commonwealth." This was true in peace as well as war. The ruler needed funds to pay adequate salaries to government officials—in making this point Contzen intimated the importance he attached to a bureaucracy—and sometimes to buy off unruly subjects. Contzen realized a ruler's need to give pensions, in effect, payoffs, to troublemakers, especially when they had a following. So he sanctioned a widespread practice.[58]

The prince raised money chiefly through taxes, not domain lands or government monopolies. Like Botero, Contzen advocated the imposition of regular direct and indirect taxes and so affirmed a feature of the developing state. Despite his attribution of the right to levy taxes to a sovereign ruler, Contzen recommended that the estates be consulted and that they have a part in the actual collection of taxes, as was the case in many German territories.[59] Contzen joined Botero in denying that tax revenues should be foregone when a specific cause for the levy of a tax ceased. Those who doubted the need for building up a cash reserve by regular taxation did not deserve the name *politicus*, he wrote. Contzen seemed to think excise taxes and customs duties were the fairest taxes, but he warned against taxes on necessities that burdened the poor, and he considered import duties also from the perspective of assisting local production. The concession of tax exemptions was "a mortal sin," a point he seemed to make with the nobility in mind. Subjects were bound in conscience to pay just taxes. That a tax was unjust was extremely difficult to determine, since the people did not have access to all the information available to the prince. Doubt about the justice of a tax never sufficed to warrant withholding payment.[60] So Contzen bolstered the power of the state.

Lucrative tax revenues assumed the productive economic activity of the subjects. Contzen urged strongly the development of agriculture, mining, industry, and trade, and as a mercantilist he recommended governmental measures to promote them. Agriculture was for him the most important and most basic economic activity, but he also showed Botero's enthusiasm for industry and trade. He expanded agriculture to include herding, fishing, and salt mining along with farming, all activities that drew products from land or sea. He favored small, privately owned plots of land, stressing the importance to the state of a productive and contented peasantry and the incentive given them by ownership of their own land. The government should annually inspect farms, awarding prizes to the most enterprising producers and determining penalties for the negligent. Reclamation projects were in order, to bring more land under cultivation, and protection was to be provided the peasants against the depredations of nobles and soldiers. Contzen made the interesting suggestion that the peasants have their own village courts, under princely oversight, and not be required to travel to cities for justice—did not merchants have their own courts?[61] As for mining, Contzen was confident that the Germans had not yet exhausted their mineral deposits, and he called for renewed prospecting. His comments showed considerable knowledge of the metallurgical map of Germany.[62]

But if agriculture was the most fundamental form of economic activity, industry and trade were the most profitable. Contzen sought to counter prevailing social attitudes. He rejected the view that mercantile activity was somehow tainted, and he lauded the contribution of merchants to the wealth, and thus to the power, of the state. The unfortunate lack of status enjoyed by artisans and craftsmen he traced back to the ancient Greeks. A partial remedy for the situation, Contzen suggested unrealistically, was for the nobility to take up the industrial arts, so demonstrating his antipathy toward the nobility. They should also be encouraged to take up business activity. Contzen also considered the influx of gold and silver into the Iberian Peninsula to have been unhealthy and artificial and to have resulted only in higher prices.

His models for successful economic activity were Venice, Florence, and Nuremberg. Germany already surpassed all other countries, he noted, in the size and number of its cities. This development should be ardently fostered, since populous cities, which were centers of trade and industry, contributed greatly to the power of a state. He suggested a number of German cities with potential for growth, including Coblenz and Mainz, and he looked across the border at the flourishing wool trade in the Netherlands and argued that the Germans could do the same if they took advantage of the opportunities at hand. As it was, they bought too many foreign goods, with consequent losses to their own economy. A state ought not import foreign goods superior to its own without taxing them. The 1629 edition of the *Ten Books* called for the establishment of trading companies (*collegia*), in imitation of the highly successful Dutch ventures with which Contzen had become familiar, perhaps through reading in Scribani's *Christian Politician* about Dutch commercial prowess.[63]

A puritan streak ran through Contzen. He was an advocate of contemporary sumptuary laws, which also exemplified the efforts to impose discipline upon the population. He praised the sumptuary legislation issued in 1615 by the archbishop-elector of Mainz, which regulated in detail, for example, what might be served at a wedding or baptismal feast. But his rationale was different from that of Machiavelli or Botero, both of whom warned of luxury and ease that undermined devotion to the state and had helped topple the mighty empire of Rome. Contzen was more concerned with economics. Prodigal spending dissipated the state's wealth, impoverished people, and hindered, we would say today, capital formation.

Like the Calvinists, he associated wealth with frugality of life. "The peasant, the citizen, the tailor, the carpenter complain that they are not able to rise [economically] because of the difficulty of the times. Yet the same persons dress like nobles, eat like rich men, build like princes, raise their families like magistrates, and never realize that their way of life is the source of their poverty." Part of the problem was competition in the display of wealth. Contzen even suggested the sale of special privileges, for example, to wear a ring, and so was an early advocate of luxury taxes.[64] Rather than encouraging the prince to construct magnificent edifices to impress the people, Contzen was hostile to such projects, and he criticized the Romans for their construction of such useless structures as triumphal arches. Nor did he see a need for such undertakings to provide work for growing urban populations, as had Botero.[65]

But everyone should have useful work, even the nobility. There should be no begging. This was an ambitious goal at a time when beggars and vagabonds constituted up to 25 percent of the population in Catholic territories in Germany.[66] Yet if rulers exploited all the opportunities at hand, he contended, there would be plenty of work, and there would be funds left over to support those who really were unable to work. Look what the Flemings did with their wool industry. There would always be some people who simply could not make their way economically themselves or who refused to work. Both sorts should be put to work at forms of forced labor in mines or on construction projects.[67]

Contzen was no more a militarist than was Lipsius. There was no greater evil than war. He deplored a culture in which more honor was given to soldiers for killing people than for saving their lives. Common to all wars, including just ones, was the collapse of discipline, the breakdown of morals, and the flourishing of vice. War turned human beings into beasts, the extreme tension of combat leading to release in violent excesses. War impoverished states and often provoked domestic political crises, bringing ruin to victors as well as vanquished. Those who were eager or enthusiastic for war were so only because they knew no other way of life.[68]

But evil as war was, given the human condition, it was permitted, and was, in fact, inevitable. For this reason a vigorous, well-trained army was essential to the material power of a state. Contzen rejected out of hand the position that "a leader in war cannot be just."[69] With his customary vigor of expression, he branded pacifists as heretics and traitors, and he elaborated Scripture passages to prove his point. In the Gospel neither Christ nor Peter had voided the military oaths of the centurions. Following Augustine, he explained that the Sermon on the Mount did not prohibit resistance to an enemy but the motivation of that resistance by hatred, anger, or revenge. A prince who had been attacked should maintain an attitude of benevolence toward a foe, much like a father toward a disobedient child. In the 1629 edition of the *Ten Books* Contzen, perhaps enriched by experience, argued that neither the diadem nor the scepter protected the kingdom, only the sword. An unarmed scepter just invited trouble. "Here I boldly pronounce: he who desires peace, let him prepare for war."[70]

Contzen's treatment of the just war was generally traditional, though with peculiar nuances. He prohibited the intervention of one state in the affairs of another more strictly than most Scholastics. Required for a just war were the normal conditions: declaration by legitimate authority, a just cause, right intention, and reasonable certainty of success. A sovereign state was the judge in its own case, since there existed no higher authority to which it was subordinate. Contzen made no mention of possible papal mediation, avoiding a discussion of the indirect power of the pope in temporal affairs.[71] He had no sympathy for a prince's ambition for military glory, and there was no effort in the *Ten Books* to accommodate either this desire or the tactic of distracting or uniting subjects by a foreign military venture. A ruler ought not to be on the lookout for an opportunity to go to war. Even in a just cause he ought to take up arms with sorrow. One state might not intervene in the affairs of another to protect a religious minority, since this infringed upon sovereignty; in Germany to do so would have violated the Peace of

Augsburg, though Contzen did not mention this. Nor would Contzen allow that the conquest and projected betterment of an allegedly inferior people justified war against it. Who was and who was not a barbarian was a highly subjective judgment, and opinions varied widely over time. The Romans themselves were once barbarians, then the Spanish, French, and Germans; now the Asians and Africans were thought to be such. Oddly, Contzen did not note the Indians of America at this point.[72]

In a portentous clause, however, Contzen qualified his prohibition of intervention and raised the possibility of a holy war. For him war was normally not a suitable way to advance the cause of religion. But he did affirm that war could be declared "at the express command and order of God."[73] In such a case intervention fit the definition of a holy war. Contzen the biblical scholar made this point, it seems, in order to accommodate into his theory the instances when the Hebrew kings had taken up arms at the behest of God, and he cited an example of this. His allowance for a holy war in the fashion of the Old Testament and his providentialist pragmatism combined later to influence the course of the Thirty Years' War.

Like Lipsius, Contzen favored an army of career soldiers, but unlike Lipsius and Botero, he had nothing to say about militias or reservists in support of regular armies, perhaps reflecting their recent ineffectiveness and certainly anticipating the practice during the Thirty Years' War where their part was insignificant. Attractive as it was in theory, in reality the citizen army of Machiavelli was unworkable. The suddenness and length of modern war required a standing army. It was to be composed of volunteers; only those who wanted to serve would make good soldiers, Contzen noted with insight. Native troops were preferable for two reasons; their loyalty was greater and, significantly, their salaries remained within the country. If a prince wanted a steady stream of recruits, he would have to see that the military enjoyed status and honor and that veterans received proper care.

But Contzen was realistic enough to see that a ruler could not expect enough volunteers from his own country, so that he would have to include foreigners in his army. The principle of voluntary service took priority over the desire for a completely native army, which Contzen also feared more than Botero or Lipsius because of the political dangers armed subjects could pose for a prince. Thus he approved of the multinational armies of the day. Foreign troops were particularly useful in the event of rebellions, and at the time Contzen wrote, Emperor Ferdinand II was quelling the uprising in his lands only with their help. Discipline and order were to be instilled by a severe regime of training. Contzen was inclined to differ with Lipsius in that he felt modern armies were superior to ancient ones. One major modern deficiency was that no effective shield had yet been devised against the bullet: "So much the more ingenious was man's mind in harming rather than helping others."[74]

Another feature of the early modern state, an organized bureaucracy, received much more extensive treatment from Contzen than from previous anti-Machiavellians, even though the increasing role they assigned to government implied a growing number of officials. Botero and Ribadeneira, under the heading of prudence, had insisted on the prince's need for counsel and assistance. Lipsius's brief chapter on prudence from others had distinguished between councillors (*consiliarii*) and assistants (*administri*), of which the latter comprised both public officials and attendants at court, and he elaborated the qualities of both.[75] His student Chokier, in turn, maintained this distinction and allotted nearly a third of his volume to princely officials. But none of them was as thorough, or sometimes as confusing, as Contzen. It was often difficult to determine in this context when he was prescribing or when he was merely describing ancient or current practices.

There was a certain contradiction between Contzen's advocacy of absolute government and a main theme of his teaching on bureaucracy, the division of power. His thought fit almost perfectly the mentality and style of Maximilian of Bavaria. Contzen's argument for absolute government was based largely on the need for vigorous and effective authority to bring order to the chaotic political and religious situation. He insisted that the prince govern personally and oversee the regular operation of government to the extent possible. Above all, he was to retain close control of finances in his own hand. Yet Contzen was highly pessimistic about human nature. "The avid desire for status and power has no end nor limit, no one suffers to be placed under another except by force of necessity. Only man can neither govern himself nor bear that another govern him."[76] Hence a ruling prince had to distribute power and responsibility in such a way that it was never concentrated in one person. Moreover each official in the bureaucratic structure must report to and be carefully checked either by the prince or another official. There was a check on everyone but the prince himself.

Contzen's treatment of civil administration was filled, or better, cluttered, with extended digressions and historical examples, especially from the Roman Empire. But the main lines stood out. The highest obligation of the prince was to select competent and honest subordinates, who were in effect his "eyes, hands, feet, and other living organs," Contzen added in the 1629 edition of the *Ten Books*.[77] At the head of government, just beneath the prince, there was to be a council or a number of councils whose function was to assist him directly in the government. The office of councillor, or senator as Contzen called it, was distinct from offices associated with the ruler's person, but often in current practice the two types of office were held by the same person. For purposes of efficiency Contzen did recommend the designation of one chief minister who would mediate, to a degree, between the ruler and the council, but he imposed limits on his authority by denying him, for example, any power over the military. At the level of administration, then, in the interest of avoiding excessive power and of providing checks, there were to be three hierarchies of officials, the executive officers or governors, the judges, and the financial officers.[78]

Contzen laid out a program by which younger men could serve a form of apprenticeship and undergo a gradual introduction into government, for example, by attending occasional council sessions or participating in embassies. He recommended, as had Machiavelli, that officials always have the opportunity to rise higher in the bureaucracy on the basis of merit. The obverse of this was that they be ready to serve in a lesser capacity after leaving a higher post. Otherwise those with experience would be lost to public service. Contzen criticized the Roman practice, approved by Machiavelli, of frequent, even annual transfer of officials. This hindered continuity in administration and prevented officials from knowing the people with whom they were dealing. On the other hand, an excessively long tenure in office could result in the formation of an independent power base; this was to be forestalled.[79]

Law and education were for the Counter-Reformer Contzen powerful means to direct citizens or subjects to virtue, and their virtue was both the goal of the state and the source of its power. So the good and the useful overlapped. The purpose of law was to make the citizens happy (*felices*) by making them virtuous and in so doing to promote the common good. "Therefore, there is no virtue acts of which cannot in some way be commanded by law; the civil law can also forbid all sins" that are external actions, not, however, thoughts and desires, which lie outside its ken. Contzen went out of his way to insist that the making of good men, not merely good citizens, was the function of law. So he attributed more responsibility to the state than did Suarez or the Scholastic tradition generally.[80] In particular law was to coerce those who did not act virtuously on their own. Contzen favored the regulation of many areas of life by law, and he laid the basis in his chapters on law for his support elsewhere of sumptuary legislation. Moreover, these laws bound in conscience; there were no merely penal laws. Yet Contzen was well aware of the limitations of law, and he reminded his readers that it must be accommodated to the circumstances and the capacity of the population. He cited a recent law of Louis XIII in France restricting the sale of offices. If France was not yet ready for such a measure, its reversal would be harmful to the status of the law. Better to show more prudence in issuing a law in the first place.[81]

Contzen ascribed to the state a great deal of authority over education. "It is necessary that the prince care for the formation of young men in morality." A mistrust of parents ran through his discussion of education, and the church itself played a secondary role. He even suggested that those with illnesses like epilepsy or leprosy might be forbidden to marry because of the burden their children might cause the state.[82] Contzen was thorough. He began his treatment of education with the proper nurture of infants, including the merits of breast-feeding, and he finished with problems of university organization. When writing of the population as a whole, his emphasis was on moral education. Those destined to study the arts and sciences—they were all young men, for Contzen had little to say about women's education—were to be chosen carefully, according to criteria of talent and moral character, not of birth or status.[83] Contzen's appreciation of the importance of social attitudes came through again in his stipulation that teachers, like soldiers, were to be accorded honor and status as well as generous salaries. He showed a special interest in Jesuit colleges, and he printed extensive passages of rules for students from the *Plan of Studies* (*Ratio Studiorum*).[84]

A main feature of the *Ten Books* is providentialist pragmatism, to which I alluded earlier. Contzen vigorously attacked Machiavelli's denial of Christian providence, devoting nearly a third of book 1 to the task. But there was in the *Ten Books* little of the wrestling with the mystery of providence that characterized Lipsius's and Ribadeneira's works. Contzen contended near the start of book 1 that God punished the evil ruler and rewarded the good one not only in the next world but in this one too. "The greater part of the punishments are reserved for the future [life]; yet meanwhile so many temporal evils precede those eternal ills, that no one can doubt that it is God who governs mortal things, judges, rewards the good, punishes the impious."[85] Without categorically stating that God inevitably saw to the suitable recompense of the virtuous and the malicious ruler in this world as well as the next, Contzen came closer to doing so than any other anti-Machiavellian. "Examples show that the good prosper whereas the impious meet an unhappy end" read a chapter title in book 2, where the examples came from the Old Testament and especially, via Bozio's *On the Fall of Peoples and Kingdoms*, from the history of the Roman Empire.[86] They indicated that Contzen had in mind a positive divine intervention in history.

We have already noted that, on the basis of his understanding of the Old Testament, in his discussion of the just war Contzen allowed for a divine summons to take up arms in the cause of religion. The victory of Ferdinand at the White Mountain he interpreted as a reward for the emperor's piety, a remark that was not merely rhetorical. Contzen did not completely lose sight of the biblical truth that the good Christian would inevitably encounter adversity in the world—indeed, he expressly alluded to it in the *Mirror of the Court*[87]—but in his anti-Machiavellian zeal he came close to doing so. Contzen's providentialist pragmatism contributed to a disaster for himself, Maximilian, and the forces of the Counter-Reformation, and it in turn provoked a change in attitudes about providence.

The publication of the *Ten Books* in 1621 led eventually to Contzen's summons to Munich in 1623 to serve as confessor to Maximilian of Bavaria, newly raised to the dignity of an imperial elector. The volume had impressed Maximilian, who kept a personal copy in his own private quarters in his residence.[88] He and Contzen shared the conviction that government was an esteemed Christian vocation—the most important of human works, as Contzen wrote on the first page of the *Ten Books*'s dedication. Maximilian, for his part, was a deeply religious person. At the same time, as a Renaissance prince he was possessed of a vigorous determination to be an effective ruler and to secure recognition as such. In the ten years following his accession in 1598, he had reformed its chaotic finances and turned Bavaria into the best-administered and most powerful territory in the empire.[89] Now he had fulfilled the long-standing Bavarian ambition to be received into the empire's electoral college. His need was to reconcile his desire for a life of piety with his pursuit of political achievement. His father, Duke William, had apparently failed to achieve this integration, having abdicated in favor of his son, allegedly so that he might lead a life of retirement and devotion.[90] Maximilian found in Contzen a priest well acquainted with the realistic demands of politics who could help him reconcile them with those of religion. This was precisely the anti-Machiavellian intent.

Many of Contzen's ideas on government and politics were obviously congenial to Maximilian. They shared the belief in the need for the unity of the state in the Catholic religion and an aversion to the Calvinists as the source of disruption in the empire. Most of Contzen's polemics had been directed against the Calvinists of Heidelberg, the university of

Maximilian's rival for the electoral title, his cousin, Frederick V. Contzen ascribed to the prince considerable control over religion in the state and so endorsed Maximilian's practice. The elector undoubtedly welcomed Contzen's form of absolutism. He was in the process of vastly curtailing the power of the Bavarian estates without completely eliminating them. During the war, with Contzen at his side, he firmly established his right to levy taxes without their consent, while leaving to them the major role in tax collection, positions advocated by Contzen.

Both Maximilian and his confessor felt that princely government should be highly personal. Both saw as crucial for a powerful state the accumulation of princely treasure. Contzen recommended that the prince himself keep a jealous watch over his *aerarium*. This was one of Maximilian's arcana. As he wrote to his cousin, Queen Margaret of Spain, through her confessor in 1611, the secret of his financial success was his own personal management of his treasury. "Under the eye of the master the steed grows strong."[91] The Law for Morality and Religion and the Code of Maximilian of 1616 had brought to Bavaria the type of detailed, regulative legislation advocated by Contzen. Whether Maximilian ever understood the bond between sound government finance and a broad tax base and the consequent need for a policy of economic development is not clear. There were new efforts after Contzen's arrival in Munich to foster trade and industry, for example, in the reorganization of the Council of Commerce in 1626. But these initiatives were victims of the war.[92]

Thus it was not surprising that Contzen enjoyed considerable influence as Maximilian's confessor. To be sure, their dealings in the confessional itself were closed to view, but Contzen, while not attending privy council meetings, served in effect as a minister with special competence for moral and religious issues. When he arrived in Munich in early 1624, events seemed to have borne out Maximilian's device, "The Lord of Hosts is with us [*Dominus virtutum nobiscum*]," and confirmed that religious duty and political utility coincided. He had taken the initiative in 1609 in organizing the Catholic League to defend Catholic interests in the Empire, and the league was instrumental in the defeat of the Bohemian rebels at the White Mountain in 1620. For this Emperor Ferdinand rewarded his older cousin Maximilian with the electoral title formerly held by the unfortunate Frederick of the Palatinate, who had unwisely accepted the Bohemian Crown from the rebels. During the 1620s, as the war spread, the fortunes of Ferdinand, Maximilian and the Catholic party improved steadily. By the winter of 1627–28 they dominated the Empire.

At this point there developed among the Catholics a split between militants and moderates. Under the influence of thinking like Contzen's, the militants discerned the finger of God in the Catholic victories. The Lord was calling them to reverse what the Catholics considered the illegal gains made by the Protestants since the Peace of Augsburg and to restore the politico-religious status of 1555. He was summoning to a holy war. The moderates wanted a peace settlement that would consolidate Catholic gains even at the expense of concessions to the Protestants. The continuation of the war only endangered the gains already made and multiplied the people's suffering. The two parties joined issue expressly on the role of providence in history. The moderates accused the militants, correctly, of claiming implicitly to possess a divine revelation for the guidance of Catholic policy. What was the basis for this claim, they asked. In the Old Testament, to be sure, God had promised victories to his people, but there was no evidence for such a promise in the current situation.[93]

The militants won the struggle, and the result was the fatal Edict of Restitution, issued by Emperor Ferdinand in 1629 at the urging of Maximilian and the other Catholic electors. It decreed the return to the Catholics of all the ecclesiastical lands seized by the Protestants since 1555, a measure that was perhaps legally correct but indefensible politically. Contzen's influence was a major factor in Maximilian's support for the edict at the time of its promulgation and of its strict maintenance at the Electoral Convention of Regensburg in 1630, when moderates at the Catholic courts argued for compromise. Contzen assured Maximilian that God would more than offset the hostility that an aggressive Catholic policy would incite among hitherto moderate Protestant rulers, and this confidence along with the belief that the Catholics were called to exploit an opportunity (*occasio*) offered them by God's providence appeared in Maximilian's initial endorsement of the edict sent to the elector of Mainz in late 1627.[94] In a memorandum written for Regensburg, Contzen exhorted the Catholics to firmness with the example of Old Testament heroes. "In a cause as holy as was that of the Maccabees," he wrote, "it behooves us to hope for a favorable outcome of the war rather than to yield our bodies and souls to the heretics and to endanger posterity too."[95]

Within a year of the end of the meeting at Regensburg, Gustavus Adolphus trounced the Catholic forces at Breitenfeld and so reversed the whole course of the war. The months following marked the nadir of Maximilian's reign, as Gustavus's troops ravaged Bavaria and in May 1632 entered Munich. In a lengthy piece entitled "A Consideration about the Persecution of the Church of Christ throughout Germany," Contzen confronted the reversal of fortune at Breitenfeld and the issues raised by it much as had Ribadeneira the defeat of the Armada in his *Treatise on Tribulation*. His "Consideration" remained in manuscript because the Jesuit censors refused to allow its publication on account of its scathing criticism of the clergy. It was not the literary masterpiece that Ribadeneira's *Treatise* had been, nor did it breathe Ribadeneira's Neostoic acceptance of defeat. Suffering was a part of the Christian life, Contzen recognized, it served as a test of faith, a means of detachment from the world, and reparation for sin. Their sins were the reason for the Catholic defeat, especially the sins of the clergy, whom Contzen excoriated, and he rejected out of hand the argument that the Protestant victory showed that God favored their side. Rather, the Lord punished the Catholics as his dear children; the Protestants he cast off as apostates. Contzen encouraged the continuation of the struggle while calling all to penance and reform of life. God permitted the defeat of a just cause only temporarily, and of the justice of the Catholic cause there could be no doubt.[96]

The Catholic victory at Nördlingen in 1634 reestablished a balance between the Catholic and Protestant forces in the empire, and at the Peace of Prague in 1635 Ferdinand and Maximilian gave up the militant program of restoration, thus preparing the way for the Peace of Westphalia in 1648. Contzen died in 1635, having been replaced as Maximilian's confessor by Johannes Vervaux, a Jesuit from Lorraine, who belonged to the moderate party. Vervaux was the author of Maximilian's foremost political testament, the *Paternal Advice* (*Monita Paterna*), written in 1639 and first published in Vervaux's *Annals of the Bavarian People* in 1662.[97] This testament was the Wittelsbach anti-Machiavellian manifesto, whether it was first meant as a private document for Maximilian's new-born heir or from the start as a public statement intended to enhance the reputation of the House. The author made use of Lipsius's marvelous aphoristic expressions, but Contzen's influence was predominant, with one exception. There was not a word of providentialist pragmatism in it. The prince was persistently reminded that reward or punishment would follow in the next life according to his deeds in the present one. Absent was the conviction that God directed human affairs toward the success of the just prince who championed his cause. Vervaux and Maximilian had repudiated Contzen's version of providentialism, a fact later confirmed by Maximilian's own statement and Vervaux's condemnation of the militant theology, without mention of Contzen by name, in the *Annals*.[98]

Contzen's militancy in his promotion of the Catholic restoration in Germany should not close our eyes to the value and influence of his political thought in the seventeenth century. Contemporaries, including such Protestants as Marcus Friedrich Wendelin in his *Three Books of Instructions on Politics* (Frankfurt, 1637) and later Rudolfus Godofredus Knichen in his *The Work of Politics in Three Books* (Frankfurt, 1682) saw in him the confuter of Machiavelli.[99] The Protestant author Johann Angelius Werdenhagen in his *General Politics* (Amsterdam, 1632) preferred Contzen to Bodin or Althusius.[100] Contzen set forth in a systematic if eclectic and occasionally confusing fashion a comprehensive program for the Catholic, absolutist state of the Counter-Reformation. No Jesuit or Catholic thinker had produced anything similar in scope. The volume fit the Counter-Reformation, and Reformation, emphasis on close cooperation of church and state in the formation of a virtuous, disciplined population. Contzen made a convincing argument for the compatibility of Christian morality with effective politics. His argument on the basis of intrinsic pragmatism was forceful. He recognized the need for power in a state and pointed out effective, moral methods for its acquisition and maintenance. In particular he stood out as an early mercantilist. Not as a political theorist but as a teacher of state building Contzen rated a high place among those Catholic writers who sought to fit the early modern state into the larger Christian vision of the world.

Contzen's influence reached to the limits of Catholic Europe, but it was felt most strongly in central Europe. It acted principally upon three social groups: Catholic clergy and religious, especially Jesuits, among whom were many teachers and preachers; the Catholic nobility, especially in the Austrian lands and south Germany; and scholars and university professors, Protestant as well as Catholic.[101] Several works appeared that were in effect condensations of Contzen, the chief being Stephen Menochius's *Sacred Politics or Political Instructions drawn from the Holy Scriptures*, first published at Lyon in 1625 and followed by two further editions by 1629.[102] Many authors borrowed heavily from him, for instance, the Louvain professor and student of Lipsius Nicolas Vernulaeus (Vernulz), who issued his *Political Instructions* in the first of many editions at Louvain in 1623 and followed this with other works, which in turn were well received at the courts of Vienna and Munich.[103] In faraway Spain, the Jesuit anti-Machiavellian Claudio Clemente named Contzen in 1637 along with Ribadeneira and Mariana as the most important contemporary representatives of the Christian teaching on the state.[104] Certainly he deserves a place of honor in the anti-Machiavellian tradition.

Chapter 7

Carlo Scribani: The Flemish-Hispanic Connection (1624)

The title page of Carlo Scribani's *Christian Politician* (Antwerp, 1624),[1] created by Rubens, proclaimed the anti-Machiavellian theme. To the left of the central cartouche, which was inscribed with the title and the dedication to Philip IV of Spain, stood a female figure representing Christian Politics. She held in one hand a scepter and in the other a rudder, emblems of strong and prudent government. The halo about her head and the eagle of Jupiter grasping thunderbolts at her feet indicated the divine as well as the powerful character of her rule. To the right stood her counterpart, the female figure of Abundance, with her cornucopia nestled close to her. An angel breathed on her face and another shackled her foot, showing the divine favor she enjoyed and her bond with the Christian ruler (see Ill. 6).[2] So Christian politics and abundance or prosperity were joined.

Yet the *Christian Politician* bore distinctive traits. Scribani devoted even less attention to issues of political philosophy than other anti-Machiavellians. Nor did he present a comprehensive plan for a Catholic state as Contzen had. His volume was less systematically constructed than the others, amounting almost to a collection of essays in a manner reminiscent of Montaigne and anticipative of Saavedra, a format making it easier to accommodate inconsistency and ambivalence without breaking the fundamental anti-Machiavellian mold. He had gathered more direct experience of the court prior to writing than had earlier anti-Machiavellians—Botero and certainly Contzen acquiring more after the publication of their volumes—and this showed perhaps in the *Christian Politician*. He was less sanguine about the correlation of the good with the useful. A Christian could be a successful *politicus*, that was his thesis as the book's title showed, but it was a struggle.

More than other anti-Machiavellian works the *Christian Politician* was a decided attempt to influence policy with specific proposals. Scribani dedicated it to the novice King Philip IV of Spain, whose accession to the throne in 1621 had generated an outpouring of reform proposals from the *arbitristas* intended to reinvigorate the faltering Spanish monarchy. That same year Archduke Albert died, who since 1598 had been coruler of the Netherlands with his wife Isabella, and the Twelve Years' Truce between Spain and the Dutch Republic was allowed to lapse. Since 1609 it had fostered a modest prosperity in the southern Netherlands loyal to Spain and a flourishing cultural life centered around the court of Brussels.[3] But now the seemingly interminable civil war broke out anew and interlocked with the conflict in Germany. At this important juncture in the history of Spain and its relationship to the Netherlands, the *Christian Politician*, which was being written in 1621, was meant to convey proposals for reform to the young king and to make recommendations for Spanish policy toward Scribani's own Netherlands. The war there had become for Madrid the central issue that any effective reform program would have to address. Thus the *Christian Politician* must also be seen as a Flemish contribution to the *arbitrista* literature at the start of Philip's reign.[4]

Carlo Scribani always identified himself as a Netherlander.[5] He was born at Brussels on November 21, 1561, the child of Hector Scribani, an Italian nobleman who had accompanied Margaret of Parma to the Netherlands in 1559, and Maria van der Beke, daughter of a wealthy patrician of Ghent. By 1579 he was a student at the Jesuit college in Cologne, where many Catholics of the Netherlands sent their sons after the outbreak of the civil war and where he preceded Adam Contzen by several years. He entered the Jesuits at Cologne in 1582 and was ordained a priest in 1590 by his uncle, Laevinus Torrentius (or Lieven van der Beke), bishop of Antwerp, a humanist ecclesiastic whom we have met as a correspondent of Lipsius.[6]

Nearly all his life as a Jesuit Scribani held major administrative positions within the order, first in Antwerp, then in Brussels. Two volumes he published in 1610, *Antwerpia* and *Origins of Antwerp*, manifested his affection for the city. Journeys to Rome on business of the Society in 1611 and 1615 enabled him to make the acquaintance of leading ecclesiastical figures, including Maffeo Cardinal Barberini, to become Pope Urban VIII in 1623, the dedicatee of Scribani's *The Prodigal Adolescent* (Antwerp, 1621) and *The Suffering Christ* (Antwerp, 1629).[7] In 1619 Scribani moved to Brussels, the seat of the court and a center of European diplomacy, to serve as rector of the college there, returning to Antwerp however to conclude the negotiations with Rubens over the ceiling paintings for the magnificent new Jesuit church.[8] It was during this period in Brussels that he wrote the *Christian Politician*. After his term as rector, Scribani retired to Antwerp in 1625, free from administrative cares. There, after a long period of illness and growing disenchantment with Spanish policy, he died on June 24, 1629.[9]

A prolific writer, Scribani published nineteen books, most in Latin but several in Flemish. This was an amazing feat when one considers his administrative responsibilities. Undoubtedly he possessed a great capacity for work; he himself tells us that he stole time from the night in order to write.[10] His publications fell into four categories. The volumes about Antwerp have been mentioned. Then there were his polemical works, the most significant of which was *Honor's Amphitheater*, published anonymously in 1605 as a response to charges of the French Calvinists against the Jesuits. For this he received a letter of naturalization from Henry IV of France, a distinction of which he was to remind French critics who twenty years later accused him of anti-French bias.[11] To this category as well belonged his *Posthumous Defense of Justus Lipsius* (Antwerp, 1607), written at the request of Lipsius himself, to defend him against Calvinist attacks following his return to the Catholic church. While admitting that Lipsius had not been constant in his practice of the Catholic faith, Scribani argued that he had always been Catholic at heart and that his return to Catholicism had been genuine.[12] Scribani's devotional books and books on the religious life constituted a third type of publication. Among these were the *Divine Love* (Antwerp, 1615) and *The Religious Physician: On the Illnesses and Cures for Souls* (Antwerp, 1618), which subsequently was translated into Spanish by the well-known ascetical writer, Louis de la Palma.[13]

Scribani's explicitly political works made up the final category of his publications. In addition to the *Christian Politician*, these included two much shorter propaganda pieces, *The Truthful Belgian: The Beginnings, Progress, and Desired End of the Civil War among the Belgians* (Antwerp, n.d.) and *The Reformed Batavian Apocalypsis* (Antwerp, n.d.), both published anonymously in Latin and Flemish probably right after the appearance of the *Christian Politician* and followed by several editions.[14] Aimed at different audiences in the Netherlands, they too sought to influence the course of events. *The Truthful Belgian* gathered together Scribani's ideas about the Dutch War, which were scattered throughout the *Christian Politician*, and often expressed them in the same words.[15] Scribani described poignantly the suffering the Flemings had undergone as a result of the seemingly unending war and the dashed hopes for peace after the lapse of the truce. Criticism of Spanish policy was harsher than in the *Christian Politician*, certainly because of the latter's dedication to Philip IV and its broader audience. The duke of Alba came in for special strictures, because Scribani felt he had treated the freedom-loving Netherlanders as slaves and had made little effort to understand their mentality.[16]

The Batavian Apocalypse was directed to a Dutch audience and was subsequently prohibited in the United Provinces. It was couched in the form of a letter from a Dutch Calvinist to a friend extolling the Dutch achievement of empire but lamenting the lack of religious freedom and the increasing power of Maurice of Nassau, who dominated the territory more thoroughly than any earlier ruler ever had.[17]

Scribani's attitude toward the war was typical of those Netherlanders who remained loyal to Spain. Three elements characterized it. First, there was attachment to the Catholic religion. Scribani saw in heresy stemming from Germany and France the source of the Netherlands' woes. The war was for him primarily a religious one, to protect the Catholic church from Calvinist attack. Second, there came loyalty to the Spanish Habsburg crown, which constituted the legitimate government in continuity with the Burgundian rulers. Archduke Albert and Archduchess Isabella had governed jointly from 1598 until Albert's death in 1621, winning a great deal of popular support. Indeed, Albert was idealized and eulogized throughout the *Christian Politician* as the perfect Christian ruler—Scribani had prepared eighteen inscriptions for the archduke's tomb at Isabella's request[18]—and Isabella retained considerable popularity until her death in 1633.[19] Moreover, the Habsburgs had shown themselves to be the champions of the Catholic cause in Europe. But Scribani's loyalty did not keep him from criticizing their policies.

The last element determining his attitude toward the war was his love of the Netherlands. Scribani was a patriot, loyal to the Burgundian and Habsburg tradition of all seventeen provinces. He was proud, in a way, of the manner in which the Dutch had held their own against the mightiest king on earth for over sixty years, and he admired their love of freedom. Religion remained the point of difference. Scribani had hoped that the truce would lead to a permanent peace. Once the war was renewed, he urged Spain to make all the efforts necessary for a victory that would reunite all the provinces, a victory to which he still looked at the time of his death in 1629.[20]

Scribani undoubtedly played a part in the political events of his day, even though sparse sources make difficult the determination of its precise nature. This was only to be expected from a man of his contacts and vigorous personality holding the responsible positions he did in a state where the rulers were as fully committed to the Counter-Reformation and as well-disposed to the Jesuits as were Albert and Isabella.[21] In 1619, the year of his move from Antwerp to Brussels, he assisted in mediating disputes between dissident factions and the government in both cities.[22] A letter of 1626 referred poignantly to four friends from his earlier days in Antwerp, now deceased, all of whom had held important municipal or provincial offices.[23] For at least ten years, dating back to 1617, Scribani served as a contact and conduit of funds for Spanish agents and spies, especially the Portuguese Manuel Sueyro, operating in Flanders and in the Dutch Republic.[24] This arrangement enabled Madrid to bypass the government of Albert and Isabella, which it did not always trust, and may have initially given Scribani entrée to the count-duke of Olivares.

After his transfer in 1619 to the residential city of Brussels his political influence probably increased. The archdukes had long looked to him for counsel in matters of conscience and worship, and other major figures from far and near sought his advice: Maximilian of Bavaria; Wolfgang William, duke of Palatinate-Neuburg; Peter Aloysius Carafa, the nuncio in Cologne; Cardinal Cueva, marquis of Bedmar and Spanish ambassador in the Netherlands; and certainly not least of all, Olivares himself, with whom he carried on at least a sporadic correspondence between 1624 and 1627, years following the publication of the *Christian Politician*.[25]

Scribani's contacts bridged both sides of the Flemish-Spanish relationship. As their surviving correspondence attests, he was a close friend of Peter Peckius, chancellor of Brabant from 1616 until his death in 1625. Peckius was given increased responsibility by Albert in the archduke's last years and employed frequently for diplomatic missions, including the last-minute attempt to negotiate an extension of the truce with the Dutch in 1621.[26] The outstanding general Ambrogio Spinola, in effect the first minister of the archdukes from 1602 to 1627,[27] visited Scribani regularly even when he was still in Antwerp. Both Peckius and Spinola were the source of policy recommendations made by Scribani in the *Christian Politician*, and Spinola almost certainly is the "great man" referred to several times in the context of these proposals.[28] Both were lauded by Scribani in the *Christian Politician*, and in 1624 they undertook efforts to secure the cardinalate for him, which, however, he discouraged.[29] Another of Scribani's likely contacts and possibly one of the other sources referred to anonymously in the *Christian Politician* was Diego Mexía, who was made first marquis of Leganés by his cousin and patron Olivares in 1627. He had long served in the Netherlands prior to his return to Spain at the accession of Philip IV in 1621. After Olivares sent him back to the Netherlands in 1627, to implement the Union of Arms there, a plan in which Scribani had a part as we shall see, he played an increasingly important role in the administration. Sometime in 1627

Leganés, in the name of Olivares and accompanied by Spinola, visited Scribani on his sickbed in Antwerp.[30] A connection with Leganés would further help explain Scribani's contact with Olivares.

Clearly, the *Christian Politician* was Scribani's most important work. A laudatory reference in the dedication to the Spanish statesman Baltasar de Zúñiga, uncle of Olivares and architect of the new regime, who had died in Spain on October 7, 1622, and ecclesiastical approvals for publication dated May 11 and 20, 1623, indicate that the book was completed in late 1622 or early 1623. Thus Scribani was certainly at work on it during the crucial year, 1621. He must have determined at this critical moment to put his views before the new king and the count-duke, who also received accolades in the dedication. Support for the war was flagging in the Spanish Netherlands, and Scribani himself had been disappointed at the failure to renew the truce.[31] Perhaps he had earlier begun a general anti-Machiavellian work and only at this time intro-duced his specific proposals. As he told Philip IV in the dedication itself, he dedicated the book to the king at the urging of his friend Peckius and of Cardinal Cueva. Both apparently agreed with the positions espoused by Scribani, who saw himself speaking for all loyal Netherlanders.

Scribani dispatched copies of the *Christian Politician* to both Philip IV and Olivares, as well as to a number of rulers and dignitaries. The king himself, for reasons that will become clear, indicated through Olivares that while he considered the book a masterpiece, he would have preferred that Scribani had served him as a private councillor and not published his advice for all the world to read, and Olivares himself com-plained that no personal letter had accompanied the copy he received.[32] Perhaps Scribani figured that only through such a book could he get the ear of the king and his minister in Madrid. Subsequently, in a letter of late 1626 or early 1627 to the count-duke, Scribani reiterated in concise fashion proposals for Spanish policy in the Netherlands found through-out the *Christian Politician.*[33] The extent to which he may have actually influenced Spanish action is nearly impossible to determine. He did ad-vocate strongly the general direction of Olivares's policy toward greater unification of the Spanish monarchy and vigorous prosecution of the war in the Netherlands, and if he did not cause the initiation of new policies, he may well have confirmed Madrid in them.

In the dedication, Scribani besought the king to persevere in his efforts for victory and a just peace in the Netherlands, and he exhorted him to confidence in God. "It is for other kings to give themselves to the hunt of animals and birds, but for the Spanish [king] to hunt new worlds for God and glory," he continued in a passage that irked Paris, where

Louis XIII's penchant for the chase was well known,[34] and perhaps hinted that the youthful Philip moderate his well-known lust for the hunt. He urged him to be mindful of "the most blessed Belgian provinces which he had received from his courageous [forebears] Maximilian, Charles, and Philip," and of the historical bonds that had grown fast between Spain and the Netherlands. The Netherlands were essential to the maintenance of Spain's position in the north of Europe and vital to the existence of its maritime empire. "To think about what ought to be done is for other kings, to carry out is Spanish," he wrote, tactfully calling attention to the inaction on reform proposals. "To wish and to attack often in vain is their lot, forever to hold on to what has once been occupied is the Spanish way, is your way," he added with an obvious allusion to the Netherlands.[35] Perhaps because of these and similar remarks some Flemings apparently thought that Scribani had been too fulsome in his praise of the Spaniards. In a letter to Peckius he defended his admittedly exaggerated plaudits, "What do they [my critics] want? That they [the Spaniards] be damned? and not warned?" and in a marvelous chapter of psychological insight in the *Christian Politician* he showed that he understood well how to mix in praise when making points with princes.[36]

But Scribani's concern with contemporary affairs should not close our eyes to the essential and more general nature of the *Christian Politician* as an anti-Machiavellian work. His goal was "to portray this Christian Politician, not merely a politician [*politicus*], but a man among every manner of men Christian in faith, piety, and morals," that is, a Christian *politicus*.[37] He wanted to depict for posterity "as in a mirror" good princes and men outstanding for their military or civic achievements.[38] The Christian life could be lived in every state of life, Scribani insisted at the start, "even under the diadem virtue takes its seat," as the example of many saintly rulers from the past and of Archduke Albert himself showed. Divine love was the basis of virtue, and it could be found in any individual, he wrote echoing Francis de Sales's *Introduction to the Devout Life*. Later he conceded that a life apart from politics was a safer way to salvation, and he remarked that a man who remained in private life would certainly be happier than one who devoted himself to public affairs. Profound cynicism about politics and life at court surfaced regularly throughout the book. Yet Scribani vigorously condemned those who preferred their private comforts to the public service.[39] There was in him an element of ambiguity about political life. Arduous as it was and dangerous for the soul, it was necessary and it could be lived in a virtuous fashion.

The *Christian Politician* circulated less than the other volumes featured in this study. Scribani's difficult Latin alone, much more complicated than Lipsius's or Contzen's, must have daunted many readers while pleasing those who delighted in convoluted Baroque style. No translations were forthcoming. Yet the volume was read. It became an important presentation of Catholic political thought in seventeenth-century Europe. Drexel included it in his canon. An instruction of 1639 for the education of Maximilian of Bavaria's nephew, Johann Franz Karl, called for the reading of "a good proven historian or the *Politics* of Lipsius or Fr. Carlo Scribani."[40] Two further editions quickly followed the original of 1624, one at Lyons in 1625 and another at Antwerp in 1626. But it never approached the influence of Contzen's *Ten Books*, in part certainly because it fell far short of his comprehensiveness.

The *Christian Politician* was divided into two books. The first, although entitled "On the conduct of the prince's subjects," treated of ministers and courtiers only, the second of rulers themselves. As Scribani himself noted, there were no significant changes in the new editions, the most notable being the reversal of the order of the two books and their publication in separate volumes.[41] The first book in the 1624 edition used here comprised twenty-seven chapters, the second forty-six, but the chapters in the second book were normally shorter than in the first, so that the first book took up nearly two-thirds of the whole.

The volume was a series of chapters or essays on individual issues. The topic of a chapter might be a virtue, but more frequently it was a statement or a question, such as "Love is stronger than fear" (2:13) or "What will a king do when about to undertake a foreign war?" (2:32). In both books the order of chapters was loose, though in the second there was a general progression from the virtues through councillors and officials to war and the military. Topics were discussed from different perspectives in different places, and this along with a failure to define terms clearly and the book's organization made for inconsistencies. Of particular note was a sixty-two-page chapter on the conduct of ambassadors that surely reflected a particular interest of Scribani and Peckius and probably an increasing general interest in diplomatic practice. Juan de Vera y Figueroa had published *The Ambassador* in 1620, and Contzen added five chapters on ambassadors to the 1629 edition of the *Ten Books*.[42]

Scribani wrote more out of his own experience and made less use of authorities than any earlier anti-Machiavellian. "You will gather all of me in it [the book]," he wrote Peckius, with whom he had surely spent long hours discussing its contents, "indeed you will find me and yourself, become as we have over a long time now one soul."[43] Sometimes he provided a reference to a source, normally he did not. No Scholastic author of either the Middle Ages or the sixteenth century was mentioned, not even Scribani's slightly older Jesuit teacher and colleague in Louvain, Leonard Lessius. Bernard of Clairvaux was the medieval author to whom he was most inclined, and he appeared only rarely. Of the modern writers, Machiavelli himself received only two fleeting mentions, and it is doubtful that Scribani had read him.[44] Nor was the name of Lipsius mentioned once in the whole volume, even though Scribani had written in his defense and probably known him personally. Yet there was some evidence of his influence and traces of Neostoic themes as the frequent citation of Seneca and Epictetus would suggest. Scribani knew of Contzen's *Ten Books*, but it does not seem to have had any influence on him, and he made no identifiable use of Botero or Ribadeneira.[45]

Scribani was a well-trained humanist with a mastery of Latin literature, especially the historians; he was not a Scholastic. His heavy reliance on Roman writers as a source of examples helped him to make a case common to the anti-Machiavellians: the policies he advocated were in accord with reason. Polybius, Sallust, Suetonius, and even Tacitus were called to the bar, but Scribani showed a penchant for less well known historians of the imperial period, such as Lampridius, Eutropius, and Florus. After the Roman writers, the Bible, both New and Old Testaments, was the source from which he most regularly drew.

The form of government Scribani presupposed throughout was a sovereign principality or kingdom, and he discussed neither the merits of the traditional forms of government nor the place of the estates, which indeed had ceased to function in any meaningful way on the federal level in the southern Netherlands.[46] He had made the transition to absolutism, despite his exaltation of the freedom-loving Netherlanders and his occasional use of the term *cives*, which recalled a civic tradition in the cities with which he certainly was familiar. Rivalry or conflict Scribani considered to be the normal relationship among sovereign states. "It is enough for kingdoms to exist for them to find an enemy," he wrote.[47] There was nothing said about an international order, much less of a papal mediatory role in conflicts among states. Although he included a flattering, three-page tribute to his friend Maffeo Barberini, now Pope Urban VIII, Scribani assigned the pope no effective function in international politics nor even in appointments to ecclesiastical office.[48] These, despite the provisions of the Council of Trent, he put in the hands of the prince, while encouraging him to select qualified candidates as Archduke Albert had always done.[49] So he made a further concession to absolutism.

Scribani denied along with the other anti-Machiavellians and most contemporaries any right of active resistance to a tyrannical prince. His experience of the long civil war in the Netherlands seems to have been the determining factor in his firm adherence to this position. To be sure, a subject was prohibited from carrying out unjust commands, but "to rebel against an impious prince was itself impious."[50] From Roman history Scribani drew a number of examples of insurrectionists who had come to an evil end, including Brutus and Cassius. He advised prominent figures to lie low and avoid the court during the reign of a tyrant. A vicious ruler was God's punishment upon a people for its sins, and the ultimate resort was to the Lord in prayer. If the worst scenario possible were to unfold, then the subject should rather allow himself to be put to death than to raise his arm against his prince.[51]

"My mind at least was to lead to virtue [*virtutem*], to lead away from vices [*vitiis*]," Scribani wrote in the preface of the *Christian Politician*, "to dissuade from what is harmful [*noxiis*] and to urge on to what is useful [*profutura*], and everywhere prepare for eternal life." Pragmatism, intrinsic and providentialist, was characteristic of his thought, even though it was expressed less clearly and less often than in other anti-Machiavellians. Christian virtue and political success were not always easy partners. For Scribani, too, a prince could not govern without the support of the people. "The welfare [of the prince] lies in the goodwill [*benevolentia*] of the people," he wrote,[52] and this goodwill or support was won and maintained by virtue that included prudence. Thus there arose the anti-Machiavellian equation: virtue was essential to winning the support of the people, what others called reputation, and this support was necessary for effective government. But Scribani did not relate this support or reputation explicitly to power as other anti-Machiavellians did, although the implicit connection was there.

Scribani understood popular support differently from other anti-Machiavellian writers, let alone Machiavelli. He was the only anti-Machiavellian clearly to place more emphasis on love than fear, devoting a chapter to the proposition "love is more powerful than fear."[53] Popular support consisted in love (*amor*) and veneration (*veneratio*), and the two overlapped to a good degree. Virtue was the way to win both, especially from people who were themselves noble of character. Scribani contended that those who loved the king would stick by him in ill as well as good fortune, whereas those who were held to him by force would desert as soon as the opportunity presented itself. Out of slaves would come enemies. Moreover, a ruler who governed by fear was himself besieged by it and needed constantly to exercise caution. This was not a happy life.

Veneration, closer to love than fear, was the product especially of innocence of life and majesty, of which Archduke Albert represented the perfect mix. Just as Scribani thought of a ruler as a father to his people, so he likened the veneration of a people for its ruler to the reverence of a son for his father as the parent advanced in years. Indeed, Scribani wrote of a prince's need for popular support as he did of his need for friends, thus confusing the personal and the political. "For neither armies nor treasuries are as much the bulwarks of kingdoms [*regnorum*, not *regum*] as friends."[54] The context here was not the friendship of foreign princes, though this came up later in the chapter, but the support of subjects, whom Scribani seems to have understood at this point to be the major figures of the realm.[55] Rewards were more useful than punishments in governing or leading a people, he insisted in opposition to much contemporary wisdom.[56] This attitude he maintained, even though he had few illusions about the fickleness of the people and readily admitted that some could only be held in check or prodded to action by punishments and threats of punishments.[57]

Scribani's insistence on the prevalence of love over fear seems attributable to three reasons. The first was personal. He sensed the power of love, especially the love of friendship, which was based on virtue. The greater part of a chapter of the *Christian Politician* was devoted to a discussion of friendship along the lines of Cicero's famous treatise, and warm expressions of friendship were frequent in his letters.[58] As a devotional writer he quite properly established love, and certainly not fear, as the basis of all virtuous activity and the whole spiritual life. One of his books bore the title *Divine Love*. Second, there was his tendency to personalize politics, as we have seen in the traditional image of the king as father and in the blending of friendship with popular support. This was perhaps unavoidable in a man of his personality who was close to a court where government still was often a matter of personal allegiances.

Another equally important reason for the primacy of love was Scribani's political outlook, evident in his conscious effort to influence policy in Madrid. Scribani recognized that Spain simply could not govern, certainly not the distant Netherlands, through fear and intimidation. Spain had to win the loyalty of the people. Precisely in the chapter on love and fear he went on to argue that one way for the king of a far-flung empire to do this was to incorporate representatives of all his realms into his councils. So he picked up on a point that Santa María had made, and before him, with explicit reference to the Spanish monarchy, Mariana.[59] By giving all the peoples of a monarchy representation in its councils the ruler assured them that he considered their interests. If an empire was ruled by one people only, the other peoples would see themselves as slaves and toss off the yoke when opportunity arose. "Whoever rules over many peoples, let him flee the name of lord and take on that of father." The application to the Spanish monarchy was obvious, although Scribani did not make it explicit. But he added that Archduke Albert had given an example in the Netherlands of how to win the affection of different groups.[60]

Scribani's message to Philip and to Olivares was to give the Flemings and other peoples of the monarchy representation at court and so deepen their loyalty. Only in this way could Madrid hope to maintain its power in the Netherlands. Indeed, at this very moment, Olivares was profoundly concerned with creating greater unity within the monarchy— he saw this as essential to its preservation—and in his Great Memorial to the king of December 25, 1624, he recommended a larger voice for the kingdoms and provinces other than Castile.[61] The incorporation of non-Castilians into the government of the monarchy remained a goal throughout the Olivares regime, but it was pursued with little energy because of the determined opposition it encountered. The Spanish Habsburgs were unable to create an "international service nobility" at the time when their Austrian cousins were accomplishing just that.[62]

A ruler's virtue had to be genuine, Scribani argued. He was so much in the public eye that it was impossible to deceive his subjects. Like the sun, he could not hide.[63] Yet Scribani well knew that support depended as much on what people thought of the prince as on what he actually was. The importance of appearances did not elude him. "Since empires depend for the most part on their reputations [*opinionibus*], those things are to be kept at a distance which customarily diminish the reputation [of the ruler]."[64] Indeed, the veneration a prince received was due more to his reputation than his actual power.[65]

It was the task of prudence to foster this image or reputation. A prince ought to advertise his virtues, but in such a way that he did not seem to do so, and to take diligent measures to hide his vices. The proper mixture of accessibility and reserve had to be found in dealing with the people; excessive familiarity certainly had to be avoided. A prince ought to be ready to correct an error but rarely to admit that he had committed one; such frankness hurt his image. He should never engage in a contest with subjects—literary, artistic, or even athletic—since it was not fitting that the ruler come out second best.[66] But a royal mystique was alien to Scribani. He had nothing to say about creating an aura of mystery about the ruler or enhancing his reputation through outstanding deeds, military or otherwise, calculated to impress the people with his greatness. He did share Botero's and Olivares's view that patronage of the arts and sciences was a way to promote princely reputation, and he certainly approved Olivares's efforts to this end on behalf of Philip IV.[67] In this respect as well Archduke Albert and Archduchess Isabella showed the way.

Loosely attached to prudence were other precepts scattered throughout the book that Scribani laid down for rulers and men of politics. Particularly significant was what he had to say about the institution of favorite or *valido*, a minister to whom the ruler assigned the major task of government and who was also bound to him by close ties of friendship. Early seventeenth-century Europe had seen a number of all-powerful first ministers: Cardinal Melchior Khlesl in Austria; the duke of Luynes in France; the duke of Buckingham in England; and especially the duke of Lerma in Spain. All eventually ended in disgrace, Lerma and Khlesl before Scribani wrote. Starting with the ascendancy of Lerma, the advisability and qualities of a *valido* had become a significant issue for Spanish political writers, and views differed. There were two elements to the discussion, the political and juridical—the king's need to shift some tasks of rule to others—and the personal—his emotional need for a friend with whom to share the burdens of government. Juan de Santa María, for example, fearful that a *valido* would dominate the king, argued that he should share the burden and task of rule with several rather than one. All agreed that he could not divide his sovereignty or his responsibility before God.[68]

Scribani, who was obviously aware of the issue, condemned the practice of appointing a *valido* as inimical to both king and favorite, and despite his recognition of the king's need for friendship, he evaluated the position chiefly from the political perspective. His words must be seen as advice to the court of Spain where Olivares, aware of its liabilities as well as its advantages, was gradually occupying the post.[69] Princes had different abilities, Scribani contended, but a ruler should generally keep the reins of government in his own hand. To turn over governmental authority to one man was to endanger his crown. He ought to allot equal power and authority to several ministers and stir up a spirit of competition among them; so they served as a check on one another and kept the prince informed of the others' activities. Thus he remained firmly in charge. Furthermore, by giving up the power to distribute offices a ruler forfeited an opportunity to bind people to himself. If they felt they owed their offices to the *valido* instead of the ruler, their loyalty would presumably be to the former.[70] As it was, both Philip and Olivares were long uncomfortable with the term *valido* to characterize their relationship, also because the term was associated with the duke of Lerma and his relationship to the indolent Philip III. Recent scholarship has discovered that the king played a much more active role in government than was hitherto thought to be the case.[71] Perhaps Scribani's words helped move him in this direction.

Scribani advised any candidate for *valido* to decline the role, if at all possible. The favor of princes was not constant, as many ancient and current examples exhibited, Sejanus under Tiberius, Piero della Vigna under Emperor Frederick II, and Thomas More under Henry VIII. Moreover the *valido* was the regular target of those discontent with the government and envious of his position. If he did assume the office, it would be wise to imitate the steward in the Gospel and make friends outside the government who would cushion his eventual fall.[72]

Scribani's prudence had the further task of guiding minister, diplomat, or king through the murky world of political deceit and two-facedness so that he would survive and prosper without losing his integrity. Scribani had no illusions about life at court, and he encouraged the man who desired a secure and peaceful life to flee from it. Here his ambivalence about politics reappeared. Lying was taken for granted; whoever desisted from it on principle was considered a "bumpkin [*rusticus*]."[73] Professions of friendship had to be taken with great caution. From his own experience Scribani was profoundly aware of the value of information to the government, of keeping secret its own intentions and plans and discovering those of others. Rivalry among states produced intense competition for information, "for in general to have known the enemy's plans is to have conquered him," and this competition was at the root of most deceit.[74] Bribery flourished. "Gold is the betrayer of a lord or a kingdom," Scribani wrote cynically, "it alone suffices to overturn or purchase a kingdom. Nor is there anything so sacred that gold will not violate; [for it] one will even hand over a parent to the enemy."[75]

Scribani's treatment of the ethics of deceit was scattered through the *Christian Politician*; it displayed a combination of idealism and realism that was not without its ambiguities. An initial rigorist stance often underwent considerable modification as Scribani delved more deeply into an issue. Yet he admitted that situations could arise from which even the most clever exercise of prudence could not extricate a minister without his having to choose clearly between morality or advantage. At issue was not the preservation of the state but the career or life of a minister. Even if refusal meant dismissal or death, a minister could not carry out an immoral command. "[In such a predicament] you are able to die bravely," Scribani wrote. "Neither fraud nor savagery is able to hold sway over any soul. And there is more praise and glory in a brave death than in a life of cowardice softened by flattery."[76] He did not advert to the Lipsian categories of deceit, but he did cover all but one of them, and they are useful for organizing what he said on the matter. Left undiscussed was injustice or the violation of positive law, probably because of Scribani's absolutism.

The first weapon against the wiles and deceits of politics was mistrust of others. "He overcomes who mistrusts," Scribani wrote, warning against "two-tongued" or false friends and displays of "excessive courtesy."[77] Within limits that were extremely difficult to define, one had to fight fire with fire. Scribani allowed and even required dissimulation, while absolutely condemning the lie. Yet the line he drew between them was difficult to follow, partly because of inconsistent terminology.[78]

God forbade a lie, Scribani argued with a citation from Scripture, but his emphasis was not on the divine prohibition. Nor was his case built primarily, as it was by most moralists, on the destruction of trust and confidence that lying generated. Dissimulation, too, undermined confidence. Scribani's argument was an appeal to the sense of honor. To lie was a servile vice, it was dishonorable. People often took pleasure in deceiving a simple or naive person, but they challenged anyone who dared call them a liar, esteeming this to be a grave insult. Moreover, those who regularly lied often respected those with a reputation for truthfulness and preferred to deal with them.[79]

Dissemblers or dissimulators "brought forth one thing from their mouths and hid another in their minds." Scribani warned his readers to avoid them. They were those who did not want to lie openly, and so took refuge in dissimulation, "so that you are able to promise yourself nothing certain from their candor and so do not know whether to believe what they say or not."[80] But, alas, dissimulation was necessary; one had to admit the well-known dictum, "he did not know how to govern who did not know how to dissimulate."[81] Scribani could not accept "that Stoic rigor" which condemned all dissimulation. Certainly it had been necessary at the court of Tiberius. Moses in his leadership of the Jews through the desert had resorted to it, and even Jesus in the Gospel had done so when he concealed his identity from the disciples on the way to Emmaus and then feigned to continue further than they when he had no intention of doing so.[82] "And who would either rule prudently or live happily here [that is, on earth], if he were compelled to pour out whatever came into his thoughts, no matter the cost in possessions, honor, or blood? Who would not think that he was allowed to conceal what was harmful when it was question of the whole state, or the safety of his wife and children or his wealth?"[83] Dissimulation was necessary to protect government secrets. It was important to keep others guessing about one's intentions and counsels, "so that we neither deny openly nor admit openly."[84] It was a fact to be regretted, but one simply could not get along in politics or at court without dissimulation.

Scribani, like Contzen, considered bribery a necessary instrument of policy. "For to hope for everything from virtue alone is to deceive yourself; seek another world." The one exception he made was in the courts; no age had sanctioned the use of bribes to influence the outcome of decisions at law. This he forbade.[85] Gifts served to strengthen the loyalty of a prince's friends.[86] They were useful to the courtier striving to advance, and there was little they could not achieve when it came to obtaining vital information from foreign courts. The prince should spare no expense in ferreting out enemies' designs. "With gold an ambassador will bring back enemy kingdoms for his lord. He does this who lays bare the counsels of kingdoms for his master, and these he is able to lay bare with gold; nothing is more certain. Nor is anything easier than to win over with money one of the scribes or servants of the secretaries [of enemy states]. Try it: you will bend [him] any way you want. Nothing is impervious to gold, not even the marriage bed."[87] Scribani advised princes to require ambassadors to report all gifts, although they ought to allow them to retain conventional ones, and recommended that ambassadors write all confidential letters themselves, not entrust them to secretaries.[88]

Scribani insisted that a prince or statesman stand by his commitments. A prince, and an ambassador too, ought to be slow in making a promise, but "once made he will be faithful to it; every pledge of a prince ought to be taken as sworn and every promise as sacrosanct."[89] This was essential if there was to be any trust among individuals or states. Without mentioning the mutinies of Spanish soldiers provoked by the failure to pay them on schedule, Scribani asserted the absolute need to be faithful to the terms on which soldiers had been hired and to pay them promptly.[90] Archduke Albert, he felt, had given a marvelous example of fidelity. In 1609, as negotiations for the Twelve Years' Truce were coming to a conclusion, a young French noblewoman and her husband had fled to the court of Albert, who agreed to protect them. He stood faithfully by this promise despite the threats of "a most powerful king," and a danger that the talks with the Dutch might collapse. The reference was to the duke and duchess of Montmorency, who sought refuge at the court of Brussels from the aggressive, amorous advances of Henry IV to the young Charlotte, whose beauty captivated the court when she debuted at a grand ball in Brussels. Henry threatened to invade the Netherlands in pursuit of her, a move that might well have brought the Dutch in on his side and so ended any thought of a truce.[91]

But, typically, Scribani did leave the prince a way out of agreements.

"I want the prince to be constant but not stone or steel." Certainly a ruler was not obliged to carry out an immoral promise, such as the one Herod made to Salome that cost John the Baptist his head. More importantly, there were times when a prince made an unwise commitment, perhaps having been tricked into it. A prudent man could find his way out of such a situation. "For there can never be lacking to a prince a way to correct a mistake." Certainly it would be wrong to go to war and shed blood because of blind adherence to a promise made in anger.[92] Obviously, a clever ruler could easily exploit this loophole. Perhaps Scribani should have paid more attention to the Scholastics, who taught that changing circumstances might release a ruler from an agreement.

With Spain in mind, but from a Flemish perspective, Scribani made proposals for the mercantilist development of a powerful state. He was aware of the *arbitrista* literature, although not necessarily of its contents in any detail. Remarks about the artificiality of the income in precious metals from the New World, which were becoming a topos in anti-Machiavellian literature, were not found in the *Christian Politician*; in fact, there was scarcely mention of the New World. Nor did Scribani bring up Spanish interests in Italy or in the growing conflict in Germany. He did not have the broad vision of the Spanish monarchy that Olivares had from Madrid. His concern was almost exclusively with the Netherlands and with the Iberian Peninsula as it was related to the Netherlands; in this he was similar to Spinola.[93] Scribani's proposals generally reiterated or expanded on those of others rather than adding new ones. There was no shortage of ideas in Spain, there was inability to implement them.

Economic growth enriched the citizens while at the same time providing the tax base necessary for the government's indispensable *aerarium*. Reflecting his own urban background, Scribani said nothing about agriculture and put all his emphasis on the development of the industrial arts, in which he saw the source of wealth, as indeed they had been in Flanders. His words sounded like Botero. "When the [industrial] arts grow, the province grows, not only in the treasury and in wealth but in the multitude of people; from these strength is added to the kingdom, and royal taxes increase notably everywhere, for the size of the public treasury generally depends upon the number of the population."[94] His claim that a kingdom acquired more widespread glory from its industrial products than from its scholarship or military exploits was tailored to a Spanish readership. Such was the case with the Netherlands, he wrote, which had earned renown through its engravings in gold, silver, and bronze and through its printing, the invention of which he attributed to the Netherlanders. Goods from all over the world poured into the Netherlands, and her products reached the four corners of the earth. Scribani lauded the creativity of the Netherlanders, and he urged his prince to be receptive to new inventions and projects; indeed, Spain had shown great openness in the case of Columbus.[95]

Spanish policy amounted to "a kind of folly." Spain exported raw wool and silk and then bought it back as finished products. This was precisely the reverse of what ought to be done. To be sure, Spain lacked craftsmen and artisans, but this only demonstrated the need to encourage immigration. Nor did Scribani make any allusion to their religion. In 1615 neither he nor Lessius had objected to the settlement of English textile workers in Antwerp, provided they did not practice their religion publicly.[96] "It was, generally speaking, lamentable to strip yourself in order to clothe another." Many suggestions had been made to remedy this situation, but nothing had been done, complained Scribani once again about Spain's inaction on reform. Indeed, Olivares did establish in 1625 a commission on population and trade (*junta de población y comercio*).[97]

"What else will I say? I see gold nearly abandon all Spain and copper hold sway. Perchance this is a sophisticated joke in a serious matter." So Scribani was conscious of the currency problems bedeviling Spain, which were provoked in part by the minting and circulation of copper vellon. In 1627 he dispatched to Olivares a detailed plan for currency reform, which he also published in later editions of *The Truthful Belgian*. The plan, which he attributed to a certain Melchior Pais, showed definite similarities to options Olivares and Spanish councillors were then considering.[98] "When, O country dear to me will you see the light," he continued, "having broken out of the darkness of your riches? When will you apply remedies to this sick body, for your own benefit, for that of Belgium and of the world? Have you not played at this too long? Shake off your sleep and come to yourself."[99]

Scribani's esteem for the artisans as a productive group in society was coupled with an aversion to the nobility that occasionally came to the surface. Offices should be awarded on the basis of service to the state not accident of birth. "There is nothing more scandalous than those great men who solely on the basis of the glory won by their forefathers expect for themselves the rewards due to virtue when through indolence and luxury they have consumed their paternal inheritance." Louis XI of France was said to have made his physician his chancellor.[100] Furthermore, the barbarous custom of duelling was destroying the finest of the nobility. Could there be a more foolish or worthless death? Scribani urged the king to proceed against the practice with the vigor Albert had shown in the Netherlands.[101] Should the prince ever have to take sides among the clergy, the nobility, and the people, he would be wise to choose the first and the last, since the nobility did not possess adequate authority without the clergy nor adequate strength without the people, and they often provoked the people with their haughtiness.[102]

"Money is the sinews of every civil war," Scribani wrote in a variation of the commonplace. How the failure to pay the troops in the Netherlands had hurt the Spanish cause! At this point Scribani introduced a plan to raise the funds necessary to support a greatly enlarged army that would, he hoped, break the deadlock and win the war in the Netherlands.[103] His plan seems to have influenced the famous Union of Arms, initiated by Olivares in the mid-1620s to compel each of the constituent elements of the Spanish monarchy to carry its weight and so to forge a tighter unity. The idea and figures, which dated from 1615, before the resumption of conflict, he attributed to "a great man," probably his friend Spinola.[104] Each kingdom or province of the monarchy was assigned a number of troops, infantry and horse, that it would be expected to raise and support, to a grand total of 221,000, of which 90,000 would serve at any one time. Some might object, Scribani realized, that only with great difficulty would Catalonia, Aragon, and Portugal be persuaded to make proportionate contributions to the war effort. Indeed, the subsequent attempt to compel them to do so proved to be the downfall of Olivares and almost the collapse of the monarchy. Exaggerating the ability of Philip to attract allegiance, Scribani pleaded with him to trust his people and make this appeal. Its success, however, did presuppose reforms, such as the recruitment of ministers from all over the monarchy, which he had recommended. A royal visit to the kingdoms of the monarchy would inspire generosity, he contended, and Philip did subsequently undertake a journey to the estates of the Crown of Aragon but with little success.[105]

As their contribution to the projected Union of Arms, Scribani, still using the figures of 1615, proposed that the Flemings contribute and support 23,000 native troops for their own defense. When they finally accepted the Union in 1627, they agreed to provide 12,000 soldiers, along with 500,000 more *escudos* per year.[106] But the novelty of Scribani's proposal consisted in the organization of a distinctive Flemish force rather than in the number of troops or amount of funds to be supplied. His proposal represented an attempt to foster a greater sense of identity among the inhabitants of the Spanish Netherlands. Scribani called, as did Lipsius, for a permanent force complemented by a militia whose service would be determined by a regular rotation. In this, he added, we would merely be imitating the Dutch, who indeed at the turn of the century had introduced progressive military reforms suggested in the works of Lipsius. Scribani made light of the danger of arming the Flemings in this way, and typically, he exaggerated their enthusiasm to fight. No people were more loyal to God and country, he asserted, demonstrating a patriotism that seemed to comprise all Netherlanders, Dutch as well as Flemings. "Certainly, if one is permitted to speak the truth, no province in the world is more suited to wage war, no [province] brings forth so many armies of the bravest soldiers, no province equips such powerful fleets." The people were eager to end the interminable war and would be willing to make the effort to do so.[107] But there is no evidence that the Spaniards permitted the formation of a large Flemish force.

Sea power was a topic Scribani took up in the context of a state's military strength, the first anti-Machiavellian to do so, and once again he put forward specific proposals of "a great man" that fit neatly into Madrid's thinking at the time. Since the late sixteenth century there had been advocates of a Spanish fleet in northern waters, Federigo Spinola, Ambrogio's brother, having proposed one back in 1593.[108] Privateers supported by the Spaniards and operating out of Ostend and Dunkerque had begun preying on Dutch shipping in 1621. The way to weaken the Dutch was to attack them in their trade. In 1623 a commission on commerce (*junta de comercio*) was formed. Out of it emerged the following year the Admiralty of Commerce (*Almirantazgo de Comercio*), which undertook a program aimed at the aggressive promotion of Spanish commercial interests in the north, the stifling of Dutch trade and an effective embargo on Dutch imports into the Iberian Peninsula, and then the preparation of a fleet in northern waters to secure these objectives. Scribani's proposal in the *Christian Politician* for the deployment of a fleet seems to have influenced Olivares's subsequent efforts in the north. But he did not venture to suggest the joint Spanish-Austrian Habsburg and then Polish *armada*, with which Olivares eventually aimed to secure control of the North and Baltic Seas and strangle Dutch commerce. The implementation of these ambitious plans was entrusted to a fellow countryman of Scribani, the adventurous Gabriel de Roy, and they remained alive even after the reverses suffered by the Habsburgs in the late 1620s. But in the long run they produced little in the way of results.[109]

Naval power was essential for the security and prosperity of a far-flung empire like that of the Spanish as well as for the promotion of the greater unity of all its parts, which Scribani considered necessary if it was to flourish. Control of the sea enabled the king to dispatch aid rapidly to areas in difficulty and made it easy to carry a war to enemy shores. Charles V had encouraged his son Philip to build up Spanish power on the seas. Scribani confessed that he had learned the lesson of sea power chiefly from the Dutch, in whose achievements he could not help taking pride. Who would have believed that this people, small in numbers, could hold at bay the most powerful king in Europe for over half a century and nearly rule the world with their naval power? "Great souls, and if God were with them along with piety and the rightness of their cause, worthy of empire."

Experts maintained, according to Scribani, that thirty ships stationed along the coast of Flanders could control the sea and dominate the north of Europe. Certainly this would cost money, but if the Dutch could raise the funds for their navy, why could not the King of Spain? Scribani's "great man" outlined a plan similar in structure to the Union of Arms. Each royal city or town throughout the monarchy should be required to support one ship. So approximately one hundred ships could be put in service. If this were thought impractical, then it would certainly be possible for each kingdom or major province to support three ships. This would supply forty-five ships which, added to twenty-five to be supported directly from the royal treasury, meant a total of seventy, which was exactly the number of ships Olivares was reported in April 1624 to want to put in operation.[110] With these, Scribani wrote, "I promise dominion of the entire sea." But this was not all. The privateers already operating out of Dunkerque would continue to harass Dutch shipping and fishing. So the Spaniards would be able to blockade the United Provinces, cut off their trade, and so bring the Dutch to their knees, and all this with a minimum of bloodshed.[111] But it was not to be so.

There was no formal discussion in the *Christian Politician* of the criteria for a just war, much less an attempt to designate current conflicts just or unjust. Scribani agreed with the ancients that war could be healthy for a state in that it promoted discipline and patriotism, but he shared the general anti-Machiavellian aversion to war that followed from his experience of the period's civil and religious conflicts.[112] He condemned vigorously the "lust to rule [*libido dominandi*]" that was at the root of so many wars and was, he thought, unusually prevalent in his own day. Rulers created the "most beautiful" pretexts of religion and liberty to justify their wars of aggression. Scribani lamented in particular wars among Christians, which were responsible for the continued success of the Turks.[113]

States would always have enemies, and Scribani accepted the conventional dictum, "Any king who wants peace will prepare for war." A ruler needed a standing army—we have already seen Scribani's advocacy of one for the Spanish Netherlands—"either for the protection of himself and his own or for the intimidation of his enemies."[114] He went on to make recommendations for this army, most drawn from ancient examples applicable to the contemporary situation in the Netherlands. Scribani welcomed foreign troops but added, perhaps with the intent to put in another word for a native Flemish force, that they should never outnumber those of the ruler's own kingdom. The presence of soldiers from many nations encouraged a healthy competition within the army. Officers had to demand strict discipline; this had been an important factor in Roman success. Its advantages in winning the support of the population, both the prince's own and that of lands he might occupy, were obvious. But to maintain order among the soldiers it was necessary to keep them busy and to pay them on time. They should be well clothed, since this fostered a sense of pride, and, here Scribani reiterated a point made by Botero, they should feel confident that they and their families would be cared for after their retirement or death. Several pieces of Scribani's advice were calculated to help the ruler keep firm control of his military. He ought to retain all major military appointments in his own hand and not name great magnates to high commands, since this only tempted them. Nor should anyone be allowed to retain a major command for a long period of time. In addition, he recommended that the prince have his own spies with the army to keep him informed of the mood and movements of the troops.[115]

Surprisingly, Scribani had little to say about the role of religion in the state. Apart from a digression in which he accused the Dutch Protestants of opposing freedom of religion lest much of the population return to Catholicism, he did not take up toleration, and he scarcely mentioned the words *heresy* or *heretics*.[116] Neither in his fulsome dedication to Philip IV nor in his regular praise for the Archduke Albert did he single them out precisely as champions of the church against the heretics, and he bemoaned the wars among Christians as the basis for Turkish power. Nor did he at any time exploit the standard argument that religious unity was necessary for a powerful state, much less discuss the ways a ruler ought to proceed in order to bring it about. His acceptance back in 1615 of English artisans in Antwerp showed his awareness of the need for economic development and his inclination toward the Lipsian position that heretics who lived quietly ought not to be disturbed.

Perhaps Scribani felt the issue of toleration to be too delicate for him to discuss. The negotiations to extend the truce with the United Provinces had broken down partly over this question, and it remained a constant point at issue between the Spaniards and the Dutch. Scribani obviously longed for the end of the war. He probably did not want to take a clear position that would lengthen the conflict, and he certainly did not want to take the responsibility for prolonging it. On the other hand, he did not assert, as had Lipsius and Ribadeneira and by now Martin Becan, Contzen's predecessor in Mainz, that under certain circumstances a ruler might tolerate heresy for the greater good. In addition, Scribani seems to have thought, correctly, that many Dutch were at least close to Catholicism; recent research indicates that up to 1650 nearly 50 percent of the United Provinces' population remained Catholic.[117] Once the war ended, many others would freely return to the Catholic church. Then, too, with the victories of Emperor Ferdinand II and Maximilian of Bavaria in Germany, many Catholics sensed in the mid-1620s that Protestantism's hour had struck.

Scribani did include a chapter entitled "Religion and Piety as the Foundations of Kingdoms." But the treatment was restricted to a discussion of the ruler's piety as a source of prosperity and triumph. "How valuable piety is in Kings and what benefits it brings to those [Kings] who love and cultivate it, we are taught by histories from all ages." Scribani brought forward the standard examples from previous times, including Constantine, Theodosius, and Clovis, and he ended with Ferdinand II, the new Moses, whose piety was legendary among contemporary Catholics. Just as the Hebrew armies defeated the Amalekites as long as Moses extended his arms in prayer, so at the White Mountain "the Emperor prayed and God conquered in the Bavarian [Maximilian] and Bucquoy [the imperial general]." Once again we approach the idea of holy war, inasmuch as God is seen as participating in the battle. But Archduke Albert provided the finest example of the pious ruler.[118] Scribani's esteem for Albert and contemporary Catholic rulers like Ferdinand and Maximilian was one reason for his failure to assert the rights of the church vis-à-vis the state. Like Contzen and William Lamormaini, confessor of Ferdinand II, he expected more from pious Habsburg and Wittelsbach princes than he did from the hierarchy.[119] As we have seen, he took it for granted that the ruler was responsible for ecclesiastical appointments, and he saw in church revenues a ready source of financial support for the troops to be levied under the Union of Arms.[120]

Scribani certainly believed that God was in charge of the world's events. His was a moderate providentialist pragmatism. He was careful to avoid saying that God inevitably assigned victory and prosperity to the religious prince who championed his cause. In fact, in the dedication to Philip IV, he stated clearly that this was not always the case, perhaps intending after the Armada's defeat to dissipate Spanish doubts that God really was on their side or perhaps merely wanting to acknowledge what was clear from experience. Good Christian princes could expect setbacks. This had been the case with David and Solomon in Old Testament times and with Edward the Confessor of England and St. Louis of France. But these were temporary or unusual occurrences.

Scribani allowed for the situation in which a statesman might be forced to choose clearly between his moral convictions and his advantage. He discussed at least two such cases, but in neither of them was the choice the ultimate one between moral compromise or the preservation of the state; it was rather a matter of the career or even life of an individual. But his response to them permits us to infer, to a degree, what he would advise when it was question of the state. In one case, which we have already seen, Scribani asserted that a minister was bound to accept loss of his career and even death rather than commit a fraudulent or savage act commanded by his prince. In fact, such a death would bring true glory. Another case involved a minister or courtier who had been wronged by a colleague. He could not return evil for evil. Scribani advised him to take measures to reduce the harm he had suffered; this was the part of prudence. He ought to dissemble the injury if this were possible and helpful; if not, then to defend his innocence. But he ought to condemn no one. There would almost always be some people who would see his side of the case, and often enough his patience and charity would win him admirers.

But, ultimately, one had to entrust oneself to God's providence in such a situation; the Lord could draw good out of evil in ways beyond man's understanding. This was Scribani's basic answer.[121] So, we can infer, would he advise the Christian ruler, or the Christian state, confronted with the choice between immoral conduct or the demise of the state. The point is not that he would recommend to the state or to the prince as ruler of the state the same material norms of conduct and so confuse personal and political morality; it is that he would not permit clearly immoral actions. Neither for him nor for other anti-Machiavellians was the preservation of the state the ultimate good. But clearly such a choice would rarely if ever present itself in such a stark fashion. The prudent ruler would know how to avoid predicaments of this kind.

Scribani frequently used the term fortune, but he assigned it different meanings and made no attempt to reconcile it systematically with the providence of God. In the dedication, for example, it was nearly identical with providence. Generally it expressed for him the fickleness, changeability, and transitory character of earthly affairs. He exhibited a vision of world history reminiscent of Lipsius. "Let us run through the Histories of the ancients and see in them the various vicissitudes in every manner of fortune, as she raises up, makes sport of, smiles upon, and punishes [rulers or states]." Beginning with the Romans, Scribani watched rulers and states pass in review as they rose and fell. "Such is the game of fortune. Its victims are Kings; for whatever has enjoyed greatness throughout the world, the drama continues as the cruel part of the tragedy follows, so that you think her [fortune] to trample upon the glorious part of the story, scepters, diadems, and the dignity of the purple."[122]

From this Scribani drew two lessons. The first downgraded man's ability to plan for the future and suggested the importance of what other writers had called *felicità* or good luck. According to Scribani, the prudent man looked to the start of a venture, not its outcome. Beginnings were in our power, but results often depended upon the vagaries of fortune, which no man could foresee. Consequently, a ruler ought never to punish a councillor when his advice did not result in success. His counsel may well have been the best in the circumstances, but fickle fortune intervened to alter the situation and foil prudence. "Good luck," he averred pessimistically, "more often accompanied imprudence than prudence."[123] Secondly, and much more generally, for Scribani the wise and prudent man allowed himself to be neither elated by success nor overwhelmed by adversity. Good fortune was particularly dangerous, since it put one off guard. Scribani's ruler or man of politics exercised a Christian, Neostoic constancy in ill fortune as well as good and looked for permanent prosperity only in eternal life.[124]

Carlo Scribani's *Christian Politician* represented the contribution to the anti-Machiavellian tradition from Flanders or the Spanish Netherlands, where Counter-Reformation culture flourished in the first third of the seventeenth century. The main anti-Machiavellian theme that the Christian could prosper as ruler or politician predominated, even though Scribani was inclined to limit the overlap of the good and the useful and was sensitive to the opposite pulls they could exercise on a man of politics. Closer to the court than previous authors, he displayed an unadorned vision of life there and struggled with the ethics of deceit. His lack of clarity in this and other areas was due in part to his preference for the essay style and its lack of system.

Scribani wrote from the perspective of a Fleming loyal to Spain, and he addressed Philip IV with specific proposals for policy, perhaps serving as a mouthpiece for leading figures in the Netherlands like Spinola. He was a Flemish *arbitrista*, who seems to have represented or even to have attempted to create a sense of identity for the Flemings and sometimes for all Netherlanders. The political situation apparently colored his broader views. His argument that the love of his subjects was more useful to a ruler than their fear grew in part out of his determination to make the Spaniards realize they had to gain the allegiance of the Flemings if they hoped to win the war in Flanders, and his virtual silence on toleration and the need for religious unity in the state resulted from the delicacy of the issue in the relationship between Spain and the Netherlands. His background and his esteem for Albert made him a loyal if critical servant of the Habsburgs. His portrait by Van Dyck, now hanging in the Kunsthistorisches Museum in Vienna, correctly shows him to have been a man of substance and influence (see Ill. 5).

Chapter 8

Diego Saavedra Fajardo: Climax of the Tradition (1643)

"If any prince has come to ruin, it was not because he was good but because he did not know how to be good." So read in capsule form the rejoinder to Machiavelli of the Spanish writer and diplomat Diego Saavedra Fajardo.[1] Such a prince or man of politics lacked the prudence that dictated how he was to exercise the virtues in the complex conditions of political life. Saavedra proposed to teach this prudence in his *The Idea of a Politico-Christian Prince Represented in One Hundred Emblems*, which though first published in Munich in 1640, appeared in its definitive form only at Milan in late 1643 and under date of 1642.[2] Because of its attractive form as much as its content, it was to enjoy many editions and translations in the years that followed. The very title of the volume, like Scribani's, declared Saavedra's intent to reconcile Christianity and politics. This was a goal he shared with a host of seventeenth-century Spanish authors of various approaches—Maravall lists sixty authors writing roughly between 1590 and 1700, the great majority in the first half of the century—many of whom advanced the Spanish anti-Machiavellian tradition begun by Ribadeneira and as *arbitristas* were concerned with the reform of the monarchy. Included in this multitude were the literary figures Francisco de Quevedo of the satiric pen and the Jesuit moralist Baltasar Gracián, whose main political works, more significant for their style than their content, appeared in 1626 and 1640 respectively.[3] Of all these Saavedra was preeminent.

Saavedra himself was a man of vast political experience, and he issued the *Politico-Christian Prince* as his long diplomatic career reached its peak. At the time he served as Spanish resident at the court of Maximilian of Bavaria, attending to political and military affairs throughout the western half of the empire in the midst of the Thirty Years' War. In 1643 he would be named chief Spanish delegate to the peace conference assembling in Münster and Osnabrück that would eventually conclude the momentous Peace of Westphalia in 1648. In his preface he tells us that during his "continual journeys through Germany and other provinces" he wrote down at night, after completing his official correspondence, what he had pondered on the road in the course of the day, and the result was this volume.[4]

The *Politico-Christian Prince* like Scribani's *Christian Politician* took a special interest in Spain. Saavedra made fewer specific proposals for reform and was further removed from the *arbitristas*, but upon him, a Spaniard writing nearly twenty years after Scribani, the future of the Spanish monarchy and its place in history weighed more heavily. To its service he had dedicated his life, and it now appeared to be caught up in a dynamic of inevitable decline. After many years encouraging and aiding Spain's foes in Italy and Germany, Richelieu's France had formally declared war on Spain in 1635. Disaster struck the reeling monarchy with the Dutch rout of the Spanish fleet at the Battle of the Downs off the coast of England in October 1639 and again the following year with revolts in Catalonia and Portugal. No wonder that Saavedra's concern, like that of other anti-Machiavellians, was primarily for the preservation of the state.

A frequently noted characteristic of the *Politico-Christian Prince* has been its ambivalence and ambiguity, not on principles but on such individual issues as the use of dissimulation or the war in the Netherlands. The same was true of Scribani's *Christian Politician*, and in both cases one reason was the format. Saavedra's volume, like Scribani's, was essentially a collection of essays, the order of which was often arbitrary; both volumes exhibited similarities to Montaigne's *Essays*. Saavedra's thought was dialectical. Statements in one essay modified and qualified from a new perspective those in others, occasionally to the point of contradiction.[5] Individual essays frequently dealt with more than one topic and sometimes presented two sides of an issue without really making clear where the author stood. Terminology lacked consistency and precision. Perhaps this was the price to be paid for the volume's attractive format and pithy language in the manner of Lipsius.

But there was a more profound reason for Saavedra's ambivalence. Overlapping sets of competing pulls or claims created a tension in him that fostered ambiguity. He wanted to be true to Christian principles and to meet the needs of the state. These two claims and the resulting tension were common to all the anti-Machiavellians—indeed their goal was to reconcile them—but the struggle appeared more difficult for Saavedra. He experienced another set of claims together with his fellow Spaniards of the governing class, not least of all the count-duke of Olivares.[6] Proud of Spanish traditions and customs, he was aware of newer, more practical, more reasonable approaches to reality. The need for reform at home was evident to him, but he was hesitant to accept the withdrawal from foreign commitments that reform seemed to imply. Occasionally this pair of claims shaded over into a nascent conflict between the claims of reason and those of religion as understood in Spain, and this despite Saavedra's acceptance of the fundamental harmony between the two. He remarked that the expulsion of the Moriscos from Spain in 1609 had caused astonishment in other princes when they saw "the grandeur of the nobility preferred to advantage and religion to human prudence."[7] These opposing tugs yanked at Saavedra when he already felt the weight of a declining Spain above him. No wonder he fell into ambivalence and ambiguity as he sought to do justice to the situation. Precisely this ambivalence made his book attractive to Baroque readers, giving expression as it did to tensions they themselves experienced in a changing Europe.

Shortly after the completion of his studies, Saavedra entered upon his career as a diplomat, and he was to spend only two years in Spain between 1612 and 1646. Thus he possessed a European perspective unusual for a Spaniard. Little is known of his early life. He was born into an old noble family on May 6, 1584, in the southern Spanish town of Algezares, in Murcia. At sixteen he began studies in canon law at Salamanca, where he received his licentiate in 1606. Later, from 1617 to 1621, he held a canonry in the prestigious cathedral of Santiago de Compostela in northern Spain, but he seems never to have received major orders.[8] By 1612 he resided in Rome, where he was attached to, and thought to dominate, Gaspar de Borja y Velasco, a Spanish cardinal at the Curia, who served as acting ambassador to the papal court from 1616 to 1619 and as ambassador from 1631 to 1635. Apart from a brief visit to Madrid in 1622–23 and nearly eighteen months there in 1630–32, Saavedra remained in Rome until 1633, holding major positions in the Spanish embassy.[9] His long stay provided him with a marvelous opportunity to learn the world of seventeenth-century diplomacy at its center. Later in the *Politico-Christian Prince* he described the members of the court of Rome as men who "dissembled without [showing] feeling in their words or faces, who appeared simple but were clever and circumspect, who knew how to obligate [others] without committing themselves, who were mild-mannered in negotiations and pliant in [reaching] agreements, secretive in their designs and persevering in their resolve, friends of all and intimates of none," indeed, perfect diplomats.[10]

The affairs of Sicily and Naples passed through Rome, and Saavedra was principally occupied with them in his first years in the embassy. Thus he was thoroughly familiar with Spanish policy in Italy, and he championed it vigorously in the *Politico-Christian Prince*. Indeed, Saavedra's vision of the Spanish monarchy emphasized its Mediterranean base in the two peninsulas, Sicily, and North Africa; in this he consciously returned to the policy of Ferdinand the Catholic, which experienced a revival for a time under Philip III and the duke of Lerma, especially from 1608 to 1614, just when Saavedra was first in Rome.[11] The Netherlands and the Americas took a definite second place for him.[12] With Borja, Saavedra participated in two papal conclaves, the one electing Gregory XV in 1621 and the other, Urban VIII in 1623. On March 8, 1632, Borja made his memorable protest in secret consistory against Urban's pro-French policy, to which he attributed the Catholic defeat at Breitenfeld the previous September, which had decisively turned the tide against the Catholics in the war. Saavedra had been recalled to Madrid for discussions about policy toward the pope, and he had not yet returned at the time of the protest. He certainly approved of its gist, if not its vigorous tone, as is clear from his remarks in the *Politico-Christian Prince*. He did, however, take the initiative subsequently to pour oil on the troubled waters.[13]

Meanwhile, Saavedra had been active on the literary front, even though his first published book was to be the *Politico-Christian Prince*. In 1612 he completed his only nonpolitical work, *The Commonwealth of Letters*, an imaginary visit atop Mount Parnassus to a community of writers, artists, and scientists of the ancient and modern world; it was published only in 1655 but circulated widely in manuscript before then. One cannot help but notice its similarity in form to Boccalini's *Reports from Parnassus*, which had long circulated in manuscript before its publication in 1612. The book revealed Saavedra as "a master of Spanish prose," his style less involved than Quevedo's or Gracián's because of his aim to reach a wider audience, and it went through well over a dozen editions after his death.[14] He produced three lengthy propaganda pieces for Spanish policy, which, however, were neither attributed to him nor published until modern times.[15] We must also presume that Saavedra participated in the intellectual life of Rome, where Lipsius had found stimulation a half-century earlier and where the humanist tradition of Marc Antoine Muret was still alive.[16] His use of Molinism when discussing the fate of the Spanish monarchy in the *Politico-Christian Prince* testified to familiarity with the theology of the Jesuit Luis de Molina, which vigorously affirmed free will, and awareness of the controversy over grace and free will between Dominicans and Jesuits, the repercussions of which were still felt in Rome during Saavedra's years there.[17] A lengthy, unfavorable allusion to Galileo in the *Politico-Christian Prince* showed him to be abreast of the affair that long agitated the city and came to its unfortunate conclusion the year of his departure, 1633.[18]

Two main works were to come from his pen subsequent to the publication of the *Politico-Christian Prince*, both political in inspiration and composed during his time in Münster. The *Follies of Europe*, a brief dialogue probably written in 1643 but not published until 1648, was a defense of Habsburg policy, and the *Gothic Crown*, published in Münster in 1646, was the first part of a major historical work, the *Gothic, Castilian, and Austrian Crown*, completed by others after his death. In this Saavedra's purpose was threefold: to complement the *Politico-Christian Prince* with further instruction in politics, to provide historical underpinning for current Spanish claims, and to win the goodwill of the Swedes—there was talk at the time of a Spanish-Swedish understanding—by showing the alleged common origins of the Swedish and Spanish crowns.[19]

The year 1633 saw Saavedra enter the most active period of his life. Olivares was intensifying his efforts to secure closer cooperation between Madrid, Vienna, and the German Catholic princes in order to reverse the tide running against the Catholics after the catastrophe of Breitenfeld in 1631. Saavedra himself appears to have suggested the need for a Spanish representative at the court of Maximilian of Bavaria.[20] The king then appointed him to the post, which he took up in July 1633. His basic task was to win Maximilian's cooperation with the Habsburg states and to counteract any French overtures to him, but many further assignments came his way. He helped prepare the way first for the advance of a Spanish army into Alsace under the duke of Feria in 1633 and then the following year for the conjunction of the Cardinal Infant's army with the king of Hungary's that led to the Catholic victory at Nördlingen in September 1634, once again establishing a balance between the two sides in the war.[21] At the court of Maximilian, Saavedra found Adam Contzen sympathetic to his proposals, and he became acquainted with the confessor of Maximilian who died in 1635.[22] We must assume that they discussed political questions and that Saavedra came to know the *Ten Books on Politics*.

Until 1642, working out of his base in Munich, Saavedra journeyed about western Germany, over to Vienna, and down to Switzerland and northern Italy on the business of Madrid. He represented Spanish interests at the Electoral Convention of Regensburg in 1636–37, and again at the Imperial Diet of Regensburg in 1640–41. His first-hand experience was the basis for his vivid description of the horrors of war in the *Politico-Christian Prince*, where he charged both sides with atrocities against friend and foe alike that outdid anything of which the Spaniards might have been guilty in the New World.[23] Saavedra succeeded in bringing some order into the military and political affairs of the Free County of Burgundy, attempted to end French recruitment of troops in Switzerland, and at the end of 1637 laid the groundwork for the switch of the duchess of Mantua over to the Spanish side in the war. All the while he continued his efforts with Maximilian. He never did secure a formal alliance, but, especially in his first years in Bavaria, he facilitated a good deal of practical cooperation with the elector.[24]

Finally, at the turn of the year 1642–43, he returned to Madrid for the first time in nearly ten years. His arrival preceded by only several weeks the fall from power on January 24, 1643, of the count-duke of Olivares. Saavedra's correspondence shows that he was on good terms with Olivares, and sometime between 1640 and 1643 he dedicated to him a revised manuscript of *The Commonwealth of Letters*. But in the second, final edition of the *Politico-Christian Prince* published in late 1643, Saavedra deleted two passages highly laudatory of Olivares.[25]

Saavedra had scarcely settled back in Madrid when he was dispatched as Spanish plenipotentiary to Münster, where the peace congress was beginning to assemble. His extensive experience in Germany made him a logical man for the post. At Münster he worked propagandistically for the Spanish cause, as we have seen, and he displayed initiative in making contacts with other delegates. But his more than two years in Münster were frustrating, largely because Madrid kept him on a short leash, insisting that he clear his actions with the marquis of Castel Rodrigo, the governor of the Netherlands, in Brussels. As the negotiations moved ahead with the presentation of formal proposals for peace in 1645, Saavedra was replaced by the count of Peñaranda, which amounted to an enhancement in status for the Spanish representative.[26] After the publication of the *Gothic Crown* in 1646, he returned to Madrid. There he died on August 24, 1648, two months before the signing of the Peace of Westphalia, "one of the most representative figures of his age." Today he is remembered more as a writer and political thinker than as a diplomat, but his writings can only be understood against the background of his diplomatic experience.[27]

The *Politico-Christian Prince* was an immensely popular book during the second half and especially the third quarter of the seventeenth century. Besides the original Munich edition of 1640 and the revised Milan edition of 1642, which served as the basis for all future editions, sixteen Spanish editions appeared before the end of the century, including two at Antwerp (1655, 1677) and three at Amsterdam (1658, 1659,

1664). The first Latin translation, by Saavedra himself, came out in Brussels in 1649, and it was followed by eleven editions, all before 1669, apart from the later Jena edition of 1686. Four editions in Italian were published at Venice between 1648 and 1698, and German (Amsterdam, 1655; Cologne, 1674), Dutch (Amsterdam, 1662, 1663), French (Paris, 1668), and English (London, 1700) editions all eventually saw the light of day.[28] The book was obviously read across confessional lines, having a major impact on the German Baroque novelist and dramatist Daniel Casper von Lohenstein.[29] The English translator, James Astry, begged pardon for Saavedra's Catholicism, then added that as a statesman he was less bigoted than most Catholics. The book's title, Astry pointed out, indicated its direction to kings and rulers, but it was also valuable for statesmen and politicians, officers and soldiers, merchants and seamen, and, indeed, for "all persons of learning, sense, or reason."[30]

Saavedra's volume was lengthy, running to 735 pages in quarto in the Milan edition and including one hundred plates. The book was not an original work of political thought; in fact there was little new in it. Nor was it the first political emblem book. Saavedra made use of an earlier volume that he must have come to know in Germany, the *Political Emblems* (*Emblemata Politica*) of Jacob Bruck Angermunt, published at Strasbourg and Cologne in 1618.[31] He followed his own advice, "Teach by giving pleasure,"[32] that is, make the lessons attractive. This was a principle of Baroque pedagogy emphasized by the Jesuits in their influential *Plan of Study*, and its application by Saavedra helps explain the book's popularity. Long considered a masterpiece of Spanish literary style, the *Politico-Christian Prince* as an emblem book delighted its readers with an appeal to eye as well as ear and assisted them with a visual aid to artificial memory.[33] Both its message and its style appealed to the Baroque reader.

The emblem or *empresa*, as employed by Saavedra, was a Baroque variation of what we today call the essay. It comprised three elements, a concise symbol or figure with a Latin motto or legend as caption, which together Saavedra called the body of the emblem, followed by a written exposition on the theme introduced by the body. The symbol and motto were meant to be unclear but not arbitrary, so as to stimulate the interest and curiosity of the reader and draw him into the topic. In the case of Saavedra, a new emphasis was given to the exposition at the expense of the symbol and motto, so that they became a mere introduction to the exposition, which was essentially an essay.[34]

A good example of a Saavedran emblem was no. 50, devoted to the highly relevant topic of the *valido* or favorite (see Ill. 9). The representation pictured against the background of a flat rural landscape a single steep mountain reaching into the clouds and being struck by lightning. The motto read "[near to] Jupiter and Lightning [*Jovi et Fulmini*]." At the start of his essay, then, Saavedra likened the favorite to a mountain rising above the common ground, close to Jupiter and his favors, but at the same time much more exposed to heat and sudden storms. The favorite occupied an exalted position, yet a lonely and perilous one. The favor and affection of a prince could be lost as quickly as they were won, as recent examples showed, such as the duke of Lerma in Spain, the marshall d'Ancre in France, the duke of Buckingham in England.

Saavedra neither advocated clearly nor rejected the choice of a favorite, unlike Scribani nearly twenty years before, who had condemned the institution. He developed two lines of thought, first analyzing the different foundations on which a favorite's position might be based and the weakness of each. A prince who selected a favorite, for example, in recognition for his service to the crown, often came to resent his obligation of gratitude and to see it as an infringement on his majesty and freedom of action. The author then provided favorites with concrete advice. A great danger was the schemes they concocted to preserve their position. A favorite became like a hypochondriac who searched constantly for ways to stay well and ended up ruining his health. Better to follow the ways of nature, that is, serve the prince with a good and faithful heart, expect dismissal, and when it came, as it almost certainly would, accept it in a constant spirit. In an undoubted allusion to Olivares, Saavedra added in the 1642 edition that for the favorite who conducted himself as Saavedra outlined, the fall would be "glorious." So he paid some tribute to the count-duke. But he closed by reiterating his warning of the previous emblem that a prince guard carefully lest a favorite secure excessive power and influence and bring his government into disrepute.[35]

Saavedra's goal was to help teach the crown prince, the eleven-year-old Prince Baltasar Carlos, and other princes, the "science of rule," which he later called "the science of sciences" and identified with a "reason of state" that was in harmony with the plan of God.[36] But he did not overlook the formation of ministers and statesmen and the government of republics. His book "was composed of aphorisms and maxims of state, because these are the stones out of which arise political constructions," but he always discussed them in their relationship to one another and their practical application to circumstances. Saavedra was wary of general precepts for princes, and insisted that the science of government was rooted in experience and reflection on experience.[37]

Saavedra had determined to write, he tells us, at the importunity of friends and colleagues who begged him to distill his own experience for the benefit of others. But history constituted the vast source of experience. Like Machiavelli in his introduction to the first book of the *Discourses*, Saavedra wrote in his dedication that just as painters and sculptors looked to the ancient world for models, so must students of politics. Yet he preferred examples from modern times because "the state of affairs had changed less and one could imitate [recent actions] with less danger and with greater success arrive at a political and informed judgment, this being the most reliable benefit of history."[38]

His two main sources, according to Saavedra, were Tacitus and the Bible, and indeed of the 1,853 citations in the *Politico-Christian Prince*, more than one-third (688) were from Tacitus and nearly another third (553) from the Bible, the remainder distributed among a number of ancient authors, philosophers, and a few historians.[39] Saavedra belonged to the influential school of the Spanish Tacitists and among them to the group that pursued the reconciliation of Tacitean realism with Christian principles.[40] His use of the Bible manifested a penchant for the wisdom literature, especially Proverbs and Ecclesiasticus or the Wisdom of Sirach, and a reluctance to draw examples from the historical books, compared to Contzen and Scribani. Mariana's *History of Spain* and the *Seven Books* (*Siete Partidas*), a Castilian law code from the thirteenth century with much historical material, were major sources because, as Saavedra wrote, they told of Baltasar Carlos's ancestors, whose failures as well as successes he noted.

Saavedra remained silent about his modern sources. Machiavelli he cited only to repudiate, and in his one explicit reference to Lipsius he rejected, ostensibly, the Fleming's acceptance of deceit.[41] But his sources certainly included Lipsius, Botero, Contzen, and probably Ribadeneira and Scribani, and like them he took over fundamental features of his political philosophy from the Scholastic tradition, as one might expect from a student of Salamanca. He borrowed from Machiavelli and even more from Lipsius, whose influence permeated Spain. A telltale sign of Botero was the frequent pairing of "prudence and valor" as the princely virtues. Like Botero and Ribadeneira, he regularly used the term "reason of state," which the northern Europeans Lipsius, Contzen, and Scribani all shunned. Ribadeneira's *Christian Prince* must have been known to him as a Spaniard, and Scribani's *Christian Politician* was popular in Germany precisely during Saavedra's stay there.[42]

The *Politico-Christian Prince* was composed of separate essays, 101, despite the title. For the Milan edition the author added one, revised their order, and divided them into eight sections. Just as in Contzen's *Ten Books on Politics*, there existed a rough similarity to the organization of Lipsius's *Six Books on Politics*. But there was no equivalent in

Lipsius of the first (nos. 1–6) and eighth (nos. 100–101) sections of the *Politico-Christian Prince*, which treated the education of the ruler and, a significant note of the Baroque, his old age and death.[43] Saavedra's final emblem concluded with a portrait of Ferdinand the Catholic, the embodiment of the perfect prince for him as for Gracián in his *The Politician Ferdinand the Catholic* and a sharp contrast with Scribani's idealization of the Habsburg Archduke Albert. It stood after a fashion as a summary of the volume and is useful for interpretation when the text appears ambiguous.

His roots in the Spanish and Scholastic political traditions led Saavedra to bring out the limited character of government more than the other anti-Machiavellians. Themes of Bellarmine and especially Suarez underlay his remarks on the origins of political authority. It was bestowed by God upon the king who was his representative in temporal affairs and enjoyed a special closeness to him.[44] But, and this is the point Saavedra emphasized, authority came, according to the provisions of the natural law, to the king or his line through the consent of the people. They submitted to the ruler, so that he would provide for them "political felicity," that is, peace, justice, and abundance. This was the purpose of government. The prince did not possess "absolute power" (*poder absoluto*). He was subject to the common good and the interests of his people, and he was bound by the natural law. The people had either explicitly reserved some power to themselves or it remained with them by virtue of the natural law as protection against "a notoriously unjust and tyrannical prince." Saavedra did not attack the delicate issue when or how a people might proceed against a tyrant, but he did note an instance from Mariana's *History of Spain* when the failure to provide justice cost a Castilian king his crown.[45]

Saavedra clearly preferred monarchy as a form of government, republics being riddled by factionalism and unreliable in foreign affairs because of undue popular pressures.[46] But he understood monarchy to be tempered by aristocratic and democratic elements, neither of which, however, was given sharp form. There was an indication of aristocratic restraint on the king in the discussion of his relationship to his councillors. Although he insisted that the prince himself actually make decisions, he expected him generally to follow his council. In fact, at one point he spoke of "obedience" to his council.[47]

Strictly speaking, a sovereign prince could impose taxes, provided they were just, without formal popular approval, but it was the part of prudence to explain the need for them and to win the assent of the people. Where there were constitutional restraints on a prince, as in France and Spain where consent was required for taxation, the king was to respect them. The exception was in critical cases of necessity, when, Saavedra seemed to say—he was not fully clear on the point—the ruler could proceed without consent but was to do all he could to explain the need to the people. Such necessity usually arose in time of war. So Saavedra seemed to side, if cautiously, with Olivares, who appealed to necessity in his efforts to extract funds from the Spanish kingdoms.[48]

"To maintain his own state is the obligation [of the prince], to conquer another [state] is voluntary," Saavedra wrote, warning against the ambition that urged to conquest. The tragic figure of Frederick of the Palatinate exemplified the prince who overreached himself. Moreover, it was no less difficult to reform a state, and so preserve it, than to found a new one, Saavedra continued, perhaps with the Spanish situation in mind, and the process always took time.[49] "Reason of state" dictated the means to maintain the state. It called for the exercise of virtue, understood to be a combination of moral virtue and political acumen, as with the other anti-Machiavellians. Virtue generated popular support or reputation, and it created power, reputation itself being a major element of power. Virtue did this by achieving the goal of government, the "public felicity" of the subjects. So there appeared in the structure of Saavedra's thought the connection between the good and the useful, and the association of virtue, reputation, and power, which we have found to characterize the anti-Machiavellians.

Reputation's vital part in government can be seen in Saavedra's emblem no. 31, which showed a single, straight Corinthian column topped by an elaborate royal crown (see Ill. 7). The motto read "resting upon reputation" (*existimatione nixa*). The column remained standing, he explained, balanced by its own weight. But once it began to totter, it would fall, the more rapidly the heavier it was. "In no other way do empires maintain themselves than with their own authority and reputation. But once they begin to lose this, they begin to fall, without their power sufficing to maintain them; rather, their very greatness hastens their fall." Saavedra then turned to a metaphor from contemporary medicine to make his point. "The spirits and natural heat [that is, the equivalent of the nervous system] of a man enable him to stand upright; the short pedestal of the feet would not suffice of itself. What else is reputation than a light spirit struck in the minds of all, which upholds the scepter." Reputation was the support of the people in which their obedience was rooted. Without it rulers could not govern nor could kingdoms endure.[50]

Reputation was even more vital than an uninterrupted hold on the territory of the state. The territory could be regained, but reputation, existing as it did in the hearts of the subjects, could not. So Saavedra interpreted the victory of the Venetians in the War of the League of Cambrai in 1508–9 when most European powers had been aligned against them. The "valorous and prudent" Senate determined not to resort to "unbecoming means," that is, a Turkish alliance, and so to compromise its reputation. Soon the Venetians recovered their territories.[51] Saavedra's views were not distant from those of his countryman Baltasar Zúñiga, who during the negotiations over the extension of the truce with the Dutch was alleged to have said that "in my view, a monarchy that has lost its *reputación*, even if it has lost no territory, is a sky without light, a sun without rays, a body without a soul."[52]

Typically, Saavedra added qualifications. He did not intend that a ruler be easily swayed by public opinion. There was a distinction to be made between genuine reputation and the applause of the mob, for whom he had little but contempt.[53] A government based on the shifting moods of the people would not long endure. Tiberius did not allow himself to be bothered by the murmuring of the mob over his residing at Capri. The policy of princes was often beyond the understanding of the people. The ruler should look to his reputation over the long term. Time often revealed humble actions to have been heroic and submission and obedience to have been courageous. Yet, and here Saavedra explained himself further, the ruler was well advised to disdain the opinion of the crowd only when it was a matter of the public good, which the people could not be expected to grasp. The outcome of his policy would then increase his reputation. Otherwise he ought to accommodate to the crowd as much as possible. In fact, the prince ought to listen carefully to public opinion and, far from attempting to suppress complaints and "murmuring," to pay close attention to them and to the pamphlets and satires directed against his government, as they often contained more than a degree of truth.[54]

Reputation or popular support was a combination of love and fear, the exact mix of which Saavedra left vague in his discussion of the topos. At first he showed a clear preference for love, but then, as was often the case, he modified his initial position allowing for the importance of fear properly understood. The affection of his subjects was "the most trustworthy guard" a prince could have about him. Indeed, Saavedra pointed to the structure of his thought when he wrote that "in this book are found scattered throughout all the ways by which [a prince] gains the goodwill of his subjects," the most efficacious being religion, justice, and liberality. Who would undergo risks for the prince if he did not love him, and who would defend the crown? But there had to be an element of fear, Saavedra conceded realistically, not servile fear but the fear born of respect and veneration, with which love was easily paired. If not, love could well degenerate into contempt. Moreover, a ruler could more readily control the fear of his subjects than their love. Nor could the prince ever hope to win the affection of all, Saavedra admitted, as had Botero and other anti-Machiavellians.[55]

The people wanted a prince of high moral quality; this increased their "respect and esteem" for him and won the favor of God's providence. A prince could not feign this moral virtue, certainly not before God but not before man either, Saavedra argued. Indeed, it was more difficult to keep up the appearance of virtue than to acquire the reality. A prince could not escape the gaze of his people. Domestics, for one, would let out his secrets, and once it came out that a ruler was not what he claimed to be, that, in fact, he was a hypocrite, his reputation would suffer more than ever. "To commit vices was fragility, to dissimulate virtues [*sic*], malice." Generally, people could understand vices, but they hated hypocrisy. Contzen had made a similar point.[56].

Yet appearances were important, and a ruler could not overlook this. "There is no monarchy so powerful," Saavedra wrote, "that it is not sustained more by opinion than by truth, more by esteem than by power."[57] It was not hypocrisy but a healthy respect for virtue and good example to attempt to conceal the vices a king might possess.[58] Throughout Saavedra, like other anti-Machiavellians, gave the ruler tips about the enhancement of his reputation. If he did not enjoy the arts, he ought to affect doing so because of "reason of state."[59] He could not possibly be up to date on all matters all the time. Thus it was unwise for him to be readily accessible to all, since those with a particular concern would see that he was not fully informed about their matter and would then think him uninformed on other matters too. For this reason many Roman emperors had insisted on the submission of written memorials by those bringing business before them. But there was little in Saavedra, in contrast to Botero, about the creation of a mystique or sense of mystery around the ruler. Finally, for the maintenance of popular consent there was still no substitute for good government. Saavedra looked at justice, mercy, and the rule of law from this perspective,[60] but he focused on prudence. It was especially to instruct in prudence that he had written the *Politico-Christian Prince*.

Prudence was for Saavedra, as for the anti-Machiavellian tradition generally, the master virtue for the prince or *político*, and it enjoyed a variety of overlapping meanings. Existing in the mind, not in the will, as did the other virtues, it served as the needle of the compass for the helmsman of the ship of state. Without it, Saavedra agreed, a prince's virtues could become as dangerous as his vices. Prudence's task was to accommodate government to the people.[61] It taught the prince to distinguish between public and private virtue. The practice of mercy, for example, could never be excessive in a private individual, but it could be in a ruler or minister if it undermined justice. To assist another was always praiseworthy in a private person, but it was reprehensible in a prince to come to the aid of another ruler and so risk the welfare of his own state "without sufficient advantage and reason of state."[62]

Prudence sometimes signified the same as reason, which for Saavedra often was opposed to passion or the affections and was meant to control them.[63] Then it came close to moderation. Prudence, or reason, moderated the ruler's ambition and gave him a sense of his limitations. He should not try to exact from his subjects the obedience that could be expected from a monastic community. Usually it was the ruler's pride that urged him to attempt an excessively absolute style of government. "The rigor of rule did not have to be as it ought to be but as it could be; even God adapted to human weakness."[64] Moderation was a theme to which Saavedra regularly returned. Princes should not be deceived into harshness or severity by a desire to restore a situation of earlier days when things were allegedly better; "it is a vice of human nature to consider the past better [than the present]," and even if it were, in the present, one had new customs and practices with which to deal. For the second time Saavedra cited Tacitus's dictum, "So long as there are human beings, there will be vices."[65]

Prudence as moderation shaded over into prudence as caution, where it was opposed to and paired off with valor, thus combining the two as they had been combined by Botero and designated the two chief princely virtues. The prince ought to proceed slowly when making changes in religion or government. Spain offended in this regard in its attempt to integrate the Moriscos, who subsequently united against the Spaniards, who in turn thought it necessary to expel them in 1609. So Spain lost a useful population.[66] But there were times when it was wise, or prudent in a higher sense, to act on a healthy impulse that could not be fully justified by reasoned analysis, to allow oneself to be drawn by circumstances to heroic decisions or actions. "One could not prevent everything with prudence, nor would great ventures be undertaken if one always prudently considered all the circumstances and dangers." Excessive prudence or caution would never bring greatness. Saavedra drew on his own experience when he described how Cardinal Borja had not hesitated to travel to Naples at a time of rebellion there, despite the protests of his aides, who feared for his safety. "Something has to be left to chance," he responded to their remonstrances. One reason for French success was their ardor or boldness, which contrasted with Spanish prudence, Saavedra added.[67]

But when should one undertake bold ventures and when hold back waiting for the opportune moment? The whole of "political science," which Saavedra nearly identified with prudence in this context, consisted in timing, knowing how to ride the waves of fortune, a term to which we will return later. "There is no state so abandoned by fortune," he wrote, perhaps with Spain in mind, "that valor [or boldness] cannot preserve and expand, when it is advised by a prudence that takes into account the circumstances, knows how to use them well, and turn them to [the benefit of] the state's greatness."[68]

Saavedra's prudence also took in what Lipsius had treated under "mixed prudence" or the various degrees of deceit. He rejected explicitly Lipsius's tolerance of any practice that departed from virtue governed by prudence.[69] But in practice the two were not distant. What Lipsius saw to be touched by malice Saavedra considered to be prudence or astuteness, a term that for him did not have the negative connotation it carried for most anti-Machiavellians. Saavedra's less systematic method, the dispersion of his treatment throughout his volume, and his less precise use of terms generated confusion. Lipsius, for example, had used the word deceit (*fraus*) as a general term for the practices he included under mixed prudence, and deception (*deceptio*) for a lie. Saavedra used the term deceit (*engaño*) for both. Certainly his ideal was expressed in his final portrait of Ferdinand the Catholic, "who did not deceive but led others to deceive themselves by the equivocal nature of his words and treaties, making use of them in such a way (when it was fitting to overcome malice with cleverness) that he was able to withdraw from them without failing in fidelity. A lie never touched his majesty."[70] This was a fine line to walk, and Saavedra in his casuistry did not always hold to it.

A healthy or prudent mistrust of others had to characterize a prince or statesman, who lived in a world peopled by the envious, the ungrateful, the deceitful, and the ambitious. But, Saavedra added, he had to have confidence in some men if he were to govern at all (see Ill. 10). "Not to trust anyone was the suspicion of a tyrant, to trust everyone the indiscreetness of an imprudent prince." One could have a good opinion of a person and still have room for mistrust based not so much on the individual's character as on the general weakness of human nature. Saavedra repeated the affirmation of Botero that neither blood ties nor friendship among princes created bonds strong enough to withstand the claims of interest.[71]

To lie was forbidden the prince or man of politics because it undercut the trust necessary in human society. But to dissimulate was absolutely essential for Saavedra as for Scribani, especially if a government were to maintain the secrecy necessary for the successful outcome of its policies. Saavedra took as the motto of emblem no. 43 "that he might know how to reign" (*ut sciat regnare*), and elaborated on the familiar dictum, "He who does not know how to dissimulate does not know how to reign" (see Ill. 8). The difference between lying and dissimulating was slight, and Saavedra himself was not always clear on it. Indeed, for him the unexpressed and blurred yet real distinction between the two seems to have been between the concealment or acquisition of information and the active propagation of falsehood, what we would today call "disinformation." A ruler, of course, had no obligation to reveal his intentions or plans. Sometimes a prince even kept his ministers in the dark, as had both Tiberius and Philip II. Saavedra argued that a prince might assert certain goals as pretexts, provided they were not at odds with his real goals, which themselves were just but would be endangered if they were known.[72] Sometimes the people ought not to be given the real reasons for princely decisions but fed "some apparent pretext." If they ever knew, he wrote, what went on in the councils of princes, they would realize that they were governed by men of no greater ability than themselves and so lose respect for authority. Decision making ought to be surrounded by secrecy and an element of mystery.[73]

For purposes of eliciting valuable information or the true feelings of others, Saavedra sanctioned what came very close to a lie. Techniques he recommended were the praise or blame of an individual or even a false statement about one's own intentions, in order to draw out the feelings of others. Thus, to test the reaction of Roman senators, Tiberius indicated that he did not desire to accept the imperial throne. Another method was the putting of questions that implied a state of affairs that one knew did not exist, the more questions the better, since they were likely to confuse one's interlocutor and induce him to blurt out secrets.[74] Better, however, Saavedra remarked, that a prince leave such practices to his ministers if at all possible, since they did not accord well with his dignity.[75]

Saavedra laid nowhere near the emphasis Scribani did on the use of money and gifts as bribes. He justified bribes in two instances. Ambassadors, whom Saavedra twice characterized as "public spies," could, without offending against either God's law or the law of nations, pay out funds to ministers in foreign countries in order to secure information about unjust plans against their own prince.[76] Princes might also, "without political scruple," fund rebels in another state or an attack on that state by a third party, provided they were engaged in a just war with the other state. The same reasons that justified the war justified such actions. Here Saavedra implicitly condemned Richelieu's support of the Habsburgs' enemies and perhaps Olivares's occasional funding of French Huguenots before a state of war existed between the two countries. But to stir up the subjects of another prince could prove dangerous, he warned, since it taught one's own to be traitors.[77] Later, in a passage redolent of Contzen, he wrote laconically that in war "victory was bought more cheaply with it [money] than with blood," thus apparently approving the bribery of enemy officers and soldiers.[78]

Considering the space Saavedra devoted to dissimulation, it is surprising how little he said about fidelity to promises and agreements. There was no indication of the Scholastic position that permitted withdrawal from a treaty under certain circumstances. Perhaps the astuteness of Ferdinand the Catholic was all that was needed. Promises and agreements had to be kept, he stated almost in an aside, for the sake of public faith and reputation.[79] This included agreements with heretics and with rebels, though in the latter case the ruler might let them feel the full rigor of the law once they committed another offense.[80]

Saavedra allowed a ruler to set aside constitutional requirements of positive law in order to levy taxes in cases of necessity, as we have seen. Perhaps he came closest to Machiavelli when discussing a mode of conduct that also fell into Lipsius's category of injustice. The situation was one of popular rebellion in which a minister was blamed by the people for a policy for which the prince was really responsible, a not uncommon occurrence. In such a case a prince was justified in not undeceiving the people and punishing the minister. "Innocence will suffer but without guilt on the part of the prince. In great events there is scarcely any remedy without some injustice, which is compensated for by the general benefit [gained]."[81] This sounded like approval in principle of evil means in order to achieve a common good. Yet it would be unfair to make too much of this statement, tucked away as it was in an essay devoted to instructions on how to handle a rebellion. Saavedra may have meant no more by punishment than the minister's removal from office and have expected as a matter of course that a minister assume responsibility in such an instance out of loyalty to his prince.

As an alternative to the "politics of these times," which "took for granted malice and deceit at every turn," Saavedra expressly called for a policy of economic development that "represented a true reason of state." The prince who wisely looked to the long-term economic welfare of his subjects obtained their support and developed the tax base that was essential to a powerful state and especially its military. Like Contzen, Saavedra made it clear that the accumulation of treasure was not avarice in a ruler.[82]

Precisely this "economic prudence" had been lacking in Spain. Most of what Saavedra had to say about the economy was fitted to the distressing Spanish situation, and he joined the chorus lamenting Spain's economic woes. Through its continual wars and lack of a well thought out policy, Spain had allowed the riches that would have made her invincible to pass to other nations. Saavedra, like Contzen and now some of his own countrymen, considered the discovery of the Indies a misfortune for Spain because it had made the country dependent upon an artificial source of wealth and led to the neglect of its own agriculture and industry. "Mount Vesuvius produces more on its slopes than the mount of Potosí from its interior even though it be of silver." Spain had mismanaged the wealth from the New World, vastly overspent, and then greatly aggravated the situation by regularly debasing the coinage. It had an extremely unfavorable balance of trade, exporting raw materials and importing finished products, and it suffered from a steady depopulation for which Saavedra gave a number of reasons including the wars, the colonies, and a foolish tax policy.[83]

The proposals Saavedra made for the revival of Spain's economy, scattered through several essays, echoed the *arbitrista* literature and in many cases reforms that Olivares had attempted to introduce or at least contemplated. They were not particularly original. What they did show was a sense for the economy as a whole and the interrelatedness of its parts. In contrast to Botero and Scribani, who came from urban areas, Saavedra paid much more attention to agriculture and husbandry than to industry, as did Spanish and French mercantilists generally.[84]

The tax burden on peasants and craftsmen, who were the most productive groups in the population, ought to be lightened, and taxes ought not be imposed on necessities of life but on luxury goods and imports where foreigners would pay them. Saavedra descried the procedures of tax collectors and tax farmers who, he argued, in their exploitation and mistreatment of the people did more harm than the impositions themselves, but he had little to offer in the way of an alternative system of tax collection.[85] He understood well the monetary woes of Spain, but his only recommendation was the general one that coinage be maintained at a standard value corresponding to that assigned it by other nations.[86] He did encourage the formation of trading companies on the Dutch model, an area where Olivares had taken an initiative with little success, and the further development of Spanish naval power to protect its commercial interests.[87]

Saavedra shared the opinion that "the strength of kingdoms consists in the number of their subjects." Among his suggestions to reverse Spain's depopulation were the curtailment of the flow of people to Madrid, where they were coming in an unprecedented degree in order to live from the court, and with reservations, the recruitment of foreign immigrants. His ambivalence appeared in his hesitation about immigration because of the harm it might do to religious and cultural unity,[88] and it turned up again in his attitude toward Spain's foreign policy. Much as he detested the war and realized how Spain's exertions in the Netherlands and Germany were exhausting the country, he did not come down clearly on the side of peace, as we shall see. In this he was much like Olivares himself.[89]

Saavedra saw as one way to revive agriculture, craft production, and trade the cultivation of a spirit of work or "work ethic." Like Contzen, he was sensitive to the importance of social attitudes and the need to change them. He sought to foster a form of piety that emphasized work and obedience, that is, one that would benefit the temporal welfare. Spain lacked necessities, he argued, not because of lack of resources but because of an unwillingness to work. Everyone wanted to become a noble, and too many entered religious life. There were too many feast days that took peasants and craftsmen from their tasks. Saavedra complained of the superstitious practices of popular piety, which, he felt, oppressed the mind and the spirit and wasted time in gatherings and pilgrimages and which were accompanied by all sorts of vices and abuses.[90] He called for education that was more practical and directed to participation in industry and commerce; here again the Dutch were the model. Spain had more than its share of theologians and lawyers.[91]

Saavedra's often cautious and ambiguous proposals were rooted in the intractability of the problems Spain faced and manifested his realism. This can be seen in his treatment of the nobility. He lamented the lack of outstanding leaders among them, a common complaint in the Spain of the 1630s and one often on the lips of Olivares.[92] While Saavedra would like to have modified their tax immunity, he realized this was impossible. This was what they saw as distinctive of themselves, and to tamper with it would raise a political furor.[93] He urged that others be given a chance at high position, noting that neither Columbus nor Cortés had been nobles. He then suggested that the prestigious posts in the civil administration be reserved for them but not the high military commands, because they lacked the requisite experience and courage. But after reflecting that soldiers might well be reluctant to follow a commoner into battle, he seemed to prefer the nobility for the major military commands too. It was easier, he concluded, to reform the old nobility by giving them opportunity for service and rewards than to create a new nobility; politically there was no real alternative. Nor did he want to enlarge the nobility because precisely the widespread desire to enter the noble class subverted the development of a work ethic. So he ended advocating a clearer line between nobility and commoner that would be difficult to cross.[94]

The laws of primogeniture in Spain were also at issue in this context. On the one hand, Saavedra admitted they were essential for the maintenance of the nobility as a group. But, on the other hand, they induced many nobles to enter the church or the military, where they had no family and so contributed to depopulation, and they impoverished many others and so contributed to the wide discrepancy between rich and poor, both causes of Spain's weakness. His suggestion was to preserve the estates of the older nobility, without clearly identifying who these would be, and to require the division of those of the newer nobility among the heirs.[95]

Preparedness was the price of peace. The *Politico-Christian Prince* recognized the need for a strong and disciplined military. Like many others, Saavedra insisted on a navy to protect what he hoped would be a growing Spanish foreign trade. Military seminaries or academies he recommended for the large cities. These were not intended for the nobility as were the seminaries envisioned by Olivares in the mid-1630s and most of the academies that had sprung up elsewhere since the late sixteenth century,[96] but for orphans, runaways, and young vagabonds, who would be trained for the service after the fashion of the Turkish Janissaries. Similar institutions he suggested for sailors in the shipyards. So the seminaries served a social as well as a military purpose, to reduce the accumulation of beggars and vagabonds in the Spanish cities.[97] Should financial resources be lacking, Saavedra looked to the church. One-third of all pious donations could be applied to them, "because those who defend the altars deserve no less than those who incense them." Saavedra showed no hesitation about using ecclesiastical resources for military purposes. This was also evident from his novel suggestion that the military orders be entrusted with manning and financing the Mediterranean and Atlantic fortresses that Olivares foresaw to safeguard the merchantmen he hoped would be built.[98]

Saavedra wanted to remain faithful to the principles of the just war but also, as had been the case with Botero and Lipsius, to accommodate two traditional conceptions, that a ruler ought to expand his territory and that war promoted the life of a vigorous state. War was for Saavedra unreasonable in a profound sense, the result of man's failure to control his passion for wealth and power. His paean to peace resounded in the hearts of many during the Thirty Years' War, it was "the sum of all the goods God gave to mankind, just as war was the worst evil." But valuable as peace was, a prince "ought not for its sake commit injustice or suffer indignities."[99]

The dictum of Tacitus's Germanic king that private persons preserved their own property whereas kings fought for the property of others, had to be understood according to "reason and prudence." A prince who wished to make his fortune in war ought to wait for a "legitimate opportunity" to do so, the implication here also being that one would appear in time.[100] But Saavedra did not point to a war with the Turks as had Botero; they were not a concern in Spain at the time. To initiate other than a just war was to yield to the passion for rule and dominion, and from this Saavedra sought to dissuade the prince with a number of utilitarian arguments. To violate the laws of justice was to expose oneself to aggression from others and to return to a state of anarchy where one could easily be the loser. Furthermore, as Saavedra could have seen from Spanish experience had he not read it in Botero, to acquire excessive power was to unite others against you and generate further war. But above all, Saavedra sought to impress upon the prince that he would find a greater challenge and more reputation in preserving his state in peace and governing it well than in venturing into unpredictable wars.[101]

War and the threat of war were essential, according to Machiavelli and many others, if a state were to keep alert, maintain a civic spirit, and avoid the softness that foreshadowed decay. Saavedra rejected this line of thought for republics, arguing that in their case wars frequently provoked internal conflicts out of which arose military leaders who then grabbed power. But he allowed it a good deal of validity for large monarchies; in fact, we would think he had accepted it were it not for his clear preference for peace expressed elsewhere. In monarchies, where social tensions were greater, wars appeared necessary to distract subjects from domestic difficulties, Saavedra concluded—hastily it would seem—from the examples of ancient Rome and modern Spain. Rome's civil wars had begun, he claimed, once its conquests had ceased. As for Spain, the war in Flanders had brought an end to Spain's civil wars and—here Saavedra echoed a sentiment of the duke of Osuna, viceroy of Naples during his years in Rome—had been a valuable training ground in the military arts.[102]

But if he thought Spain had garnered some benefit from the long struggle with the Dutch, his overall verdict was unclear. The losses in men and money in those remote and inclement provinces had been so great and Spain's successes so few, Saavedra wrote, "that one could doubt whether it would be better to be conquered or to conquer" or whether it would be desirable to seek some way to put out that fire, so voracious of blood and gold, and to direct resources to the navy; this would make it possible to control the Atlantic and the Mediterranean with sea power and to limit efforts on land to the unification of the monarchy and to the Mediterranean. But, Saavedra went on in a manner typical of his twisting lines of thought, love for Spain's subjects in the Netherlands, the desire to free them from the servitude they mistakenly called liberty, and the intent to preserve true religion carried more weight than did reason of state. In this instance valor overruled reason and prudence.[103]

No peace would ever last, Saavedra asserted, that was not basically fair to both parties; thus fairness was in the interest of both.[104] He rejected the new idea of the balance of power as a means to preserve the peace. He saw the idea to have emerged in Italy as a weapon against the Spaniards, and he applied it only to Italy and not to the whole of Europe. Who would oversee a balance of power and maintain rough equality among the Italian states, jealous and fearful of one another as they were? If one state did grow disproportionately and was attacked by the others, who would preside over the division of the spoils? Spain had long preserved the peace in Italy. The Italians would be better advised to keep their eyes on the power seeking to expand, namely France, not on the power already well established in Italy. It was the former that constituted a source of unrest and a danger to peace in the region, as Ferdinand II, grand duke of Tuscany, had lately come to recognize, according to Saavedra.[105]

Justice and the law, reward and punishment, were columns upholding the state, but they would hang in the air if they did not have under them the firm foundation of religion. Only the punishments and rewards provided by religion were adequate to engender the internal respect for authority and obedience to law necessary in a political community. Who would live content with his lot in life, refrain from crime, honor agreements if it were not for the sanctions and hopes of religion? The ancients had recognized this, some like Numa manipulating the people through religion. This Saavedra did not approve, and he warned his readers of unnamed contemporaries who used religion for political purposes. Following Augustine, he acknowledged that God had rewarded some non-Christian peoples with enduring empires, not for their false religion but for the sincerity of their worship and their moral virtue. How many more benefits would come to the state through the practice of the true Christian religion.[106] Later he added a new twist to the argument against Machiavelli that Christians made courageous soldiers. The truly brave or heroic person was the one who mastered his affections or passions and channeled them properly. The "Stoic sect" had taught this, but Christianity had done so much more effectively. Like Ribadeneira, Saavedra then listed a multitude of Christian, mostly Spanish, commanders and generals as proof that Christianity produced outstanding soldiers.[107]

Saavedra's remarks on the need for religious unity in a state were nuanced. He insisted on religion as a powerful unifying force and on the prince's duty to foster this unity, and he attributed Spain's greatness to its loyalty to the Catholic faith. But none of his examples illustrating the divisiveness of religious diversity was drawn from the period following the Reformation, and nowhere were there assaults on the heretics. In fact, Saavedra's examples drawn from the Netherlands might have served as counterexamples. Philip II could have maintained his rule there intact and avoided the overwhelming costs of the war had he been willing to concede liberty of conscience. But he preferred "the honor and glory of God to his own greatness." Likewise Philip IV at the start of his reign refused to renew the truce with the Dutch advocated by some councillors and suggested by "the ordinary reason of state." The king declared "he did not want to besmirch his reputation by upholding for one hour peace with rebels against God and his crown," Saavedra reported with apparent approval.[108]

But elsewhere he approached a position similar to the *políticos*, as had Lipsius and Ribadeneira. Novelties in religion should be spotted and quickly uprooted lest they spread and threaten the prince's rule. Saavedra recognized a problem with this procedure. The understanding was free, and it violated human liberty to impose belief. Moreover, some argued that punishment of those failing in faith ought to be left to God. Yet the dangers to religion and the state were such that it seemed better "to oblige the subjects . . . to hold it for [a matter] of greater sanctity and reverence [of God] to believe rather than to understand the things of God," he wrote, giving expression to his suspicion of speculative thought as a source of heresy.[109] Yet if heresy had acquired a firm foothold among the people, prudence ought to be applied rather than fire and sword, especially since often the use of force only rendered dissidents more obstinate and violent themselves, nor "does reason always surrender to force."[110] Once again he expressed his doubts about policy in the Netherlands.

The spiritual and temporal powers were to work together in harmony, each within its delimited sphere, according to Saavedra. "This [the temporal power] covers itself with the authority of that [the spiritual power], and that [the spiritual power] maintains itself with the power of this [the temporal power]." The ruler ought to stay out of matters of religious practice and doctrine. Christianity was a universal religion, and if each prince introduced his own variations, unity would be undermined and the people confused. In quarrels with the pope or disputes over ecclesiastical jurisdiction, the people usually took the other side or at least a great deal of harmful conflict was stirred up. For this reason it was better to avoid fights with the church, yet Saavedra the Spaniard added, as Botero had not, that the ruler should not hesitate to assert his rights when principles were at stake.[111] The ruler's task was to see to the enforcement of ecclesiastical decrees, using punishments when necessary, especially when the temporal as well as the spiritual welfare was involved.[112] Not once, however, did Saavedra explicitly mention the Inquisition in the whole of the *Politico-Christian Prince.*

Saavedra did show, in two areas at least, inclination to put the church more at the specific service of the state. Both we have already seen, the development of a piety that encouraged discipline and work and the use of church property. Saavedra issued the normal injunctions against confiscation of church property without good reason and provided examples of punishments visited upon rulers who violated them. But it was different in cases of necessity. Natural reason showed that rulers might make use of church property when it was question of the preservation of the state, with the understanding that compensation would be made when possible. Ecclesiastics "were a part, yes the most noble and principal part, of the commonwealth," and they were expected to contribute to its defense. This was the case especially in Spain, where the kings had been the outstanding benefactors of the church. The Holy See, recognizing this, had been generous in granting privileges to the kings of Spain, as Saavedra illustrated with examples from the eleventh to the fifteenth centuries. The kings for their part ought to use the funds for the reasons for which they were given, but they did not have to be scrupulous about this.[113] Saavedra also complained about excessive benefactions to the church, thus removing wealth, especially landed wealth, from profitable exploitation, and he lauded the regulations Venice had issued to curb donations to the church, which had provoked the famous interdict of 1605 and the subsequent contest with the papacy.[114] The unduly large numbers of people entering religious life also came in for his cautious criticism, since this contributed to depopulation.[115]

The papacy was the subject of an essay by Saavedra. More than any of the anti-Machiavellians, he accorded it a continuing role in international affairs, but there was a catch. His views were certainly colored by his long experience in Rome and by Spanish unhappiness with Urban VIII. The papacy served as an arbiter among the kingdoms of Christendom, he wrote, the pope was the "common father" (*padre commune*) of kings, a term Urban regularly applied to himself. Papal recognition gave them a certain legitimacy, Saavedra continued in a way redolent of the curialist theory of the origin of temporal authority, and it brought them blessings. But his authority was one voluntarily accepted. The pope possessed two swords, but he made use of the temporal one through the princes who defended the church. They had a duty to support, obey, and protect him. But as soon as the pope resorted to force himself, his efforts became counterproductive. "Unarmed, the papal dignity is more powerful than armies," as Leo the Great demonstrated when he turned Attila back from Rome. If the faithful had made it possible for the pope to raise an army, this was only to protect his own security and to benefit the universal church. When the pope forgot this and became involved in normal politics—in 1641 papal troops invaded the small principality of Castro, beginning a war that ended in humiliation for Urban VIII three years later—the tiara became a helmet, he was treated as any other prince, and his authority to mediate disputes among princes was forfeit. "His pastoral duty is not war but peace."[116]

Saavedra drew out what he considered to be the implications of the pope's role as common father for contemporary politics, especially in Italy. To be the common father was not to be neutral. To be neutral was to be for no one; in the face of evil, this was a form of cruelty. A father who did nothing during a quarrel of his sons became a cause of the damage they did to each other. He had to act, first with love and then, if necessary, with severity. So with the pope and princes. If they did not obey his admonitions, and there was danger his authority would be undermined and his ability to mediate compromised, then he had to take the side of the party with a just cause.[117] In other words, the popes were expected to support Spain in Italy against the French.

A ruler who practiced religion and justice won the favor of God for the conservation of his state, Saavedra affirmed regularly.[118] He shared the view widespread in Spain that the glory and power of the Spanish monarchy was a divine reward for the piety of the Spanish kings.[119] The Lord had fought alongside the Hebrew kings in the great battles of the Old Testament. Saavedra found modern parallels to them and paid his respects to the holy war, referring to Maximilian's pious general, Count Tilly, "the Christian Joshua," to whom the Lord gave an astounding victory over the Protestants at Stadtlohn while he assisted at Mass, and to Emperor Ferdinand II, to whom God granted the glorious victory at the White Mountain while he participated in the divine office.[120]

But Saavedra, too, was well aware that history was infinitely more complex than this. In an effort to understand the workings of God's providence in the history of kings and nations, Saavedra arrived at an eclectic philosophy of history that, typically, was not fully elaborated in any one place but dispersed throughout the *Politico-Christian Prince*. This he then applied to the Spanish monarchy as he saw it in decline. As sources Saavedra drew on the biblical tradition, Lipsius, and Machiavelli. Like both authors and many thinkers of the sixteenth and seventeenth centuries, he was concerned to avoid a providentialist determinism and to save the activity of free will. To do this he finally turned to the controversial theological doctrine of Molina.

Saavedra's first principle and starting point was that God's providence governed the world.[121] But how then did one explain that upright and honest rulers championing God's cause suffered defeat? One response was similar to Ribadeneira's following the defeat of the Armada and to Contzen's following Breitenfeld. God allowed this as a test of faith or a punishment and correction for the prince and his people. Usually in such cases the setback was only temporary, and "the same divine sun . . . will return and magnify with its light his [that is, the prince's] grandeur," as had happened with Emperor Ferdinand II.[122] Perhaps the current setbacks for the House of Habsburg were only temporary, Saavedra wrote. "But I do not know whether I would venture to say that in Pharaoh himself and in his kingdom it appears that the [Kingdom of] France and the punishment which that divine sun of justice threatened is prefigured, and that we ought to hope, given the other miraculous demonstrations made for the conservation and greatness of the House of Austria, that after calming his anger toward it, he will dissolve the mists beclouding its august spires, thus revealing above them in triumph the imperial eagle."[123] At another point he saw in Richelieu a scourge sent by God for Christendom and the House of Habsburg. Sometimes for impenetrable reasons of his providence, God allowed defeat and failure to overtake good and upright rulers and peoples, Saavedra admitted.[124] There was mystery in divine providence.

Saavedra made use of the concepts of fortune and occasion or opportunity and a theory of the rise and decline of states as had Lipsius and, before him, Machiavelli. He never strictly defined fortune in the *Politico-Christian Prince*, but in the *Gothic Crown* he called it "that series and eternal disposition of divine Providence in human affairs."[125] In the *Politico-Christian Prince* fortune, then, was identified with the "conjunction of causes," which raises up empires and then brings them down.[126] Occasion was usually a particular point of time in this chain of causes, "which passes quickly never to return."[127] Political prudence, as we have seen, was above all the ability to ride the waves of fortune, to know when to allow oneself to be carried by the winds, when to buck them.[128] Indeed, it could even force an opening for opportunity.[129] The ruler had to know when to intervene energetically against unhealthy developments in the state, when to overlook them and allow them to heal of themselves; for those ambitious for office, it was necessary to know when to wait for their opportunity and when to seize it, because fortune was quick and elusive. Constancy, meanwhile, enabled the ruler or politician neither to lose heart in adversity nor to grow overconfident in success.[130]

For Saavedra, as for Lipsius, just as there was nothing permanent in nature, so there was nothing in politics that endured. "Monarchies are no different from living things or vegetables. They are born, they live, they die as these, without any fixed period of existence. And so, their declines are natural." Yet he later qualified this natural character of the decline of states, more or less in accord with Machiavelli, by contending that two factors were always at work in the process, God's providence (or for Machiavelli, fortune) and secondary causes, the latter being "human imprudence or blind passions." No state ever fell without culpable human failure in government, or, in Machiavellian terms, the loss of *virtù*.[131] In a youthful, growing empire, where the desire for glory and dominion remained vigorous, quick, decisive action was the rule. Ardor lessened once an empire achieved maturity; then endowed with respect and authority, it could allow itself time in taking action as it enjoyed what it had acquired. But once an empire had peaked and begun to decline, the fall was inevitable. Yet here Saavedra held out hope for Spain. Monarchies rose and fell at a different pace. By decisive, restorative action decline could be delayed and extended over a long duration.[132]

Saavedra integrated much of what he had to say on providence and history in essays number 87 and 88, where he also took up explicitly the relationship between providence and free will. The flow of history depended on God's providence. God now raised up and pulled down kingdoms, he granted opportunities; it was no longer fortune that did this. God attained his goals, making use of and frustrating human prudence and valor as he willed. He had wished to elevate, for example, Cosimo de Medici to leadership in Florence. Efforts to prevent this by Cosimo's foes, including his exile, only served to strengthen his position, and the timely death of Niccolò da Uzzano, the enemy who had urged his exile, opened the door for his successful return to the city.[133] Thus God achieved his goal.

The same was true of Spanish history. God had wished to exalt the monarchy of Spain as he had the Roman Empire in the ancient world. So he had raised up heroic figures, such as Ferdinand the Catholic, Columbus, Hernando Cortés, the Pizarro brothers, and many others. But now following the death of so many outstanding personalities like the marquis of Spinola, Gonzalo de Córdoba, the marquis of Aytona, the duke of Lerma (a general in Flanders, not the former *valido*) and others, the dearth of leadership in Spain pointed to God's design. "O profound providence of that eternal Being! Who would not conclude from this to the decline of the monarchy of Spain." Later he added words that seemed to express his own feelings and those of many contemporaries, "Unfortunate were great subjects born into a collapsing monarchy. They were not put to use or, [if they were] they could not resist the weight of the fall and were brought down by it, having lost the chance for glory and honor and often being blamed for what in any event had to be." The longer a state existed, the closer it was to its end.[134]

But this was not Saavedra's last word. He was not a determinist nor would he accept "dead resignation." We must not be passive, he encouraged his countrymen. So had Lipsius argued, but from a slightly different perspective. He had called for action because not knowing whether the illness of the state was fatal, we were obliged to work to heal it as long as life remained, and he had pointed to the survival of the individual and of humanity should the state go under, thus lessening the degree of the disaster. Saavedra turned at this point to the Machiavellian image of the river, to which he likened the "series and connection of causes moved by the first cause." We could not directly withstand its current, but we could learn to adjust to it and to ride with its flow. It was prudence that guided us at this critical point. This was not to attempt to undo the divine decrees. That would be "mad presumption." Here Saavedra turned to high theology, specifically to a form of Molinism. God in his eternal decree ordaining the course of history, had foreseen "our courage, our virtue, or our neglect, our imprudence, and tyranny." Mankind or specifically human actions created a part of that chain of causes that was history. In no way did God take away human free will. He issued his divine decrees and determined the flow of history only after taking into account our free actions, which he had from all eternity foreseen. Thus in a very real way we influenced and contributed to the course of history. We had to act.[135] So Saavedra encouraged his countrymen to take some heart as they fought to hold off the decline of the monarchy.

Anti-Machiavellianism peaked with Saavedra. Not that he offered the most complete program for a powerful Christian state—that Contzen had done. Contzen's was the most effective response to Machiavelli on the level of intrinsic pragmatism, even if his practical vision was restricted to central Europe. Saavedra asserted forcefully the anti-Machiavellian conviction that a Christian could prosper in politics, and he showed the frequent overlap of the good and the useful, although he avoided these terms. His struggle to understand providence and to encourage his fellow Spaniards at a time of crisis was poignant and convincing, and his expression was masterful. His appreciation of the complexities and ambiguities of political practice came regularly to the fore, and his use of the essay form rather than a systematic treatise served to intensify this appreciation. In his effort to reconcile politics and morality, more artistically than systematically, and in his simultaneous respect for recalcitrant reality, Saavedra reflected the experience of his contemporaries, and perhaps of moderns too, as they grappled with issues of political ethics. So he earned his reputation as a great Baroque writer and, according to one historian, has appeared "to modern minds the most influential political thinker of Habsburg Spain."[136]

Chapter 9

Anti-Machiavellianism, Counter-Reformation, and the Baroque

Machiavelli's claim that the sincere Christian could not succeed in politics startled, then scandalized and scared Europeans of the sixteenth century. This was more so the case because the assertion touched an element of experience that seemed to give it the ring of truth. Guicciardini was one who answered "Amen" to Machiavelli, Thomas Cromwell another, Montaigne perhaps a third. But if Machiavelli was right, one had to accept a cleavage between Christianity and the world of politics that sundered the unified vision of life still shared by most Christians, and the serious Christian had to abandon politics. Assuredly, tension between Christianity and the world was hardly new; it had been felt at least since the struggle of the early church, reflected already in the New Testament, to find the proper attitude toward the Roman state and then toward classical culture in general. But Machiavelli raised the issue anew in acute fashion. The anti-Machiavellian response was essentially a statement about the place of the Christian in the world, and it was an integral feature of the Counter-Reformation and the culture of the Baroque.

The response to Machiavelli gathered force slowly, largely because his writings became known only gradually. Pole, Osorio, Caterino, and others rose up to challenge aspects of his position, especially his denial of Christian providence and his reduction of religion to a means of social control, and the Scholastics of the Silver Age dealt with him at a distance and in passing, as it were, demonstrating that his view of the state did not fit the Christian conception of life and the role of the state therein. It was the anti-Machiavellians who descended into the trenches to do battle with him on his own terrain. They endeavored to work out a program for the effective development and preservation of a state that was in accord with Christian principles, that is, a Christian statecraft. Despite the *anti* in anti-Machiavellian, theirs was an eminently positive venture.

We have dealt with the six leading anti-Machiavellians in this book and discussed others who entered the lists and contributed to the anti-Machiavellian tradition. Their books were widely read. They helped form the political culture of the day as they reached the politically active class directly or through the classroom, not only rulers but councillors and magistrates of city and state, diplomats, military officers, intellectuals, and ecclesiastics. Contemporary interest in issues of political morality and in the fundamental issue of the relationship of Christianity to politics was intense and was itself a feature of the era. The title of a lecture published by the Englishman, Thomas Stapleton, professor at Louvain, put the issue well: *An Academic Speech, Are Contemporary Politicians to be Considered among the Number of Christians* (Munich, 1608).[1]

The anti-Machiavellian writers tell us much about and help us to interpret the Counter-Reformation and the culture of the Baroque, which to a degree overlap not only chronologically but in intent and content. By Baroque culture, as we indicated at the start, we mean the culture of Catholic Europe from approximately 1590 to 1680; these were the years when the anti-Machiavellian writers were popular, with the intensity of the debate over Machiavelli diminishing somewhat after 1650.[2] Under Counter-Reformation we understand the movement within the Catholic church, from roughly the middle of the sixteenth to the start of the eighteenth century, to reform, to combat Protestantism, and to accommodate to the changing culture and society of early modern Europe. So it extends at both ends beyond the period strictly under discussion. Both Baroque culture and Counter-Reformation wrestled with the changes that had overtaken Europe, some rapidly, some gradually, in the sixteenth century, the Counter-Reformation to adapt the church to the challenges they posed, Baroque culture to assimilate them into a new synthesis, especially an intellectual vision and stable political settlement. The anti-Machiavellians contributed to both by elaborating a Christian reason of state suitable for the new world of the sovereign states and so attempting to reunite what Machiavelli had severed, Christianity and politics.

Judging anti-Machiavellianism to be a major element of the Counter-Reformation and of Baroque culture, what do we learn about both of them from it? This is the question of our final chapter.

But before we turn to it, we must first make a brief detour to discuss another issue that naturally arises to confront us, why did writers in France not produce any significant anti-Machiavellian works? Certainly, issues of political morality were alive there, as we have seen. Machiavelli's *Prince* and *Discourses* continued to be published in France after the issuance of the Index of 1559, and Botero and especially Lipsius were immensely popular authors there. Ribadeneira's *Christian Prince* was translated in 1610, and other anti-Machiavellian works appeared later in French, Ammirato's in 1618, Bellarmine's in 1620 and 1625, Marquez's in 1621.[3]

The answer to our query seems to lie primarily in the distinctive political and religious situation in France, first in the religious wars that reached their peak just as Botero and Lipsius published their main political works in 1589 and then in the gradual and not uncontested movement toward absolutism and divine right monarchy that followed right up into the reign of Louis XIV. A secondary reason that we can only suggest is that the optimism characteristic of the Counter-Reformation elsewhere was not so prominent in France, where Augustinianism and Jansenism were very much at home.

The nature and future of the French monarchy was at issue during these years, and it drew the attention of France's primary political thinkers. The Calvinist François Hotman had published his *Franco-Gallia* in 1573, the year following the St. Bartholomew's Day Massacre, placing the estates above the king, and six years later the *Defense of Liberty against Tyrants* (*Vindiciae contra Tyrannos*) of Philippe du Plessis-Mornay claimed the right of subjects to rebel when they were oppressed. Meanwhile Bodin's *Six Books of the Republic* came down vigorously on the side of absolutism in 1576, although his volume looked well beyond the French scene. Pierre de Belloy has been called "the first in France to expound with any fullness of theory what may conveniently be called, *par excellence*, the theory of the divine right of kings." He published his *Catholic Apology* in 1585 and his *On the Authority of the King* two years later.[4] Botero and Lipsius both subscribed to absolutism in addition to putting forth anti-Machiavellian programs during the reign of Henry IV, and this undoubtedly enhanced the popularity of their volumes. French authors of the early years of the seventeenth century, like Pierre Charron in his *On Wisdom* of 1601, which was dependent on Lipsius, were concerned with political ethics, but they produced no significant programs for the government of a state and often focused on issues of law and sovereignty.[5]

Later Richelieu's controversial policies at home and abroad became issues. Both he and Louis XIII were thoroughly convinced that their measures to strengthen the monarchy and assert France's role in Europe were well within the bounds of Christian morality,[6] and so much the more, that a Christian politics was possible. Richelieu fostered writers who defended his policies. But their emphasis was then on the achievements of his program and a defense of its morality and his status as a

Christian statesman rather than on the more general issue of a Christian politics and the elaboration of a program of state building. This was the case, for example, with two important publications of 1631, the year after Richelieu's triumph over his domestic enemies in the Day of Dupes: the *Prince* of Jean Louis Guez de Balzac, and the *Minister of State* of Jean de Silhon. Balzac in particular stretched the limits of royal power, especially when it came to preventive detention and even execution of potential troublemakers,[7] and both saw Richelieu as the ideal minister. Neither book was directed against Machiavelli, nor did either employ the categories of the good and the useful, let alone locate a frequent harmony between them.[8] In fact, right at the opening of the *Minister of State* Silhon pointed out that God's providence did not always favor the just cause as the victories of the Protestants and Turks made clear. "There was nevertheless," he added shortly afterwards, "nothing strange about the fact that there were so few good men among so many occasions of sin or that the science of governing was so rare, since it was so difficult."[9] Such statements, of course, further exalted the achievement of Richelieu.

There were to be sure more general treatments of politics in France during this period, but they do not qualify as properly anti-Machiavellian works, let alone as major ones. In 1621 the priest Etienne Molinier, who had preached at the coronation of Louis XIII, issued his *The Political Virtues*, which was directed against Machiavelli and aimed, as the title indicates, to show that *politique* and virtue belonged together.[10] But this was a brief undistinguished work that drew heavily on Scripture as it treated various virtues of the "politick person" and did not aim, as the author stated in his preface, to deal with the "art of policy," that is, to outline a plan for the creation and maintenance of a state. Such was the explicit goal of the anonymous *Councillor of State*, later attributed to the diplomat Philippe de Béthune, which appeared in 1633, though it may well have been written long before then.[11] This volume developed clearly and systematically a comprehensive program for state building, wherein the reader easily recognizes the signs left by the author's reading of Lipsius and especially Botero. But the *Councillor of State* was not written to provide an alternative to Machiavelli nor to argue to a harmony between the claims of the good and the useful.

Machiavelli himself determined the issues for the anti-Machiavellians and so decidedly left his mark on the Counter-Reformation and the Baroque. His impact on thought and language remained vigorous.[12] Much agreement existed between him and the anti-Machiavellians, not only on issues but on answers too, as we have shown. The basic issue, whether a Christian could be a successful ruler or politician, was laid out by Machiavelli, which is not to deny that contemporary political circumstances brought it to the surface in a more fundamental sense. He gave it voice and deserves much of the credit for making political morality a dominant issue of the Baroque. Machiavelli exhibited a Renaissance confidence in the capacity of man to plan and exercise effective government, and the anti-Machiavellians displayed a similar confidence. Machiavelli defined the state in terms of power and so focused political thought on power. While retaining the Aristotelian and Scholastic purpose of the state, peace and order, material prosperity, and the promotion of virtue, the anti-Machiavellians proposed to show that their program led to a powerful state more effectively than did Machiavelli's. Power was not evil. It was, as Machiavelli declared, an absolute necessity for a prince or state in a hostile and chaotic world. The anti-Machiavellians accepted and fostered his reorientation of political thought toward power, and in doing so they assumed to a significant degree his criterion of utility—that is, usefulness for the development of a powerful state—as the test for the validity of a political program. They recognized to an extent beyond the Scholastics the new sovereign state of Machiavelli and Bodin and the competition and rivalry among these states.

Many lesser, related issues, which if not initially raised by Machiavelli were sharply reformulated by him, set the topics for treatment by the anti-Machiavellians. Machiavelli's famous statement in *The Prince* that what was important was not that the ruler have certain virtuous qualities but that he seem to have them, raised the question of the relationship between appearance and reality, and it became a standing concern for the anti-Machiavellians and for the Baroque. The social role of religion, the use of deceit in politics, the relative value to a prince of the love or fear of his subjects, "men and money" as the basis of power, the composition of an army, and the relationship of ruler or state to fortune or providence were all issues brought to the surface by Machiavelli that set the agenda for the anti-Machiavellians and found echoes in Baroque culture.

In its affirmation that the Christian could succeed in politics, anti-Machiavellianism manifested a fundamentally optimistic vision of the Christian's relationship to the world. This form of optimism must be considered a principal feature of the Counter-Reformation and the Baroque. This is not to deny the presence of an Augustinian, Jansenist countertendency, especially in France, but we must avoid projecting on to the rest of Catholic Europe the situation in France, where Baroque culture never really took hold.[13] The first principle of anti-Machiavellian statecraft was that the good (*bonum honestum*) and the useful (*bonum utile*) were found together in the real world. Machiavelli had radically separated them in his insistence that the successful politician could not long remain on the path of Christian moral virtue. The very titles of Scribani's and Saavedra's volumes, combining Christian with the often suspect term politician or *politicus*, testified to the opposite conviction. The two basic arguments the anti-Machiavellians employed were what we have called intrinsic or immanent and providentialist pragmatism. This was the fundamental form of their thought. Its most basic appearance was in the connection they found between virtue, reputation, and power, which emerged as three key, interrelated concepts of the anti-Machiavellians and of the Baroque period. In a broad sense they reappeared in five main elements of anti-Machiavellian statecraft, in that the good, virtue, produced the useful, reputation and power. But before we take these up, a word must be said about the absolutism of the anti-Machiavellians, which reflected a common feature of the Baroque and Counter-Reformation conception of government.

The period of the religious wars saw a clear shift in European political thought toward absolutism, the two most well-known examples being Bodin and Hobbes, and the anti-Machiavellians were a part of this trend. All six we have discussed in detail were absolutists, who generally favored monarchy as a form of government tempered by vague aristocratic or democratic elements, Botero and Scribani assuming this without discussion, the others stating it if only indirectly. The anti-Machiavellians broke with the general Scholastic tradition of estates and of a right to resistance, the Spaniard Mariana being an exception in this regard. Yet theirs was not the ideology or trappings of divine right kingship as espoused in England by James I or by the French tradition leading to Bossuet, despite occasional echoes of this in Lipsius or Contzen. Consent remained the basis of government, but in fact could no longer be effectively withdrawn. The reason for anti-Machiavellian absolutism was practical. Only a strong monarchy could restore and maintain order in the age of religious wars and growing cities. This was especially true when one took account of the many-headed mob, who were perceived as an increasing threat to authority and social order.

For the anti-Machiavellians there was no effective way a king could be coerced, either by the people, by another prince, or even by the pope. His sovereignty protected him against the last two, and there were no domestic institutional checks on him. Only God could take kings to task. A prince could impose taxes without the consent of a representative body, although he was always wise to seek popular acceptance of levies. The appeal to resistance usually led to war and a chaotic situation worse than an oppressive government. Tyranny was more endurable than anarchy. Hesitant on these issues were the Spanish authors Ribadeneira and Saavedra, not to mention Mariana, probably because of their nearness to the Spanish and Scholastic traditions. Ribadeneira explicitly avoided the issue of the need of consent for taxation, and only with great reluctance did Saavedra accept the right of the king in cases of necessity to override the cortes on tax issues.

But if the anti-Machiavellians placed no institutional restraints on the ruler, they insisted on his adherence to natural law and his responsibility before God. They urged him to heed the advice of his councillors. Nor did some hesitate to warn that a tyrannical ruler did, in fact, often lose his crown. There were two ultimate checks on him. One was his conscience, educated in piety and virtue, and sometimes formed with the help of a theologian or confessor. The second arose out of his need for popular support or reputation. Here the need for consent reappeared in a nonjuridical form.

The first element of anti-Machiavellian statecraft was to acquire and maintain reputation, which was essential to a ruler. It was the same as consent or popular support, and it constituted the most basic ingredient of a ruler's power after virtue, which itself was the source of reputation. Reputation was power. Machiavelli had insisted on the need of popular support for a prince or government—this was a main theme of *The Prince* and the *Discourses*—and the anti-Machiavellians took over this democratic element in their vision of government. Occasionally they wrote of the importance of reputation for foreign policy, as when Contzen noted that battles could be won on the force of reputation alone when enemies refused to challenge a ruler. But their principal attention was given to reputation's importance for the ruler's relationship to his own people. It was more vital to a ruler's power than was money, army, or lands, although these were important factors in its creation. When a Baroque ruler or statesman like Maximilian or Olivares argued that reputation demanded a certain policy, he meant that the basic interest of the state required it. Richelieu too, familiar with the anti-Machiavellian tradition, recognized the overriding value of reputation. Advising Louis XIII in his *Political Testament*, he claimed that history showed that princes of great reputation achieved more than those who might have surpassed them in military forces, riches, or other forms of power. Better to risk the state itself rather than reputation, "the greatest force of sovereigns [*le plus grand force des souverains*]," he wrote at one point, insisting on the need for fidelity to agreements.[14]

Reputation existed in the wills of subjects as a combination of love and fear, where fear designated respect, reverence, and awe, more than fear of punishment or terror. As a group the anti-Machiavellians struck a healthy balance between love and fear with a slight tilt toward fear. Botero and Scribani were the only two who directly addressed the question of which was the more important, with Botero closest to Machiavelli's insistence on fear and Scribani at the other extreme.

Virtue was the way to reputation and power. Just as for Machiavelli's *virtù*, anti-Machiavellian virtue was the instrument by which the ruler gathered and sustained reputation or popular support. Lipsius went so far as to call the good will and reverence of the people itself the prince's "virtue." The virtue of a prince or man of politics was a combination of moral virtue and political skill guided by prudence, which stood out, often paired with valor, as the leading virtue of the Baroque ruler or man of politics. It generally counseled moderation in government; a ruler ought not expect the obedience of monks from his subjects, Saavedra warned, and the attempt to compel it usually resulted from his own pride. One of prudence's many demands was that a prince or statesman acquire a particular knowledge of individual states, especially his own, with a view to adapting principles or formulating policy for them. From this it was but a short step to an individualized "reason of state" for particular states. All in all, the ruler who through the exercise of his virtue provided "abundance, peace, and justice," in the words of Botero, or in other terms, secured the common good of the subjects, would have their support. The duty of the ruler to advance the common good coincided with his advantage, to increase his reputation and so his power, in the clearest form. In this way he maintained the consent of his subjects and guaranteed the de facto continuance of his rule.

Machiavelli, however, had declared that what counted in the case of some virtues like truthfulness or liberality and certainly in the case of religion was the appearance, not the reality itself. The prince must be thought to possess them, but to exercise them zealously was to invite ruin. Here there arose the issue of the relationship between appearance and reality, which fascinated the anti-Machiavellians as it did Baroque thinkers and artists, for example, in the illusions created by Baroque art like the false dome painted on the ceiling of the Church of San Ignacio in Rome. The anti-Machiavellians generally argued that it was not possible to deceive the people, in the long run, with the illusion of virtue, and that the discovery of the attempt to deceive stigmatized the prince as a hypocrite. Statecraft required a virtue that was genuine, because only it could safely secure reputation.

Yet the anti-Machiavellians readily admitted the importance of appearances in politics, Saavedra going so far in his dialectical fashion as to assert that "there is no monarchy so powerful that it is not sustained more by opinion than by truth."[15] Botero in his short treatise on reputation distinguished genuine from artificial reputation and urged the ruler to promote the latter. This was necessary, and acceptable, as long as he remained within the realm of verisimilitude. Contzen insisted on the necessity, and morality, of promoting the ruler's image and advertising his virtues, and most anti-Machiavellians suggested practices and demeanor for doing this. Machiavelli had urged heroic and stunning deeds, like those of Ferdinand of Aragon, to augment a ruler's reputation and create a sense of wonder and awe in subjects, but only Botero incorporated this into his program, seeking to produce an aura of mystery about the prince. Patronage of the arts was recommended by Botero and Scribani, and both Botero and Lipsius favored the pageants and popular entertainments of the day to impress the people and enhance the ruler's reputation. Thus appearances were crucial to a ruler's standing, but they did not take the place of the reality of virtue or power.

In the harsh, competitive world of court and politics, a second element of anti-Machiavellian statecraft was the donning of a fox's skin or the exercise of cunning or deceit. The anti-Machiavellians were as aware of this need as Machiavelli. Deceit as a part of prudence was essential for the political survivor, and its licit and illicit use was a topic that captivated anti-Machiavellian writers and was a preoccupation of Baroque culture. Casuistry flourished in the effort to arrive at a realistic ethic. Lipsius arrayed practices of "mixed prudence" under the heading of deceit and attributed to them different degrees of malice or departure from virtue. But his statement that a drop of water did not spoil the wine indicated that he did not consider them all immoral, and certainly others did not. Ribadeneira preferred the figure of an antidote used against a viper's poison. They scrutinized practices to determine what was and what was not permitted, and generally they linked their condemnation of a practice with its lack of utility. Often in this gray area they failed in clarity; neither were they all of the same mind. Two opposing statements set the tone for the discussion: Botero's assertion, reiterated by Saavedra, that in politics interest always prevailed over other considerations and the conviction that trustworthiness was essential to a ruler's or statesman's reputation. Moreover, mutual trust had to exist in a viable society, domestic or international.

Yet a healthy mistrust was required for life in government or at court, as a defense against the deceit of others. Dissimulation was absolutely necessary for the ruler or man of politics, but lying was prohibited by all except Lipsius, who with an uneasy conscience allowed it under extreme circumstances for the good of the state. Yet the anti-Machiavellians had great trouble clearly distinguishing lying from dissimulation, and they disagreed about equivocation. Information they realized to be a precious asset in the political struggle, and they judged dissimulation to be necessary for the protection of secrets. In fact, the basic distinction between dissimulation and lying came out to be between the conceal-ment of information or the preservation of secrets and the active propa-gation of falsehood. Bribery was deemed acceptable and encouraged by the anti-Machiavellians who considered it, usually in two forms, pen-sions or gifts by rulers to maintain the loyalty of restive subjects and payments to foreign officials, civil or military, to secure information or win their allegiance. Scribani most aggressively recommended bribery as a way to obtain vital information and most insistently warned the ruler to establish security measures for his own officials. He also outlawed the use of bribery in the courts, and the constant insistence on the provision of justice to subjects indicates that this practice was generally considered out of bounds because it corrupted an essential function of the state.

Perfidy or infidelity to agreements and injustice or departure from law were the two most serious forms of deceit taken up by Lipsius. The anti-Machiavellians generally demanded adherence to agreements as nec-essary for the preservation of trust and reputation. Richelieu also insisted on this, breaking explicitly with many "politiques." Large powers, he claimed, were usually more faithful to alliances because they could less afford the loss of reputation that unfaithfulness brought in its train.[16] The one exception, for Lipsius, was in negotiations with rebels, where his hatred for rebellion induced him to permit a ruler to make promises he had no intention of keeping. Contzen refused to allow either this or the argument that promises made under duress did not bind, since they could be used to invalidate many agreements and would thus corrode the trust necessary for political relationships. Yet nearly all the anti-Machiavellians acknowledged the truth of Botero's statement that agree-ments not founded on common interest would not long endure and rec-ognized the pressure of necessity. In order better to reconcile principle with fact, they would have done well to recur to the Scholastics, who generally were more flexible regarding withdrawal from commitments. Scribani moved farthest in this direction. The reason why others did not lay precisely in utility, that is, in their fear that it would impair a prince's reputation for trustworthiness.

Anti-Machiavellian authors had relatively little to say about depar-ture from the law. They were resolute in not countenancing departures from natural law, a point Lipsius clarified in the 1596 edition of the *Six Books*, but they usually followed the Scholastic tradition acknowledging the force of necessity when dealing with positive law—for Aquinas him-self necessity was not subject to positive law—and their absolutism inclined them in this direction. A case illustrating an acceptable procedure in the face of necessity according to the anti-Machiavellians was the controversial decision of Emperor Ferdinand II in 1634 to order the arrest, and if this were impossible in the circumstances as was likely, the execution, not the murder, of his enigmatic general, Wallenstein. Ferdinand, a genuinely conscientious man, did not act arbitrarily. He submitted all the evidence available to a committee of three imperial councillors, two of whom were known to be supporters of the general. The committee judged him to be guilty of insubordination and treachery and a threat to the security of the state, and they recommended the procedure Ferdinand followed. A formal trial was not possible, not least of all because of Wallenstein himself, who officials in Vienna knew would not submit to arrest. Though he seems to have overridden positive law, Ferdinand cannot be said to have acted against the natural law.[17]

Economic development constituted the third element of anti-Machiavellian reason of state, which they saw as a moral alternative to Machiavelli's unacceptable practices. Power and virtue went together, and for these architects of a Baroque and Counter-Reformation state as for Machiavelli two sources of power were money and men. But they understood both of them in a broader sense than he did, economic growth as well as ready funds, an economically productive population as well as soldiers. Five of the six writers emphasized economic growth as a way to a powerful state, and in doing so they advocated expanding the state's activity. The accumulation of treasure was indispensable to a prince, and the foundation for this was the wealth of his subjects as a tax base. The good and the useful converged, the ruler's duty to foster the benefit of his subjects and his need for revenue. Botero and Contzen deserve a prominent place among the early mercantilists. Both presented comprehensive plans for the economy, encompassing agriculture, industry, commerce, and tax policy, both calling for the imposition of regular taxes whether there existed an immediate need for funds or not and so fostering a feature of the modern state, regular taxation. Ribadeneira, Scribani, and Saavedra were not as systematic or complete as Botero and Contzen, but the promotion of economic reform was fundamental to their programs.

The most critical factor in the production of wealth were the human resources of a state. Botero, the founder of demographic studies, though well aware of the social problems caused by the growing population in Italian cities and of the limits to the number of people a region could support, still saw in a well-trained and growing population the principal source of a country's productivity and wealth. The most populous areas of Europe were the wealthiest, North Italy, the Netherlands, France. The promotion of agriculture, essential to feed a growing population, but especially the development of industry and the growth of cities were seen as crucial. Two major anti-Machiavellian themes were severe criticism of Spain for its export of raw materials and import of finished goods, for the artificiality of its income from the New World, and for its crushing taxation, and admiration for the initiatives of the Dutch and the Flemish in industry and trade.

Generally, the anti-Machiavellians saw the need to foster social attitudes favorable to a work ethic, a further area of government activity. Saavedra recommended a style of piety that would put more emphasis on work and less on pilgrimages and feast days. Scribani wished that Spanish nobles would see a source of honor in business activity, and Ribadeneira, Contzen, Scribani, and Saavedra were all critical of a nobility that did not pull its weight but also conscious of the political obstacles to challenging their privileges. Contzen exalted the contribution merchants made to society, and he advocated a frugal, "puritan" style of life that would generate savings and capital for investment.

The anti-Machiavellian concern for economic progress tells against the arguments, considerably weakened already, that Counter-Reformation Catholicism was responsible for the failure of Catholic states, especially the Italian states and Spain, to keep pace economically with the Protestant countries of the north during the seventeenth century. The principal explanation for the shift of economic hegemony from Italy northwards must be sought elsewhere: in the loss of markets in the Levant and northern Europe due to the Thirty Years' War and mercantilistic measures taken by northern states; in high prices due to a rigid guild system; in economic recession that encouraged investment in land and offices; in the growth of world trade and the importance of Atlantic ports; in social attitudes regarding honor associated with the Baroque but little connected with religion.[18] Nor did the Catholic position on usury present any meaningful restriction on the sources of credit or economic growth, certainly not after 1600.[19] Yet Catholic attitudes in some areas did impede economic progress. Saavedra gently called attention to them when he complained of the exaggerated numbers entering the clergy and religious life in Spain, the excessive lands held by the church, and the many feast days free from work. Another attitude uncongenial to economic growth appeared when the desire for religious uniformity clashed with the need to retain or recruit economically productive subjects. To this we shall return when we take up toleration.[20]

In a world where war was unavoidable and the need for preparedness constant, a vigorous military was the fourth feature of an anti-Machiavellian reason of state. It was a source of power, to be exercised according to the norms of virtue and discipline if it were to be effective.

The anti-Machiavellians were initially drawn into a discussion of the military by Machiavelli's contention that Christians made poor soldiers. They argued that war was a legitimate, even necessary Christian activity, and they showed that Christianity had produced many great soldiers and military leaders, from Constantine to Charles V and Alexander Farnese, not to mention the heroes of the New World. Pacifism was sharply rejected—it corresponded to Machiavelli's view of Christianity—and so was Machiavelli's militarism and thirst for conquest and glory. An awareness of the horrors of war characterized the anti-Machiavellians, most of whom had experienced them at first hand on a scale Machiavelli had not. They accepted the fact of war and the need for defense, and they endeavored to submit war to the restraints of law and humanity. In general, they took over, with little elaboration except for Lipsius and Contzen, the principles of the just war theory as found in the contemporary Scholastics, devoting relatively little space, however, to the manner of conducting a just war as opposed to the grounds for initiating one.

Apart from Botero's summons to a war against the Turks, who were not heretics but infidels occupying Christian territory and threatening further advances, the anti-Machiavellians manifested no enthusiasm in their volumes for holy or religious war, as one might have expected them to do in the age of religious wars. Ribadeneira and Contzen merely mentioned the possibility of such wars in passing, though both were involved in the promotion of holy war, Ribadeneira prior and Contzen subsequent to his writing. No anti-Machiavellian demonstrated zeal for religious war against the heretics in his writing. Scribani warned against those who urged war for the sake of religion, and Saavedra was at most half-hearted in his support for war against the Dutch rebels. One reason for this was anti-Machiavellian respect for the sovereign state, which did not brook intervention by an outsider. Nor was there any clear mention in the anti-Machiavellians of the exercise of the indirect power of the papacy toward European states.

Botero, Lipsius, and Saavedra did make an effort to incorporate into their thought contemporary ideas about war found in Machiavelli. They conceded that war and conquest were a source of glory for a ruler and that war served to invigorate a state or at least to distract subjects from domestic difficulties, but they besought princes to await a legitimate opportunity, that is, a just cause, to undertake a campaign for these purposes. Richelieu said in essence the same in his *Political Testament*, although he did not mention war as a means to obtain princely glory.[21] The usual remark that opportunity would soon present itself must not be seen as cynicism but as a statement of fact following from consciousness of the contemporary political situation. It also represented a further effort to establish the relationship of the good with the useful, the pursuit of justice with glory and reputation or domestic political advantage. Yet Botero and Saavedra each argued further that the development of his own state enhanced the reputation or popular support of a ruler more than did a victorious war, a point implicit in others, and Botero, it would appear, ingeniously organized his whole *Reason of State* to show that a ruler could acquire the glory of expanding his state by developing its human and material resources more than by foreign conquest.

As with economic development, the anti-Machiavellians enlarged the role of government as they took up and elaborated on points of military organization made by Machiavelli. The citizen army he championed did not prove feasible. They generally wanted at least a minimal professional force, and Lipsius's *miles perpetuus* combined with rotating reservists, which Contzen and Scribani endorsed, was to have an influence on the development of many states, as was his advocacy of Roman order and discipline on the evolution of armies. The anti-Machiavellians usually accepted Machiavelli's preference for native troops over foreigners. For Botero they were necessary to preserve the genuine independence of a prince, who could not afford to rely on foreigners for defense, and for Lipsius, like Machiavelli, they were more likely to demonstrate loyalty to the prince. But most anti-Machiavellians considered foreigners a necessary complement to native soldiers and denied Machiavelli's position that unity of language and culture was essential for an effective army. In fact, for Botero the multinational composition of contemporary armies fostered healthy diversity and competition. For Contzen the principle of voluntary service prevailed over the principle of native troops; better foreign volunteers than native conscripts. A new idea introduced by Botero and advanced by others was the need to provide for wounded and retired soldiers and for their wives and children. Attention to these concerns would make soldiers into more loyal and more vigorous fighters. Do we have here the origins of the *Invalides*?

The anti-Machiavellians fostered unity in the Catholic or at least Christian religion as a fifth characteristic of statecraft. During the age of the Baroque and Counter-Reformation the power of government grew, in Catholic areas as well as Protestant, with the help of religion. Indeed, government activity on behalf of religion has recently been called a "motor" for the development of the German states equal in importance to the growth of the military and the introduction of regular taxation.[22] Religion was certainly a principal integrating factor in the nascent multiethnic Habsburg monarchy as it emerged under Ferdinand II.[23] Machiavelli recognized the valuable political function of religion, and the anti-Machiavellians found his cynical advocacy of the manipulation of religion for political ends to be perhaps the most repulsive feature of his thought. Yet their own stress on the ways Christianity was useful to prince and government tended ironically to transform religion into an instrument of the state with harmful long-term results.

Christianity was a stalwart support of the state because it insisted upon the divine origin of authority and the subjects' duty of obedience and allegiance except when they might be ordered to obey a command clearly against God's will. In this regard Botero and Contzen contrasted Catholicism with Calvinism, which they saw on the basis of recent history as subversive of authority by its very nature. Christianity was, in virtue of the fear of punishment and hope of reward it held out, the only effective deterrent from crime and prop of the social order, especially with regard to the common people or mob. Lipsius, Contzen, and to a lesser extent Saavedra shared Machiavelli's view that fear engendered by religion and the threat of its punishments was the most potent force compelling obedience to the laws and the practice of virtue, especially in straitened circumstances. Their highlighting of fear contrasted with Scribani's accent on love, and it contributed to the presentation of Christianity as a religion of fear, which characterized some strains of the Counter-Reformation.[24]

The anti-Machiavellians accepted the contemporary consensus that unity of religion was highly desirable, if not essential, as a bond uniting the citizens of a powerful state and that heresy necessarily generated social and political unrest and upheaval. Yet with the exception of Contzen, who envisioned a steady Catholic march toward victory over Protestantism in Germany, and possibly Scribani, who did not address the issue, they all conceded that at a certain point, where protracted conflict was the alternative, the greater good was served by toleration. Paradoxically, often their concern for utility led them to this. Religion was useful as a bond among the subjects, but when it lost its utility as such—it having become obvious that further conflict in the interest of religion only barbarized the people, undermined all religion, and destroyed the state—then toleration was acceptable. Thus the anti-Machiavellians came to accept the view of most *politici*. Ribadeneira's acceptance of toleration and the manner he came to it were especially noteworthy. It was precisely through this type of argument from the greater common good that Catholics in some areas came to accept and justify toleration during the Counter-Reformation. It prevailed, for example, at the conference of theologians convoked in Vienna in 1635 by Emperor Ferdinand II to evaluate the terms of the Peace of Prague, which in turn anticipated the Peace of Westphalia.[25]

At this point it is useful to return to economic development and the failure, in general, of Catholic states to keep up with Protestant ones. There were many nonreligious reasons for this, as we have seen. One reason that can be attributed to religion seems to have been the lack of toleration in Catholic states that resulted in the exile or departure of economically productive groups or the refusal to recruit them. The anti-Machiavellians and such other Catholic thinkers as Molanus and Becan advocated toleration in cases where the greater good, religious or political, called for it, but this was rarely stretched to include greater economic development. Lipsius's advocacy of toleration for quiet dissidents pointed to implicit economic benefits, and his fellow Netherlander Scribani in his advice for the city of Antwerp allowed for the immigration of English craftsmen who practiced their religion unobtrusively.[26] Saavedra showed his frequent ambivalence in his attitude toward the recruitment of foreign craftsmen for settlement in Spain, and he feared that the economic benefits they would bring would not outweigh the harm they would do to religious and cultural unity. Generally, this unity had a higher priority for the anti-Machiavellians, despite their esteem for economic development. Perhaps the clearest example of this in practice was the departure of nearly one hundred thousand Protestants from the Austrian lands under Ferdinand II in the first third of the seventeenth century.[27] The Revocation of the Edict of Nantes in 1685 was a case for itself.

Religious unity remained the ideal for the anti-Machiavellians, and for most politicians too. Generally, the anti-Machiavellians called for firm treatment of dissenters when this was feasible, and Botero and Contzen proposed detailed programs for the maintenance of Catholicism and for its introduction into newly acquired lands. The state had the major part in the implementation of these programs, and this led in practice to an augmentation of its role in religious matters and so in its power. Indeed, the measures of the Counter-Reformation, dependent as they were on the state, gave impetus to bureaucratic growth.[28] In Spain one need only think of the apparatus created by the Inquisition, though it was not mentioned by the anti-Machiavellians. Both Botero and Contzen required patience in the process of winning over the people and underlined the positive measures to be employed: clergy of high moral quality, effective preachers, genuine care for and adaptation to the people, and education. Schools, in particular the Jesuit colleges, were accorded a significant role in the process, to gain the youth and so win the population in the long run. Generally, the anti-Machiavellians kept this long-range perspective in view.

When it came to pressures to conform, Botero wrote that these were political measures aimed not at conversion but at the prevention of rebellion and so they were the task of government. The most severe penalty any anti-Machiavellian suggested, apart from Lipsius, was exile. They were aware that faith was a free act and that attempts to impose it could create hypocrites and false conversions. This was one reason why Lipsius opposed prying into consciences and recommended the sufferance of quiet dissenters. Contzen's principal argument in defense of the use of force followed Augustine's *"compelle intrare* [force them to enter]." Those who first participated under pressure in external rituals or practices of the church would gradually assimilate the suitable interior attitudes, and they would then be grateful to those who applied the pressure. This was a psychology frequently at work in the Counter-Reformation. That pressures could and sometimes did have an opposite effect is evident.

Both Botero and Saavedra warned rulers to avoid conflicts with the pope because the people usually sided with him and this harmed princely reputation. But no anti-Machiavellian assigned to the pope a role in international affairs with any teeth, except perhaps Saavedra, and his principal purpose in reminding the pope of his function as *"padre commune"* was largely to convince him to exercise it against France. The anti-Machiavellians of the Counter-Reformation virtually excluded the pope from international affairs, thus anticipating the direction of the Peace of Westphalia, and generally speaking they fostered the *Staatskirchentum* that would characterize the late seventeenth and eighteenth centuries. Scribani encouraged Philip IV to appoint worthy candidates to ecclesiastical positions, assuming appointment to be the function of the ruler, and in none of the anti-Machiavellians was there a suggestion of efforts made after Trent to regain control of these appointments. Scribani and Saavedra sanctioned the widespread use of church property for government revenue.

Education and the development of a bureaucracy were important yet less central features of anti-Machiavellian statecraft. The emphasis was placed on moral, religious, and practical education. Contzen devoted one of the *Ten Books* to the topic, where he stressed moral development. He wanted schools to be available for male students of character and ability, and he dealt with issues from infant care to university administration. Saavedra, content that Spain had a sufficiency of lawyers and theologians, favored a more practical education as in the United Provinces and encouraged the foundation of technical schools, especially for training soldiers and sailors. Botero saw education largely under the rubric of religious instruction and lauded the work of the Jesuit colleges.

In the education of the ruler himself, anti-Machiavellians underscored the value of history as a source of the experience leading to prudence. Their books teemed with examples to instruct and to inspire.

The expansion of the role of government called for by the anti-Machiavellians assumed a growing number of officials. But only Contzen elaborated at length on the organization of a bureaucracy down to the local level. Others discoursed on the selection of councillors, their qualifications, and proper employment. Ribadeneira, writing under Philip II, wanted Prince Philip to learn to delegate more authority, but generally the anti-Machiavellians encouraged more personal government by the prince and were concerned to prevent concentration of power outside him. Their suspicion of human nature resulted in a primitive separation of powers under the prince. Botero and Lipsius advocated a clear distinction between councillors, who advised the ruler, and administrators, who as governors or generals possessed jurisdiction or executive power. An issue of special importance to Spain in this context was the *valido*, with Scribani opposing the institution and Saavedra hedging on the issue. Botero, Ribadeneira, and Contzen urged princely surveillance of judges and tax collectors, those officials who most frequently came into contact with subjects, Botero even through the use of informers, which Scribani recommended for the army. Contzen outlined a system of controls whereby all officials reported to or were visited by either the prince himself or another official. Only the prince remained above this network, checked only by his conscience and his reputation. Anti-Machiavellian confidence in him contrasted with its suspicion of subordinate officials.

Thus the contents of anti-Machiavellian statecraft reveal much about the mentality of the Counter-Reformation and Baroque. But perhaps its general characteristics are more informative still about both.

The anti-Machiavellians reflected contemporary interest in the role of providence in history, which led them into a philosophy or theology of history. This was in part a legacy of Renaissance and Reformation, for which the issue of man's free will and its relationship to God's activity was central, and it remained one for Catholic thinkers of the Counter-Reformation as the drawn-out controversies over grace and free will between Jesuits and Dominicans and between Jesuits and Jansenists showed. With his interpretation of history in terms of fortune and *virtù*, Machiavelli had brought up the issue from a new perspective. The anti-Machiavellians responded incorporating elements of his thought as they did so. Ribadeneira and Contzen avoided the word fortune, but the others showed no hesitation in using it.

The anti-Machiavellians asserted first of all the fact of divine providence in history. This was known, ultimately, only with the help of faith, not by reason alone, and so was distinct from the rest of their argument. Christian reason of state demanded government in accord with religion and morality, because God usually rewarded rulers with political success or failure as their deeds merited. Many examples convincing to the person of faith were brought forward in support of this position. Contzen in the *Ten Books* scarcely allowed for instances to the contrary and so championed an extreme providentialist pragmatism. But it was obvious to most anti-Machiavellians that this did not always obtain. Lipsius and Ribadeneira were profoundly engaged personally by the question of God's providence, because of the war in the Netherlands and the defeat of the Armada respectively. So the anti-Machiavellians strove to develop a vision of history that would account for the defeat of Christian kings and rulers who appeared to be championing God's cause. The question was ultimately a form of the perennial problem of why evil exists.

First, there was the argument of the Old Testament that defeat was a punishment for sin into which the good had fallen, by which God corrected them and drew them back to the right path, or that it was a warning, a testing, a purification, lest they become too enamored of this world and forget the Lord. In these instances God often made use of an evil or pagan prince to chastise and discipline his people. So Ribadeneira interpreted the catastrophe of the Armada and Contzen, in his treatise on "The Defense of the Church Persecuted in Germany," the victory of Gustavus Adolphus at Breitenfeld. Lipsius's variation on the argument was especially noteworthy. All men were sinners, and the true state of a person's soul was known only to God. Thus no one could ever claim that punishment was undeserved or God unfair. If one considered the social nature of man and looked at kingdoms, empires, cities as social units over a long period of time, retribution for their crimes nearly always caught up with them. Neither the Jews nor the Romans had escaped this.

The second approach to the problem, not completely distinct from the first, was that essentially of Augustine and Aquinas as found chiefly in Ribadeneira. God granted success to Christian and non-Christian, to good and evil rulers alike, to manifest its transitory character and that of all earthly achievement. The genuine reward of the Christian ruler was the peace and joy of a good conscience in this world and eternal life in the next. If taken alone, this position virtually abandoned providentialist pragmatism, but in the context it was called upon to explain those instances where providentialist pragmatism did not seem to apply.

Finally, there was Lipsius's theory of the rise and fall of states and kingdoms, which exercised a powerful influence on the Baroque period, and for which he drew on Neostoicism and to a degree on Machiavelli himself. It was fitted into a broader vision of Christian providence. According to Lipsius, the rise and decline of states occurred in a pattern similar to the stages of human life. This was a natural process, carried forward in part by calamities such as wars and natural catastrophes, which could not be construed as punishment and which, Lipsius asserted with some hesitancy, resulted in greater good. The collapse of a kingdom or state was not the ultimate tragedy, since individuals and the human race survived, and new states arose in place of old ones. This process was to be accepted with constancy as God's will, but constancy did not mean passivity. On the contrary, the duty of ruler or citizen, who could not be sure which stage the process had reached, was to struggle on behalf of the state until the outcome was beyond doubt and only then surrender to what was clearly God's purpose.

Echoes of this attitude can be heard in the statement attributed to the future Emperor Ferdinand II in the Baroque classic, *The Virtues of Emperor Ferdinand II*, as he faced a crisis in 1616, "All mortal things have their own time; to be born, to grow, to pass away; it may be that the rule of the Austrians is included in this; and if this should seem good to God, he [Ferdinand] would not only not resist but not be sad that God chose by his will to distribute empires and kingdoms now to these people, now to those. Human resources and power are at his disposal, and He gives them and takes them away as He will."[29]

Fifty years later Saavedra adapted this theory to the situation of Spain, which he was convinced had passed its peak and entered upon evident and inevitable decline. But decline proceeded at a different pace with different states, and it could be slowed down by vigorous human activity. Decisive action could alter history. This was not to resist God's will but, according to the Molinist theology to which Saavedra resorted, to participate in the course of providence and affect the flow of history by virtue of God's foresight of human actions from all eternity in the light of which he formulated his decrees. So Saavedra forcefully asserted the power of human free will.

The anti-Machiavellians shared with Machiavelli a decidedly low opinion of human nature, though they were not quite as pessimistic as he was. Variations on his theme that men were generally "ungrateful, changeable, simulators and dissimulators, runaways in danger, eager for gain" sounded often enough. Politics was governed by the law of the jungle, hence the need to be always on guard and to protect oneself with mistrust and dissimulation. Like their adversary the anti-Machiavellians demonstrated contempt for the mob, for the control of which religion, and especially the sanctions of religion, were necessary, and bread, entertainment, and pageantry were useful. Fear, to be sure a fear characterized by reverence and respect more than terror, was generally a more valuable element in popular support than love.

Yet paradoxically, the anti-Machiavellians expanded the reach and activity of government and in doing so manifested a great confidence in its ability to direct a society toward the order and discipline desired by the Baroque after the changes of the sixteenth century. This was a form of optimism they inherited from Machiavelli and the Renaissance, which it is legitimate to see as a forerunner of the Enlightenment. Anti-Machiavellians were optimistic about the capacity of government, and church, to create an orderly and prosperous society out of unpromising human material. The two working together could restore religion, inculcate attitudes of obedience, loyalty, and diligence, and impose social discipline. Mercantilistic measures could bring wealth to a country, and regular taxation income to the prince, the anti-Machiavellians contended, and training and discipline could create effective and well-behaved armies composed of a core of professional troops augmented by reservists. International order was possible. For Contzen the part of education was of particular importance, and he and others advocated the effort to change social attitudes by inculcating a work ethic and supported sumptuary laws with their often detailed regulation of life.

Nor were the anti-Machiavellians writing in a vacuum. The effort to impose order and social discipline characterized the period, and anti-Machiavellian works like Botero's, Lipsius's, and Contzen's were virtually handbooks of how to go about this. From roughly the mid-sixteenth to the early eighteenth centuries, church and government, in Protestant and Catholic regions and in some areas more effectively than in others, worked to create bureaucratic structures and well-disciplined populations, and so, it has been argued, helped prepare the way for later industrial society.[30] Between the late sixteenth and the late eighteenth centuries, the image of the German gradually changed from the coarse, beer-swilling peasant to the punctual, industrious worker.[31] Nor can one overlook the many mercantilist initiatives undertaken, with varying degrees of success, and the growing efficiency of tax collection. Armies grew and, especially after the Thirty Years' War, became better organized. Anti-Machiavellian optimism, in this form, contributed to a mentality that supported the growing activity of government during the Baroque and after.

The contents of anti-Machiavellian statecraft were arrived at by arguments based chiefly on reason, as the very term "reason of state" was meant to indicate by Botero. The English Jesuit Persons used the term precisely in the sense of "the rules of politics insofar as they were accessible to the natural light of reason" in his *Conference about the Next Succession* (1595).[32] Baroque culture and the Counter-Reformation esteemed reason. This was a reason in harmony with faith; no conflict was perceived between the two. Furthermore, the criterion for the validity or reasonableness of an argument came increasingly to be utility, in that the good and the useful were, for practical purposes, nearly equated. The desire to meet Machiavelli on his own terms explains, of course, this style of argument, which pointed toward the Enlightenment. The anti-Machiavellians drew on non-Christian authorities and examples precisely to show that their argument was based on reason, not faith, and here they turned especially to the Romans as had Machiavelli. They confirm the conception of the seventeenth century as "the Roman Century." In addition, in their pursuit of examples they searched other historical eras, the Christian and Byzantine Empires, the Middle Ages, even contemporary China, and so extended historical knowledge, even if they showed little critical sense. Figures about whom they wrote turned up regularly in the drama of the Baroque, and their examples became commonplace.

Anti-Machiavellian statecraft aimed at the preservation of the state, and this feature reflected a culture that sought entities and structures that would endure in the face of time and change. The other side of the Baroque sense of the transitoriness of things was the pursuit of permanence and stability. Machiavelli himself spoke of the foundation and preservation of states, but as the *Discourses* clearly showed, his primary interest was in the creation of a state that would stand the test of time. The challenge was to endure, and for Machiavelli, to meet this challenge expansion was necessary. After the first sentence of the *Reason of State* Botero never again mentioned a state's foundation and developed his own notion of its expansion. Preservation, however, meant change not stagnation, as the need for increased government activity showed, but a change that took place gradually—as summer moved, not directly into winter, but through fall—and for which a prudent ruler prepared his people. Yet eternal life for a state was not possible, all including Machiavelli himself recognized. Even the most magnificent of empires perished. The Baroque theory of the rise and decline of states was an attempt to come to terms with this fact and to discover a pattern in the life of states and the limits of their existence, an issue of unusual interest in contemporary Spain.

Anti-Machiavellian statecraft was the product not of philosophers and theorists but of political writers and moralists or casuists who sought by careful analysis the application of general principles to new and specific situations. The anti-Machiavellians shared the contemporary concern with moral practice, with how to live morally in the changing world of the early seventeenth century, and they found counterparts in writers like the Spaniard Baltasar Gracían, the French moralists Jean de la Bruyère and La Rochefoucauld, and in the Catholic, and Protestant, moral theologians who focused more and more on specific issues of moral conduct.[33] Related to these were the spiritual writers like Francis de Sales and Louis de Puente, who attempted to show the practice of the full Christian life in different states and callings. Moral practice involved casuistry, which can go to excesses, and Pascal pilloried the Jesuits for making Christian life too easy. But casuistry is essential in any complex society, and especially in a changing society, where people attempt to live in a moral fashion. This is much clearer to us today when it is evident that issues like the morality of nuclear weapons or of medical or business practice can only be resolved, and then only approximately, by the careful analysis of situations and application of principles.

Lastly, anti-Machiavellian statecraft was an effort at an intellectual synthesis that succeeded only in part and that betrayed a degree of strain or artificiality, an attribute often associated with the Baroque. This brings us back to what was said early in this chapter about the basic anti-Machiavellian view that the Christian could achieve political success. In a narrower field they pursued the same unity that the systematic philosophers of the seventeenth century did, the late Scholastics, especially Suarez, then Descartes, Hobbes, Leibniz, and many lesser lights. The search for unity was a feature of the culture. What Machiavelli had separated the anti-Machiavellians hoped to reunite, politics and Christian morality, the useful and the good. They succeeded, in that they demonstrated that Christians could and often did prosper in politics without compromising themselves. This was of great significance. Far from being necessarily "dirty," as Machiavelli claimed, politics was a worthy vocation in which a Christian could live out a life of service. Contzen above all proclaimed this. The Christian was not to retreat from the world of politics, as some Christian thinkers advocated, but to play an active role in it. The anti-Machiavellians displayed creativity in showing how the Christian might retain his integrity and be an effective politician as, to take only one example, in the proposals of Botero and Contzen that earned them a foremost position among early mercantilists. Theirs was a specification of the Counter-Reformation spirituality of Ignatius Loyola and Francis de Sales.

But beyond this fundamental optimism there were two further tendencies found in the anti-Machiavellians, often in the same authors, both of which seem to have characterized the Baroque. One tendency inclined to force the good and the useful together in a manner that gave credence to an element of strain in the Baroque. Botero and Contzen can be singled out here. It simply is not true to experience that in this world, to use slang terms, "the good guys always win" any more than it is true that "nice guys finish last" always, as Machiavelli claimed. Neither Machiavelli nor the anti-Machiavellians ring true in this regard. The piling up of examples illustrating that in this world God punished princes who did not suppress heresy or were unfaithful to pacts and rewarded those who acted in an opposite fashion seemed intended to overpower the reader rather than to persuade him.

But all six anti-Machiavellians, except Contzen in the *Ten Books*, realized in the end the limitations of the arguments from pragmatism. They exhibited a sense for the tension between the good and the useful, and they struggled with providence. This was the second tendency. Lipsius, Ribadeneira, Saavedra grappled with providence's mystery. Lipsius agonized over his allowance of a lie or an overriding of the law under pressure of necessity, and he reacted violently when charged with "Machiavellizing." Scribani acknowledged explicitly that the Christian politician might be forced to choose between career and fidelity to principle. But a more pronounced recognition of this and of the truth that the genuine Christian would encounter adversity and contradiction, that is, the cross, would have been desirable. The conflict brought on by the good and the useful did take on sharper form in Lipsius and in the last two writers, Scribani and Saavedra, who, at the time of writing, possessed more experience of politics than the others. Scribani and Saavedra abandoned the systematic method of the earlier writers in favor of largely independent essays on matters of state and politics. Their adoption of this form may be interpreted as an attempt to create an artistic unity—and Saavedra's *Politico Christian Prince* was certainly a work of literature—where an intellectual synthesis was deemed impossible, and so more easily to slide over or downplay inconsistencies, which did appear more frequently in them. On the one hand, they were more faithful to experience in that they brought out more clearly conflict between the good and the useful; on the other, to the extent they put forward a purported unity of the two, they too displayed a forced character. Thus they best expressed both tendencies.

This brings us to our final consideration, the significance of the anti-Machiavellians. First, they constituted a major aspect of the church's effort to accommodate to the changing world of the sixteenth century and especially to the sovereign states of early modern Europe. Part of Counter-Reformation reform was the attempt to define the church's relationship to the world and the way Christians could live their lives in it. The church faced similar challenges in other, related fields at this time, as we have seen. To evaluate the whole Counter-Reformation from the perspective of its accommodation would burst the limits of this volume, but certainly the anti-Machiavellians deserve great credit for affirming a Christian's place in the world and for showing how a Christian could work effectively in politics. They helped release into the world the energies of many genuine Christians with consequences that have benefited the world in ways it is impossible to measure but which can be more fully appreciated if we consider the alternative, the abandonment of the world to the Machiavellians. This is one of the glories of the Counter-Reformation and the Baroque.

There was, however, one drawback in their work that had long-term, unhappy consequences, even though one can understand the historical circumstances in which it took place. The anti-Machiavellian emphasis on the convergence of the state's or the increasingly absolute ruler's interest in power and the good of religion or, in other words, on the usefulness of religion to the development of the state fostered a mentality that saw in the church an instrument of the state. In this sense, the anti-Machiavellians excessively accommodated to the world. They tied the church too closely to the states of the Old Regime, which was to come under growing criticism in the course of the eighteenth century and to enter upon a period of gradual collapse at the quake of the French Revolution and its aftershocks, with disastrous results for the church. It had become identified in the eyes of many, in different degrees in different parts of Europe to be sure, with the state and the social system. Even today in many of the formerly Catholic states of Europe—Spain, Austria, France, Belgium, and parts of Germany and Italy—the long tradition of its close association with the state still burdens the church. The temptation to align itself with the power of the state is one the church of the Counter-Reformation and Baroque did not adequately resist.

Finally, to end on a positive note, at a time of growing cynicism about politics, when it was seen increasingly, due in no small part to Machiavelli, as necessarily compromising, and the term politician or *politico* frequently connoted underhandedness or irreligion, the anti-Machiavellians reasserted the tradition dating back to Aristotle and Cicero of the dignity of the vocation to politics and the importance to it of moral virtue. For a state or a society to flourish, it needed leaders and citizens who were persons of virtue, where virtue denoted both moral qualities and political ability. Thinkers of the Enlightenment and the American Founding Fathers once again reaffirmed this truth firmly upheld by the Counter-Reformation, which is much more than a truism. Our own day has seen once again the rampant growth of cynicism about politics and politicians. A reading of the anti-Machiavellians reminds us that politics without virtue is suicidal and that the political vocation is an honorable one.

Notes

Preface

1. *Machiavellism*, p. 49. For a recent evaluation of Meinecke's ground-breaking volume, see Stolleis, "Friedrich Meinecke's 'Die Idee der Staatsräson' und die neuere Forschung," esp. pp. 56–59.

Chapter 1

1. *Machiavelli: The Chief Works*, translated by A. H. Gilbert, pp. 57–58. All translations of Machiavelli and page references are from this volume unless otherwise noted, but book and chapter numbers are given for those using other editions. The Italian text I have used is *Il principe e le opere politiche*, introduction by Delio Cantimori.

2. *Prince*, 17 (p. 62).

3. *Discourses*, 2:2 (pp. 330–31); see also 3:1 (p. 422) along with many other texts. For recent discussions of Machiavelli and Christianity, see Hulliung, *Citizen Machiavelli*; Brown, "The Historian as Philosopher"; and the classic essay by Berlin, "The Originality of Machiavelli," which also evaluates many interpretations of Machiavelli.

4. *Prince*, 7 (p. 31).

5. *Discourses*, 1:9 (p. 218).

6. De Mattei, *Dal premachiavellismo all'antimachiavellismo*, pp. 44–48.

7. On the *Imitation of Christ*, see Stephanus Axters, *The Spirituality of the Old Low Countries*, trans. from the Dutch by Donald Attwater (London, 1954), pp. 71–76, and Louis Bouyer, Jean Leclercq, and François Vandenbroucke, *The Spirituality of the Middle Ages*, vol. 2 of *A History of Christian Spirituality*, trans. from the French by the Benedictines of Holme Eden Abbey, Carlisle (London, 1968; rpt. New York, 1982), pp. 436–38, 503.

8. *Utopia: A New Translation. Backgrounds. Criticism*, translated and edited by Robert M. Adams (New York, 1975), pp. 22–30, esp. 28–30.

9. *Menosprecio de corte y alabanza de aldea* and *Relox de príncipes*, usually translated in the sixteenth century as *Dial of Princes*; the theme *contemptus mundi* was only one among many in the works of this complex figure. See esp. Redondo, *Guevara (1480?-1545)*, pp. 78, 374–77, 402–5, 430–31, 663, 695–96.

10. Kiesel, "*Bei Hof, bei Höll*," pp. 91–93, 105.

11. On the abdication of Charles V, see Heinrich Lutz, *Christianitas Afflicta* (Göttingen, 1964), esp. pp. 412–15; on William's abdication, see Albrecht, "Das konfessionelle Zeitalter," pp. 404–6.

12. Church, *Richelieu and Reason of State*, pp. 72–75; Keohane, *Philosophy and the State in France*, pp. 112–16. See esp. Book 3, Essay 1, "Of the Useful and the Honorable," in *The Complete Works of Montaigne*, trans. Donald L. Frame (Stanford, 1957), pp. 599–610.

13. Stegmann, *L'héroisme cornélien*, 2:174; on the origins of the term "reason of state," see De Mattei, *Il problema della "ragion di stato,"* pp. 1–49.

14. See Chapter 4.

15. I use the term Counter-Reformation in this broad sense to comprise these three aspects of the movement within the Catholic church; specifically, it encompasses Catholic reform. On this controversial issue of terminology, see John W. O'Malley's "Introduction," in *Catholicism in Early Modern History*, pp. 3–7, and the literature cited there.

16. For the Baroque as a period in European history, see Maravall, *Culture of the Baroque*, pp. 3–15, esp. 3–4. I have drawn heavily on this and other works of Maravall, as the bibliography indicates.

17. To Francesco Vettori, Dec. 10, 1513, cited in Hale, *Machiavelli and Renaissance Italy*, pp. 130–32.

18. Machiavelli's understanding of the state at a time when both the term and the reality were changing is a matter of controversy. Nor is it a question merely of the term *lo stato* in the *Prince*, where it meant predominantly "political command over men," but also of terms such as *il vivere civile* for "body politic" in the *Discourses* and of the reality to which they refer in both works (see J. H. Hexter, "The Predatory Vision: Niccolò Machiavelli. *Il Principe* and *lo stato*," in *The Vision of Politics on the Eve of the Reformation: More, Machiavelli, and Seyssel* [New York, 1973], pp. 163, 167, 170). Recent scholarship has tended to push the origins of the modern state further back into the Middle Ages; see, for example, Joseph Strayer, *On the Medieval Origins of the Modern State* (Princeton, 1970). For our purposes it is legitimate to use the term state here to denote both government or rule as well as the people and territory ruled and their organization (see Münkler, *Im Namen des Staates*, pp. 171–73, esp. 173).

19. *Discourses*, 1:1, 2 (pp. 192, 197); 3:41 (p. 519); see also *Prince*, 18 (p. 67); 24 (p. 88); 25 (p. 91).

20. Mesnard, *L'essor de la philosophie politique*, pp. 50–53.

21. *Discourses*, 1:3 (p. 201).

22. Ibid., 2:Preface (p. 323).

23. Ibid., 1:5 (p. 206), 37 (p. 272); 3:21 (p. 477).

24. Machiavelli's inconsistent use of the term fortune makes it impossible to determine its precise nature for him, whether it was merely the propitious coming together of natural events, as Russo writes (*Il principe*, pp. 39–40), or a personal or impersonal force. See Skinner, *Machiavelli*, pp. 23–29; for the evolution of the understanding of fortune from the ancient period through the Renaissance, including Machiavelli, see Doren, "Fortuna im Mittelalter und in der Renaissance."

25. *Discourses*, 2:29 (pp. 407–8).

26. *Prince*, 6 (p. 25); 25 (pp. 89–92); *Il principe*, ed. Russo, pp. 71–72, 195–96; *Discourses* 2:29 (pp. 406–8).

27. *Prince*, 25 (pp. 90, 92).

28. *Discourses*, 2:30 (pp. 411–12).

29. *Discourses*, 1:Preface (pp. 322–23); 2:1 (pp. 324–27). See Mesnard, *L'essor de la philosophie politique*, p. 20.

30. *Discourses*, 1:39 (p. 278); see also 1:Preface (pp. 190–92).

31. 3 (p. 15). I use here the translation of Luigi Ricci, revised by E. R. P. Vincent, in *Machiavelli: The Prince and The Discourses*, introduction by Max Lerner (New York, 1940), p. 9. It seems better to translate *vezziaggare* as "caress" than as "treat generously."

32. Skinner, *Foundations*, 1:184; see also p. 138. This may go too far, inasmuch as Machiavelli appears to exclude from *virtù* certain modes of acting that, while necessary for the prince, cannot be subsumed under *virtù* or win him glory, as is seen, for example, in his discussion of Agathocles, the despicable tyrant of Syracuse (*Prince*, 8 [pp. 35–36]; see also *Discourses*, 1:26 [p. 254] and 3:40 [p. 518]). In this case scholars are pursuing a nonexistent consistency in Machiavelli. What is of concern to us is not the precise definition of *virtù* but the qualities required for a ruler whether they belong under *virtù* or not. For a discussion of *virtù* in Machiavelli, see John Plamenatz, "In Search of Machiavellian *Virtù*," in *The Political Calculus*, edited by Anthony Parel (Toronto, 1972), pp. 157–78. For a discussion of *gloria* in Machiavelli, see Victor A. Santi, *La "gloria" nel pensiero di Machiavelli* (Ravenna, 1979), esp. pp. 22–52, and the review by Russell Price, *Renaissance Quarterly* 35 (1982): 82–86, who argues that Santi excessively systematizes Machiavelli and associates *gloria* too closely with morality.

My discussion of Machiavelli is much indebted to Skinner's *Foundations* and to his *Machiavelli*.

33. *Prince*, 15 (p. 58).

34. *Prince*, 18 (p. 66); see also *Discourses*, 1:26 (pp. 253–54).

35. *Prince*, 18 (pp. 64–65); *Discourses*, 2:13 (pp. 357–58).

36. *Prince*, 16 (pp. 59–61); 17 (pp. 61–63); 7 (p. 31); *Discourses*, 3:5 (p. 428).

37. *Prince*, 19 (pp. 67–76); 17 (pp. 62–64); *Discourses*, 3:21 (p. 477). A chief function of religion, soon to be discussed, was to instill fear in the people.

38. See n. 29 above; *Prince*, 3 (p. 14); 5 (pp. 30–33); *Discourses*, 2:23 (pp. 388–92).

39. Murillo Ferrol, *Saavedra Fajardo*, p. 311.

40. *Prince*, 18 (pp. 65–66).

41. Ibid., 21 (pp. 81–84); *Discourses*, 3:20 (p. 476).

42. *Discourses*, 1:20 (p. 246), 58 (pp. 313–18); 2:2 (pp. 328–33); 3:9 (p. 453), 17 (p. 471).

43. *Prince*, 12 (p. 47); *Discourses*, 1:4 (p. 202).

44. *Discourses*, 1:2 (pp. 195–201), 3 (pp. 201–2), 4 (202–4), 49 (pp. 295–97); 3:27 (pp. 489–92); *Prince*, 4 (p. 25).

45. *Discourses*, 1:16 (p. 237), 34 (p. 268), 45 (p. 288); 3:3 (p. 425).

46. Ibid., 1:12 (p. 227).

47. Ibid., 2:2 (pp. 330–31); 3:1 (p. 422). For an alternative, militant interpretation of Christianity occasionally suggested by Machiavelli, see Headley, "On the Rearming of Heaven," pp. 399–400, and the literature there cited.

48. Ibid., 1:12 (pp. 226–29).

49. Ibid., 1:11 (p. 224).

50. Ibid., 1:11 (pp. 223–26), 12 (pp. 226–27), 14 (pp. 231–33); 2:2 (p. 331).

51. *Prince*, 13 (p. 54). The citation is from the *Annals*, 13:19.

52. *Discourses*, 2:10 (pp. 348–51).

246 / Notes to Pages 13–19

53. Ibid., 2:2, 3.

53. Ibid., 2:2, 3.
54. *Prince*, 12–13 (pp. 46–55); *Discourses*, 1:43 (p. 286); 2:20 (pp. 381–83), 30 (pp. 409–12); 3:33 (p. 502).
55. *Discourses*, 1:6 (pp. 207–11); 2:4 (p. 337), 19 (pp. 379–80), 25 (p. 399); 3:16 (pp. 468–70).
56. Ibid., 3:17 (p. 471). Skinner, *Machiavelli*, pp. 73–74, and much more so Hulliung, *Citizen Machiavelli*, pp. 26–27, 35, 46–60, esp. 58–60, 95–98, 225, show Machiavelli's insistence on conquest as a means to preserve a republic and win it glory. Behnen, "Der gerechte und der notwendige Krieg," pp. 50, 56–63, esp. 57, discusses the necessity of war, and conquest, for Machiavelli's state while remarking on the near impossibility of distilling a consistent theory of war from his writings.
57. This includes editions where the *Prince* and the *Discourses* were printed together. Gerber, *Machiavelli: Die Handschriften, Ausgaben und Übersetzungen seiner Werke*, 2:3–34, 48–67; 3:30–33; D'Addio, *Pensiero politico di Scioppio*, pp. 258–65; Hubert Jedin, *Geschichte des Konzils von Trient*, vol. 4, *Dritte Tagungsperiode und Abschluss* (Freiburg, 1975), part 2:233.
58. Lutz, *Ragione di Stato*, pp. 48–62, publishes the chapters of the *Apologia ad Carolum Quintum Caesarem* dealing with Machiavelli. On Pole and Machiavelli, see Donaldson, "Machiavelli, Antichrist, and the Reformation," esp. pp. 211, 215–26.
59. Donaldson, "Machiavelli, Antichrist, and the Reformation," p. 215.
60. *Summa theologica*, 2-2, question 47, articles 10–12, *Opera Omnia*, 8:358–60; see de Paz, *La prudencia política según Santo Tomás*, pp. 17–20, 38.
61. *De nobilitate christiana libri III* (Florence, 1552), p. 217.
62. Ibid., pp. 200–242; D'Addio, *Pensiero politico di Scioppio*, pp. 276–79; see also Prosperi, "La religione, il potere, le élites," pp. 515–22.
63. *De libris a Christiano detestandis et a Christianismo penitus eliminandis* (Rome, 1552). The section dealing with Machiavelli is published in Italian translation in Firpo, *Il pensiero politico*, pp. 613–20; D'Addio, *Pensiero politico di Scioppio*, pp. 271–75.
64. D'Addio, *Pensiero politico di Scioppio*, pp. 280–84; De Mattei, *Dal premachiavellismo all'antimachiavellismo*, pp. 225–28.
65. Rathé, "Gentillet and the First 'Anti-Machiavel,'" pp. 186–88 (the citation is on p. 186, n. 1).
66. Kelley, "Murd'rous Machiavel," pp. 546–58; De Mattei, *Dal premachiavellismo all'antimachiavellismo*, pp. 230–31.
67. *Discours contre Machiavel*, p. 11.
68. Ibid., pp. 125, 131–46, 195, 221–26.
69. Ibid., pp. 48, 249–51.
70. Ibid., passim, e.g., pp. 150, 156, 258, 325–29, 332, 353–55, 367–68, 394, 442.
71. Mesnard, *L'essor de la philosophie politique*, pp. 539–45; Keohane, *Philosophy and the State in France*, pp. 80–81.
72. For the general historical background in the late sixteenth century, see especially J. H. Elliott, *Europe Divided, 1559–1598*, and the books of Marvin O'Connell, Peter Clark, Eric Cochrane, Henry Kamen, and John O'Malley listed in the bibliography. Theodore K. Rabb's *The Struggle for Stability in Early Modern Europe* provides the best introduction to the controversial "seventeenth-century crisis" theory and outlines a broad interpretation of the sixteenth and seventeenth centuries in European history that is to this author largely convincing.

73. Delumeau, *Rome au xvi siècle*, pp. 56, 59.
74. Maravall, *Culture of the Baroque*, pp. 104–25, esp. p. 118.
75. *De Subventione Pauperum*.

Chapter 2

1. Gerber, *Machiavelli: Die Handschriften, Ausgaben, und Übersetzungen seiner Werke*, 2:33, 81–82, 105–6; 3:115. A very limited, incorrectly dated edition of the *Prince* appeared at Venice, probably in the early seventeenth century, and in 1630 and 1648 partially expurgated editions of the *Discourses* appeared there.

Italian editions of these two works along with the *Art of War* and the *History of Florence* did appear in London between 1584 and 1588, and they appeared five times between about 1588 and 1630 and again twice in 1679 and 1680, mostly at Geneva. In these editions place and date of publication were usually concealed; see ibid., 2:83–105.

2. Ibid., 3:21, 35, 39–48, 65–75, 82–85, 103–4. Dutch translations of each came out at Leiden in 1615 and again in 1652.

3. Paul F. Grendler, *The Roman Inquisition and the Venetian Press* (Princeton, 1977), p. 168; Stegmann, *L'héroisme cornélien*, 2:161.

4. Procacci, *Fortuna del Machiavelli*, pp. 64–69, 278, 328–32; D'Addio, *Pensiero politico di Scioppio*, p. 562; J. G. A. Pocock, ed., *The Political Works of James Harrington* (Cambridge, 1977), introduction, esp. pp. 15–42, and Pocock's *Machiavellian Moment*, pp. 384, 450. Harrington's *Commonwealth of Oceana* appeared in 1656.

5. Raab, *The English Face of Machiavelli*, pp. 56–61, 70, 77–78, 90.

6. *Atheismus triumphatus seu reductio ad religionem per scientiarum veritates* . . . of which the original title was "Recognoscimento filosofico della vera universale religione contra l'anticristianesimo machiavellistico"; Headley, "On the Rearming of Heaven," esp. pp. 387–91, 394–404.

7. On Campanella, see also Luigi Firpo, "Campanella, Tommaso," in *Dizionario biografico degli Italiani* (Rome, 1974), 17:372–400.

8. *De robore bellico diuturnis et amplis catholicorum regnis; De ruinis gentium et regnorum; De antiquo et novo Italiae statu; De imperio virtutis sive imperia a veris virtutibus non a simulatis debent* . . . . The first named discussed at length Machiavelli's *Art of War*. On Bozio, see P. Craveri, *Dizionario Biografico degli Italiani* (Rome, 1971), 13:568–71.

9. *Judicium de Nouae militis Galli, Joannis Bodini, Philippi Mornaei, et Nicolai Machiavelli quibusdam scriptis*; De Mattei, *Dal premachiavellismo all' antimachiavellismo*, pp. 240–42; Donnelly, "Possevino's Papalist Critique," p. 32.

10. This is the case with an edition paginated consecutively with a Latin translation of the *Prince, Nicolai Machiavelli Florentini Princeps . . . diligenter emendatus* (Frankfurt, 1608), p. 197. See also Gerber, *Machiavelli: Die Handschriften, Ausgaben und Übersetzungen seiner Werke*, 3:60.

11. This is the case with the Italian edition I have used, which is bound with his *Il soldato christiano* and a number of other treatises; see the Bibliography. For the publication history of the *Judicium* and the *Il soldato christiano*, the latter of which was first published in 1569 at the request of Pius V for use by the troops sailing against the Turks, see Sommervogel, *Bibliothèque de la Compagnie de Jésus*, 6:1065–66, 1075–76.

12. De Mattei, *Dal premachiavellismo all'antimachiavellismo*, p. 240.

13. *Il soldato christiano*, p. 181; see note 11 above.

14. Ibid., pp. 182–87. For the relevant passages in Aquinas, see his *On Kingship*, translated by Phelan, nn. 54–66, 76–86, 91. I have preferred in my text to translate Aquinas's *De regimine principium* as *On the Government of Princes*.

15. Lewy, *Constitutionalism and Statecraft*, pp. 26–28, 156.

For a good treatment of many Italian anti-Machiavellian writers, see De Mattei, *Il problema della "ragion di stato"* and *Il pensiero politico italiano*, 2 vols. Both these works are collections of articles that have appeared in numerous periodicals since the 1930s. Unfortunately, they are not acknowledged as such nor do they indicate the place of original publication. The articles in the first work were originally published as a series entitled "Il problema della 'Ragion di Stato' nel seicento" in the *Rivista internazionale di filosofia del diritto* from 1949 (vol. 26) to 1961 (vol. 38). I have not attempted to trace the place of original publication for the two-volume work.

For a good overview of Spanish anti-Machiavellians, see Maravall, *La philosophie politique espagnole au xvii siècle*. For further literature, see the Bibliography.

16. Evennett, *Spirit of the Counterreformation*, pp. 43–44, 128–32 (Editor's Postscript by John Bossy); Cognet, *La spiritualité moderne*, pp. 21–22, 274–82; de Guibert, *The Jesuits*, pp. 125–29, 156–57, 180–81. See also Trevor-Roper, "Religion, the Reformation, and Social Change," pp. 34–36.

17. *Perfeccion del cristiano en todos los estados* (Valladolid and Pamplona, 1612–16); *La cour sainte* (Paris, 1624). For the publication history of both, see Sommervogel, *Bibliothèque de la Compagnie de Jésus*, 6:1285–89; 2:906–17. For this feature of Counter-Reformation spirituality, see de Guibert, *The Jesuits*, pp. 255–56, 273–74, 295–301, 313–18, 370–71, 255–56.

18. Stegmann, *L'héroisme cornélien*, 2:61; Valentin, "Gegenreformation und Literatur," passim. See also the conclusion of his imposing *Le théâtre des Jésuites*, 2:946–61, esp. 958–61.

19. De Mattei, *Il pensiero politico italiano*, 1:17–18, 24–27, 32, 43, 48–50, stresses this point for Italian writers and indicates the continuity with the Renaissance. He pays particular attention to the well-known dialogue of Paolo Paruta, *Della perfezione della vita politica* (Venice, 1579), on pp. 35–38.

20. Tierno Galvan, *El Tacitismo en los escritores políticos españoles*, p. 41; Chabod, *Botero*, p. 37; Rubenstein, "The History of the Word *Politicus*," pp. 55–56.

21. "Politischen, . . . maulchristen mit ihren Schreckpotaten," cited in Sturmberger, *Kaiser Ferdinand II. und das Problem des Absolutismus*, p. 33.

22. *The First Part of a Treatise concerning Policy and Religion*, 2d ed., English Recusant Literature 1558–1640, vol. 175 (Douai, 1615; rpt. Menston, 1974), dedicatory epistle. The spelling in the quotation is modernized. I am grateful to my graduate student, Fr. Vincent Costello, for this reference.

23. Stegmann, *L'héroisme cornélien*, 2:159–202, esp. 159–69, 202; see also Church, *Richelieu and Reason of State*, pp. 54–72.

24. Fumaroli, *L'âge de l'éloquence*, pp. 27, 520.

25. Stolleis, *Arcana Imperii und Ratio Status*, p. 29; De Mattei, *Il pensiero politico italiano*, 1:6–7, 9–10, 20–21.

26. Stegmann, *L'héroisme cornélien*, 2:63, 659.

27. *El gobernador cristiano, deducido de las vidas de Moysen y Josue, príncipes del pueblo de Dios*. The letter of June 11, 1604, is printed at the start

of the volume, which went through at least five further Spanish editions before 1783 and a French translation (Nancy, 1621).

28. *El embajador*; on the book and the author, see Mattingly, *Renaissance Diplomacy*, pp. 181–91.

29. *El embajador*, p. 74 (mispaginated 77).

30. Ibid., pp. 74 (mispaginated 77)–80, esp. 74–75.

31. See, for example, R. H. Tawney, *Religion and the Rise of Capitalism* (New York, 1926), pp. 227–53.

32. Leites, *Conscience and Casuistry*; Mosse, *The Holy Pretense*; L. Vereecke, "Moral Theology, History of," in *New Catholic Encyclopedia* (Washington, 1967; rpt., Palatine, Ill., 1981), 9:1119–22; E. Dublanchy, "Casuistique," *Dictionnaire de Théologie Catholique*, vol. 2, part 2 (Paris, 1932), 1859–77, esp. 1871–77.

33. On Pascal in particular and the early conflict between Jansenists and Jesuits in general, see Guardini, *Pascal for Our Time*, esp. pp. 192–97, and Richard M. Golden, "Jesuit Refutations of Pascal's *Lettres Provinciales*," in *Church, State, and Society under the Bourbon Kings of France*, ed. Richard M. Golden (Lawrence, Kansas, 1982), pp. 83–124. There is an enormous literature on the topic; see Delumeau, *Catholicism*, pp. 99–128.

34. Ilting, "Macht, Gewalt," pp. 854–56.

35. See, for example, Evennett, *Spirit of the Counter Reformation*; Reinhard, "Gegenreformation als Modernisierung?"; Delumeau, *Catholicism*.

36. On usury and business ethics, see Noonan, *The Scholastic Analysis of Usury*, pp. 199–362, and Wilhelm Weber, *Wirtschaftsethik am Vorabend des Liberalismus: Höhepunkt und Abschluss der scholastischen Wirtschaftsbetrachtung durch Ludwig Molina (1535–1600)* (Münster, 1959); on toleration, Lecler, *Toleration and the Reformation*; on the Galileo Affair, Giorgio de Santillana, *The Crime of Galileo* (Chicago, 1955), and Jerome J. Langford, *Galileo, Science, and the Church*, rev. ed. (Ann Arbor, 1971); on the Rites controversies, see Francis Rouleau, "Chinese Rites Controversy," *New Catholic Encyclopedia* (Washington, 1966, rpt. 1981), 3:611–17; Vincent Cronin, "Malabar Rites Controversy," ibid., 9:97–99; Charles E. Ronan and Bonnie Oh, eds., *East Meets West: The Jesuits in China, 1582–1773* (Chicago, 1988); and George H. Dunne, *Generation of Giants* (Notre Dame, 1962).

Another aspect, of course, of the Catholic church's relationship to contemporary culture in the early modern period had to do with its attitude toward popular culture, a topic of much current interest; see Delumeau, *Catholicism*, and Peter Burke, *Popular Culture in Early Modern Europe* (New York, 1978).

37. Skinner, *Foundations*, 2:171–73, brings out well the relationship between the anti-Machiavellians and the Scholastics.

38. Ibid., 135–38; Copleston, *History of Philosophy*, 3:Part 2, pp. 153–72.

39. Mesnard, *L'essor de la philosophie politique*, pp. 617–18, 658–60, 670–73.

40. Ibid., and pp. 454–72.

41. *De legibus et Deo legislatore, Opera Omnia*, vols. 5–6; Rommen, *Staatslehre des Suarez*, p. 242.

42. Brodrick, *Robert Bellarmine*, pp. 62–63, 70.

43. Mesnard, *L'essor de la philosophie politique*, pp. 639–44; Brodrick, *Robert Bellarmine*, pp. 249–63, 264–302 passim; Bouwsma, *Venice and the Defense of Republican Liberty*, pp. 339–482.

44. *De officio principis christiani libri tres*; Sommervogel, *Bibliothèque de la Compagnie de Jésus*, 1:1243–44. The Latin version was also published in 1619

at Antwerp, Cologne, and Lyons, and there were two French translations, one at Lyons in 1620 and the other at Paris in 1625. Sommervogel overlooks the Spanish translation (Madrid, 1624).

45. Mesnard, *L'essor de la philosophie politique*, pp. 636–37. Rommen, *Staatslehre des Suarez*, pp. 118–31; the citation of the *De legibus et Deo legislatore*, Book 3, chap. 2, n. 7, is on p. 124, n. 25.

46. Copleston, *History of Philosophy*, 3:Part 2, pp. 167–68, 215–20; Mesnard, *L'essor de la philosophie politique*, p. 628; Arnold, *Staatslehre des Bellarmin*, pp. 115, 123–36, 153–56, 199–227, 264–65; Skinner, *Foundations*, pp. 154–56.

47. *The King and the Education of the King*, 1:6 (pp. 144–48); Mesnard, *L'essor de la philosophie politique*, pp. 551–52, 538–39; Lewy, *Constitutionalism and Statecraft*, pp. 71–73, 133–36, contends that Mariana's position differed inconsequentially from that of other Jesuits. See also Ford, *Political Murder*, pp. 157, 182–83.

48. *De regimine principis*, nn. 44–52; Ford, *Political Murder*, pp. 124–25.

49. Arnold, *Staatslehre des Bellarmin*, pp. 241–54.

50. Copleston, *History of Philosophy*, 3:Part 2, 220–22; Rommen, *Staatslehre des Suarez*, pp. 224–34.

51. *De legibus et Deo legislatore*, Book 3, chap. 2, nn. 2–5 (*Opera Omnia*, 6:216–17); see Giacon, "Machiavelli, Suarez, e la ragion di stato," who cites the above passage, p. 186. Suarez distinguishes between commanding immoral acts and permitting or tolerating them in order to avoid greater evils. The latter the state must sometimes do.

52. Brodrick, *Robert Bellarmine*, pp. 105–11.

53. Suarez, *On the Three Theological Virtues*, treatise 3, disputation 13, section 2, *Selections*, pp. 805–8; Mesnard, *L'essor de la philosophie politique*, pp. 470, 630; Arnold, *Staatslehre des Bellarmin*, pp. 102–5.

54. Suarez, *A Defense of the Catholic and Apostolic Faith*, Book 3, chap. 23, paragraphs 9–12, 18–23, in *Selections*, pp. 691–93, 698–702; Copleston, *History of Philosophy*, 3:Part 2, pp. 165–67; Arnold, *Staatslehre des Bellarmin*, pp. 348–60; Rommen, *Staatslehre des Suarez*, pp. 256–63, 269. For a critique of this power, in addition to Rommen, see Brodrick, *Robert Bellarmine*, pp. 294–97, who relies on John Courtney Murray, "Bellarmine and the Indirect Power," *Theological Studies* 9 (1948): 491–535.

55. Mesnard, *L'essor de la philosophie politique*, pp. 463–72.

56. Rommen, *Staatslehre des Suarez*, pp. 249–69, 285–95; Arnold, *Staatslehre des Bellarmin*, pp. 97–98, 272–74, 335–38, 348, 351, 353; Mesnard, *L'essor de la philosophie politique*, pp. 646–57.

57. *On the Three Theological Virtues*, treatise 3, disputation 13, section 1, in *Selections*, pp. 800–805. The citations are on pp. 800 and 805. Arnold, *Staatslehre des Bellarmin*, pp. 280–86.

58. There is an immense literature on the just war. A good comparative study of Scholastic thinkers is Walters, "Five Classic Just-War Theories." See also Johnson, *Just War Tradition*.

59. *On the Three Theological Virtues*, treatise 3, disputation 13, section 2, in *Selections*, pp. 805–10. The citations are on pp. 808 and 809. Arnold, *Staatslehre des Bellarmin*, p. 286.

60. Arnold, *Staatslehre des Bellarmin*, pp. 286–89. There is a movement here from a moral to a more juridical concept of war; see Rommen, *Staatslehre des Suarez*, p. 301. Vitoria had already dropped right intention as a requirement for a just war; see Vitoria, *Obras*, pp. 757, 797–800.

61. *On the Three Theological Virtues*, treatise 3, disputation 13, sections 4 and 6, in *Selections*, pp. 816–23, 828–30. The citations are on pp. 816 and 818.

62. Ibid., section 7, in *Selections*, pp. 836–51. The citations are on pp. 840 and 846.

63. Ibid., pp. 852–53.

64. Rommen, *Staatslehre des Suarez*, p. 262; Arnold, *Staatslehre des Bellarmin*, p. 341.

65. Lecler, *Toleration and the Reformation*, 1:268–69, 386, 398–401, 403–5, 422; Mecenseffy, *Geschichte des Protestantismus in Österreich*, pp. 51–54.

The papacy neither condemned nor acknowledged the Peace of Augsburg, tacitly accepting it; see Repgen, *Die römische Kurie und der westfälische Friede*, 1:82–86; see also 136–53.

66. Lecler, *Toleration and the Reformation*, 2:66, 84–87, 99–102, 107–10.

67. *The Six Bookes of a Commonweale*, Book 4, chapter 7 (pp. 535–39), and p. A13 (introduction). See Skinner, *Foundations*, 2:253–54, and Allen, *A History of Political Thought in the Sixteenth Century*, pp. 429–30, both of whom underplay the distinction between private and public. Lipsius will pick up this distinction, and it is implicit in the position of Aquinas in the next paragraph.

68. 2-2, question 10, article 11, *Opera Omnia*, 8:92–93. A different reason was given for the toleration of Jewish rites; they prefigured the Christian faith and so gave witness to it.

69. Lecler, *Toleration and the Reformation*, 1:301; 2:228–33, 235–38, 499; Molanus, *Libri quinque*, pp. 39–44, 128–32, 148–49, 165. Lecler fails to note Aquinas's application of this to heretics.

70. *De triplici virtute theologica, fide, spe, et caritate*, treatise 1, disputation 20, section 3 (*Opera Omnia* 12:516).

71. Ibid., disputation 16, section 4, and disputation 19, sections 1–6 (pp. 416, 460, 462, 473–74, 486, 490).

72. *On the Three Theological Virtues*, treatise 1, disputation 18, sections 2–4, in *Selections*, pp. 749–69.

73. *De triplici virtute theologica fide, spe, et caritate*, treatise 1, disputation 20, section 3, and disputation 23, sections 1–2 (*Opera Omnia* 12:509–17, 579–81). The citations are on pp. 509, 514, and 515.

Chapter 3

1. "Botero e stato maraviglioso, poi ch'egli ha accommodato tanto l'honestà della causa, e il giusta, e'l dovere, col profitto de' Prencipi, che percio egli merita in questo fatto lode immortale" in *Discorsi sopra la ragion di stato del Signor Giovanni Botero*, p. 64.

2. De Mattei, *Il problema della "ragion di stato,"* p. 65; Stegmann, *L'héroisme cornélien*, 2:174.

3. Stegmann, "Apologie du statu quo institutionnel," pp. 230–31, and his *L'héroisme cornélien*, 2:173–74.

4. *Discorsi sopra la ragion di stato del Signor Giovanni Botero*, Proemio; Tierno Galvan, *El Tacitismo en los escritores políticos españoles*, p. 44.

5. Dollinger, "Maximilian von Bayern und Justus Lipsius," pp. 281–83.

6. Ibid., p. 259, n. 80; Sturmberger, *Kaiser Ferdinand II. und das Problem des Absolutismus*, p. 20.

7. Behnen, " 'Arcana—Haec Sunt Ratio Status': Ragion di Stato und Staats-

räson," p. 181; Fischer, *Giovanni Botero*, p. 95.

8. De Mattei, *Il problema della "ragion di stato,"* pp. 64–91; Murillo-Ferrol, *Saavedra Fajardo*, p. 187; for a similar modern criticism, see Bouwsma, *Venice and the Defense of Republican Liberty*, p. 301. Much of the early criticism of Botero was directed against his definition of reason of state.

9. *Delle cause della grandezza delle città*, 1:10 (p. 360); 2:12 (p. 396). All references to Botero's *Reason of State*, *Greatness of Cities*, and *Additions to the Reason of State* are taken from Firpo's edition of the *Ragion di stato*. The first numbers are to book and chapter, those in parentheses to pages. Translations are my own.

10. For biographical data on Botero, see Firpo's commentary in *Ragion di stato*, pp. 33–40, and his "Botero, Giovanni," pp. 352–60.

11. *De regia sapientia libri tres* (Milan, 1583), Dedication, cited by De Luca, *Stato e chiesa*, p. 27.

12. Fischer, *Giovanni Botero*, p. 6; De Luca, *Stato e chiesa*, pp. 50–52.

13. Magnuson, *Rome in the Age of Bernini*, p. 16.

14. Firpo in Botero, *Ragion di stato*, p. 37; Chabod, *Botero*, pp. 39–40.

15. *Delle cause della grandezza delle città*, 1:1 (p. 345); 2:11 (pp. 388–92, 396); 3:2 (pp. 401–3); Fischer, *Giovanni Botero*, p. 56; Firpo in Botero, *Ragion di stato*, pp. 461–63, 465.

16. Firpo, "Botero, Giovanni," pp. 357–58 (quotation); Fischer, *Giovanni Botero*, p. 14 (and n. 26), 84, 91; Chabod, *Botero*, pp. 84, 186–93.

17. Fischer, *Giovanni Botero*, p. 13.

18. *Relationi universali*, part 4, book 2 (pp. 145–52); 2:4 (p. 134); 3:1 (p. 110); 4:1 (p. 32) (but see also the comments on the economic devastation of Granada caused by the expulsion of the Moors, 1:1 [p. 7]); see below, at n. 103; De Luca, *Stato e chiesa*, pp. 11, 17, 74–81, 88, 104; Chabod, *Botero*, pp. 114–21.

19. De Mattei, *Il problema della "ragion di stato,"* pp. 70–71.

20. Bernardino M. Bonansea, *Tommaso Campanella: Renaissance Pioneer of Modern Thought* (Washington, 1969), pp. 28, 312, 389; Donnelly, "Possevino's Plan," esp. pp. 188–90, 197.

21. Kenneth M. Setton, *The Papacy and the Levant*, vol. 4, *The Sixteenth Century from Julius III to Pius V*, Memoirs of the American Philosophical Society, no. 162 (Philadelphia, 1984), pp. 1097, 1100; *Die Hauptinstruktionen Clemens VIII für die Nuntien und Legaten an den europäischen Fürstenhöfen, 1592–1605*, ed. Klaus Jaitner (Tübingen, 1984), 1:xvii–xxii.

22. Firpo in Botero, *Ragion di stato*, p. 18.

23. For this date, see Stegmann, "Apologie du statu quo institutionnel," p. 225, and De Mattei, *Il problema della "ragion di stato,"* p. 278.

24. On the term "reason of state," see chap. 1, n. 13.

25. Savelli, "Tra Machiavelli e S. Giorgio," pp. 261–64.

26. Delumeau, *Rome au xvi siècle*, pp. 56, 59; N. S. Davidson, "Northern Italy in the 1590s," pp. 158–59; Burke, "Southern Italy in the 1590s," pp. 180–82; Magnuson, *Rome in the Age of Bernini*, p. 9.

27. See Stegmann, "Apologie du statu quo institutionnel," esp. pp. 241–48.

28. Many of these writers are discussed at length in De Mattei, *Il problema della "ragion di stato"* and *Il pensiero politico italiano*.

29. Firpo in Botero, *Ragion di stato*, pp. 457–67. Firpo considers the Venetian edition of 1598 to be definitive, while noting that the changes Botero made after 1589 were mostly the addition of new examples. See n. 4 above for the 1591 Spanish translation missed by Firpo.

30. *Discorso sopra C. Tacito*, Proemia; Schellhase, *Tacitus in Renaissance Political Thought*, pp. 123–27, 142–45; Chabod, *Botero*, p. 39. Ammirato did not mention Botero by name, but the inference is clear. Ammirato was an anti-Machiavellian in the same sense as Botero, but they differed in this and in other points; see De Mattei, *Scipione Ammirato*, pp. 116–17, 121.

31. *Ragion di stato*, Dedication, pp. 51–53.

32. Elliott, "Self-Perception and Decline," p. 55 (rpt., p. 255), and his *The Revolt of the Catalans* (Cambridge, 1963), pp. 183–84, 572; Elliott and Peña, *Memoriales y cartas del Conde Duque de Olivares*, p. xiii; Tierno Galvan, *El Tacitismo en los escritores españoles*, pp. 30, 36–37.

33. A reading of Cochrane's recently published *Italy, 1530–1630*, esp. pp. 106–202, makes this clearer than ever.

34. Stumpo, "Finanze e ragion di stato," pp. 181–82, 205–6.

35. *Ragion di stato*, 1:1 (p. 55). Machiavelli wrote "Tutti li stati, tutti e' dominii che hanno avuto et hanno imperio sopra li uomini, sono stati e sono o republiche o principati" (p. 15).

36. Ibid.

37. Ammirato, *Discorso sopra C. Tacito*, book 12, chap. 1 (pp. 228–42); Spontone, *Dodici libri del governo di stato* (Verona, 1599), book 5 (pp. 122–24). See De Mattei, *Scipione Ammirato*, pp. 121–51, and *Il problema della "ragion di stato,"* pp. 64–91, and Meinecke, *Machiavellism*, pp. 119–29, esp. 120, 127.

38. *Ragguagli di Parnaso*, book 2, *ragguaglio* (report) 87, p. 290.

39. De Luca, *Stato e chiesa*, pp. 58, 100, 143.

40. *Ragion di stato*, 1:1 (p. 55); see De Luca, *Stato e chiesa*, p. 60.

41. *Ragion di stato*, 1:6 (pp. 60–63).

42. Ibid., 1:1 (p. 55); 1:8 (p. 67); *Delle cause della grandezza delle città*, 3:3 (p. 405).

43. According to Münkler, *Im Namen des Staates*, p. 270, Guicciardini and Alonso de Castro, *Tractado de republica* (Burgos, 1521), were the first political writers to give the concept of interest a prominent place in their analysis.

44. *Ragion di stato*, 2:6 (p. 104); see also 8:13 (p. 262); *Aggiunte, Della neutralità*, pp. 445–46.

45. *Ragion di stato*, 1:5 (pp. 58–59).

46. Firpo in Botero, *Ragion di stato*, p. 469.

47. Cited in Parker, *Europe in Crisis*, p. 156.

48. *Testament politique*, esp. pp. 143, 355, 373–75, 450; John H. Elliott, "A Question of Reputation? Spanish Foreign Policy in the Seventeenth Century," *Journal of Modern History* 55 (1983): 477–78.

49. For two uses of *potenza*, see below, at n. 86, and *Aggiunte, Della riputazione del prencipe*, 2 (p. 443), where it is used as a synonym for the Latin *potentia*.

50. *Ragion di stato*, 7:1 (pp. 221–22); *Discourses*, 2:10 (pp. 348–51); *Prince*, 10 (p. 42). This is not to deny that Machiavelli also saw the need for general population growth; see *Discourses*, 2:3 (pp. 334–45).

51. *Ragion di stato*, 3:1 (p. 147).

52. Ibid., 1:8 (pp. 67–68); 3:1 (pp. 147–48, quotations); *Delle cause della grandezza delle città*, 3:3 (p. 405); *Aggiunte, Della riputazione del prencipe*, 1:2 (p. 416).

53. *Aggiunte, Della riputazione del prencipe*, 1:2 (pp. 415–16); 1:3 (pp. 418–22); see Aristotle, *Politics*, 5:10 (pp. 238–40).

54. *Ragion di stato*, 2:15 (p. 133); *Aggiunte, Della riputazione del prencipe*, 1:4 (pp. 422–24).

55. *Ragion di stato,* 2:11 (pp. 120–26, quotation on p. 120); *Aggiunte, Della riputazione del prencipe,* 2 (p. 443).

56. *Ragion di stato,* 1:11 (p. 71); 2:1 (p. 95); 2:14 (p. 132).

57. Mulagk, *Phänomene des politischen Menschen,* pp. 121–28, 221–25.

58. Magnuson, *Rome in the Age of Bernini,* p. 11; Barbara McClung Hallman, *Italian Cardinals, Reform, and the Church as Property* (Berkeley, 1986).

59. *Ragion di stato,* 1:11 (p. 71, quotation); 1:12 (p. 72); 1:14 (pp. 74–76); 1:15 (pp. 76–78); 1:16 (pp. 79–83, quotation on p. 80); 1:17 (pp. 83–86); 1:18 (pp. 87–88).

60. See *Discourses,* 3:28 (pp. 492–93).

61. *Ragion di stato,* 1:19 (p. 89); 1:20 (pp. 89–92, quotation on p. 90); 1:21 (pp. 92–93); 1:22 (pp. 93–94).

62. Ibid., 2:1 (p. 95); 2:8 (p. 114, n. 2); 2:2 (pp. 95–98); 2:3 (pp. 98–100); 2:4 (p. 100); 2:5 (pp. 100–103). Quotations are on pp. 95 and 99.

63. The transition from a general to a particularized reason of state is a theme of Meinecke's *Machiavellism* and of Münkler's *Im Namen des Staates.* Meinecke sees it first developing in the France of Richelieu; see esp. pp. 146–51.

64. *Ragion di stato,* 2:6 (pp. 104, 108–9, 111).

65. *Aggiunte, Della neutralitrà,* p. 453.

66. *Ragion di stato,* 2:6 (pp. 106–7, 110).

67. Ibid., 2:11 (p. 121); 5:1 (p. 177).

68. Ibid., 2:10 (p. 118); 2:11 (pp. 122, 125); see the *Prince,* 21 (pp. 81–82).

69. Maravall, *Culture of the Baroque,* pp. 104–25.

70. Magnuson, *Rome in the Age of Bernini,* p. 10.

71. *Ragion di stato,* 3:1 (pp. 147–50); 3:2 (151–52); 3:3 (152–53, quotation on p. 153).

72. Ibid., 4:3–6 (pp. 160–74).

73. *Discourses,* 1:37 (pp. 272–75); 3:25 (pp. 486–88).

74. *Ragion di stato,* 2:14 (p. 132); 2:17 (pp. 141–45, quotations on pp. 144 and 145); on contemporary sumptuary laws and luxury taxes, see Stolleis, *Pecunia Nervus Rerum,* esp. pp. 9–18, 36–37, 45–48, 50–55.

75. *Ragion di stato,* 2:14 (p. 132); 2:15 (pp. 133–35); see Coreth, *Pietas Austriaca,* pp. 18–21.

76. *Ragion di stato,* 2:16 (pp. 135–37).

77. Ibid., and pp. 137–38, quotation on p. 137.

78. See Reinhard, "Zwang zur Konfessionalisierung?," esp. pp. 268–70; Schilling, *Konfessionskonflikt und Staatsbildung,* pp. 365–66, and his "Reformation and the Rise of the Early Modern State."

79. *Ragion di stato,* 2:16 (pp. 138–41).

80. Ibid., 5:2 (pp. 179–81). For Suarez on this point, see *On the Three Theological Virtues,* treatise 1, disputation 18, section 3, in *Selections,* pp. 763–67. He distinguishes, for unbelievers, between compulsion, which is prohibited, and inducements to the faith, which must be used with prudence because of the danger of false conversions.

81. *Ragion di stato,* p. 182, n. 1.

82. Ibid., 5:3 (pp. 181–83); 5:4 (pp. 183–85); 5:6 (misnumbered 7) (pp. 188–90); 5:7 (pp. 190–95); 5:8 (pp. 195–96).

83. Ibid., 5:9 (pp. 196–202).

84. Ibid., 7:1 (pp. 221–23).

85. Stolleis, *Pecunia Nervus Rerum,* pp. 71–72.

86. *Ragion di Stato,* 7:3 (p. 225).

87. Magnuson, *Rome in the Age of Bernini*, pp. 8–11.
88. For a brief history of this phrase, which dated from classical times, see Stolleis, *Pecunia Nervus Rerum*, pp. 63–71.
89. *Ragion di stato*, 7:2 (pp. 223–24); 7:3 (pp. 225–26). The quotation is on p. 225.
90. June 21, 1598, *Briefe und Akten zur Geschichte des Dreissigjährigen Krieges in den Zeiten des vorwaltenden Einflusses der Wittelsbacher* 4 (Munich, 1878), 479–80, cited in Bireley, *Maximilian von Bayern*, p. 15.
91. *Ragion di stato*, 7:10 (pp. 233–37).
92. In his *Réponse au paradoxe de Monsieur de Malestroit*; see Allen, *A History of Political Thought*, p. 395.
93. *Ragion di stato*, 1:15 (pp. 76–79); 7:5 (p. 229); 7:9 (p. 233); Fischer, *Giovanni Botero*, pp. 74–76; Noonan, *The Scholastic Analysis of Usury*, pp. 249–50, 279–80, 360–62, 407–8.
94. *Ragion di stato*, 7:5 (p. 229); 7:6 (pp. 229–31); 7:7 (p. 231); on extraordinary revenues see also *Aggiunte, Della neutralità*, p. 452.
95. Magnuson, *Rome in the Age of Bernini*, p. 45.
96. Hale, *War and Society*, pp. 234–40.
97. Stolleis, *Pecunia Nervus Rerum*, pp. 107–8.
98. Ibid.; Stumpo, "Finanze e ragion di stato," pp. 188, 192–93, 224.
99. Fischer, *Giovanni Botero*, pp. 78–79, 81, 91–92; N. J. Davidson, "Northern Italy in the 1590s," p. 161.
100. *Ragion di stato*, 7:4 (pp. 226–28).
101. Ibid., 7:12 (pp. 238–42); 8:2 (pp. 243–46).
102. On this decline, see Casey, "Spain: A Failed Transition," pp. 209–11.
103. *Ragion di stato*, 7:12 (pp. 240–41); 8:9 (p. 259); see also *Delle cause della grandezza delle città*, 1:3 (p. 348).
104. Ibid., 8:3 (pp. 246–50).
105. Magnuson, *Rome in the Age of Bernini*, p. 9.
106. Viner, *Role of Providence*, pp. 32, 36–38. I am grateful to Prof. Albert O. Hirschmann of the Institute of Advanced Study at Princeton for this reference.
107. *Ragion di stato*, 1:10 (p. 356).
108. Parker, *Military Revolution*, pp. 72–75.
109. *Ragion di stato*, 9:11 (pp. 294, 297–98, 300–301); 9:12 (pp. 301–3); 9:17 (pp. 307–9); Machiavelli, *Discourses*, 3:12 (pp. 459–62).
110. *Ragion di stato*, 9:2 (pp. 269–75, citation on p. 273); Schulze, "Die deutschen Landesdefensionen im 16. und 17. Jahrhundert," pp. 129–49, esp. 139.
111. *Ragion di stato*, 9:13 (p. 304); Parker, *Military Revolution*, p. 60.
112. *Ragion di stato*, 9:7 (pp. 285–86); 9:8 (pp. 286–88). The quotation is on p. 286.
113. Ibid., 10:3 (pp. 321–22).
114. Ibid., 10:9 (pp. 335–40, quotations on pp. 336, 337).

Chapter 4

1. Most important in this regard is the work of the late Gerhard Oestreich. See the Bibliography and especially his posthumously published *Neostoicism and the Early Modern State*.
2. Gerlo and Vervliet, *Inventaire de la correspondance de Juste Lipse*; Wol-

fram Prinz, "The 'Four Philosophers' by Rubens and the Pseudo-Seneca in Seventeenth-Century Painting," *The Art Bulletin* 55 (1973): 410–28, esp. p. 412. Simone Zurawski, "Rubens's *Apologia* of Justus Lipsius, and Reminiscences of Erasmus," unpublished paper delivered at the Sixteenth Century Studies Conference, Arizona State University, Tempe, October 1987.

3. *Politicorum sive civilis doctrinae libri sex* (Frankfurt, 1590), preface to the reader, p. 10. This is the text of the *Politicorum* used here unless otherwise indicated (henceforth *Politics* in the text, *Politicorum* in the notes). The same volume includes the *Ad libros politicorum breves notae* (Frankfurt, 1590), paginated consecutively with the *Politicorum* (henceforth *Brief Notes* in the text, *Breves notae* in the notes). In all Lipsius's works cited here the book and chapter are indicated, as well as the page of the edition consulted.

4. For general biographical material on Lipsius, see Saunders, *Justus Lipsius: The Philosophy of Renaissance Stoicism*, pp. 3–55. As Oestreich, *Neostoicism and the Early Modern State*, p. 65, remarks, no complete biography of Lipsius will be possible until his enormous correspondence has been edited. A start on this has been made with the multivolume *Justi Lipsi Epistolae*, eds. A. Gerlo, M. A. Nauwelaerts, and H. D. L. Vervliet, now in progress.

5. De Nave, "Peilingen naar de oorspronkelijkheid van Justus Lipsius' politiek denken," pp. 451–52.

6. Hescher, "Justus Lipsius," p. 201.

7. Schellhase, *Tacitus in Renaissance Political Thought*, pp. 15, 119.

8. Wansink, *Politieke wetenschappen aan de Leidse Universiteit*, p. 5.

9. Oestreich, *Neostoicism and the Early Modern State*, p. 13. The text I have used unless otherwise indicated is *De constantia libri duo*, 3d ed. (Frankfurt, 1590) (henceforth *Constancy* in the text, *Constantia* in the notes); it is bound in with the *Politicorum* (see n. 3 above).

10. Tracy, "With and Without the Counter Reformation," p. 547; Wansink, *Politieke wetenschappen aan de Leidse Universiteit*, p. 15.

11. "Certificat d'orthodoxie de Lipse, délivré par J. à Campis, recteur du Collège des Jésuites à Liège," Liège, July 9, 1591, in Lipsius, *Correspondance conservée au Musée Plantin-Moretus*, no. 22 (documents), pp. 254–56 and notes; Hescher, "Justus Lipsius," pp. 201–3; Lipsius's personal religious views of these years are still in controversy and are perhaps impossible to ascertain; nor is it necessary to do so for purposes of this book. See Oestreich, *Antiker Geist und moderner Staat*, pp. 43–47, and Güldner, *Das Toleranz-Problem in den Niederlanden*, pp. 120–23, 128–38.

12. Oestreich, *Neostoicism and the Early Modern State*, pp. 57–60 (quotation on p. 60).

13. De Nave, "De polemiek tussen Justus Lipsius en Dirck Coornhert."

14. Güldner, *Das Toleranz-Problem in den Niederlanden*, pp. 119–20.

15. See, for example, letters no. 15 (pp. 86–89), no. 93 (p. 391), and no. 98 (pp. 416–17), written to various Spaniards between 1595 and 1604, in Lipsius, *Epistolario*.

16. Oestreich, *Neostoicism and the Early Modern State*, p. 58; Gottigny, "Juste Lipse et l'Espagne," p. 107. The text I have used is the *Monita et Exempla Politica* (Antwerp, 1606) (henceforth *Advice* in the text, *Monita* in the notes).

17. "Compte rendu de la mort de Lipse par Fr. von den Broeckius," May 9, 1606, in Lipsius, *Correspondance conservée au Musée Plantin-Moretus*, no. 23 (documents), pp. 256–61; von den Broeckius was also present.

18. Preface to the reader, p. 9.

19. *Monita*, 1:1 (p. 1–3).

20. *De una religione, adversus dialogistam liber, in quo tria capita libri quarti politicorum explicantur;* see above, n. 3.

21. Fumaroli, *L'âge de l'éloquence*, pp. 153–58, 224.

22. Oestreich, *Neostoicism and the Early Modern State*, pp. 99, 104–5; Breuer, *Oberdeutsche Literatur*, pp. 133–34, 138; Press, "Stadt und Territoriale Konfessionsbildung," pp. 284–96.

23. To Manuel Sarmiento de Mendoza (Salamanca), Mar. 14, 1600, in Lipsius, *Epistolario*, no. 72, pp. 294–95; the phrase "velut theatrum hodiernae vitae" is found in Lipsius's preface to his commentary on Tacitus; see Kühlmann, *Gelehrtenrepublik und Fürstenstaat*, p. 55, and n. 12.

24. Dedicatory Letter, p. 9; Preface to the reader, p. 11.

25. Lipsius to Torrentius, May 6, 1584, *Epistolae*, no. 342, 2:113; see Güldner, *Das Toleranz-Problem in den Niederlanden*, p. 84, n. 123.

26. *Constantia*, Preface, pp. 3–7, quotations on pp. 4, 5; Güldner, *Das Toleranz-Problem in den Niederlanden*, p. 87.

That Lipsius added this preface with a certain reluctance is evident from letters to Abraham Ortelius (Antwerp), *Epistolae*, no. 365 (Aug. 23, 1584), 2:143, where he referred to those who wanted it inserted as "certain champions of piety [who are] short on piety and certainly on prudence," and to Janus Gulielmus (Paris), ibid., no. 375 (Sept. 19, 1584), pp. 154–55.

27. Gottigny, "Juste Lipse et l'Espagne," p. 90, n. 1.

28. *Constantia*, 1:4 (p. 23).

29. Ibid., 1:11 (pp. 33–37, quotation on p. 36); 1:22 (pp. 58–60).

30. Kühlmann, *Gelehrtenrepublik und Fürstenstaat*, pp. 129–32.

31. Hescher, "Justus Lipsius," p. 202; Güldner, *Das Toleranz-Problem in den Niederlanden*, p. 127.

32. *Politicorum*, p. 8.

33. *Breves notae*, p. 251; see above, n. 3.

34. *Politicorum*, Preface to the reader, pp. 9–13, quotation on p. 10.

35. Coron, "Les 'Politicorum sive civilis doctrinae libri sex,' de Juste Lipse," pp. 56–57.

36. Preface to the reader, p. 11.

37. *Essays*, 1:26, cited in Lipsius, *Epistolario*, p. 10. The translation is mine. See *The Complete Works of Montaigne*, trans. Donald M. Frame (Stanford, 1957), p. 108.

38. Preface to the reader, pp. 12–14, 17; 4:1 (pp. 87–88).

39. Kühlmann, *Gelehrtenrepublik und Fürstenstaat*, pp. 189–90, 215–18, 228–33.

40. De Nave, "Peilingen naar de oorspronkelijkheid van Justus Lipsius' politiek denken," pp. 450–70, esp. pp. 466–68, 480–83; Oestreich, *Neostoicism and the Early Modern State*, p. 41.

41. Oestreich, *Neostoicism and the Early Modern State*, p. 41.

42. Ibid., pp. 76–89; Rothenberg, "Maurice of Nassau," pp. 34–38; Reinhard, "Humanismus und Militarismus," pp. 186, 191–95, 199–203; I. A. A. Thompson, "The Impact of War," p. 276.

43. Güldner, *Das Toleranz-Problem in den Niederlanden*, pp. 97–111, 122–23.

44. *Monita*, Preface, pages unnumbered.

45. Ibid., 1:6, 7 (pp. 44–46).

46. Ibid.

47. Ibid., 1:2 (pp. 9–10).

48. *Politicorum*, 2:2 (pp. 44–46); see also 4:5 (pp. 95–99).

49. For example, Lipsius to Theodorus Leeuwius (The Hague), in *Epistolae*, no. 426 (June 28, 1585), 2:214–16; Lipsius to Heinrich von Rantzau (Breitenburg), in ibid., no. 511 (Jan. 3, 1587), p. 324.

50. *Politicorum*, 2:2 (pp. 45–46); *Monita*, 2:7 (p. 119). See De Nave, "Justus Lipsius, schrijver 'in politicis,'" p. 595.

51. *Politicorum*, 2:10 (pp. 55–56); *Monita*, 2:9 (pp. 123–28). See De Nave, "Justus Lipsius, schrijver 'in politicis,'" p. 598; see also below, at n. 80.

52. *Politicorum*, 6:5 (pp. 239–43, quotation on p. 242).

53. Ibid., 1:7 (p. 46).

54. *Politicorum*, 2:1 (p. 43).

55. Ibid., 1:1 (p. 26).

56. Ibid., 4:1 (pp. 87–88).

57. Ibid., 4:5–6 (pp. 95–101).

58. Ibid., 4:8–9 (pp. 103–7, quotations on pp. 103, 107).

59. Ibid., 4:9 (pp. 107–8), 11–12 (pp. 142–44, quotation on p. 143).

60. Ibid., 4:8 (pp. 103–6); see also 2:15 (pp. 64–66), 17 (p. 67).

61. Ibid., 4:9 (pp. 107–11).

62. Ay, *Land und Fürst im alten Bayern*, pp. 166–68; Herbert Hassinger, "Die Landstände der öst. Länder. Zusammensetzung, Organisation, and Leistung," *Jahrbuch des Vereins für Landeskunde von Niederösterreich und Wien* 2 (1964): 989–1035, esp. pp. 989, 994, 1015, 1020, 1022–24, 1033–35.

63. *Politicorum*, 4:11 (pp. 129–36).

64. Ibid., 4:9 (pp. 113–16, quotation on p. 116), 12 (p. 145); 5:15 (p. 202).

65. Ibid., 4:9 (pp. 116–17).

66. Ibid., 1:6 (p. 36); *Breves notae*, p. 261; *Monita*, 1:6 (p. 45).

67. *Politicorum*, 4:13 (p. 148).

68. Ibid. (pp. 147–50).

69. Ibid. (p. 148).

70. See above, at n. 53.

71. *Politicorum*, 4:14 (p. 150).

72. *Ragion de stato*, 5:5 (p. 186).

73. *Politicorum*, 4:14 (pp. 151–53).

74. Ibid. (pp. 153–54).

75. Ibid., 5:17 (p. 216).

76. Ibid., 6:4 (p. 238).

77. Ibid., 4:14 (pp. 154–55).

78. Ibid., (p. 156).

79. Ibid., 2:14 (pp. 62–63); 4:14 (pp. 156–57). In the *Monita*, 2:13 (p. 261), he stated explicitly, "therefore utility favors fidelity."

80. De Nave, "Justus Lipsius, schrijver 'in politicis,'" p. 612–13, and n. 208.

81. *Politicorum*, 4:14 (pp. 157–60, quotations on pp. 157, 160).

82. *De una religione*, 2 (pp. 43–44).

83. See above, Chapter 2, at n. 63.

84. *Summa Theologica*, 1–2, question 96, article 6, in *Opera Omnia*, 7:187.

85. *Politicorum*, 4:2 (p. 89); *Breves notae*, 3 (p. 255, quotation).

86. *De una religione*, 2 (p. 23–24); *Monita*, 1:2 (pp. 3–4).

87. *Monita*, 1:2 (p. 4), 3 (p. 13).

88. *Politicorum*, 1:2 (p. 27).

89. Güldner, *Das Toleranz-Problem in den Niederlanden*, p. 126.

90. *Monita*, 1:3 (13–21).

91. *Politicorum*, 4:2 (pp. 89–91, quotation on p. 89), 3 (p. 91); *De una religione*, 2 (pp. 20, 24, 30–35), 3 (pp. 48–49).

92. Güldner, *Das Toleranz-Problem in den Niederlanden*, p. 154.

93. See *Politicorum*, 6:4 (p. 238).

94. *De una religione*, 3 (pp. 56–61).

95. *Politicorum*, 4:3 (pp. 92–93, quotations on p. 92), 4 (pp. 93–94).

96. Lipsius to Coornhert, Apr. 1, 1590, printed in *De una religione*, pp. 12–14; Lipsius to an unnamed third party, ibid., pp. 15–16; ibid., 3 (pp. 54–56). See also Güldner, *Das Toleranz-Problem in den Niederlanden*, pp. 103, 108–15.

97. For a detailed discussion of these changes, see Güldner, *Das Toleranz-Problem in den Niederlanden*, pp. 123–27.

98. Oestreich, *Neostoicism and the Early Modern State*, pp. 58, 80; Parker, "Military Revolution, 1560–1660," pp. 95–103, esp. pp. 95, 103.

99. *Politicorum*, 5:3 (pp. 165 [mispaginated 156]–66).

100. Ibid., 5:4 (pp. 167–69).

101. Ibid., 5:5 (pp. 169–72).

102. Ibid., 4:9 (pp. 111–13). On the usefulness of foreign war as an antidote to domestic strife, see also 6:7 (p. 247).

103. *The King and the Education of the King*, 3:2 (p. 290).

104. See *Summa Theologica*, 2–2, question 40, article 3, in *Opera Omnia*, 6:316.

105. *Politicorum*, 5:17 (pp. 216–17); Bireley, *Religion and Politics*, pp. 188, 272.

106. *Politicorum*, 5:18 (pp. 218–21), 19 (pp. 221–24, quotations on pp. 222, 223), 20 (pp. 224–27).

107. Oestreich, *Neostoicism and the Early Modern State*, p. 71.

108. Hale, *War and Society*, pp. 65–68.

109. *Politicorum*, 4:7 (pp. 102–3); 5:11 (pp. 181–84); Oestreich, *Neostoicism and the Early Modern State*, pp. 70–71.

110. *Politicorum*, 5:9 (pp. 178–80), 10 (pp. 180–81).

111. Ibid., 5:12 (pp. 184–88), 13 (pp. 188–97, quotation on p. 189), 15 (pp. 202–3, quotation on p. 202).

112. Oestreich, "Antike Literatur."

113. Parker, *Military Revolution*, pp. 18–20.

114. *Politicorum*, 5:13 (pp. 188–97; quotation on p. 195).

115. *Constantia*, 2:6 (pp. 70–71), 7 (pp. 72–74, quotation on p. 73), 8 (pp. 74–76).

116. Ibid., 1:13 (p. 41).

117. Ibid., 1:19 (p. 52).

118. *Politicorum*, 1:4 (p. 31); see also the addition in the 1604 edition published at Antwerp, p. 24; *Monita*, 1:5 (p. 23).

119. *Constantia*, 1:21 (p. 57).

120. Ibid., 1:15 (pp. 43–44).

121. Ibid., 1:16 (pp. 44–46).

122. *Politicorum*, 6:2 (pp. 231–32).

123. *Constantia*, 1:22 (pp. 58–60, quotation on p. 59); see also *Politicorum*, 1:4 (p. 33).

124. *Constantia*, 2:11 (pp. 79–81 [mispaginated 82], quotation on p. 81).

125. Decree on Justification, Session 6, January 13, 1547, chaps. 9 and 12, canons 12–16, in *Enchiridion Symbolorum: Definitionum et Declarationum de Rebus Fidei et Morum*, 36th rev. ed., ed. Henricus Denzinger and Adolfus

Schönmetzer (Freiburg, 1965), nos. 1533–34, 1540, 1562–66 (pp. 372–75, 379).

126. *Constantia*, 2:16 (pp. 89–90). In the edition used here, chapter 14 has been divided into two chapters, 14 and 15; this is not the case in all editions. As a result, from this point on the numeration of chapters differs in different editions.

127. Ibid., 2:14 (pp. 85–87), 15 (pp. 87–88, quotations on pp. 86, 87).

128. Ibid., 2:17 (pp. 91–94). The citation is on p. 94.

129. Oestreich, *Neostoicism and the Early Modern State*, pp. 57–58. There were seventeen editions of Bodin in the French between 1576 and 1753, nine in the Latin between 1586 and 1650, and Italian, German, and English translations. There were eight editions of Althusius between 1603 and 1654, and no translations. Oestreich makes this statement only of Lipsius; I have extended it to Botero. His influence has not been as systematically studied as that of Lipsius.

130. Oestreich, *Antiker Geist und moderner Staat*, pp. 190–91, 216; for the reception of Lipsius especially in Protestant Germany, see Stolleis, "Lipsius-Rezeption."

131. Church, *Richelieu and Reason of State*, pp. 75–78; Oestreich, *Neostoicism and the Early Modern State*, pp. 58, 106–9.

132. "Monita Paterna," in Schmidt, *Geschichte der Erziehung der bayerischen Wittelsbacher*, nos. 2, 3, 5, 7, 47 (pp. 117, 119, 137); Dollinger, "Maximilian von Bayern und Justus Lipsius," esp. pp. 235–36, 281–89, 294–96.

133. Gottigny, "Juste Lipse et l'Espagne," p. 144, citing Bataillon, *Erasme et l'Espagne* (Paris, 1937), p. 815.

134. Corbett, "The Cult of Lipsius," pp. 145–46, 148–49.

135. Siedschlag, *Der Einfluss der niederländisch-stoischen Ethik*, esp. pp. 164–89; Elliott, *The Count-Duke of Olivares*, pp. 22–23, 93, 105, 181, 246, 280, 454. Botero's influence on Richelieu would be a fruitful area of study.

Chapter 5

1. Rey in Ribadeneira, *Historias de la contrarreforma*, pp. ciii, 878; Gottigny, "Juste Lipse et l'Espagne," pp. 5–7, 282. Martin and Parker, *The Spanish Armada*, pp. 255–56, 258, 260, 263–64; for what Philip actually said, see pp. 256, 258.

2. Elliott, *The Count-Duke of Olivares*, pp. 89–94, and his "Self-Perception and Decline," pp. 41–61, rpt. in Elliott, *Spain and Its World*, pp. 241–61; Gordon, "Morality, Reform, and the Empire," pp. 3–19.

3. *Tratado de la tribulación*, 1:23 (pp. 403–6), 24 (p. 408); Gottigny, "Juste Lipse et l'Espagne," pp. 256–67, esp. pp. 266–67; Blüher, *Seneca in Spanien*, pp. 269–72, 281–82.

4. For biographical information on Ribadeneira, see the documents and commentary in the two-volume *Monumenta Historica Societatis Jesu, Ribadeneira* (hereafter, *MHSJ*), and Rey's introduction to Ribadeneira, *Historias de la contrarreforma*.

5. Martin and Parker, *The Spanish Armada*, pp. 83–84.

6. See Persons to Ribadeneira, Paris, Sept. 10, 1584, along with the comments of the editor, in *Letters and Memorials of Father Robert Persons, S.J.*, edited by Leo Hicks, S.J., (London, 1942), 1:227–35.

7. Brodrick, *Robert Bellarmine*, p. 14.

8. Toledo, Feb. 16, 1580, in *MHSJ*, 2:22–28. See the same volume for other

letters to Quiroga. According to Prat, *Histoire du P. Ribadeneyra*, p. 291, Philip II intended to send Ribadeneira to Portugal to negotiate over the succession, but he excused himself.

9. Loomie, *Spanish Elizabethans*, p. 111.

10. See the correspondence in *MHSJ*, vol. 2.

11. Rey in Ribadeneira, *Historias de la contrarreforma*, pp. xl, cxxiv.

12. *Jerusalem Conquistado* (1611), cited in ibid., p. lxxxiii.

13. Ibid., p. 22. According to Eduard Fueter, *Geschichte der neueren Historiographie*, 3d ed. (Munich and Berlin, 1936), p. 283, "Der Humanismus hat keine Biographie hervorgebracht, die sich dem Werke Ribadeneiras an die Seite stellen liesse."

14. *Illustrium Scriptorum Societatis Jesu* (n.p., 1602). For a complete list of the works of Ribadeneira, see Rey's introduction to Ribadeneira, Historias de la contrarreforma, pp. xlii–xliv, and for the *Flos Sanctorum*, see ibid., p. lxxxi.

15. *Historia eclesiástica del scisma de Inglaterra.*

16. De la Fuente in Ribadeneira, *Obras escogidas*, pp. 177–78, and Rey, in Ribadeneira, *Historias de la contrarreforma*, pp. 855–71.

17. *Exortación para los soldados y capitánes que van a esta jornada de Inglaterra, en nombre de su capitán general*, in *MHSJ*, 2:347–70; see Martin and Parker, *The Spanish Armada*, pp. 107, 148, 161–62, and Garrett Mattingly, *The Armada* (Boston, 1962), p. 148.

18. *MHSJ*, 2:356, 368.

19. Ribadeneira to Ana de Guzmán, May 1588, in *MHSJ*, 2:92–95.

20. Cited in Martin and Parker, *The Spanish Armada*, p. 260; de la Fuente in Ribadeneira, *Obras escogidas*, p. 358.

21. *Tratado de la tribulación*, dedication, p. 359.

22. Ibid., 2:1–2 (pp. 411–14, citation on pp. 413–14).

23. Ibid., 2:6–21 (pp. 418–47, esp. pp. 418–23, 426, 432, 444–46).

24. *Historia eclesiástica del scisma de Inglaterra*, 2:27–29, 32 (pp. 341–45, 349–52).

25. See Sommervogel, *Bibliothèque de la Compagnie de Jésus*, 6:1735–36. For the English translation, which bears no date, see Clancy, *Papist Pamphleteers*, p. 228. For the Latin translation, see Brants, " 'Le Prince' de Machiavel dans les anciens Pays-Bas," pp. 89–91; for the French, see Thuau, *Raison d'état et pensée politique*, p. 87.

The text of *The Christian Prince* that I am using is found in Ribadeneira's *Obras escogidas*, edited by de la Fuente, pp. 449–587.

26. Rey in Ribadeneira, *Historias de la contrarreforma*, p. lxxxvii; Prat, *Histoire du P. Ribadeneyra*, p. 605.

27. *Wittelsbach und Bayern* (Munich, 1980), vol. 2, *Um Glauben und Reich*, ed. Hubert Glaser, part 2, *Katalog der Ausstellung*, p. 524.

28. Clancy, *Papist Pamphleteers*, pp. 180, 228.

29. *An sit utilitas in scelere vel de infelicitate principis machiavellani contra Machiavellum et politicos ejus sectatores*, p. 59.

30. *The First Part of a Treatise concerning Policy and Religion*, 2d ed., English Recusant Literature, 1552–1640, vol. 175 (Douai, 1615, rpt. Menston, 1974); *The Second Part of a Treatise concerning Religion and Policy*, 2d ed., English Recusant Literature, 1552–1640, vol. 180 (Douai, 1615, rpt. Menston, 1974); Clancy, *Papist Pamphleteers*, pp. 180–86.

For a brief sketch of the long and eventful life of Fitzherbert, from 1552 to 1640, see *Letters of Thomas Fitzherbert, 1608–1610*, ed. Leo Hicks, S.J., Publications of the Catholic Record Society, vol. 41 (London, 1948), pp. 1–3. I am grateful for assistance from my student, Fr. Vincent Costello, who wrote his master's essay on Fitzherbert.

31. Madrid, late 1588, in *MHSJ*, 2:105–10; see Rey in Ribadeneira, *Historias de la contrarreforma*, p. 1355.

32. Schellhase, *Tacitus in Renaissance Political Thought*, p. 152.

33. *The King and the Education of the King*, 2:6 (p. 208).

34. *Príncipe cristiano*, dedication and preface, pp. 452–55.

35. Ibid., preface, pp. 455–56.

36. Galino, *Los tratados sobre educación de príncipes*, pp. 13–16, 24–25. Giles of Rome, or Aegidius Romanus, composed his work for Philip the Fair of France about 1285.

37. Gottigny, "Juste Lipse et l'Espagne," pp. 270–97.

38. *Tratado de república y policía christiana*, c. 1 (pp. 3, 7); Elliott, *The Count-Duke of Olivares*, pp. 95, 105–6, 108.

39. *Príncipe cristiano*, 1:21 (p. 490); 2:9 (p. 534).

40. *The King and the Education of the King*, 1:8 (pp. 161–62).

41. *Príncipe cristiano*, 1:1 (pp. 458–59).

42. Ibid., 1:8 (p. 467).

43. Ibid., 1:15 (pp. 478–82).

44. Ibid., 1:17 (p. 482).

45. Ibid., 1:27 (pp. 500–502).

46. Ibid., 1:26 (p. 498).

47. Ibid. (p. 499).

48. 2–2, question 10, article 11 in *Opera omnia*, 8:92–93.

49. Geoffrey Parker, "Why Did the Dutch Revolt Last So Long?" in *Spain and the Netherlands 1559–1659: Ten Studies* (Glasgow, 1979), p. 53; see also Kamen, "Toleration and Dissent in Sixteenth-Century Spain," pp. 19–23.

50. Loomie, *Spanish Elizabethans*, p. 196.

51. *Príncipe cristiano*, 1:26 (p. 499).

52. These paragraphs do not appear in the text in the *Obras escogidas*, but they are found in the text edited by Rey, *Historias de la contrarreforma*, pp. 1263–65.

53. Marquez, *El gobernador cristiano*, 2:33 (pp. 358–59). The texts were Aquinas's *Compendium of Theology*, 2–2, question 10, article 8, ad 1, and article 11 (*Opera omnia*, 8:89, 92–93) and Augustine's *Against the Epistle of Parmenianus*. There is a discrepancy between the two in the citation of Augustine, but a subsequent reference by Marquez to Ribadeneira on a related minor point makes clear that he had *The Christian Prince* as he wrote.

54. *The King and the Education of the King*, 1:10 (pp. 170–79); 2:14 (pp. 257–63); 3:16 (pp. 361–73).

55. See his chap. 37 (pp. 238–42).

56. *Príncipe cristiano*, 2:1–3 (pp. 518–24); the citation is on p. 521.

57. Ibid., 2:23 (p. 552).

58. Ibid., 2:31, 32 (pp. 562–66, esp. 562).

59. Ibid., 2:23 (pp. 553–54), 31 (p. 562), 33 (p. 567); see also 2:14 (p. 541–42). The quotations are on pp. 553–54.

60. See Elliott, *The Count-Duke of Olivares*, pp. 32, 95, 178, 295, 318–20, 386.

61. *Príncipe cristiano*, 2:24 (p. 554), 32 (pp. 564–65).

62. Ibid., 2:31 (pp. 563–64).

63. Gottigny, "Juste Lipse et l'Espagne," pp. 280–86.

64. *Príncipe cristiano*, 2:4 (p. 524).
65. D. Hughes, "Mental Reservation," *New Catholic Encyclopedia* (Washington, 1967; rpt., Palatine, Ill., 1980), 9:662–63.
66. *Príncipe cristiano*, 2:4 (p. 525).
67. Botero, *Ragion di stato*, 2:8 (pp. 113–14); Marquez, *El gobernador cristiano*, 1:14 (pp. 74–76); Aquinas, *Summa Theologica*, 2–2, question 111, article 1, in *Opera Omnia*, 9:430.
68. *Príncipe cristiano*, 2:4 (pp. 525–26).
69. Ibid., 2:15 (p. 542).
70. Ibid., 2:32 (p. 565).
71. Ibid.
72. Ibid., 2:5 (p. 526).
73. Ibid., 2:6–7 (pp. 528–31).
74. Ibid., 2:9 (pp. 532–34).
75. Ibid., 2:10 (pp. 534–35); Lewy, *Constitutionalism and Statecraft*, pp. 28–32.
76. *Príncipe cristiano*, 2:11 (pp. 537–38).
77. Ibid., 2:34 (p. 567).
78. Ibid., 2:35–38 (pp. 569–75); the citation is on p. 575.
79. Ibid., 2:39 (pp. 575–76).
80. Ibid., 2:43 (pp. 582–84).
81. Ribadeneira to Quiroga, Feb. 16, 1580, in *MHSJ*, 2:23.
82. *Príncipe cristiano*, 2:41–43 (pp. 579–84); the citations are on p. 579.
83. Ibid., 2:41 (p. 579).
84. Ibid., 2:41–42 (pp. 579–82).
85. On holy war during the period, see Johnson, *Ideology, Reason, and the Limitation of War*, esp. pp. 132–33; Roland Bainton, "Congregationalism: From the Just War to the Crusades in the Puritan Revolution," *Andover Newton Theological School Bulletin* 35 (1943): 1–20; Paul Rousset, "L'idéologie de croisade dans les guerres de religion au xvi siècle," *Schweizerische Zeitschrift für Geschichte* 31 (1981): 174–84.
86. *Arte real para el buen govierno de los reyes, y príncipes, y de sus vasallos* (Toledo, 1623), p. 4, cited in Elliott, "Self-Perception and Decline," p. 49 (rpt., p. 249); see also pp. 47–54 (rpt., pp. 247–54).
87. See ibid.
88. *Príncipe cristiano*, 1:10 (pp. 469–70).
89. Ibid., 1:11 (pp. 471–72).
90. Ibid., 2:40 (pp. 577–78).

Chapter 6

1. Breuer, *Oberdeutsche Literatur*, pp. 138–39.
2. Ul. Capitaine, "Chokier (Jean de) ou De Chokier de Surlet." There is no modern study of Chokier. I have used the edition of the *Thesaurus politicorum aphorismorum* (Rome, 1611) found in the Newberry Library in Chicago, and references are to it. I have also consulted editions found in the *Bayerische Staatsbibliothek* in Munich and in the library of the University of St. Mary of the Lake in Mundelein, Illinois.
3. *Thesaurus politicorum aphorismorum*, 1:7 (pp. 36–39); 2:9 (pp. 110–11, quotation), 18 (pp. 175–76).

4. *Consejo i consejero de príncipes*; see Fadrique Furió Ceriol, *El concejo i consejeros del príncipe y otras obras*, ed. Diego Sevilla Andrés (Valencia, 1952), pp. 32–33 (editor's introduction).

5. Seils, *Die Staatslehre des Adam Contzen*, p. 175.

6. *Politicorum*, 3:3.1 (pp. 104–5). In references to the *Ten Books on Politics* (henceforth *Ten Books* in the text) or *Libri decem politicorum* (henceforth *Libri decem* in the notes), the first numeral indicates the book, the second the chapter, and the third the paragraph.

7. Reinhard, "Zwang zur Konfessionalisierung?," esp. pp. 259–60, 265–66, 268–77; Raeff, *The Well-Ordered Police State*, pp. 43–179. On social discipline as a characteristic of the period, see Schulze, "Gerhard Oestreichs Begriff 'Sozialdisziplinierung' in der frühen Neuzeit."

8. Sigmund Riezler, *Geschichte Bayerns* 5 (Gotha, 1903): 18–19; Michael Doeberl, *Entwicklungsgeschichte Bayerns*, 2d ed. (Munich, 1908), 1:515–22; on the *Codex Maximilianus*, see *Das bayerische Landrecht von 1616*, ed. Helmut Günter (Munich, 1969).

9. Seils, *Die Staatslehre des Adam Contzen*, pp. 191–228.

10. *Methodus doctrinae civilis seu Abissini regis historia*. A German translation appeared at Sulzbach in 1672.

11. *Aulae speculum sive de statu, vita, virtute aulicorum atque magnatum*. A second edition appeared at Cologne in 1686.

12. *Politicorum libri decem, in quibus de perfectae reipublicae forma, virtutibus et vitiis, institutione civium, legibus, magistratu ecclesiastico, civili, potentia reipublicae, itemque seditione ac bello, ad usum vitamque communem accomodate tractatur*. The parallel with Lipsius appears if one starts at the end of the title. Lipsius and Contzen both treated civil and foreign war and military affairs in the last two books. Contzen's book 8, on power, dealt with issues like reputation and taxation, which Lipsius handled in his fourth book on political prudence. Contzen took up councillors and officials in book 7, as Lipsius did in book 3, under "prudence from others." Basic issues of the nature and form of government and then religion and the virtues served as the topics of Contzen's first three and Lipsius's first two books. Contzen then in his fourth, fifth, and sixth books turned to subjects barely mentioned by Lipsius, education, law, and ecclesiastical officials, the first two illustrating his concern to mold and form ordinary citizens in virtue.

13. *Libri decem*, 1:1.4 (pp. 1–2).

14. Ibid., 1:2.4 (p. 5).

15. Ibid., 1:2.6 (pp. 5–6).

16. Ibid., Dedication, unpaginated; 10:1.7 (p. 739).

17. Dedicatory Letter to Maximilian, unpaginated.

18. *Libri decem*, 10:1.3 (p. 738).

19. Ibid., 1:1.8 (p. 3); 5:1.5 (p. 271); 10:1.3 (p. 738, quotation); 10:20.1 (p. 770); 10:60.1–3 (pp. 822–34). For Contzen's use of history in the *Instruction on Civic Doctrine*, see Breuer, *Oberdeutsche Literatur*, pp. 173–80.

20. *Libri decem*, 10:32.1 (p. 787).

21. Firpo in Botero, *Ragion di stato*, p. 458.

22. Seils, *Die Staatslehre des Adam Contzen*, pp. 77–81, 171–73, 179–84.

23. *Libri decem*, 5:5.5–6 (p. 279); cf. Seils, *Die Staatslehre des Adam Contzen*, pp. 57–59.

24. *Libri decem*, 1:24.4–8 (pp. 53–56); 5:5.11 (p. 280); 5:20.1 (p. 303).

25. Ibid., 7:6.3–4 (pp. 477–78); 9:8.4 (p. 636); Seils, *Die Staatslehre des Adam Contzen*, p. 145, and n. 69.

26. *Libri decem,* 5:20.2 (p. 303); 6:2.7 (p. 335); Seils, *Die Staatslehre des Adam Contzen,* pp. 82–84.

27. *Libri decem,* 5:20.2, 6, 8 (pp. 303–5); see Seils, *Die Staatslehre des Adam Contzen,* pp. 69–72.

28. See Seils, *Die Staatslehre des Adam Contzen,* pp. 51–54, 106, 130–31, 178.

29. *Libri decem,* 8:2.3 (p. 550); 8:3.1–3 (p. 552).

30. Ibid., 8:4.1 (p. 552).

31. Seils, *Die Staatslehre des Adam Contzen,* p. 106.

32. Lipsius, *Politicorum,* 1:1 (p. 26); 1:2 (p. 27).

33. Ibid., 4:9 (p. 111).

34. *Libri decem,* 2:3.4–5 (p. 66); 2:10.2 (p. 76); 9:20.6–7 (p. 674).

35. Ibid., 1:23.6 (pp. 52–53).

36. Ibid., 6:3. 1–15 (pp. 337–40); see Seils, *Die Staatslehre des Adam Contzen,* pp. 82–88.

37. Bireley, *Maximilian von Bayern,* pp. 18–19.

38. *Libri decem,* 9:18–20 (pp. 669–74).

39. *De fide haereticis servanda.*

40. Lecler, *Toleration and the Reformation,* 1:299–303.

41. *Libri decem,* 9:22.3 (pp. 677–78); this was a theme of Contzen's polemical works.

42. Evans, *Rudolf II and His World,* pp. 156–58, 285–86, and his *Making of the Habsburg Monarchy,* pp. 62–68, 109–16.

43. *Libri decem,* 2:17, esp. paragraph 9 (pp. 92–95, quotation on p. 94).

44. Ibid., 2:18–19 (pp. 95–100).

45. See R. Po-Chia Hsia, *Society and Religion in Münster 1535–1618* (New Haven, 1984), pp. 67–69.

46. Hans Sturmberger, *Adam Graf Herberstorff: Herrschaft und Freiheit im konfessionellen Zeitalter* (Munich, 1976), pp. 261–71; Hermann Rebel, *Peasant Classes: The Bureaucratization of Property and Family Relations under Early Habsburg Absolutism, 1511–1636* (Princeton, 1983), pp. 7, 247–48, 256–57, 261–69.

47. Seils, *Die Staatslehre des Adam Contzen,* p. 106.

48. *Libri decem,* 3:5 (pp. 110–12); 3:17.2 (p. 163); 3:21 (pp. 178–80); Seils, *Die Staatslehre des Adam Contzen,* pp. 107–8, 114, 124–25, 128–29, 131–32.

49. *Libri decem,* 3:4 (pp. 106–8, quotation on p. 106); 8:5.4 (p. 555); 10:38.3 (p. 797).

50. Ibid. (1629 ed.), 7:37.5 (p. 618); on Wotton's epigram, see Mattingly, *Renaissance Diplomacy,* pp. 55, 206.

51. *Libri decem,* 3:7 (pp. 116–18); 8:24.3–4 (p. 618); 9:15.7 (p. 663).

52. Ibid., 5:5.10–11 (p. 280); 5:20.1 (p. 303); Seils, *Die Staatslehre des Adam Contzen,* pp. 67–69.

53. *Libri decem,* 3:16.19 (p. 161).

54. Ibid., 8:3.4 (p. 552); 8:4.3 (p. 553).

55. Ibid., 8:4.3, 5 (pp. 552–53).

56. Ibid., 8:4.5, 7 (p. 553); 2:13 (pp. 78–79).

57. Seils, *Die Staatslehre des Adam Contzen,* pp. 149, 155.

58. *Libri decem,* 8:5 (pp. 554–55).

59. Ibid., 8:7 (pp. 557–61).

60. Ibid. (quotations on pp. 558, 561); Seils, *Die Staatslehre des Adam Contzen,* pp. 145–49.

61. *Libri decem*, 8:11 (pp. 571–75).
62. Ibid., 8:12 (pp. 575–76).
63. Ibid., 8:10 (pp. 565–70, 647–48 in 1629 ed.); 8:15.4 (pp. 585–86).
64. On the development of luxury taxes in Germany, see Stolleis, *Pecunia Nervus Rerum*, esp. pp. 57–61.
65. *Libri decem*, 8:14 (pp. 578–83, quotation on p. 578).
66. Wilhelm Lütge, *Deutsche Sozial- und Wirtschaftsgeschichte*, 2d ed. (Göttingen, 1960), p. 333, cited in Seils, *Die Staatslehre des Adam Contzen*, p. 139.
67. *Libri decem*, 8:15.2–4 (pp. 585–86); Seils, *Die Staatslehre des Adam Contzen*, p. 139.
68. *Libri decem*, 10:2 (pp. 740–41).
69. Ibid., 10:13.1 (p. 759).
70. Ibid., 10:3.2–5 (pp. 743–45, p. 842 in 1629 ed.); 10:6.1 (p. 750, quotation).
71. Ibid., 10:4.1–7 (pp. 745–46); 10:5.2 (p. 749); 10:6 (p. 750–51), 10 (pp. 756–57).
72. Ibid., 10:6.5–8 (p. 750); 10:8.2 (p. 752).
73. Ibid., 10:6.5 (p. 750).
74. Ibid., 10:14.2 (p. 760); 10:20 (pp. 770–72), 10:28 (pp. 783–84); 10:29 (pp. 784–85); 10:59 (pp. 820–22, quotation); Seils, *Die Staatslehre des Adam Contzen*, pp. 157–61, 167–68.
75. Lipsius, *Politicorum*, 3:3–7 (pp. 72–79), 3:10–11 (pp. 82–86).
76. *Libri decem*, 7:1 (p. 463).
77. Ibid., 7:7.11 (p. 538, 1629 ed.).
78. Ibid., 7:9 (pp. 482–83); 7:12 (p. 489); 7:13 (pp. 489–94); 7:14.3 (p. 497); 7:16.1 (p. 500).
79. Ibid., 7:8 (pp. 481–82); 7:10 (pp. 484–87); 7:11 (pp. 487–88).
80. Ibid., 5:4.5–6 (pp. 277–78, quotation); 5:6 (pp. 280–81); 5:8.1, 8 (p. 283). On Suarez, see above, Chapter 2, at n. 45. Aquinas emphasizes the obligation of the ruler to direct citizens to the life of virtue more in the *De Regimine Principum*, nn. 115–20, than in the *Summa Theologica*, 2–2, question 96, articles 2–3, in *Opera Omnia*, 7:181–82, where the distinction between citizen and individual is more developed.
81. *Libri decem*, 5:8.1 (p. 283); 5:13.2, 5 (pp. 295–96); see Seils, *Die Staatslehre des Adam Contzen*, pp. 64–67, 76–77, and Moote, *Louis XIII*, p. 118.
82. *Libri decem*, 4:1 (pp. 182–83); 4:2 (pp. 183–84); 4:3.1 (p. 184); 4:5.5 (p. 189, quotation).
83. Ibid., 4:3.2 (pp. 185–86); 4:5 (pp. 188–90); 4:7 (196–99).
84. Ibid., 4:8 (pp. 199–206); 4:9 (pp. 206–9).
85. Ibid., 1:12.1 (p. 22).
86. Ibid., 2:12 (p. 77).
87. Pp. 467–72.
88. Dollinger, "Maximilian von Bayern und Justus Lipsius," p. 284, and n. 11.
89. Dieter Albrecht, *Die auswärtige Politik Maximilians von Bayern, 1618–1635* (Göttingen, 1962), p. 2.
90. On Duke William's abdication, see Albrecht, "Das konfessionelle Zeitalter," pp. 404–6, and Dollinger, *Finanzreform Maximilians I. von Bayern*, pp. 1–50.
91. Maximilian to Father R. Haller, Jan. 15, 1611, *Briefe und Akten zur*

Geschichte des dreissigjährigen Krieges, 9, ed. Anton Chroust (Munich, 1903), no. 20, pp. 51–52.

92. Bireley, *Maximilian von Bayern*, pp. 43–45, 49–50, and "Antimachiavellianism, the Baroque, and Maximilian of Bavaria," p. 147 and n. 45.

93. Bireley, *Maximilian von Bayern*, pp. 75–89, 93–107, 122–39. An example of an important moderate paper, which was presented to the Catholic electors at the Electoral Convention of Regensburg in 1630, is the unpublished "Consilium Theologicum Cuiusdam Monachi Dominicani et Celebris Professoris," *Bayerisches Hauptstaatsarchiv* (Munich), *Akten zur Geschichte des dreissigjährigen Krieges* 242, 22 folia.

94. Bireley, *Maximilian von Bayern*, pp. 76–78.

95. *Briefe und Akten zur Geschichte des dreissigjährigen Krieges*, n.s., part 2, vol. 5, ed. Dieter Albrecht (Munich, 1964), no. 170, pp. 419–23. For a detailed analysis of Contzen's role in the formation of Bavarian policy, see Bireley, *Maximilian von Bayern*.

96. "De Persecutione Ecclesiae Christi per Germaniam Consideratio," *Bayerisches Hauptstaatsarchiv* (Munich), *Jesuitica* 81, ff. 126–226; Bireley, *Maximilian von Bayern*, pp. 177–78.

97. The best edition of the *Monita Paterna* is Friedrich Schmidt, *Geschichte der Erziehung der bayerischen Wittelsbacher*, *Monumenta Paedogogica Germanica* (Berlin, 1892), 14:104–41.

98. Bireley, "Antimachiavellianism, the Baroque, and Maximilian of Bavaria," pp. 154–56, and *Maximilian von Bayern*, pp. 222–23; Vervaux, *Annales boicae gentis* (Munich, 1662), 3:215–22.

99. Wendelin, *Institutionum politicarum libri tres*, p. 7, and Knichen, *Opus politicorum in tribus libris*, col. 20, both cited in Münkler, *Im Namen des Staates*, pp. 185–86, 361–62; Seils, *Die Staatslehre des Adam Contzen*, pp. 225, 228.

100. Werdenhagen, *Politica generalis*; Seils, *Die Staatslehre des Adam Contzen*, p. 201.

101. Seils, *Die Staatslehre des Adam Contzen*, pp. 198–99; he discusses at length the influence of Contzen on pp. 191–228.

102. *Politica sacra, seu institutiones politicae ex divinis scripturis depromptae*.

103. *Institutionum politicarum libri iv*. Seils, *Die Staatslehre des Adam Contzen*, pp. 215–18.

104. *Discursus christianus politicus* (Alcala, 1637), p. 5, as cited in Seils, p. 221 and n. 257; Seils, pp. 201–2, 215–18.

Chapter 7

1. *Politico-Christianus*.

2. Max Rooses, *L'oeuvre de P. R. Rubens: Histoire et description de ses tableaux et dessins* (Antwerp, 1892), 5:119; Jay Richard Judson and Carl van de Velde, *Book Illustrations and Title Pages*, Corpus Rubenianum Ludwig Burchard, part 21, vol. 1 (London, 1979), pp. 52, 237–38, 365.

3. Pirenne, *Histoire de Belgique*, 225, 421–37, 453–55, 464–71.

4. On the *arbitrista* literature, see Chapter 5, n. 2.

5. Terminological difficulties arise at this point. The term Scribani himself employed was the Latin *Belgus*. The use of the term *Belgian* here would be anachronistic and inaccurate; Scribani designated all the inhabitants of the sev-

enteen Burgundian provinces as *Belgi*, though he was not always consistent. I use the term "Netherlander" to designate such inhabitants and the "Dutch" to designate those of the Dutch Republic or United Provinces. For the inhabitants of the southern Netherlands loyal to Spain I use the term "Flemings." It is not completely accurate, but there is no better term and it corresponds to the Spanish designation of the area as "Flanders."

6. Brouwers, *Scribani*, pp. 1–6, 19–20, 35, 48.

7. *Origines Antwerpensium; Adolescens prodigus, succumbit vitiis, redit ad se et in omnem aetatem ac fortunam a virtute instruitur; Christus patiens . . . piis exercitationibus illustratus.*

8. John Rupert Martin, *The Ceiling Paintings for the Jesuit Church in Antwerp*, Corpus Rubenianum Ludwig Burchard, part 1 (New York, 1968), p. 31.

9. Brouwers, *Scribani*, pp. 506–7 (on health); Scribani to Georgius Uwens, 1626, in Scribani, *Brieven*, no. 61, pp. 194–96.

10. Scribani to Peter Peckius, 1624, in Scribani, *Brieven*, no. 21, p. 67.

11. *Clari Bonarsci Amphitheatrum honoris in quo Calvinistarum in Societatem Jesu criminationes iugulatae*; Brouwers, *Scribani*, pp. 129–51; Scribani to Pierre Coton, S.J., 1626, in Scribani, *Brieven*, no. 58, pp. 178–82.

12. *Justi Lipsi Defensio postuma*; Brouwers, *Scribani*, pp. 170–73, and his "Scribani's verdediging van Justus Lipsius," *Philologische Studien* 4 (1933): 216–21.

13. *Amor divinus* and *Medicus religiosus: De animorum morbis et curationibus*; Brouwers, *Scribani*, pp. 303–5, 372–77.

14. *Veridicus Belgicus sive civilium apud Belgas bellorum initia, progressus, finis optatus* and *Reformata Apocalypsis Batavica*; Brouwers, *Scribani*, p. 448 and n. 87.

15. Brouwers, *Scribani*, p. 449, n. 87.

16. Ibid., pp. 448–59.

17. Ibid., pp. 460–63.

18. They are printed as a conclusion to the *Politico-Christianus*, pp. 628–31 and also in Brouwers, *Scribani*, pp. 545–48.

19. Pirenne, *Histoire de Belgique*, pp. 224–25, 249–50.

20. Brouwers, *Scribani*, pp. 465–68, 477–89, 494–99.

21. Pirenne, *Histoire de Belgique*, pp. 242–45.

22. Brouwers, *Scribani*, pp. 384–87, 474.

23. Scribani to Georgius Uwens, 1626, in Scribani, *Brieven*, no. 60, pp. 188–93.

24. Brouwers, *Scribani*, p. 474; Maurice van Durme, *Les archives générales de Simancas et l'histoire de la Belgique* (Brussels, 1964), 1:598–99, 615; Jan Joseph Poelhekke, *'t Uytgaen van den Treves. Spanje en de Nederlanden in 1621* (Groningen, 1960), pp. 114–15; Manuel Angel Echevarría Bacigalupe, *La diplomacia secreta en Flandes* (Bilbao, 1984), p. 161.

Sueyro was a linguist who translated the *Annals* and *Histories* of Tacitus into Spanish (Antwerp, 1613); see Fernández-Santamaría, *Reason of State and Statecraft in Spanish Political Thought*, pp. 190–91.

25. Brouwers, *Scribani*, pp. 285–86; see the letters, including ten to Olivares, in Scribani, *Brieven*.

26. Lefèvre, *Spinola et la Belgique*, p. 65; see, for example, Scribani to Peckius, 1624, in Scribani, *Brieven*, no. 21, pp. 65–70.

27. Lefèvre, *Spinola et la Belgique*, p. 11.

28. Brouwers, *Scribani*, pp. 282–83, 459, n. 117; Elliott, *The Count-Duke of Olivares*, pp. 246–47.

29. Brouwers, *Scribani*, p. 505.

30. Scribani to Olivares, 1627, in Scribani, *Brieven*, no. 68, pp. 221–22; on Leganés, see Elliott, *The Count-Duke of Olivares*, pp. 274–77.

31. Lefèvre, *Spinola et la Belgique*, p. 85.

32. Scribani to Olivares, 1625, in Scribani, *Brieven*, no. 36, p. 107; Brouwers, *Scribani*, p. 285.

33. Scribani, *Brieven*, no. 65, pp. 207–10.

34. Scribani to Peter Coton, S.J., 1626, in Scribani, *Brieven*, no. 58, pp. 179–82.

35. *Politico-Christianus*, dedication, unpaginated.

36. 1:11 (pp. 131–46); Scribani to Peckius, 1624, in Scribani, *Brieven*, no. 21, p. 68.

37. Preface. "Volo, me hunc Politico-Christianum manumittere . . . ." The words seemed to mean to release or liberate as a sculptor released a figure from the stone in the famous phrase of Michelangelo.

38. Ibid.

39. Ibid., 1:1 (p. 7); 2:1 (pp. 398, 400).

40. Dollinger, "Maximilian von Bayern und Justus Lipsius," p. 286.

41. Scribani to Georgius Uwens, 1626, in Scribani, *Brieven*, no. 60, p. 188.

42. *Libri decem*, 7:33–37.

43. Scribani, *Brieven*, 1624, no. 21, p. 70.

44. The references to Machiavelli are on 1:2 (p. 16).

45. Scribani to Contzen, 1624, in Scribani, *Brieven*, no. 31, pp. 89–91. Seils, *Die Staatslehre des Adam Contzen*, pp. 206–9, argues that Scribani was in some areas dependent on Contzen. Brouwers, in Scribani, *Brieven*, p. 89, and in a long personal communication to me, denies this. I think Brouwers is correct.

46. Pirenne, *Histoire de Belgique*, pp. 227–31, 405–6.

47. *Politico-Christianus*, 2:38 (p. 573).

48. Ibid., 2:28 (pp. 539–42).

49. Ibid., (pp. 534–42).

50. Ibid., 1:7 (p. 98).

51. Ibid. (pp. 95–101).

52. Ibid., 2:12 (p. 457).

53. Ibid., 2:12 (pp. 457–65).

54. Ibid., 2:13 (misnumbered 8), p. 465.

55. Ibid., 2:12 (pp. 457–65); 2:2 (p. 407); 2:18 (p. 489); 2:20 (p. 507).

56. Ibid., 2:14 (pp. 470–72).

57. Ibid., 1:8 (pp. 110–11); 1:6 (p. 85).

58. Ibid., 1:3 (esp. pp. 25–42).

59. Santa María, *Tratado de república y policía christiana*, c. 27 (pp. 143^r–143^v); Mariana, *The King and the Education of the King*, 3:4 (p. 285); Elliott, *The Count-Duke of Olivares*, pp. 175–76.

60. *Politico-Christianus*, 2:12 (pp. 463–65).

61. "Gran Memorial," *Memoriales y cartas del Conde Duque de Olivares*, 1:no. 4, pp. 92–94; see Elliott, *The Count-Duke of Olivares*, pp. 192–96.

62. Elliott, *The Count-Duke of Olivares*, pp. 593–94; on the Austrian Habsburgs, see Evans, *Making of the Habsburg Monarchy*.

63. *Politico-Christianus*, 1:6 (pp. 81–82); 1:3 (pp. 26–27, 42–43).

64. Ibid., 2:2 (pp. 406–7).

65. Ibid., 2:9 (p. 442).

66. Ibid., 2:1 (p. 395); 2:9 (p. 442); 2:15 (p. 473); 2:23 (p. 513); 2:26 (p. 624).

67. Ibid., 2:22 (pp. 522–23); Elliott, *The Count-Duke of Olivares*, pp. 174–77.

68. Stradling, *Philip IV and the Government of Spain*, pp. 4–5; Tomás y Valiente, *Los validos en la monarquía española*, pp. 5–7, 32, 122–54, esp. pp. 124, 143–44.

69. See Elliott, *The Count-Duke of Olivares*, pp. 169–70, 284–85.

70. *Politico-Christianus*, 2:29 (pp. 542–45), 38 (pp. 617–25).

71. Stradling, *Philip IV and the Government of Spain*, pp. 18–19, 50, 56. Stradling and Elliott (*The Count-Duke of Olivares*) both assert the independent role of the king, Stradling more so than Elliott.

72. *Politico-Christianus*, 1:12 (pp. 146–55); 1:11 (p. 138).

73. Ibid., 1:6 (p. 88), 13 (p. 161); see his extremely negative description of the court, 1:11 (pp. 132–34).

74. Ibid., 1:26 (p. 330).

75. Ibid. (p. 358).

76. Ibid., 1:13 (p. 161).

77. Ibid., 1:2 (pp. 18–19); 1:13 (p. 160).

78. See, for example, 1:13 (pp. 155, 158), and 2:15 (p. 476). Scribani used the term *simulatio* rather than *dissimulatio*, which he never employed. The sense is clearly that of dissimulation, but the usage generates further unclarity.

79. Ibid., 1:2 (pp. 18–19), 6 (p. 89), 13 (pp. 157–58, 160).

80. Ibid., 1:13 (pp. 158–60).

81. Ibid., 1:26 (p. 343).

82. Ibid., 1:13 (pp. 156, 162).

83. Ibid. (pp. 162–63).

84. Ibid., 1:9 (pp. 135–36), 6 (p. 93), 13 (pp. 156, 163); 2:6 (p. 430).

85. Ibid., 1:2 (pp. 20–21).

86. Ibid., 2:5 (p. 424), 13 (pp. 465–66).

87. Ibid., 1:26 (p. 358).

88. Ibid. (pp. 331–32, 336–38).

89. Ibid., 2:15 (p. 472); 1:26 (p. 342).

90. Ibid., 1:24 (pp. 260–61).

91. Ibid., 2:15 (pp. 472–74); see David Buisseret, *Henry IV* (London, 1984), pp. 173–74, and Paul Henrard, *Henri IV et la Princesse de Condé, 1609–10* (Brussels, 1870); this volume is based largely on the papers of Peckius, who must have been Scribani's source.

92. *Politico-Christianus*, 2:15 (p. 472).

93. Elliott, *The Count-Duke of Olivares*, p. 362.

94. *Politico-Christianus*, 2:24 (p. 515).

95. Ibid., 2:43 (pp. 609–11).

96. Güldner, *Das Toleranz-Problem in den Niederlanden*, p. 149.

97. Elliott, *The Count-Duke of Olivares*, p. 296.

98. Scribani, *Brieven*, nos. 72–73, pp. 231–46; Elliott, *The Count-Duke of Olivares*, pp. 252, 266–69, 305–8, 355–56, 410, 514.

99. *Politico-Christianus*, 2:24 (pp. 515–17).

100. Ibid., 2:14 (p. 471).

101. Ibid., 2:41 (pp. 583–84).

102. Ibid., 2:44 (pp. 613–14).

103. Ibid., 2:42 (pp. 596–609).

104. Ibid. (p. 596); Elliott, *The Count-Duke of Olivares*, pp. 246–48; Brouwers, *Scribani*, p. 459, n. 117. On the Union of Arms, see also Elliott and

Peña in Olivares, *Memoriales y Cartas de Conde Duque de Olivares*, nos. 9 and 10, pp. 173–97, with figures on pp. 191–92.

105. Elliott, *The Count-Duke of Olivares*, pp. 253–66.

106. *Politico-Christianus*, 2:42 (pp. 603–4); Stradling, *Philip IV and the Government of Spain*, p. 186; see also F. Prims, "De Unie van 1627," *Antwerpensia* 7 (1934): 243–50.

Parker, *The Army of Flanders and the Spanish Road*, pp. 144, 157, 272, estimates that in 1623 there were 21,041 soldiers from the Netherlands in the Army of Flanders and by 1627, over 27,000. So the 12,000 must have been either new soldiers or soldiers funded by money from the Spanish Netherlands. Parker notes the extreme difficulty of computing the amount of men or money actually contributed to the Army of Flanders by the Spanish Netherlands.

107. *Politico-Christianus*, 2:42 (p. 609).

108. Lefèvre, *Spinola et la Belgique*, p. 16.

109. Ibid., p. 82; Elliott, *The Count-Duke of Olivares*, pp. 214–20, 332–35, 360–62; Jonathan Israel, "The Politics of International Trade Rivalry during the Thirty Years' War: Gabriel de Roy and Olivares' Mercantilist Projects," *International History Review* 8 (1986): 517–49. Israel shows that the Spaniards did succeed in greatly curtailing the illegal import of Dutch goods into the Iberian Peninsula.

110. Elliott, *The Count-Duke of Olivares*, p. 215.

111. *Politico-Christianus*, 2:38 (pp. 572–78, citations on p. 575, 576).

112. Ibid., 1:24 (pp. 294–95), 26 (pp. 322–23).

113. Ibid., 1:24 (p. 294), 26 (pp. 322–23, 353); 2:1 (pp. 396–99).

114. Ibid., 2:37 (pp. 569–70), 38 (p. 573).

115. Ibid., 1:24 (pp. 254–56, 260, 267–68); 2:30 (pp. 546–47), 39 (pp. 578–81). Brouwers, *Scribani*, pp. 433–34.

116. *Politico-Christianus*, 2:19 (p. 499).

117. Tracy, "With and Without the Counter Reformation," pp. 547–48.

118. *Politico-Christianus*, 2:19 (pp. 494–500, citations on pp. 495, 497).

119. Bireley, *Religion and Politics*, pp. 30–43.

120. *Politico-Christianus*, 2:42 (pp. 598–99, 605).

121. Ibid., 1:16 (pp. 196–98).

122. Ibid., 1:21 (pp. 234–36).

123. Ibid., 1:16 (p. 194), 22 (p. 241). For a similar sentiment, see Montaigne, *Essays*, 3:8, in *The Complete Works of Montaigne*, trans. by Donald Frame (Stanford, 1957), pp. 712–13.

124. *Politico-Christianus*, 1:16 (pp. 193, 198), 18 (p. 206), 20 (p. 220).

Chapter 8

1. *Príncipe político-cristiano*, no. 18, p. 208. The first number refers to the *empresa* or emblem, the second to the page in Saavedra Fajardo, *Empresas políticas: Idea de un príncipe político-cristiano*, 2 vols. (paginated consecutively), ed. Aldea Vaquero, the edition I have used throughout. For the other works of Saavedra I have used the *Obras completas*, ed. González Palencia.

2. Aldea Vaquero in *Príncipe político-cristiano*, pp. 40–41. Aldea Vaquero conjectures that there may have been a second Munich edition in late 1640. The Munich edition(s) are rare; I have consulted the one at the Firestone Library of Princeton University.

3. *Política de Dios, gobierno de Cristo* (Madrid, 1626, and part 2, posthumously, 1655) and *El político don Fernando el Católico* (Zaragoza, 1640). These writers are discussed brilliantly as a group in Maravall, *La philosophie politique espagnole au xvii siècle*; see also Fernández-Santamaría, *Reason of State and Statecraft in Spanish Political Thought*.

4. *Príncipe político-cristiano*, p. 61.

5. On Montaigne and Saavedra, see Lopes Fanego, "Montaigne et Saavedra Fajardo," esp. pp. 35–36, 49–50. See Jover, *1635*, pp. 456–59, for contradictions in Saavedra.

6. See Elliott, *The Count-Duke of Olivares*, pp. 677–85.

7. *Príncipe político-cristiano*, no. 59, p. 591.

8. Fraga Iribarne, *Saavedra y Fajardo*, pp. 13–14; Aldea Vaquero in *Príncipe político-cristiano*, p. 15.

9. Aldea Vaquero in *Príncipe político-cristiano*, pp. 16–18; González Palencia in Saavedra Fajardo, *Obras completas*, pp. 19–20.

10. *Príncipe político-cristiano*, no. 81, p. 775.

11. Israel, *The Dutch Republic and the Hispanic World*, pp. 12–14.

12. *Príncipe político-cristiano*, no. 45, p. 419; no. 69, pp. 677–86; no. 78, pp. 748–49; no. 84, p. 799; and esp. no. 95, pp. 869–78.

13. Aldea Vaquero, in *Príncipe político-cristiano*, pp. 17–19.

14. *República literaria*. Dowling, *Saavedra Fajardo*, p. 110; Dowling, *El pensamiento*, pp. 49–52. For the editions of *The Commonwealth of Letters*, see Fraga Iribarne, *Saavedra y Fajardo*, p. 675.

15. These include the *Introducciones a la política y razón de Estado del Rey Católico Don Fernando* (1631); *Razón de Estado del Rey Don Fernando el Católico* (shortly afterwards); and *Respuesta al Manifiesto de Francia* (1635). See Fraga Iribarne, *Saavedra y Fajardo*, pp. 675–76, and González Palencia in *Obras completas*, p. 31. According to Elliott, *The Count-Duke of Olivares*, p. 489, Saavedra sent copies of the first two to Olivares in April, 1633.

16. Joucla-Ruau, *Tacitisme de Saavedra Fajardo*, pp. 37–38.

17. See Francis L. Sheerin, "Molinism," in *The New Catholic Encyclopedia* (New York, 1967; rpt., Palatine, Ill., 1981), 9:1010–13, and Thomas K. Ryan, "Congregatio de Auxiliis," in ibid., 4:168–71.

18. *Príncipe político-cristiano*, no. 86, pp. 809–10.

19. *Locuras de Europa*; *Corona gotica*. Dowling, *El pensamiento*, pp. 76–79; Fraga Iribarne, *Saavedra y Fajardo*, pp. 544–51.

20. Dowling, *El pensamiento*, p. 22.

21. Fraga Iribarne, *Saavedra y Fajardo*, pp. 201–31.

22. Bireley, *Maximilian von Bayern*, pp. 199, 203.

23. *Príncipe político-cristiano*, no. 12, pp. 165–67.

24. Fraga Iribarne, *Saavedra y Fajardo*, pp. 197–393 passim.

25. Aldea Vaquero in *Príncipe político cristiano*, pp. 41–43; González Palencia in *Obras completas*, pp. 31, 1136, 1224–25.

26. Fraga Iribarne, *Saavedra y Fajardo*, pp. 535–36, 545, 551; Aldea Vaquero in *Príncipe político-cristiano*, pp. 26–28.

27. Aldea Vaquero in *Príncipe político-cristiano*, p. 28.

28. Mario Praz, *Studies in Seventeenth-Century Imagery*, 2d ed., Sussidi eruditi, no. 16 (Rome, 1964), pp. 483–85. Five Spanish editions of the *Politico-Christian Prince* appeared in the eighteenth century, three in the nineteenth, and two in the twentieth. The editions listed here do not comprise those included in the various editions of Saavedra's *Obras Completas*.

29. Mulagk, *Phänomene des politischen Menschen,* esp. pp. 184–93.

30. *The Royal Politician Represented in One Hundred Emblems* (London, 1700), preface.

31. García de Diego in Saavedra Fajardo, *Idea de un príncipe político-cristiano,* 1:xxix.

32. *Príncipe político-cristiano,* no. 5 (motto), p. 107.

33. Saavedra indicated this as a purpose for his use of the emblem in the dedication to Prince Baltasar Carlos, p. 51. For a fascinating study of the uses of artifical memory during the period, see Jonathan Spence, *The Memory Palace of Mateo Ricci* (New York, 1984).

34. Dowling, *Saavedra Fajardo,* p. 83, and his *El pensamiento,* pp. 59–62, where the author also explains the technical difference between an emblem and an *empresa.* The terms were used interchangeably in the seventeenth century. Maravall, "La literatura de emblemas en el contexto de la sociedad barrocca," is a lucid discussion of the use and attraction of the emblem in the seventeenth century, and it has much on Saavedra.

35. *Príncipe político-cristiano,* no. 50, pp. 465–87, quotation on p. 485; Aldea Vaquero in *Príncipe político-cristiano,* pp. 42–43.

36. *Príncipe político-cristiano,* no. 5, p. 110; no. 18, pp. 203–4.

37. Ibid., preface, p. 64; no. 5, pp. 109–10.

38. Dedication, pp. 51–52; preface, pp. 61–65, quotation on p. 65.

39. Joucla-Ruau, *Tacitisme de Saavedra Fajardo,* pp. 13–15.

40. Ibid., 78–79. On Tacitism in Spain, see Tierno Galvan, *El Tacitismo en los escritores políticos españoles,* esp. pp. 32–33, which, however, has little specifically on Saavedra.

41. *Príncipe político-cristiano,* no. 43, p. 404.

42. My hunch is that Saavedra consciously imitated and further developed the format of Scribani's *Christian Politician,* but I am not prepared to argue the point at this time.

The Milan edition of the *Príncipe político-cristiano,* pp. 53–59, carries an exchange of letters in 1643 between Saavedra and Erycius Puteanus, a Flemish humanist and successor in Lipsius's chair at Louvain, who had been a friend and correspondent of Scribani; see Brouwers in Scribani, *Brieven,* pp. 73–75, 150–54. Saavedra spent a couple months in Brussels on his way to Münster in 1643.

43. Saavedra's sixth (nos. 73–95) and seventh (nos. 96–99) sections on the prince's conduct in civil and foreign war and in peace negotiations corresponded roughly to the fifth and sixth books of Lipsius on military prudence, and Saavedra's fourth (nos. 49–58) and fifth (nos. 59–72) sections on the prince's relationship to his ministers and the government of his states to the third and fourth books of Lipsius on the use of others' prudence and the civic prudence that entailed the *arcana imperii.* More tenuous was the connection between the second (nos. 7–37) and third (nos. 38–48) sections of Saavedra on the prince's general conduct and his relationship to subjects and strangers and Lipsius's first two books on basic principles of government and the virtues of the prince.

44. *Príncipe político-cristiano,* no. 18, p. 204.

45. Ibid., no. 20, pp. 219–25, esp. p. 225, quotations on p. 225; no. 21, 227–39, esp. p. 228; no. 28, p. 286, quotation.

46. Ibid., no. 10, pp. 145–51, esp. 150.

47. Ibid., no. 41, p. 389; no. 55, pp. 533–46, esp. 539–43, quotation on p. 541. Saavedra's ambivalence appeared in this context. He also lauded Philip II's decisions taken against his councillors as well as Philip's practice of occasionally

keeping his councillors in the dark about aspects of the state of affairs.

48. Ibid., no. 67, pp. 656–59; Elliott, *The Count-Duke of Olivares*, pp. 149, 481, 547, 593.

49. *Príncipe político-cristiano*, no. 59, pp. 575–79, quotation on p. 577; no. 19, p. 214.

50. Ibid., pp. 309–12. Saavedra used the same figure for reputation in the *Corona gotica*; see his *Obras completas*, p. 744. He was imprecise in his language. Sometimes reputation was support itself, an act of the will, as in Botero and Lipsius, sometimes the opinion (*opinion*) or thought of the people from which support followed. The difference for our purposes is of little significance.

I am grateful to Prof. John Boler of the University of Washington for his explanation of the medical metaphor.

51. *Príncipe político-cristiano*, pp. 309–12.

52. Cited in Elliott, "Foreign Policy and Domestic Crisis: Spain, 1598–1659," in *Spain and Its World*, p. 122.

53. See *Príncipe político-cristiano*, no. 61, pp. 612–13.

54. Ibid., no. 32, pp. 319–24; on attentiveness to public opinion, see no. 14, pp. 177–84, and no. 48, pp. 447–49.

55. Ibid., no. 38, pp. 361–68.

56. Ibid., no. 18, pp. 201–8, quotation on p. 207.

57. Ibid., no. 81, p. 768.

58. Ibid., no. 40, p. 381.

59. Ibid., no. 6, pp. 112–13; see also, no. 4, pp. 100–101.

60. Ibid., no. 11, p. 156; no. 21, p. 230; no. 22, pp. 241–49.

61. Ibid., no. 28, pp. 285–91; no. 18, pp. 208–12.

62. Ibid., no. 47, pp. 433–42, quotation on p. 434.

63. Reason in Saavedra did not denote so much the faculty of reason as opposed to faith and what could be known by reason as distinguished from what could be known by faith, although it did denote this at times; rather, it designated the faculty of reason primarily as opposed to the passions and regulative of them. This is the same meaning usually assigned reason by Richelieu in the *Testament politique*; see, for example, pp. 268, 300–301, 382. We are entering the world of Descartes and seventeenth-century France.

64. *Príncipe político-cristiano*, no. 41, pp. 385–93, quotation on p. 391.

65. Ibid., no. 85, pp. 806–8.

66. Ibid., no. 27, p. 281; no. 59, pp. 577–95, esp. pp. 580, 591.

67. Ibid., no. 87, pp. 817–22, quotations on pp. 817–18.

68. Ibid., no. 36, pp. 345–51, quotation on pp. 346, 348; no. 65, pp. 637–40.

69. Ibid., no. 43, pp. 404–5.

70. Ibid., no. 101, p. 931.

71. Ibid., no. 46, pp. 422–25; no. 51, pp. 502–5, quotation on p. 502; no. 78, p. 747.

72. Ibid., no. 44, p. 410; no. 78, pp. 749–50.

73. Ibid., no. 42, p. 397 (quotation); no. 62, pp. 617–18.

74. Ibid., no. 62, pp. 621–22.

75. Ibid., no. 45, p. 420.

76. Ibid., no. 79, pp. 756–57; no. 62, p. 617.

77. Ibid., no. 90, pp. 836–38.

78. Ibid., no. 96, p. 883.

79. Ibid., no. 51, p. 503.

80. Ibid., no. 73, p. 717, and no. 93, p. 860.

81. Ibid., no. 73, p. 712.

82. Ibid., no. 67, pp. 653–58, quotations on pp. 653, 654, 658; no. 69, p. 673; see also no. 53, p. 522.

83. Ibid., no. 66, pp. 647, 649–52; no. 68, pp. 665–69; no. 69, pp. 674–82, quotations on pp. 675, 677.

84. Marquez, "El mercantilismo de Saavedra Fajardo," pp. 282–83.

85. *Príncipe político-cristiano,* no. 67, pp. 654–55, 660–62.

86. Ibid., no. 69, pp. 681, 685–86; see Grice-Hitchinson, *Early Economic Thought in Spain,* pp. 167–68.

87. *Príncipe político-cristiano,* no. 68, pp. 665–69.

88. Ibid., no. 66, pp. 647–50, quotation on p. 647.

89. Elliott, *The Count-Duke of Olivares,* pp. 236, 325, 516, 587–90, 680–83.

90. *Príncipe político-cristiano,* no. 71, pp. 695–99; no. 27, pp. 282–83.

91. Ibid., no. 66, pp. 643–47.

92. Elliott, *The Count-Duke of Olivares,* pp. 505, 536, 567.

93. *Príncipe político-cristiano,* no. 67, p. 660.

94. Ibid., no. 17, pp. 195–200; no. 71, p. 696.

95. Ibid., no. 66, pp. 651–52.

96. Olivares, *Memoriales y cartas de Olivares,* 2:66–73; Donnelly, "Possevino's Plan," pp. 196–97, shows that Possevino had long been an advocate of such academies in Italy. See also John R. Hale, "The Military Education of the Officer Class in Early Modern Europe," in *Cultural Aspects of the Italian Renaissance: Essays in Honour of Paul Oskar Kristeller,* ed. Cecil Clough (Manchester and New York, 1976), pp. 440–61.

97. Maravall, *Culture of the Baroque,* pp. 47, 111–12, 120–25.

98. *Príncipe político-cristiano,* no. 82, pp. 781–83, 788–89, quotation on p. 789; no. 68, pp. 668–69.

99. Ibid., no. 74, pp. 719–22; no. 98, quotation on p. 899; no. 99, pp. 901–4, quotation on p. 901.

100. Ibid., no. 74, p. 723; no. 59, p. 576; Lipsius, *Politicorum,* 4:9 (p. 112) (see above, Chapter 4, at n. 102).

101. *Príncipe político-cristiano,* no. 59, pp. 575–79; Botero, *Ragion di Stato* 3:11 (p. 60).

102. *Príncipe político-cristiano,* no. 83, pp. 791–95; Israel, *The Dutch Republic and the Hispanic World,* p. 33.

103. *Príncipe político-cristiano,* pp. 794–95. Later Saavedra wrote, "Con perpetuas vitorias se perdieron las Paises Bajos, porque quiso el valor obrar mas que la prudencia" (no. 84, p. 799).

104. Ibid., no. 98, p. 897.

105. Ibid., no. 81, pp. 776–79; on the policy of Ferdinand II, who sought to steer a middle course between Spain and France, see Furio Diaz, *Il Granducato di Toscana: I Medici,* Storia d'Italia, vol. 13, part 1 (Turin, 1976), pp. 372–73.

106. *Príncipe político-cristiano,* no. 24, pp. 261–66; no. 27, p. 284.

107. Ibid., no. 26, pp. 273–78, quotation on p. 274.

108. Ibid., no. 24, pp. 264–65.

109. See ibid., no. 66, pp. 644–45.

110. Ibid., no. 27, pp. 279–84, quotations on pp. 283, 284.

111. Ibid., no. 27, pp. 265–66, quotation; no. 94, pp. 865–68.

112. Ibid., no. 24, p. 266.

113. Ibid., no. 25, pp. 267–72, quotation on p. 270.

114. Bouwsma, *Venice and the Defense of Republican Liberty,* pp. 293–

416; Frederic C. Lane, *Venice: A Maritime Republic* (Baltimore, 1973), pp. 396–98.

115. *Príncipe político-cristiano*, no. 66, pp. 646–47, 651–52.

116. Ibid., no. 94, pp. 861–65, quotations on pp. 863, 864. On the papal war with Castro, see Franz Xaver Seppelt, *Geschichte der Päpste*, vol. 5, *Von Paul III. bis zur französischer Revolution*, 2d ed., prepared by Georg Schwaiger (Munich, 1959): 279–82.

117. Ibid., pp. 864–65.

118. For example, no. 59, p. 579.

119. Ibid., no. 97, p. 893; see Straub, *Pax et Imperium*, pp. 56, 61.

120. *Príncipe político-cristiano*, no. 18, pp. 201–5, quotation on p. 203.

121. Ibid., no. 18, pp. 203, 207; no. 87, pp. 817–22. On Saavedra and providence, cf. Mulagk, *Phänomene des politischen Menschen*, pp. 153–65.

122. *Príncipe político-cristiano*, no. 18, p. 204.

123. Ibid., no. 75, p. 730.

124. Ibid., no. 50, pp. 485–87; see also no. 26, p. 276.

125. *Obras completas*, p. 745.

126. *Príncipe político-cristiano*, no. 34, p. 337; no. 88, p. 824.

127. Ibid., no. 59, p. 579; no. 64, p. 630, quotation.

128. Ibid., no. 36, pp. 345–51.

129. Ibid., no. 59, p. 579.

130. Ibid., no. 34, pp. 335–39; no. 80, pp. 759–62.

131. Ibid., no. 60, pp. 598–99. Here Saavedra wrote, "I do not know whether I dare to say that there would be perpetual empires if in princes will [or desire] were always in tune with power and reason with events." Machiavelli would say that such permanent harmony was impossible, given man's nature, and so a perpetual empire was impossible. Lipsius, on the other hand, would have to say, because of his stricter analogy with the natural world, that even if such harmony were possible, an empire because of its very nature would still eventually collapse.

132. Ibid., and no. 64, pp. 630–33. Saavedra wrote without elaboration that smaller states followed a different pattern of rise and fall than did great monarchies. Perhaps this reflected the difficulty Machiavelli had in fitting Sparta and especially Venice into his conception of the rise and fall of states.

133. Ibid., no. 88, p. 826.

134. Ibid., no. 87, pp. 820–21.

135. Ibid., no. 88, pp. 824–28.

136. Stradling, *Philip IV and the Government of Spain*, p. 304.

Chapter 9

1. *Oratio academica an Politici horum temporum in numero christianorum sint habendi*. This short piece was published posthumously, Stapleton having died in 1598.

2. De Mattei, *Il problema della "ragion di stato,"* pp. 278–93, esp. 278, 282; Stolleis, *Arcana Imperii und Ratio Status*, p. 29.

3. See Church, *Richelieu and Reason of State*, pp. 57–72, where further similar works are mentioned.

4. *Apologie catholique*; *De l'autorité du roi*; Allen, *A History of Political Thought*, p. 383.

5. Church, *Richelieu and Reason of State*, p. 78.

6. Church, *Richelieu and Reason of State*; Moote, *Louis XIII*. This is a main thesis of both books.

7. Church, *Richelieu and Reason of State*, pp. 241–49.

8. In the second part of *Le Ministre d'Estat*, published in 1643 to defend Richelieu's policies, Silhon did make use of the categories of good and useful and rejected what he felt were Machiavellian positions; see Church, *Richelieu and Reason of State*, pp. 431–35, and Siedschlag, *Der Einfluss der niederländisch-stoischen Ethik*, pp. 154–64, who considers this a separate volume.

9. Book 1, discourse 1, pp. 4–6; discourse 2, p. 14.

10. *Les politiques chrestiennes: ou Tableau des vertus politiques considerées en l'estat chrestien*; for this I have used the English version, *A Mirrour for Christian States: or A Table of Politick Virtues Considerable amongst Christians* (London, 1635).

11. Church, *Richelieu and Reason of State*, pp. 279–82.

12. On the development of a particular political language, see J. G. A. Pocock, "The Concept of Language and the *Métier d'Historien*," pp. 19–38, and specifically on Machiavelli, pp. 33–36.

13. See Valentin, *Le théâtre des Jésuites*, 2:958.

14. Pp. 372–74, 355 (quotation); see also p. 450. Richelieu placed more weight on the role of reputation in international affairs than did the anti-Machiavellians generally. In him we find a similar association of virtue, reputation, and power.

15. *Príncipe político-cristiano*, no. 81, p. 768.

16. *Testament politique*, pp. 354–55.

17. Bireley, *Religion and Politics*, pp. 202–4; Sturmberger, *Kaiser Ferdinand II. und das Problem des Absolutismus*, pp. 35–37. The manner in which Wallenstein was actually killed as he lay in bed is another matter.

18. See Carlo M. Cipolla, "The Economic Decline of Italy," in *The Economic Decline of Empires*, ed. Carlo M. Cipolla (London, 1970), pp. 196–214.

19. Noonan, *The Scholastic Analysis of Usury*, esp. pp. 249–50, 279–80, 360–62, 407–8.

20. See Trevor-Roper, "Religion, the Reformation, and Social Change," esp. pp. 23–24, 28–29, 33–34, 38–40. He distinguishes between Catholic teaching and the "social forms" of the Counter-Reformation state, the latter impeding economic progress. For a positive view of the Counter-Reformation also with regard to economic development, see Reinhard, "Gegenreformation als Modernisierung?," esp. pp. 236, 239, 245–51.

21. Pp. 381–82.

22. Schilling, *Konfessionsbildung und Staatsbildung*, p. 365. See also his "Reformation and the Rise of the Early Modern State"; Reinhard, "Zwang zur Konfessionalisierung?" and "Reformation, Counter-Reformation."

23. See Evans, *Making of the Habsburg Monarchy*, and for the specific role of Ferdinand, Bireley, "Ferdinand II, Founder of the Habsburg Monarchy," in *Crown, Church and Estates in Central Europe 1526–1711: Between Reformation and Baroque*, ed. Trevor Thomas and R. J. W. Evans (London, in press).

24. Cf. Delumeau, *Le péché et la peur*. Exaggerated fear as a characteristic of early modern religion, Protestant as well as Catholic, is a theme that runs through much of Delumeau's recent work.

25. Bireley, *Religion and Politics*, pp. 212–19.

26. Even Contzen, in a case put to him by Maximilian, recommended concessions for the sake of "the common good" to two Calvinist brothers in the recently occupied Upper Palatinate who owned a textile firm upon whom nearly

one thousand people depended for work. See Bireley, *Maximilian von Bayern*, pp. 51–52.

27. Mecenseffy, *Geschichte des Protestantismus in Österreich*, p. 173.

28. See, for example, the classic of Felix Stieve, *Das kirchliche Polizeiregiment in Baiern unter Maximilian I* (Munich, 1876).

29. William Lamormaini, *Ferdinandi II Romanorum Imperatoris Virtutes* (Vienna, 1638), pp. 29–30, cited in Bireley, *Religion and Politics*, p. 15.

30. Reinhard, "Gegenreformation als Modernisierung?," pp. 231–36, 239–40; Raeff, *The Well-Ordered Police State*; see also Peter Burke, *Popular Culture in Early Modern Europe* (New York, 1978), pp. 207–22, 213, 218–22, and Schulze, "Gerhard Oestreichs Begriff 'Sozialdisziplinierung' in der frühen Neuzeit," esp. pp. 292, 302.

31. Münch, *Ordnung, Fleiss, und Sparsamkeit*, pp. 14, 33–38.

32. Cited in Clancy, *Papist Pamphleteers*, p. 181.

33. See also Anthony Levi, *French Moralists: The Theory of the Passions 1585 to 1649* (Oxford, 1964), pp. 7–8.

Bibliography

Primary Sources

Ammirato, Scipione. *Discorsi sopra C. Tacito*. Florence, 1594.

Aquinas, Thomas. *De regimine principum ad Regem Cypri et De regimine Judaeorum ad Ducissam Brabantiae: Politica opuscula duo*. 2d rev. ed. Edited by Joseph Mathis. Turin, 1948. Rpt. Turin, 1971.

——————. *On Kingship to the King of Cyprus*. Translated by Gerald B. Phelan. Revised by I. Th. Eschmann. Toronto, 1949.

——————. *Summa Theologica*. In *Opera omnia cum commentariis Thomae de Vio Caetani*. Vols. 6–9. Rome, 1891–97.

Aristotle. *The Politics of Aristotle*. Edited and translated by Ernest Barker. New York, 1962.

Balzac, Jean Louis Guez de. *Le prince*. Paris, 1631.

Bellarmine, Robert. *De officio principis Christiani*. In *Opera omnia*, vol. 8, pp. 87–235. Paris, 1873. Rpt. Frankfurt, 1965.

Béthune, Philippe de. *Le conseiller d'estat*. Paris, 1633.

Boccalini, Traiano. *Ragguagli di Parnaso*. 3 vols. Edited by Giuseppe Rua. Scrittori d'Italia, nos. 6, 39, 199. Bari, 1910–48.

Bodin, Jean. *Method for the Easy Comprehension of History*. Translated by Beatrice Reynolds. New York, 1966.

——————. *The Six Bookes of a Commonweale*. Translated by Richard Knolles. London, 1606. Facsimile ed. Edited with an introduction by Kenneth D. McRae. Cambridge, Mass., 1962.

Botero, Giovanni. *Della ragion di stato con tre libri delle cause della grandezza delle città, due Aggiunte e un Discorso sulla popolazione di Roma*. Edited with an introduction by Luigi Firpo. Classici politici, no. 2. Turin, 1948.

——————. *Della ragion di stato, e delle cause della grandezza delle città*. Edited with an introduction by Carlo Morandi. Bologna, 1930.

——————. *The Reason of State*. Translated by P. J. Waley and D. P. Waley. *The Greatness of Cities*. Translated by Robert Peterson. In one volume. London, 1956.

——————. *Le relationi universali*. Venice, 1596.

Calderini, Apollinare de. *Discorsi sopra la ragion di stato del Signor Giovanni Botero.* Milan, 1609.

Chokier, Jean de. *Thesaurus aphorismorum politicorum.* Rome, 1611.

Contzen, Adam. *Aulae speculum sive de statu, vita, et virtute aulicorum et magnatum.* Cologne, 1630.

⸻. *De pace Germaniae libri duo.* Mainz, 1616.

⸻. *Methodus doctrinae civilis seu Abissini regis historia.* Cologne, 1628.

⸻. *Politicorum libri decem.* Mainz, 1621.

Fitzherbert, Thomas. *An sit utilitas in scelere vel de infelicitate principis machiavellani contra Machiavellum et politicos ejus sectatores.* Rome, 1610.

Gentillet, Innocent. *Discours contre Machiavel.* Edited with an introduction by A. D'Andrea and P. D. Stewart. Florence, 1974.

Guevara, Antonio de. *The Diall of Princes.* Translated from the French by Thomas North. London, 1557. Facsimile ed. Amsterdam, 1968.

⸻. *Menosprecio de corte y alabanza de aldea.* Edited with an introduction by Matias Martinez Burgos. Clasicos Castellanos, no. 19. Madrid, 1967.

Lamormaini, William. *Ferdinandi II Romanorum imperatoris virtutes.* Vienna, 1638.

Lipsius, Justus. *Ad libros politicorum breves notae.* Frankfurt, 1590.

⸻. *La correspondance de Juste Lipse conservée au Musée Plantin-Moretus.* Introduction, correspondance et commentaires, documents, bibliographie by Alois Gerlo and Hendrik D. L. Vervliet, with the collaboration of Irene Vertessen. Antwerp, 1967.

⸻. *De constantia libri duo.* 3d ed. Frankfurt, 1590.

⸻. *De una religione adversus dialogistam liber, in quo tria capita libri quarti politicorum explicantur.* Leiden, 1591.

⸻. *Epistolario de Justo Lipsio y los españoles (1577–1606).* Edited by Alejandro Ramirez. Madrid, 1966.

⸻. *Justi Lipsi Epistolae.* Part 1: *1564–1583.* Edited by A. Gerlo, M. A. Nauwelaerts, H. D. L. Vervliet. Part 2: *1584–1587.* Edited by M. A. Nauwelaerts. Brussels, 1978–83.

⸻. *Monita et exempla politica: Libri duo qui virtutes et vitia principum spectant.* Antwerp, 1606.

⸻. *Politicorum sive civilis doctrinae libri sex.* Frankfurt, 1590.

⸻. *Six Bookes of Politikes or Civil Doctrine.* Translated by William Jones. London, 1594.

⸻. *Two Books of Constancie.* Translated by Sir John Stradling. London, 1594. Facsimile ed. Edited with an introduction by Rudolf Kirk. New Brunswick, N.J., 1939.

Machiavelli, Niccolò. *Machiavelli: The Chief Works and Others.* Translated by Allan Gilbert. Vol. 1. Durham, N.C., 1965.

⸻. *Il principe.* Edited with an introduction by L. Arthur Burd. Oxford, 1891. Rpt. Oxford, 1968.

———. *Il principe e le opere politiche.* Introduction by Delio Cantimori. 3d ed. Milan, 1981.
———. *Il principe e pagine dei Discorsi e delle Istorie.* Edited by Luigi Russo. 13th ed. Florence, 1967.
Mariana, Juan de. *The King and the Education of the King.* Translated by George A. Moore. Washington, D.C., 1948.
Marquez, Juan. *El gobernador cristiano, deducido de las vidas de Moysén y Josué, príncipes del pueblo de Dios.* Salamanca, 1612.
Molanus, Joannes. *Libri quinque. De fide haereticis servanda, tres. De fide rebellibus servanda, liber unus. Item unicus. De fide et iuramento, quae a tyranno exiguuntur, qui est quintus.* Cologne, 1584.
Molinier, Etienne. *A Mirrour for Christian States: or, A table of politick vertues considerable amongst Christians.* Translated from the French by William Tyrwhit. London, 1635.
Olivares, Count-Duke of. *Memoriales y cartas del Conde Duque de Olivares.* Edited with an introduction by John H. Elliott and José de la Peña. 2 vols. Madrid, 1978–80.
Paruta, Paolo. *Della perfezione della vita politica libri tre.* Venice, 1599.
Possevino, Antonio. *Discorso contra l'impietà e perniciosissimi consigli del Machiavello.* In *Il soldato christiano con nuove aggiunte,* pp. 181–87. Venice, 1604.
———. *Judicium de Nouae militis Galli, Joannis Bodini, Philippi Mornaei, et Nicolai Machiavelli quibusdam scriptis.* Venice, 1592.
Princeps in Compendio. Vienna, 1668.
Ribadeneira, Pedro de. *Historia eclesiástica del scisma de Inglaterra.* In *Obras escogidas del Padre Pedro de Rivadeneira,* edited with an introduction by Don Vicente de la Fuente, pp. 181–357. Biblioteca de autores españoles. Madrid, 1868. Rpt. Madrid, 1952.
———. *Monumenta Historica Societatis Jesu, Ribadeneira.* 2 vols. Madrid, 1920.
———. *Pedro de Ribadeneyra. S.I. Historias de la Contrarreforma.* Edited with an introduction by Eusebio Rey. Biblioteca de autores cristianos. Madrid, 1945.
———. *Tratado de la religion y virtudes que debe tener el príncipe cristiano para gobernar y conservar sus estados, contra lo que Nicolas Maquiavelo y los políticos deste tiempo enseñan.* In *Obras escogidas del Padre Pedro de Rivadeneira,* edited with an introduction by Don Vicente de la Fuente, pp. 449–587. Madrid, 1868. Rpt. Madrid, 1952.
———. *Tratado de la tribulacion.* In *Obras escogidas del Padre Pedro de Rivadeneira,* edited with an introduction by Don Vicente de la Fuente, pp. 358–448. Madrid, 1868. Rpt. Madrid, 1952.
Richelieu, Armand Jean du Plessis, Cardinal de. *Testament politique.* Edited by L. André. Paris, 1947.
Saavedra Fajardo, Diego. *Empresas políticas: Idea de un príncipe político-cristiano.* 2 vols. Edited with an introduction by Quintín Aldea Vaquero. Madrid, 1976.

———. *Idea de un príncipe político-cristiano representada en cien empresas.* Edited with an introduction by Vicente García de Diego. 4 vols. Clasicos Catellanos, nos. 76, 81, 87, 102. Madrid, 1942–46.

———. *Obras completas.* Edited with an introduction by Angel González Palencia. Madrid, 1946.

———. *The Royal Politician represented in one hundred emblems.* Translated by James Astry. London, 1700.

Santa Maria, Juan de. *Tratado de república y policía christiana.* Madrid, 1615.

Scribani, Carolus. *Brieven van Carolus Scribani S.J. (1561–1629).* Edited by L. Brouwers. Antwerp, 1972.

———. *Justi Lipsi defensio postuma.* In *Justi Lipsi sapientiae et literarum antistitis fama postuma,* 2d ed., pp. 227–70. Antwerp, 1613.

———. *Politico-Christianus.* Antwerp, 1624.

Suarez, Francisco. *Opera omnia.* New edition. Edited by Charles Berton. Vols. 5–6, 12. Paris, 1856–58.

———. *Selections from Three Works: De legibus ac Deo legislatore, 1612. Defensio fidei Catholicae, et apostolicae adversus Anglicanae sectae errores, 1613. De triplici virtute theologica, fide, spe, et caritate, 1621.* Vol. 2, *The Translations.* Introduction by James Brown Scott. Classics of International Law, no. 20, vol. 2. Oxford, 1944.

Tacitus. *The Complete Works of Tacitus.* Translated by Alfred John Church and William Jackson Brodribb and edited by Moses Hadas. New York, 1942.

———. *Cornelii Taciti Annalium ab excessu divi Augusti Libri.* Edited by C. D. Fisher. Scriptorum Classicorum Bibliotheca Oxoniensis. London, 1906.

Vera y Figueroa, Juan de, Count of La Roca. *El embajador.* Seville, 1620. Facsimile ed. Madrid, 1947. (In this facsimile edition the author's name is given as Juan Antonio de Vera y Zúñiga.)

Vitoria, Francisco de. *Obras de Francisco de Vitoria: Relecciones teologicas.* Biblioteca de autores cristianos. Edited by Teofilo Urdanoz. Madrid, 1960.

Secondary Sources

Abel, Günter. *Stoizismus und frühe Neuzeit.* Berlin, 1978.

Albrecht, Dieter. "Das konfessionelle Zeitalter. Zweiter Teil: Die Herzöge Wilhelm V und Maximilian I." In *Handbuch der bayerischen Geschichte.* Vol. 2, *Das alte Bayern: Der Territorialstaat von Ausgang des 12. Jahrhunderts bis zum Ausgang des 18. Jahrhunderts.* 2d rev. ed. Edited by Max Spindler and Andreas Kraus, pp. 395–457. Munich, 1988.

Aldea Vaquero, Quintín, ed. *See* Saavedra Fajardo.

Allen, J. W. *A History of Political Thought in the Sixteenth Century.* London, 1928. Rpt. London and New York, 1960.

Arnold, F. X. *Die Staatslehre des Kardinals Bellarmin: Ein Beitrag zur rechts- und staatsphilosophie des konfessionellen Zeitalters.* Munich, 1934.

Ay, Karl-Ludwig. *Land und Fürst im alten Bayern: 16.–18. Jahrhundert.* Regensburg, 1988.

Behnen, Michael. " 'Arcana—Haec Sunt Ratio Status': Ragion di Stato und Staatsräson. Probleme und Perspektive (1589–1651)." *Zeitschrift für historische Forschung* 14 (1987): 129–95.

———. "Der gerechte und der notwendige Krieg: 'Necessitas' und 'Utilitas reipublicae' in der Kriegstheorie des 16. und 17. Jahrhunderts." In *Staatsverfassung und Heeresfassung in der europäischen Geschichte der frühen Neuzeit,* edited by Johannes Kunsich, pp. 43–106. Berlin, 1986.

Berges, Wilhelm. *Die Fürstenspiegel des hohen und späten Mittelalters.* Leipzig, 1938. Rpt. Stuttgart, 1952.

Berlin, Isaiah. "The Originality of Machiavelli." In *Studies on Machiavelli,* edited by Myron P. Gilmore, pp. 147–206. Florence, 1972. Printed in condensed form in *The New York Review of Books,* Nov. 4, 1971, pp. 20–32.

Bertelli, Sergio. *Bibliografia Machiavelliana.* Verona, 1979.

Bireley, Robert. "Antimachiavellianism, the Baroque, and Maximilian of Bavaria." *Archivum Historicum Societatis Jesu* 53 (1984): 137–59.

———. *Maximilian von Bayern, Adam Contzen, S.J. und die Gegenreformation in Deutschland 1624–1635.* Schriftenreihe der Historischen Kommission bei der Bayerischen Akademie der Wissenschaften, Schrift 13. Göttingen, 1975.

———. *Religion and Politics in the Age of the Counterreformation: Emperor Ferdinand II, William Lamormaini, S.J., and the Formation of Imperial Policy.* Chapel Hill, N.C., 1981.

Bleznick, Donald W. "Spanish Reaction to Machiavelli in the Sixteenth and Seventeenth Centuries." *Journal of the History of Ideas* 19 (1958): 542–50.

Blüher, Karl Alfred. *Seneca in Spanien: Untersuchungen zur Geschichte der Seneca-Rezeption in Spanien vom 13. bis 17. Jahrhundert.* Munich, 1969.

Borja de Medina, S.J., Francisco de. "Jesuitas en la armada contra Inglaterra (1588): Notas para un centenario." *Archivum Historicum Societatis Jesu* 58 (1989): 3–42.

Bouwsma, William J. *Venice and the Defense of Republican Liberty.* Berkeley, Calif., 1968.

Bozza, Tommaso. *Scrittori politici italiani dal 1550 al 1650.* Rome, 1949. Rpt. Rome, 1980.

Brants, V. " 'Le Prince' de Machiavel dans les anciens Pays-Bas." In *Mélanges d'histoire offerts à Charles Moeller.* Vol. 2, pp. 87–99. Louvain and Paris, 1914.

Breuer, Dieter. *Oberdeutsche Literatur, 1565–1650: Deutsche Literaturgeschichte und Territorialgeschichte in frühabsolutistischer Zeit.* Munich, 1979.

Brodrick, James. *Robert Bellarmine: Saint and Scholar.* London, 1961.

Brouwers, L. *Carolus Scribani S.J. 1561–1629: Een groot man van de Contra-Reformatie in de Nederlanden.* Antwerp, 1961.

————. "Scribani's verdediging van Justus Lipsius." *Philologische Studien* 4 (1933): 216–21.

————, ed. *See* Scribani.

Brown, Irene Coltman. "The Historian as Philosopher: Machiavelli and the New Philosopher Prince." *History Today* 31 (June 1981): 15–20.

Burke, Peter. "Southern Italy in the 1590s: Hard Times or Crisis?" In *The European Crisis of the 1590s*, edited by Peter Clark, pp. 177–90. London, 1985.

Capitaine, Ul. "Chokier (Jean de) ou de Chokier de Surlet." In *Biographie Nationale de Belgique*, 4:85–91. Brussels, 1873.

Carter, Charles H. "Belgian 'Autonomy' under the Archdukes, 1598–1621." *Journal of Modern History* 36 (1964): 245–59.

Casey, James. "Spain: A Failed Transition." In *The European Crisis of the 1590s*, edited by Peter Clark, pp. 209–28. London, 1985.

Chabod, Federico. *Giovanni Botero.* Rome, 1934.

Charmot, François. *Ignatius Loyola and Francis de Sales: Two Masters, One Spirituality.* Translated by Sister M. Renelle. St. Louis, Mo., 1966.

Church, William F. *Richelieu and Reason of State.* Princeton, N.J., 1972.

Clancy, Thomas P. *Papist Pamphleteers: The Allen-Persons Party and the Political Thought of the Counter Reformation in England.* Chicago, 1964.

Clark, Peter, ed. *The European Crisis of the 1590s.* London, 1985.

Cochrane, Eric. *Italy, 1530–1650.* Edited with an introduction by Julius Kirschner. New York, 1988.

Cognet, Louis. *La spiritualité moderne: L'essor, 1500–1650.* Part 1 of *Histoire de la spiritualité chrétienne*, edited by Louis Bouyer, François Vandenbroucke, and Louis Cognet. Vol. 3. Paris, 1966.

Copleston, Frederick. *A History of Philosophy.* Vol. 1, Part 2, *Greece and Rome.* Vol. 2, Part 2, *Medieval Philosophy: Albert the Great to Duns Scotus.* Vol. 3, Part 2, *Late Medieval and Renaissance Philosophy: The Revival of Platonism to Suarez.* New York, 1962–63.

Corbett, Theodore G. "The Cult of Lipsius: A Leading Source of Early Modern Spanish Statecraft." *Journal of the History of Ideas* 36 (1975): 139–52.

Coreth, Anna. *Pietas Austriaca: Ursprung und Entwicklung Barocker Frömmigkeit in Österreich.* Munich, 1959.

Coron, Antoine. "Les 'Politicorum, sive civilis doctrinae, libri sex,' de Juste Lipse. Édition critique de Livre IV." Ecole Nationale des Chartes. Positions des thèses. Paris, 1974.

Costello, Frank B. *The Political Philosophy of Luis de Molina, S.J. (1535–1600).* Library of the Historical Institute of the Society of Jesus. Rome and Spokane, Wash., 1974.

Cremer, Albert. "Les théoriciens italiens de la raison d'état, juges de Jean Bodin." *Revue d'histoire diplomatique* 89 (1975): 249–61.

Croce, Benedetto. *Storia dell'età barocca in Italia.* Bari, 1921.

D'Addio, Mario. *Il pensiero politico di Gaspare Scioppio e il machiavellismo del seicento.* Milan, 1962.

D'Andrea, A. "The Political and Ideological Content of Innocent Gentillet's *Anti-Machiavel.*" *Renaissance Quarterly* 23 (1970): 397–411.

Davidson, N. S. "Northern Italy in the 1590s." In *The European Crisis of the 1590s,* edited by Peter Clark, pp. 157–76. London, 1985.

Davies, G. A. "The Influence of Justus Lipsius on Juan de Vera and Figueroa's 'Embaxador.'" *Bulletin of Hispanic Studies* 42 (1965): 160–73.

De Guibert, S.J., Joseph. *The Jesuits, Their Spiritual Doctrine and Practice: A Historical Study.* Translated by William J. Young, S.J., and edited by George Ganss, S.J. Chicago, 1964. Rpt. St. Louis, 1986.

De la Fuente, ed. *See* Ribadeneira.

De Luca, L. *Stato e chiesa nel pensiero politico di Giovanni Botero.* Rome, 1946.

Delumeau, Jean. *Catholicism between Luther and Voltaire: A New View of the Counter-Reformation.* Translated by Jeremy Moiser with an introduction by John Bossy. London and Philadelphia, 1977.

———. *Le péché et la peur: La culpabilisation en Occident, xiii–xviii siècles.* Paris, 1983.

———. *La peur en Occident, xiv–xviii siècles. Une cité assiegée.* Paris, 1978.

———. *Rome au xvi siècle.* Paris, 1975.

De Maddalena, Aldo, and Hermann Kellenbenz, eds. *Finanze e ragion di stato in Italia e in Germania nella prima età moderna.* Annali dell'Istituto storico italo-germanico, no. 14. Bologna, 1984.

De Mattei, Rodolfo. *Il pensiero politico di Sciopione Ammirato.* Lecce, 1959.

———. *Il pensiero politico italiano nell'età della Controriforma.* 2 vols. Milan and Naples, 1982–84.

———. *Dal premachiavellismo all'antimachiavellismo.* Biblioteca storica Sansoni, no. 46. Florence, 1969.

———. *Il problema della "ragion di stato" nell'età della Controriforma.* Milan and Naples, 1979.

Dempf, Alois. *Christliche Staatsphilosophie in Spanien.* Salzburg, 1937.

De Nave, Francine. "Justus Lipsius, schrijver 'in politicis.'" *Res publica* 11 (1969): 590–622.

———. "Peilingen naar de oorspronkelijkheid van Justus Lipsius' politiek denken." *Tijdschrift voor Rechtsgeschiedenis* 38 (1970): 449–83.

———. "De polemiek tussen Justus Lipsius en Dirck Volckertsyn Coornheert (1590): Hoofdoorzaak van Lipsius' vertrek uit Leiden (1591)." *De Gulden Passer* 48 (1970): 1–40.

De Paz, Herminio. *La prudencia política según Santo Tomás.* Avila, 1974.

Dollinger, Heinz. "Kurfürst Maximilian von Bayern und Justus Lipsius." *Archiv für Kulturgeschichte* 46 (1964): 227–308.

———. *Studien zur Finanzreform Maximilians I. von Bayern in den Jahren 1598–1619.* Schriftenreihe der Historischen Kommission bei der Bayerischen Academie der Wissenschaften, Schrift 8. Göttingen, 1968.

Donaldson, Peter S. "Machiavelli, Antichrist, and the Reformation: Prophetic Typology in Reginald Pole's *De Unitate* and *Apologia ad Carolum Quintum*." In *Leaders of the Reformation*, edited by Richard L. De Molen, pp. 211–46. London and Toronto, 1984.

Donnelly, John Patrick. "Antonio Possevino's Papalist Critique of French Political Writers." In *Regnum, Religio et Ratio: Essays Presented to Robert M. Kingdon*, edited by Jerome Friedman, pp. 31–39. Sixteenth Century Essays and Studies, no. 8. Kirksville, Mo., 1987.

————. "Antonio Possevino's Plan for World Evangelization." *Catholic Historical Review* 74 (1988): 179–98.

Doren, A. "Fortuna im Mittelalter und in der Renaissance." In *Vorträge der Bibliothek Warburg*, edited by Fritz Saxl, vol. 2, part 1, 1922–23, pp. 71–144. Leipzig, 1924.

Dowling, John C. *Diego de Saavedra Fajardo*. Boston, 1977.

————. *El pensamiento político-filosófico de Saavedra Fajardo: Posturas del siglo XVII ante le decadencia y la conservación de las Monarquías*. Murcia, 1957.

Dreitzel, Horst. *Protestantischer Aristotelismus und absoluter Staat*. Veröffentlichungen des Instituts für europäische Geschichte, no. 55, Abteilung Universalgeschichte. Wiesbaden, 1970.

Echevaría Bacigalupe, Manuel Angel. *La diplomacia secreta en Flandes*. Bilbao, 1984.

Elliott, John H. *The Count-Duke of Olivares: The Statesman in an Age of Decline*. New Haven, Conn., 1986.

————. *Europe Divided, 1559–1598*. New York, 1968.

————. "Self-perception and Decline in Early Seventeenth-Century Spain." *Past and Present* 74 (1977): 41–61. Reprinted in *Spain and Its World*, pp. 241–61.

————. *Spain and Its World, 1500–1700: Selected Essays*. New Haven, Conn., 1989.

————. "The Statecraft of Olivares." In *The Diversity of History: Essays in Honor of Sir Herbert Butterfield*, edited by J. H. Elliott and H. G. Koenigsberger, pp. 117–47. Ithaca, N.Y., 1970.

Elliott, John H., and José de la Peña, eds. *See* Olivares.

Evans, R. J. W. *The Making of the Habsburg Monarchy, 1550–1700: An Interpretation*. Oxford, 1979.

————. *Rudolf II and His World*. Oxford, 1973.

Evennett, H. Outram. *The Spirit of the Counter Reformation*. Edited with a postscript by John Bossy. Notre Dame, Ind., 1970.

Fernández-Santamaría, J. A. "Reason of State and Statecraft in Spain, 1595–1640." *Journal of the History of Ideas* 41 (1980): 355–79.

————. *Reason of State and Statecraft in Spanish Political Thought, 1595–1640*. Lanham, Md., 1983.

————. *The State, War and Peace: Spanish Political Thought in the Renaissance, 1516–1559*. Cambridge Studies in Early Modern History. Cambridge, 1977.

Firpo, Luigi. "Botero, Giovanni." In *Dizionario Biografico degli Italiani*, 13:352–62. Rome, 1971.
————. *Il pensiero politico del Renascimento e della Controriforma*. Milan, 1966. (Extract from the *Grande antologia filosofica*, vol. 10. Milan, 1964.)
Firpo, Luigi, ed. *See* Botero.
Fischer, Emil Albert. *Giovanni Botero, ein politischer und volkswirt-schaftlicher Denker der Gegenreformation*. Bern, 1952.
Ford, Franklin. *Political Murder: From Tyrannicide to Terrorism*. Cambridge, Mass., 1985.
Fraga Iribarne, M. *Don Diego Saavedra y Fajardo y la diplomacia de su época*. Madrid, 1956.
Fumaroli, Marc. *L'âge de l'éloquence: rhétorique et "res literaria," de la Renaissance au seuil de l'époque classique*. Geneva and Paris, 1980.
Galino Carillo, María Angela. *Los tratados sobre educación de príncipes, siglos xvi–xvii*. Madrid, 1948.
García de Diego, Vicente, ed. *See* Saavedra Fajardo.
Gemert, Geil van. *Die Werke des Ägidius Albertinus (1560–1620): Ein Beitrag zur Erforschung des deutschsprachigen Schrifttums der katholischen Reformbewegung in Bayern um 1600 und seiner Quellen*. Geistliche Literatur der Barockzeit, Sonderband 1. Amsterdam, 1979.
Gerber, Adolf. *Niccolò Machiavelli, die Handschriften, Ausgaben und Übersetzungen seiner Werke im 16. und 17. Jahrhundert*. 4 vols. Gotha, 1912–13. Rpt. 4 vols. in 1. Turin, 1962.
Gerlo, A., and H. D. L. Vervliet, *Inventaire de la correspondance de Juste Lipse, 1564–1606*. Antwerp, 1968.
Gerlo, A., and H. D. L. Vervliet, eds. *See* Lipsius.
Giacon, Carlo. "Machiavelli, Suarez, e la ragion de stato." In *Umanesimo e scienza politica, Atti del Congresso Internazionale di Studi Umanistici, Rome-Florence 1949*, edited by Enrico Castelli, pp. 185–99. Milan, 1951.
Gilbert, A. H. *Machiavelli's 'Prince' and its Forerunners: 'The Prince' as a Typical Book De Regimine Principum*. Durham, N.C., 1938.
Gilbert, Felix. "The Composition and Structure of Machiavelli's *Discorsi*." In *History: Choice and Commitment*, pp. 115–33. Cambridge, Mass., 1977. (Originally published in *Journal of the History of Ideas* 14 [1953]: 136–56.)
————. *History: Choice and Commitment*. Cambridge, Mass., 1977.
————. "The Humanist Concept of the Prince and *The Prince* of Machiavelli." In *History: Choice and Commitment*, pp. 91–114. Cambridge, Mass., 1977. (Originally published in *Journal of Modern History* 11 [1939]: 449–83.)
————. "Machiavellism." In *History: Choice and Commitment*, pp. 155–76. Cambridge, Mass., 1977. (Originally in the *Dictionary of the History of Ideas* 3 [1973]: 116–26.)
González Palencia, Angel, ed. *See* Saavedra Fajardo.

Gordon, Michael D. "Morality, Reform, and the Empire in Seventeenth-Century Spain." *Il pensiero politico* 11 (1978): 3–19.

———. "The Science of Politics in Seventeenth-Century Spanish Thought." *Il pensiero politico* 7 (1974): 379–94.

Gottigny, Jean. "Juste Lipse et l'Espagne, 1592–1638." 2 vols. Diss., Catholic University of Louvain, 1966–67.

Grice-Hutchinson, Marjorie. *Early Economic Thought in Spain, 1177–1740.* Boston, 1978.

Guardini, Romano. *Pascal for Our Time.* Translated by Brian Thompson. New York, 1966.

Güldner, Gerhard. *Das Toleranz-Problem in den Niederlanden im Ausgang des 16 Jahrhunderts.* Historische Studien, no. 403. Lübeck and Hamburg, 1968.

Hafter, Monroe Z. "Deviousness in Saavedra Fajardo's *Idea de un príncipe.*" *Romanic Review* 49 (1958): 161–67.

———. *Gracián and Perfection: Spanish Moralists of the Seventeenth Century.* Harvard Studies in Romance Languages, no. 30. Cambridge, Mass., 1966.

Hale, John R. *Machiavelli and Renaissance Italy.* New York, 1960.

———. "The Military Education of the Officer Class in Early Modern Europe." In *Renaissance War Studies,* pp. 225–46. London, 1982.

———. *War and Society in Renaissance Europe, 1450–1620.* London and Baltimore, Md., 1985.

Hamilton, Bernice. *Political Thought in Sixteenth-Century Spain: A Study of the Political Ideas of Vitoria, De Soto, Suarez, and Molina.* Oxford, 1963.

Headley, John M. "On the Rearming of Heaven: The Machiavellism of Tommaso Campanella." *Journal of the History of Ideas* 49 (1988): 387–404.

Hescher, Hans. "Justus Lipsius, ein Vertreter des christlichen Humanismus in der katholischen Erneuerungsbewegung des 16. Jahrhunderts." *Jahrbuch für das Bistum Mainz* 6 (1954): 196–231.

Hinrichs, Ernst. *Fürstenlehre und politisches Handeln im Frankreich Heinrichs IV.: Untersuchungen über die politische Denk- und Handlungsformen im Späthumanismus.* Veröffentlichungen des Max-Planck Instituts für Geschichte, no. 11. Göttingen, 1969.

Hulliung, Mark. *Citizen Machiavelli.* Princeton, N.J., 1983.

Ilting, Karl-Heinz. "Macht, Gewalt, iv, 2." In *Geschichtliche Grundbegriffe: Historisches Lexikon zur politisch-sozialen Sprache in Deutschland,* vol. 3, pp. 854–56. Stuttgart, 1982.

Israel, Jonathan I. *The Dutch Republic and the Hispanic World, 1606–1661.* Oxford, 1982.

Johnson, James Turner. *Ideology, Reason, and the Limitation of War: Religious and Secular Concepts 1200–1740.* Princeton, N.J., 1975.

———. *Just War Tradition and the Restraint of War.* Princeton, N.J., 1981.

Jones, Joseph R. *Antonio de Guevara.* Boston, 1975.

Joucla-Ruau, André. *Le Tacitisme de Saavedra Fajardo.* Paris, 1977.

Jover, José María. *1635: Historia de una polémica y semblanza de una generación*. Madrid, 1949.

Kamen, Henry. *The Iron Century: Social Change in Europe, 1550–1660*. London, 1971.

_____. "Toleration and Dissent in Sixteenth-Century Spain: The Alternative Tradition." *Sixteenth Century Journal* 19 (1988): 3–23.

Kelley, Donald R. "Murd'rous Machiavel in France: A Post Mortem." *Political Science Quarterly* 85 (1970): 545–59.

Keohane, Nannerl O. *Philosophy and the State in France: The Renaissance to the Enlightenment*. Princeton, N.J., 1980.

Kiesel, Helmut. *"Bei Hof, bei Höll."* *Untersuchungen zur literarischen Hofkritik von Sebastian Brant bis Friedrich Schiller*. Studien zur deutschen Literatur, no. 60. Tübingen, 1970.

Koenigsberger, Helmut. *Politicians and Virtuosi: Essays in Early Modern History*. London, 1986.

Kraus, Andreas. "Le développment de la puissance de l'état dans les principautés allemandes (xvi–xvii siècles)." *Revue d'histoire diplomatique* 89 (1975): 298–319.

Kühlmann, W. *Gelehrtenrepublik und Fürstenstaat: Entwicklung und Kritik des deutschen Späthumanismus in der Literatur des Barockzeitalters*. Studien und Texte zur Sozialgeschichte der Literatur. Tübingen, 1982.

Kunisch, Johannes, ed. *Staatsverfassung und Heeresfassung in der europäischen Geschichte der frühen Neuzeit*. Berlin, 1986.

Lecler, Joseph. *Toleration and the Reformation*. Translated from the French by T. L. Westow. 2 vols. New York, 1960.

Lefèvre, J. *Spinola et la Belgique (1601–1627)*. Brussels, 1947.

Leites, Edmund, ed. *Conscience and Casuistry in Early Modern Europe*. Ideas in Context. Cambridge, 1988.

Lewy, Guenter. *Constitutionalism and Statecraft during the Golden Age of Spain: A Study of the Political Philosophy of Juan de Mariana, S.J.* Travaux d'Humanisme et Renaissance, no. 36. Geneva, 1960.

Loomie, Albert. *The Spanish Elizabethans: The English Exiles at the Court of Philip II*. New York, 1963.

Lopez Fanego, Otilia. "Montaigne et Saavedra Fajardo." *Bulletin de la société des amis de Montaigne* 11/12 (1988): 35–50.

Lutz, Heinrich. *Ragione di Stato und christliche Staatsethik im 16. Jahrhundert*. 2d ed. Münster, 1961.

Macek, Josef. " 'La fortuna' chez Machiavel." *Le Moyen Age* 77 (1971): 305–28, 493–523.

Machiavellismo e antimachiavellici nel cinquecento. Atti del Convegno di Perugia, 30 ix–1 x 1969. Florence, 1969.

Magnuson, Torgil. *Rome in the Age of Bernini*. Vol. 1, *From the Election of Sixtus V to the Death of Urban VIII*. Stockholm and Atlantic Highlands, N.J., 1982.

Maravall, José Antonio. "La corriente doctrinal del tacitismo politico en España." *Cuadernos Hispanoamericanos*, nos. 238–40 (1969): 645–67.

———. *Culture of the Baroque: Analysis of a Historical Structure.* Translated from the Spanish by Terry Cochran. Theory and History of Literature, no. 25. Minneapolis, Minn., 1986.

———. *Estado moderno y mentalidad social (siglos xv a xvii).* 2 vols. Madrid, 1972.

———. "La literatura de emblemas en el contexto de la sociedad barroca." In *Teatro y literatura en la sociedad barroca*, pp. 149–88. Madrid, 1972.

———. "Moral de acomodación y carácter conflictivo de la libertad (Notas sobre Saavedra Fajardo)," *Cuadernos Hispanoamericanos*, nos. 257–58 (1971): 663–93.

———. *La oposición política bajo los Austrias.* Barcelona, 1972.

———. *La philosophie politique espagnole au xvii siècle dans ses rapports avec l'esprit de la Contre-Réforme.* 2d ed. Translated by Louis Cazes and Pierre Mesnard. Paris, 1955.

Marquez, Javier. "El mercantilismo de Saavedra Fajardo." *El Trimestre Económico* 10 (1943): 247–86.

Martin, Colin, and Geoffrey Parker. *The Spanish Armada.* New York, 1988.

Mattingly, Garrett. *Renaissance Diplomacy.* London, 1955.

Mecenseffy, Grete. *Geschichte des Protestantismus in Österreich.* Graz and Cologne, 1956.

Meinecke, Friedrich. *Machiavellism: The Doctrine of Raison d'Etat and Its Place in Modern History.* Translated by Douglas Scott. New York, 1957.

Mesnard, Pierre. *L'essor de la philosophie politique au xvi siècle.* 3d ed. Paris, 1969.

Moote, A. Lloyd. *Louis XIII, the Just.* Berkeley, Calif., 1989.

Mora, Gonzalo Fernández de la. "Maquiavelo visto por los tratadistas españoles de la Contrarreforma." *Arbor* 13 (1949): 417–49.

Morandi, Carlo, ed. *See* Botero.

Mosse, George L. *The Holy Pretense: A Study in Christianity and Reason of State from William Perkins to John Winthrop.* Oxford, 1957.

Mulagk, Karl-Heinz. *Phänomene des politischen Menschen im 17. Jahrhundert.* Berlin, 1973.

Müller, R. A. "Fürstenspiegel des 17. Jahrhunderts: Regierungslehre und politische Pädagogik." *Historische Zeitschrift* 240 (1985): 571–97.

Münch, Paul, ed. *Ordnung, Fleiss und Sparsamkeit: Texte und Dokumente zur Entstehung der "bürgerlichen Tugenden."* Munich, 1984.

Münkler, Herfried. *Im Namen des Staates: Begründung der Staatsräson in der Frühen Neuzeit.* Frankfurt, 1987.

Murillo Ferrol, F. *Saavedra Fajardo y la política del barroco.* Madrid, 1957.

Noonan, John T., Jr. *The Scholastic Analysis of Usury.* Cambridge, Mass., 1957.

O'Connell, Marvin. *The Counter Reformation, 1560–1610.* New York, 1974.

Oestreich, Gerhard. "Die antike Literatur als Vorbild der praktischen Wissenschaften im 16. und 17. Jahrhundert." In *Classical Influences on*

European Culture, A.D. *1500–1700*, edited by R. R. Bolgar, pp. 315–24. Cambridge, 1976.

————. *Antiker Geist und moderner Staat bei Justus Lipsius (1546–1606): Der Neustoizismus als politische Bewegung.* Edited by Nicolette Mout. Schriftenreihe der Historischen Kommission bei der Bayerischen Akademie der Wissenschaften, Schrift 38. Göttingen, 1989.

————. *Geist und Gestalt des frühmodernen Staates: Ausgewählte Aufsätze.* Berlin, 1969.

————. "Justus Lipsius als Universalgehehrter zwischen Renaissance und Barock." In *Leiden University in the Seventeenth Century: An Exchange of Learning*, edited by Th. H. Lunsingh Sheurleer and G. H. M. Postumus Meyjes, pp. 177–201. Leiden, 1975.

————. *Neostoicism and the Early Modern State.* Edited by Brigitta Oestreich and H. C. Koenigsberger and translated by David McClintock. Cambridge Studies in Early Modern History. Cambridge, 1982.

O'Malley, John W., ed. *Catholicism in Early Modern History: A Guide to Research.* St. Louis, 1988.

Pagden, Anthony, ed. *The Languages of Political Theory in Early Modern Europe.* Ideas in Context, Cambridge, 1987.

Panella, Antonio. *Gli antimachiavellici.* Florence, 1943.

Parker, Geoffrey. *The Army of Flanders and the Spanish Road.* Cambridge Studies in Early Modern History. Cambridge, 1972.

————. *Europe in Crisis, 1598–1648.* Glasgow, 1979.

————. "The Military Revolution, 1560–1660, a Myth?" In *Spain and the Netherlands, 1559–1659: Ten Studies*, pp. 86–103. Glasgow, 1979.

————. *The Military Revolution: Military Innovation and the Rise of the West, 1500–1800.* Cambridge, 1988.

————. *The Thirty Years' War.* London, 1984.

See also Colin Martin.

Il pensiero politico di Machiavelli e la sua fortuna nel mondo. Atti del Convegno Internazionale Sancasciano-Florence, 28–29 September 1969. Florence, 1972.

Pereña Vicente, Luciano. *Teoría de la guerra in Francisco Suarez.* 2 vols. Madrid, 1954.

Pirenne, Henri. *Histoire de Belgique.* Vol. 4. 3d ed. Brussels, 1927.

Pocock, J. G. A. "The Concept of Language and the *Métier d'Historien*: Some Considerations on Practice." In *The Languages of Political Theory in Early Modern Europe*, edited by Anthony Pagden, pp. 19–38. Cambridge, 1987.

————. *The Machiavellian Moment: Florentine Political Thought and the Atlantic Republican Tradition.* Princeton, N.J., 1975.

Prat, F. M. *Histoire du P. Ribadeneyra.* Paris, 1862.

Press, Volker. "Stadt und territoriale Konfessionsbildung." In *Kirche und gesellschaftlicher Wandel in deutschen und niederländischen Städten der Werdenden Neuzeit*, edited by Franz Petri, pp. 251–96. Cologne and Vienna, 1980.

Procacci, Giuliano. *Studi sulla fortuna del Machiavelli.* Rome, 1965.
Prosperi, Adriano. "La religione, il potere, le élites: Incontri Italo-Spagnoli della Contrariforma." *Annuario dell'Istituto Storico Italiano per l'età moderna e contemporanea* 29–30 (1977–78): 499–529.
Raab, Felix. *The English Face of Machiavelli.* London, 1968.
Rabb, Theodore K. *The Struggle for Stability in Early Modern Europe.* Oxford, 1975.
Raeff, Marc. *The Well-Ordered Police State: Social and Institutional Change through Law in the Germanies and Russia, 1600–1800.* New Haven, Conn., 1983.
Ramirez, Alejandro, ed. *See* Lipsius.
Rathé, C. Edward. "Innocent Gentillet and the First 'Anti-Machiavel.' " *Bibliothèque d'Humanisme et Renaissance* 27 (1965): 186–225.
Redondo, Augustin. *Antonio de Guevara (1480?-1545) et l'Espagne de son temps.* Travaux d'Humanisme et Renaissance, no. 148. Geneva, 1976.
Reinhard, Wolfgang. "Gegenreformation als Modernisierung? Prologemena zu einer Theorie des konfessionellen Zeitalters." *Archiv für Reformationsgeschichte* 68 (1977): 226–52.
———. "Humanismus und Militarismus: Antike-Rezeption und Kriegshandwerk in der oranischen Heeresreform." In *Krieg und Frieden im Horizont des Renaissancehumanismus,* edited by Franz Josef Worstbrock, pp. 185–204. Mitteilung XIII der Kommission für Humanismusforschung. Weinheim, 1986.
———. "Reformation, Counter-Reformation, and the Early Modern State: A Reassessment." *Catholic Historical Review* 75 (1989): 383–404.
———. "Zwang zur Konfessionalisierung? Prologemena zu einer Theorie des konfessionellen Zeitalters." *Zeitschrift für historische Forschung* 10 (1983): 257–77.
Repgen, Konrad. *Kriegslegitimationen in Alteuropa: Entwurf einer Typologie.* Schriften des Historischen Kollegs, Vorträge, no. 9. Munich, 1985.
———. *Die römische Kurie und der westfälische Friede: Idee und Wirklichkeit des Papsttums im 16. und 17 Jahrhundert.* Vol. 1, Parts 1–2. Tübingen, 1962–65.
Rey, Eusebio, ed. *See* Ribadeneira.
Rommen, Heinrich. *Die Staatslehre des Franz Suarez, S.J.* München-Gladbach, 1926. Rpt. New York, 1979.
Rothenberg, Gunther E. "Maurice of Nassau, Gustavus Adolphus, Raimondo Montecuccoli, and the 'Military Revolution' of the Seventeenth Century." In *Makers of Modern Strategy from Machiavelli to the Nuclear Age,* edited by Peter Paret with the collaboration of Gordon A. Craig and Felix Gilbert, pp. 32–63. Princeton, N.J., 1986.
Rubenstein, Nicolai. "The History of the Word *Politicus* in Early-Modern Europe." In *The Languages of Political Theory in Early-Modern Europe,* edited by Anthony Pagden, pp. 41–56. Cambridge, 1987.
Russo, Luigi, ed. *See* Machiavelli.
Saunders, Jason Lewis. *Justus Lipsius: The Philosophy of Renaissance Stoicism.* New York, 1955.

Savelli, Rodolfo. "Tra Machiavelli e S. Giorgio: Cultura giuspolitica e dibattito istituzionale a Genova nel Cinque-Seicento." In *Finanze e ragion di stato in Italia e in Germania nella prima età moderna*, edited by Aldo De Maddelena and Hermann Kellenbenz, pp. 249–321. Annali dell'Istituto storico italo-germanico, no. 14. Bologna, 1984.

Schellhase, Kenneth C. *Tacitus in Renaissance Political Thought*. Chicago, 1976.

Schilling, Heinz. *Konfessionskonflikt und Staatsbildung. Eine Fallstudie über das Verhältnis von religiösem und sozialem Wandel in der Frühneuzeit am Beispiel der Grafschaft Lippe*. Quellen und Studien zur Reformationsgeschichte, no. 48. Gütersloh, 1981.

_____. "The Reformation and the Rise of the Early Modern State." In *Luther and the Modern State in Germany*, edited by James D. Tracy, pp. 21–30. Sixteenth Century Essays and Studies, no. 7. Kirksville, Mo., 1986.

Schmidt, Friedrich. *Geschichte der Erziehung der bayerischen Wittelsbacher: Urkunden nebst geschichtlichem Überblick*. Monumenta Germaniae Paedogogica, no. 14. Berlin, 1892.

Schnur, Roman, ed. *Die Rolle der Juristen bei der Entstehung des modernen Staates*. Berlin, 1986.

_____. *Staatsräson: Studien zur Geschichte eines politischen Begriffes*. Berlin, 1975.

Schulze, Winfried. "Die deutschen Landesdefensionen im 16. und 17. Jahrhundert." In *Staatsverfassung und Heeresverfassung in der europäischen Geschichte der frühen Neuzeit*, edited by Johannes Kunisch, pp. 129–49. Berlin, 1986.

_____. "Gerhard Oestreichs Begriff 'Sozialdisziplinierung' in der frühen Neuzeit." *Zeitschrift für historische Forschung* 14 (1987): 265–302.

Scott, James Brown, ed. *See* Suarez.

Seils, Ernst-Albert. *Die Staatslehre des Jesuiten Adam Contzen, Beichtvater Kurfürst Maximilian I von Bayern*. Historische Studien, no. 405. Lübeck and Hamburg, 1968.

Siedschlag, Karl. *Der Einfluss der niederländisch-neostoischen Ethik in den politischen Theorien zur Zeit Sullys und Richelieus*. Historische Forschungen, no. 13. Berlin, 1978.

Siegel, Jerrold. "*Virtù* in and since the Renaissance." In *Dictionary of the History of Ideas*, 4:476–86. New York, 1973.

Singer, Bruno. *Die Fürstenspiegel in Deutschland im Zeitalter des Humanismus und der Reformation*. Humanistische Bibliothek, Ser. 1, no. 34. Munich, 1981.

Skalweit, Stephan. "Das Herrscherbild des 17. Jahrhunderts." *Historische Zeitschrift* 184 (1957): 65–80.

Skinner, Quentin. *The Foundations of Modern Political Thought*. 2 vols. Cambridge, 1978.

_____. *Machiavelli*. Past Masters Series. New York, 1981.

Sommervogel, Carlos. *Bibliothèque de la Compagnie de Jésus*. 12 vols. Brussels and Paris, 1890–1909. Rpt. Louvain, 1960.

Stegmann, André. "Apologie du statu quo institutionnel chez les historiens italiens de la fin du xvi siècle." *Revue d'Histoire diplomatique* 89 (1975): 225–48.

———. *L'héroisme cornélien: Genèse et signification*. 2 vols. Paris, 1968.

Stolleis, Michael. *Arcana Imperii und Ratio Status: Bemerkungen zur politischen Theorie des frühen 17. Jahrhunderts*. Veröffentlichungen der Joachim-Jungius Gesellschaft der Wissenschaften Hamburg, no. 39. Göttingen, 1980.

———. "Friedrich Meinecke's 'Die Idee der Staatsräson' und die neuere Forschung." In *Friedrich Meinecke Heute*, edited by Michael Erbe, pp. 50–75. Berlin, 1981.

———. *Geschichte des öffentlichen Rechts*. Vol. 1: *1600–1800*. Munich, 1988.

———. "Gründzüge der Beamtenethik (1550–1650)." In *Die Rolle der Juristen bei der Entstehung des modernen Staates*, edited by Roman Schnur, pp. 273–302. Berlin, 1986.

———. "Lipsius-Rezeption in der politisch-juristischen Literatur des 17. Jahrhunderts in Deutschland." *Der Staat* 27 (1) (1987): 1–30.

———. *Pecunia Nervus Rerum: Zur Staatsfinanzierung in der frühen Neuzeit*. Frankfurt, 1983.

Stradling, R. A. *Philip IV and the Government of Spain, 1621–1665*. Cambridge, 1988.

Straub, Eberhard. "Don Diego Saavedra y Fajardo und die Rechtfertigung des spanischen Reiches." *Zeitschrift für bayerische Landesgeschichte* 34 (1971): 514–46.

———. "Das Herrscherbild im 17. Jahrhundert vornehmlich nach dem 'Mundus Christiano Bavaro Politicus.' " *Zeitschrift für bayerische Landesgeschichte* 32 (1969): 193–221.

———. *Pax et Imperium: Spaniens Kampf um seine Friedensordnung in Europa zwischen 1617 und 1635*. Rechts- und staatswissenschaftliche Veröffentlichungen der Görresgesellschaft, n.s., no. 31. Paderborn, 1980.

Stumpo, Enrico. "Finanze e ragion di stato nella prima età moderna. Due modelli diversi: Piemonte et Toscana, Savoia et Medici." In *Finanze e ragion di stato in Italia e in Germania nella prima età moderna*, edited by Aldo De Maddelena and Hermann Kellenbenz, pp. 181–231. Annali dell'Istituto storico italo-germanico, no. 14. Bologna, 1984.

Sturmberger, Hans. *Kaiser Ferdinand II. und das Problem des Absolutismus*. Munich, 1957.

Thompson, I. A. A. "The Impact of War." In *The European Crisis of the 1590s*, edited by Peter Clark, pp. 261–84. London, 1985.

Thuau, Etienne. *Raison d'état et pensée politique à l'époque de Richelieu*. Paris, 1966.

Tierno Galvan, Enrique. "Saavedra y Fajardo, teorico y cuidadano del estado barroco." *Revista Española de derecho internacional* 1 (1948): 467–76.

———. *El Tacitismo en los escritores políticos españoles del Siglo de Oro*. Murcia, 1949. Rpt. as "El Tacitismo en las doctrinas políticas del Siglo de Oro Espagnol," in *Escritos 1950–1960*, pp. 11–93. Madrid, 1971.

Titone, Virgilio. *La politica dell'età barocca.* 2d ed. Cattinisetta and Rome, 1969.

Tomás y Valiente, Francisco. *Los validos en la monarquía española del siglo xvii.* Madrid, 1982.

Tracy, James. "Miscellany: With and Without the Counter Reformation: The Catholic Church in the Spanish Netherlands and the Dutch Republic, 1580–1650. A Review of the Literature since 1945." *Catholic Historical Review* 71 (1985): 547–75.

Trevor-Roper, Hugh R. "Religion, the Reformation, and Social Change." In *Religion, the Reformation, and Social Change and Other Essays*, pp. 1–45. 2d ed. London, 1971.

Valentin, Jean-Marie. "Gegenreformation und Literatur: Das Jesuitendrama im Dienste der religiösen und moralischen erziehung." *Historisches Jahrbuch* 100 (1980): 240–56.

_____. *Le théâtre des Jésuites dans les pays de langue allemande, 1554–1680: Salut des âmes et ordre des cités.* 3 vols. European University Studies, German Language and Literature. Bern, 1978.

Viner, Jacob. *The Role of Providence in the Social Order.* Philadelphia, 1972.

Walters, LeRoy Brandt. "Five Classic Just-War Theories: A Study of Thomas Aquinas, Vitoria, Suarez, Gentile, Grotius." Ph.D. Diss., Yale University, 1971.

Wansink, H. *Politieke wetenschappen aan de Leidse Universiteit 1575–1650.* Utrecht, 1981.

Index

Absolutism: in anti-Machiavellians, 33, 222–23; in Botero, 52, 99; in Lipsius, 80–81, 99; in Contzen, 141–42, 154; of Maximilian, 158; in Scribani, 170–71; limited, in Saavedra, 197. *See also* Consent as basis of government; Right of resistance

Agriculture: in Botero, 67; in Contzen, 150; in Scribani, 178; in Saavedra, 205–6

Alba, duke of, 164–65

Albert (archduke), 163, 166; and Lipsius, 80; model prince for Scribani, 165, 168, 170, 172, 173, 174, 177, 184, 187; prohibition of duelling, 179

Albertinus, Ägidius, 2

Alexander VI (pope), 8

Althusius, Johannes, 99, 161; editions of, 260 (n. 129)

Ambassador, The, 29, 99, 169; tension between good and useful in, 30

Ambassadors: in Contzen, 169; in Scribani, 169, 177; in Saavedra, 203. *See also* Diplomats

Ammirato, Scipione, 27, 219, 253 (n. 30); and Botero, 47; on Tacitus, 50; and reason of state, 51

Angermunt, Jacob Bruck, 194

Anti-Machiavellianism, ix, x; term explained, 24–25; general features, 27–33, 216, 217, 221–22, 234–40; in France, 29, 218–20; statecraft of, 222–34; significance of, 240–42.

See also Anti-Machiavellian tradition; Anti-Machiavellian writers

Anti-Machiavellian tradition, ix–x, 3, 26–27, 29; term defined, 27. *See also* Anti-Machiavellian writers

Anti-Machiavellian writers, 26–27; knowledge of Machiavelli's works, 4; influence of Bodin, 18–19; dissemination of works of, 28–30, 218, 237; and Scholastics, 33, 221. *See also* Anti-Machiavellian tradition

Antwerp, 22, 163

Appearance and reality: in Machiavelli, 9; as issue for the Baroque, 55, 221; in Lipsius, 84; in Contzen, 148; in Scribani, 172; in Saavedra, 200; anti-Machiavellians and, 224–25. *See also* Reputation

Aquinas. *See* Thomas Aquinas, Saint

Arbitrista(s), 51, 132, 188, 189; Ribadeneira as first, 111; Scribani as Flemish, 163

Aristotle, 5, 35, 139, 140

Army. *See* Military

Astry, James, 194

Augsburg, 22

Augsburg, Peace of, 2, 20, 152–53, 159; step toward toleration, 42; and concessions to rulers, 145; and papacy, 251 (n. 65)

Augustine, Saint, 15, 76, 95; on just war, 40, 152; on lying, 87, 125, 147; on toleration, 121, 145, 146, 233